Impromptu Startup!

Brian Olah

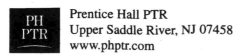
Prentice Hall PTR
Upper Saddle River, NJ 07458
www.phptr.com

ISBN 0-13-019115-9

9 780130 191151

90000

Library of Congress Cataloging-in-Publication Data Available

Editorial/Production Supervision: *Rose Kernan*
Acquisitions Editor: *Mark L. Taub*
Cover Designer: *Talar Agasyan*
Cover Design Director: *Jerry Votta*
Manufacturing Manager: *Alexis R. Heydt*
Editorial Assistant: *Michael Fredette*

© 2001 Prentice Hall PTR
Prentice-Hall, Inc.
Upper Saddle River, NJ 07458

Prentice Hall books are widely used by corporations and government agencies for training, marketing, and resale.

The publisher offers discounts on this book when ordered in bulk quantities.
For more information, contact Corporate Sales Department, phone: 800-382-3419;
fax: 201-236-7141; e-mail: corpsales@prenhall.com
Or write: Prentice Hall PTR
   Corporate Sales Department
   One Lake Street
   Upper Saddle River, NJ 07458

Printed in the United States of America
10 9 8 7 6 5 4 3 2 1

ISBN 0-13-019115-9

Prentice-Hall International (UK) Limited, *London*
Prentice-Hall of Australia Pty. Limited, *Sydney*
Prentice-Hall Canada Inc., *Toronto*
Prentice-Hall Hispanoamericana, S.A., *Mexico*
Prentice-Hall of India Private Limited, *New Delhi*
Prentice-Hall of Japan, Inc., *Tokyo*
Pearson Education Asia Pte. Ltd., *Singapore*
Editora Prentice-Hall do Brasil, Ltda., *Rio de Janeiro*

Contents

Preface

Consulting and teaching the Cognos Business Intelligence solution has led me to various companies using Impromptu and many people using its tools over the past few years. Everywhere I went, people were thirsting for more knowledge on the tools. Many have asked if someone has written a book on "this stuff." I would always answer those questions with: "You know, someone should."

The idea for writing this book first came to me while browsing around the Computer section in a local bookstore. I was looking at the latest offerings from the gurus of Data Warehousing. There were numerous books on different databases, spreadsheet applications, and programming languages, but, when I looked for a book on Cognos, I did not see one. A light bulb finally clicked on. "Why would there not be a book about Impromptu?" My search continued to the Internet, to on-line bookstores and still nothing.

Then, in the middle of summer, when most people are playing softball, golf, or working in the yard, I was exploring the option of what it would take to write a book on Impromptu. One thing led to another, and Impromtpu Startup! began.

Acknowledgments

I would first like to thank my wife, Dr. Erin Munjas Olah, for her support and understanding as I sat countless hours in front of my laptop. It was the deciation, commitment, and passion of her career that inspired me. This has been an enormous undertaking and only because of her I was able to do it. Thank you sweetheart.

I would also like to pay a special thanks to two special influences in my life. First, a special thanks to Jeff Popovich for introducing me to Computer Science back in the late 1970s. It was the initial interest he took in showing me about computers that directed my life. Next, a special thanks to the person who shaped that interest, John Gresh, my Computer Science teacher in High School. His diligence, dedication, and gift of teaching brought out the best in me.

Thanks to my family and friends, all of whom helped and supported me in their own way.

Thank you to all of the companies I worked with in the past, all of the students I have trained, and all of my peers who I have worked with over the years.

I would like to thank all of my colleagues who have contributed with ideas, support, knowledge, reviews, or just listened: Tom Hammergren, Angie Stocker, Gary Wilson, Brian Liederbach, Brad Storts, Pat Reedy, Frazer Donaldson, Ed Kendall, Aaron Hartung, and Roger Ward. Thanks to the wonderful people at Cognos for being so supportive of this effort: Rob Collins, Cassandra Moon, Brian Tinkler, Mark Godby, Mike Bagott, and Lynne Angus.

Thanks to Prentice Hall for the opportunity to put this instructional book on Impromptu out into the market. Special thanks to the team who put this book together: Mark Taub, Rose Kernan, and the gang.

Finally, I have to thank Don Humphreys, because without his technical writing skills, effort, and patience, you would not be reading this book.

Brian Olah

Introduction

Technology is evolving quicker than ever. This has led to an explosion of both information and technology on everyone's desktop at work. Common now in companies are terms like Databases, Data Warehouses, Data Marts, and probably several more terms have sprung up by the time you read this. Access to information is critical to a successful organization.

At the same time, the Information Technology (IT) departments within companies are struggling to keep pace with new hardware and computer systems to run the organization. There is just too much to do. Most companies stuff report writing into the job category of "Hey, by the way, you need to write some reports." A hard reality in companies today is that reporting is at or near the bottom on the IT To-Do list.

So, for non-IT departments to get the reports they need to run their segment of the company, oftentimes, they have had to take on report writing. This is where tools like Impromptu have evolved—to address the needs of non-technical report writers. Leveraging the common GUI environment that most people are comfortable with, tools like Impromptu have made their way into the fabric of running businesses.

Goals of the Book

This book is a practical guide to building reports in Impromptu. The main goal of this book is to provide report consumers and report writers with the knowledge and understanding of Impromptu to be able to write reports. The report writing skills and techniques taught in this book are geared toward preparing you to build reports against your own databases quickly and effectively.

A secondary goal of this book is for report writers to take report writing seriously and pay attention to the requirements and details of the report. It is often a tedious job, one that is virtually thankless. More often than not, the only time attention is paid to a report is when there is something wrong. Think about it. When was the last time that someone won a corporate award for "writing a report." Not likely.

When writing a report, attention must be placed on the requirements of that report. This is the blueprint for the report, and attention to blueprints in other lines of work, like building a house, require following the instructions to the letter. The same principles and discipline should apply with report writing. If a mistake is made with a blueprint, a homeowner may end up with a bathroom in the hallway, while a mistake in a report, if gone unnoticed, can lead to decisions made off of incorrect data.

Audience

This book is for all users of Impromptu: the casual users, the application programmers, the business managers, the data warehousing consultants, business analysts, anyone who needs to write a report in Impromptu.

In this book, three categories of report consumers are identified: report consumers, report developers, and administrators. This book addresses the reporting writing needs of the all three categories of users. Each one of these groups has a responsibility, to some degree, of writing reports. From a report consumer, a person who will just run/view reports, to the administrator, a person who technically responsible for access to the database—this book will help them gain an understanding on how to run and then build Impromptu reports. This book addresses the report consuming and writing needs for each group, from report consumers to the heavy IT administrator.

Structure

A reporting environment contains many different types of reports to answer just as many different questions and needs. Just as there are many different types of reports, the level of complexity varies within these types of reports. Learning how to build a report is just like learning anything else. Start with the basic principles, and then add to that knowledge incrementally.

In all my years of both personal experience and teaching others, I have found that it is nearly impossible to sit down, read something from cover to cover, and learn a computer application. As complex as systems and applications are, there is just too much in these tools to fully digest in such a relatively short period of time. In contrast, spending time learning the basics, the building blocks of an application, and then using and learning how to apply those skills in a familiar environment, is far more productive in the long run.

I relate this familiar environment to the users' own situation: their own database columns, their own reports, and yes, even their own computer. Building an unfamiliar report using an imaginary database does not enhance a learning environment; it essentially teaches someone how to build a report for *that* database. Unfortunately, I have experienced this first hand everywhere I have been. When people are required to learn an application, they do not normally extract the "how to" from the how to *build this report*. They focus more on build this report, which relates to the fact that *this report* means nothing to them.

Once someone learns something, whether it's from being required or from self-motivation, they have to apply that skill in a familiar setting. Then they relate the knowledge to something that matters to them—their environment, their situation, their database, and their reports.

Once users become comfortable with this knowledge, they migrate or move on to more challenging topics naturally. This produces a successful experience for the user and motivates them to learning more, at their own pace.

The structure of this book follows this principle and is divided into three parts. Each chapter covers one concept of reporting. It uses one specific example throughout each chapter. In the chapters, I do use a sample database to build these reports and exercises. Unfortunately, I had to use one to provide a framework for the flow of the concept. But, the focus of each exercise is directed to providing steps to perform a certain action or concept.

Great care has been taken in making each chapter present a specific topic, without being dependent on other chapters. This gives a user of this book the ability to use a chapter, and then be able to go back to their environment and try that particular skill.

Part I: Basic Impromptu Reporting

This group of chapters deals with introducing the user to Impromptu environment. We start with installing the tool and identifying the different types of users. Next, we show the user around the environment, explaining how to open a report, and specifically what Impromptu does during the whole process. Finally, a step-by-step walkthrough of creating a simple report provides a further explanation of the different things a report developer sees and what they do within Impromptu.

Part II: Fundamental Reporting Concepts

The second part of the book is designed to take you to the next level of reporting. Once the basics are understood, you now want to enhance a report with concepts such as summaries, grouping on columns, and filtering out undesirable information. These chapters discuss functionally how to incorporate these topics in building reports.

Part III: Advanced Impromptu Reporting

The third section unveils the hidden treasures of Impromptu, like prompting a user for refined queries, drill through to additional reports, and discuss how Impromptu handles all the columns and objects for advanced reporting.

Basic Impromptu Reporting

Part 1—Basic Impromptu Reporting will introduce you to Impromptu. These chapters will take you from the installation of Impromptu, to opening your first report, to creating a basic report on your own. These tasks may sound simple, but these chapters go into great detail on what happens when you do something or when Impromptu appears to be doing something. The level of detail covered in Part 1 provides the foundation for understanding topics covered in Part 2 and Part 3.

After completing Part 1, you will be able to open or build a basic report and successfully navigate the graphical user interface of Impromptu—the skills required to be a report consumer.

So, You Just Bought Impromptu . . . Now What?

This first chapter is designed to describe what Impromptu is and what type of reports you can expect to build. Describing what the tool is will give you a better understanding of how to apply Impromptu in your work environment. This chapter will also introduce the concept of different types of report users and how they view and use Impromptu.

In addition, this chapter walks through loading the User version of Impromptu 6.0. Finally, the chapter points out the differences between the User and Administrator versions.

This chapter covers the following information:

- What, exactly, Impromptu is
- What you can do with Impromptu
- What skills are necessary to use Impromptu effectively
- How to load Impromptu

What Is Impromptu?

Simply put, Impromptu is an end-user reporting tool. With it, you can access data from a database without having to understand complex programming languages. In fact, most users of Impromptu don't even build reports as their primary job; instead, they view and manipulate reports already created.

Figure 1.1
Load or "splash" of Impromptu.

Table 1.1

What Impromptu is	What Impromptu isn't
An end-user reporting tool	A heavily programmatic tool designed specifically for technical people.
A graphical, Windows-oriented, end-user report viewing environment.	A blue-screen text editor.
A mechanism to access many different databases.	A reporting tool designed to run a specific brand of database.

What Kinds of Reports Are Available in Impromptu?

Impromptu is a robust tool that offers users an endless supply of reports that can generally be subdivided into two categories:

- Standard reporting
- Ad-hoc reporting

Standard Reporting

These reports are the kind you run on a consistent basis without much modification. If you've ever worked in the mainframe world, you may recall receiving those nasty "green-bar" reports every Monday morning. Well, Impromptu lends itself well to this type of reporting, as Figure 1.2 shows. With Impromptu, you can generate a report and run it as often as necessary; you can even schedule reports to run at a specific time.

Figure 1.2   A Standard Report.

Ad-Hoc Reporting

Ad-hoc comes from Latin meaning "after the fact." The Information Technology (IT) world takes the term and applies it to an instance when reporting is performed, hence ad-hoc reporting. While Impromptu comes with a wide variety of prepackaged reporting templates, there may come a time when you need a different type of report from the ones provided. With its ad-hoc capability, Impromptu enables users to create new reports and customize them as often as they wish.

Figure 1.3   "Bill's Weekly Shipping" Ad-Hoc Report.

Who Uses Impromptu?

Just about anybody with any basic level of computer skill can use the simple user interface of Impromptu. In most instances, however, there are three distinct user roles for this tool:

- Administrator
- Report developer
- Report consumer

Figure 1.4   Many different people, from a secretary, to a blue collar plant manager, to a normal-looking office person, and of course the stereotypical IT person—maybe even an executive.

These roles can be filled by a wide variety of users. The user fills the role that best describes his or her level of technical skill. In the past, companies have separated technical skills into two categories: IT people and business or functional people. Impromptu goes a step further and breaks the typical mold in which only IT people can be administrators or report developers.

Table 1.2

Role	IT Person	Functional Person
Administrator	Can be. This is the typical role associated with IT people.	Can be. This is a new concept. If the functional person has the skills, there is no reason why that person cannot be an Impromptu administrator.
Report Developer	Can be. This is another typical role. Defaulted over the years due to complex programming skills, IT people have assumed the report developer position.	Can be. Impromptu breaks the mold of this stereotype. Users with Windows skills can develop their own reports.
Report Consumer	Can be. Usually is not. IT people have traditionally built reports based on instructions and requirements handed to them by someone—for someone somewhere else.	Can be. This is where everybody expects functional people to be, and they still can be with Impromptu. But with Impromptu, they can do all of the above.

Administrator

The administrator is really the "gatekeeper" of the Impromptu reporting environment. Administrators control user access to the tool, including which columns a user can access and which reports a user can run or change. The administrator also controls all of the technical features of Impromptu.

To be an administrator, you need to understand databases, including database tables and how they interrelate. You also need to understand how reports are built, even if you never actually build a single report. Understanding how reports are built helps the administrator recognize how the users will use the features of Impromptu daily, as shown in Table 1.3.

Table 1.3

Skill	Administrator	Report Developer	Report Consumer
Relate tables	X		
Assign responsibilities to users	X		
Organize the Catalog for users	X		
Build simple reports	X	X	X
Build and change complex reports	X	X	
Add user prompts to refine report results	X	X	
Build report relationships	X	X	
Open and view reports	X	X	X

Report Developer

The report developer's main job is to build both standard and ad-hoc reports. You don't have to be a technical person to be a report developer; you just need an in-depth understanding of what types of reports a user will need and how to create those reports in Impromptu. Most of the work for the report developer occurs right after the company installs Impromptu and the administrator constructs the reporting environment. After setting up all of the initial reports, the report developer becomes the maintenance expert for the system, doing things like changing reports, adding the occasional new report, scheduling batch jobs, and answering questions.

Table 1.4

Skill	Administrator	Report Developer	Report Consumer
Relate tables	X		
Assign responsibilities to users	X		
Organize the Catalog for users	X		
Build simple reports	X	**X**	X
Build and change complex reports	X	**X**	
Add user prompts to refine report results	X	**X**	
Build report relationships	X	**X**	
Open and view reports	X	**X**	X

Report Consumer

A report consumer is just that—someone who consumes or uses the reports that Impromptu produces. For the most part, these people just want to run reports and see results. They do not want to learn complex tools and steps to retrieve information. Their skills, shown in Table 1.5, reflect the desire for a simple interface and easy and quick access to the report. A report consumer could be someone in executive management or one of the company bookkeepers. Sometimes a report consumer becomes adept at using Impromptu and evolves into a report developer, or even an administrator. While that may happen in some cases, it is not a mandatory progression. You will get to see the power of Impromptu just by running reports.

Table 1.5

Skill	Administrator	Report Developer	Report Consumer
Relate tables	X		
Assign responsibilities to users	X		
Organize the Catalog for users	X		
Build simple reports	X	X	**X**
Build and change complex reports	X	X	
Add user prompts to refine report results	X	X	
Build report relationships	X	X	
Open and view reports	X	X	**X**

Where Can Each Role Find Information?

Table 1.6 highlights what parts of this book apply to a particular Impromptu user.

Table 1.6

Role	Skills	Where in the book
Administrator	The administrator skills and tasks are not covered in this book. Contact Cognos for a class on learning the skills needed to become an administrator.	Not Available
Report Developer	Build simple reports Build and change complex reports Add user prompts to refine report results Drill from one report to another.	Part 1 Part 2 Part 3 Part 3
Report Consumer	Open and view reports	Part 1

So, Who Should Do What?

Impromptu is such an easy tool to use that anybody can fill any role. But where to begin is a whole different question. The following three scenarios help to give a sense of who can and should do what in an initial deployment of Impromptu.

Scenario 1:

Scenario 1 represents an implementation of Impromptu that has a great deal of support from the Information Technology (IT) group within the company. From IT we have Mary as the *administrator*, and Bill as the *report developer*.

Additionally we have two people from the accounting department, Jill and Bob. Jill is the senior staff accountant and Bob is fresh out of college. Jill is only a *report consumer*. Bob is both a *report developer* and a *report consumer*.

Figure 1.5
Mary, IT person is the administrator,
report developers are Bill and Bob,
report consumers are Jill and Bob.

Scenario 2:

Scenario 2 represents an implementation of Impromptu in a company with a smaller IT group. They are not able to dedicate, even part-time, an individual to be a report developer; they can provide only an administrator. From IT we just have Mary as the *administrator*.

From the accounting department, we still have Jill and Bob. The difference here is that both Jill and Bob are more accomplished report developers, having used other report-writing tools. They are comfortable taking full control of developing all the reports.

Figure 1.6
Mary, IT person is the administrator, report developers and report consumers are both Jill and Bob.

Scenario 3:

In Scenario 3, an overloaded IT staff is represented. Mary is extremely busy and does not have time to take on another responsibility. She asks Jill to be the administrator, and after heavy consideration, Jill refuses because she has too much to do herself. So, Mary and Jill recruit Bob to be the administrator.

As in Scenario 2, both Jill and Bob are accomplished report developers. But now, between the two of them, they take on all of the roles of Impromptu.

Figure 1.7
Bob is the administrator, report developers and report consumers are Jill and Bob.

How Do I Load Impromptu?

There are two versions of Impromptu: the Administrator version and the User version. You can build reports in either version; the difference is that the Administrator version contains a subenvironment that allows and manages changes to a portion of Impromptu called a Catalog. The User version allows only a report developer or consumer the ability to use this Catalog.

There are two basic ways to load the system:

1. The simple way, where you just accept the default selections all the way through the installation wizard
2. The step-by-step way, where you customize the installation

Loading Impromptu

This section walks you through the installation of the Impromptu User version. After you have successfully installed Impromptu, refer to the next section, which describes the differences between Impromptu User and Administrator.

Step 1: Insert CD

First, insert the CD Cognos Enterprise Reporting: Impromptu 6.0.

Figure 1.8
The Autorun window.

The CD has an Autorun feature, shown in Figure 1.8, that immediately shows the load menu. If you do not immediately see this window, chances are you or someone has turned off the Autorun feature from the CD/DVD drive in your computer. To start the Autorun feature with this turned off:

1. Select the Start Menu.Programs.
2. Choose Windows Explorer, or Windows NT Explorer.
3. Expand the CD ROM folder.
4. Double click on Setup.

Step 2: Start Install

The main item we will be installing is the User version, as shown in Figure 1.9.

5. Select "Install Cognos Impromptu User version."

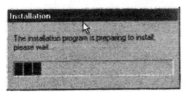

Figure 1.9
The setup install shield: "Impromptu
first load the install program."

Step 3: Welcome Screen

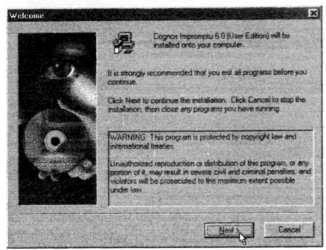

Figure 1.10
The Welcome screen warns you
about having other applications
open during installation.

The Welcome screen, shown in Figure 1.10, begins the installation screens and introduces the installation process to the user. In the past, the user was advised to uninstall previous versions of Impromptu before upgrading to a newer version. However, with Impromptu 6.0, if you are upgrading from Impromptu 3.5, 4.0, or 5.0 to Impromptu 6.0, you may leave the older version on your computer. This is critical for those of you who write reports for different groups of users—those who have older versions of Impromptu on their computers and those who have the later version.

6. Click the Next button.

Step 4: Software License Agreement

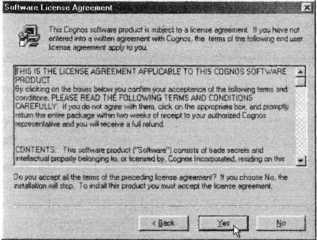

Figure 1.11
This is a standard agreement used throughout the software industry.

7. Click Yes.

Step 5: User Information

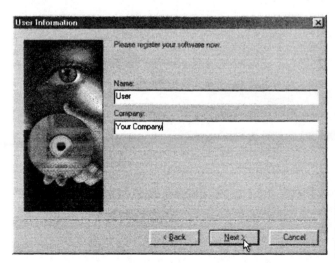

Figure 1.12
User Information allows you to modify the user name and company name.

Impromptu went to your computer's registry and retrieved the computer's user name and the default company name associated with the person logged into the computer.

8. Change either text box as desired and click Next.

Step 6: Application Destination Folder

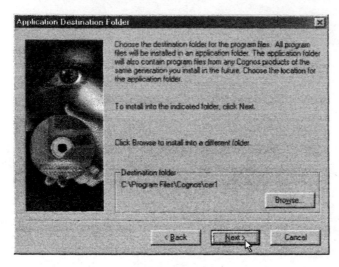

Figure 1.13
This allows you to modify where
the application will reside on
your computer.

Impromptu suggests a standard place to install the application, but you can change where Impromptu is to be installed. This is important because some computers load software in different places—for example, different hard drive letters other than the standard "C Drive."

9. Change the subdirectory as necessary and click Next.

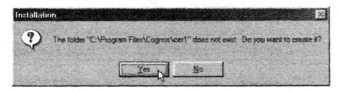

Figure 1.14
Confirms the creation of a
new subdirectory.

If you see Figure 1.15, Impromptu has determined that the subdirectory selected does not currently exist, and asks if you want to create it.

10. Click Yes.

Step 7: Documentation Destination Folder

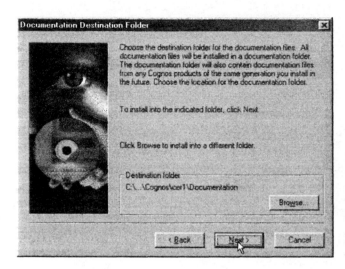

Figure 1.15
The Documentation Destination does the same thing as the Application Destination screen, the previous screen.

If you opted to load the Impromptu documentation, you will be prompted to select a destination folder. Impromptu will suggest a location, but you can choose a different one.

11. Change the subdirectory as necessary and click Next.

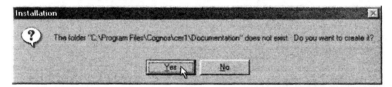

Figure 1.16   Confirms the creation of a new subdirectory.

12. Click Next.

Again, Impromptu may determine that the subdirectory selected does not currently exist and asks if you want to create it.

13. Click Yes.

Step 8: Installation Type

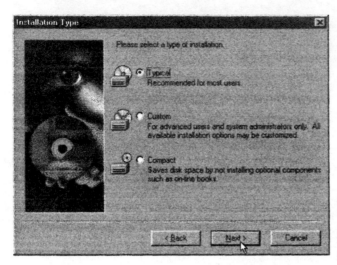

Figure 1.17
The Installation Type window
provides three options to choose
from to install the application.

14. Change the installation type as desired and click Next.

    There are three types of installations:

    • **Typical.** This is the recommended approach to installing Impromptu. It installs the
      application, all help files, a quick tour, and all of the accessory programs delivered
      with Impromptu.
    • **Custom.** The custom installation allows you to select specifically what you want to
      install and not install.
    • **Compact.** A compact installation installs only the bare essentials required to run
      Impromptu.

    Even though disk drive space is reasonably priced these days, one concern always is
how much space you have right now. Each installation requires a different amount of space,
as Table 1.7 shows.

Table 1.7

Installation	Disk Space
Typical	90.18 Meg
Custom	All selected: 97.45 Meg
Compact	48.81 Meg

What Gets Loaded?

Table 1.8 gives a breakdown of each component of the Impromptu installation along with a description and an estimated size required.

Table 1.8

Component	Description	Size
The application	The main Impromptu application	Full application: 62.54 Mb Minimum required: 26.79 Mb
User Defined Functions	User Defined Functions are functions defined outside of Impromptu. This is an advanced topic not covered in this book. For more on this folder, see the online help at http://support.cognos.com.	Maximum: 1.35 Mb
Scheduler	The Scheduler application comes with Impromptu, free of charge. It is a tool that allows you to schedule an Impromptu report to be run while the computer is unattended (e.g., late at night when no one is around or during a specific time of day). This application is not covered in this book, but it is an easy scheduling tools to use.	Maximum: 16.94 Mb
CognosScript Editor	The CognosScript Editor is a Visual Basic-like macro environment for advanced report developers and experienced programmers to use to control more aspects of a report in a scheduler. For those of you who are interested in learning more, either contact your Cognos representative for more information, or review the online documentation provided by Cognos.	Maximum: 8.87 Mb
Portfolio	Portfolio is another free application provided by Cognos. It purpose is for the report developer to create a Briefing Book environment to view reports. This is a programming language-free environment with wizards and helpers to guide you through the process.	Maximum: 20.65 Mb

Component	Description	Size
PowerPrompts	PowerPrompts is a development environment used to build powerful sequential filtering for Impromptu Web Reports—the web-based Managed Reporting Solution from Cognos.	Maximum: 13.08 Mb
Access Manager	Provides user authentication and security for all of Cognos Products. This is used by the Impromptu 6.0 User version, and no additional configuration is required. The setup and configuration of Access Manager should be reserved for administrators to perform across the company.	Maximum: 5.07 Mb

The smallest possible amount of space required to run Impromptu 6.0 User version is 26.79 Meg.

If the installation process requires you to install additional software—for example Distributed COM 1.3—you will get a message like one of the two in Figure 1.18.

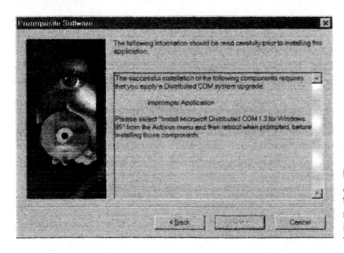

Figure 1.18
A window can display requiring that you need to install additional software, like this one requesting Distributed COM 1.3.

Just cancel out of this installation process, go back to the Impromptu Autorun window, and install software for the version of Windows you are using.

Step 9: Shortcut Folder

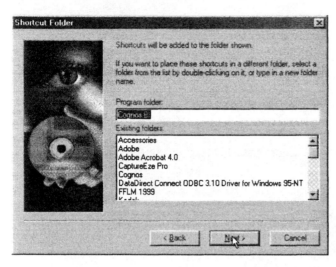

Figure 1.19
The Shortcut folder.

The Shortcut folder, shown in Figure 1.19, allows you to choose where the installation places Impromptu and its components. The default is Cognos BI.

15. Choose the appropriate destination for Impromptu 6.0 User version and click Next.

Step 10: Summary

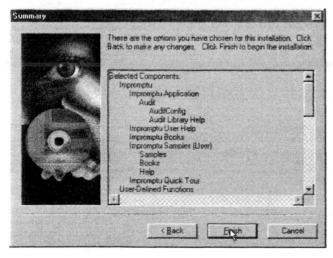

Figure 1.20
The Summary of installation selections.

16. Click Finish.

Tip

If you are concerned about having enough space to install Impromptu, look closely at the Summary window. At the bottom of the scroll-down menu is a total amount of hard drive space required to install and a total estimate of the available space. If it does not look good, use the Back key and remove some of the nonessentials, such as the Tour, Portfolio, and Cognos Script.

The Install Completes

Once you finish the installation options, Impromptu loads.

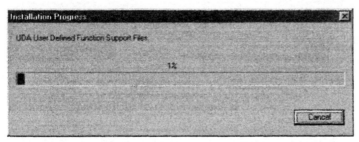

Figure 1.21   Next, the installation bar fills, taking a few minutes.

Upon completion, the installation process displays the new Cognos BI folder or the folder you assigned Cognos BI to from Step 9.

Figure 1.22
The setup is complete.

17. Click OK.

The installation process winds down, clearing out any temporary files needed to install Impromptu and closing the installation.

This gives you a chance to see the icons of the application just installed and to create a desktop shortcut, if desired.

Figure 1.23
The Cognos BI folder.

Create Desktop Shortcut

While you are here, you might as well create a shortcut on your desktop, as shown in Figure 1.24.

1. With the right mouse button, click and drag the Impromptu Icon from the Cognos BI folder to the desktop.

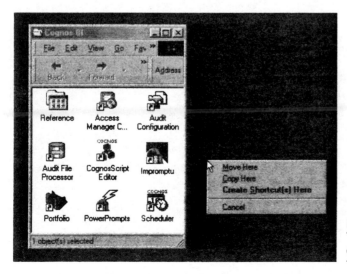

Figure 1.24
This demonstrates creating a shortcut.

2. Choose "Create Shortcut here."

Differences of Administrator Version

The main difference between the User and the Administrator versions are the number of components installed and used. The Administrator version contains three more components to properly administer the Cognos Enterprise Reporting environment. They are as follows:

- **Access Manager Admin Tools**—tools that provide the environment where the administrator gives access to groups of report developers and consumers.
- **Common Logon Server**—tools that provide the necessary environment to combine the logon security between all of Cognos' products.
- **Architect**—a metadata management tool to provide information to all of Cognos' Business Intelligence tools.

These features allow an administrator to establish and manage the proper components. Many of these components are shared with the administration of the Impromptu Web Reporting environment and the PowerPlay suite of products.

Additional Products and Services

The Impromptu install CD contains more products and services that you can load at any time. In general, these components should be installed only if an Impromptu Administrator calls for them.

Summary

At this point, you should be able to

- Recognize what Impromptu is and what it does
- Understand the different user roles within Impromptu
- Load Impromptu successfully and recognize what gets loaded

Now that you have a basic understanding of what Impromptu is, what type of reporting can be performed, and what type of users are needed, you can take the next step and learn the basic reporting principles of Impromptu.

Getting Started

T he focus of this chapter is to get you up and running in Impromptu as quickly as possible. Here we will open up a sample report and take a look at it. The process of running a report is quite simple, but once you run one and understand what occurs during the process, you will see that many things happen under the covers.

This chapter covers the following information:

- Opening a prepackaged report
- Key components of Impromptu
- Overview of the Catalog

Opening Your First Report

In this first section, you will quickly move through the process of opening a prepackaged report in Impromptu.

Start Impromptu

Going forward, every chapter begins with you either opening a report from the samples provided by Cognos or building one from scratch. For this chapter, you will just open a report.

Step 1: Open Impromptu

The rest of this book assumes that you already have Impromptu open. If you need to, dog-ear this page or stick a tab on the page to refer back to opening Impromptu.

Tip

If you decided to create a shortcut on your desktop, go ahead and double click to launch Impromptu, and proceed to Step 2: Opening a Report.

From the main Impromptu desktop:

1. Click the Start button.
2. Click Programs.
3. Click Cognos BI.
4. Choose Impromptu.
5. A welcome screen appears.

Figure 2.1
The Impromptu Welcome Screen.

6. Click the box in the lower left corner that says, "Don't show this in the future."
7. Click the Close button.

You could have used the "Open existing report" button from the initial splash screen, but in all my years of using and instructing Impromptu, I have not run across many people who consistently use it. So, for the purpose of this book, I provide instructions for opening reports "the old fashioned way"—once you are inside the program. If you do intend to use the splash screen, see Table 2.1 for a description of each option.

Table 2.1

Option	Description
Create a report using a template	This allows you to use a predefined template to build a report. Templates are covered in Chapter 4.
Open existing report	This takes you to the familiar Open dialog box to search for previously saved reports.
Take a quick tour	This gives you a guided tour through screen captures of Impromptu.

Now you are ready to open a report. For this exercise, we will use a report that comes with the standard load of Impromptu. This report is called Product Type Sales.imr. The .imr is the file extension used by Impromptu indicating that the file is a report.

Step 2: Opening a Report

As in all Windows applications, Impromptu offers two ways to open a report:

- From the menu
- From the toolbar Open icon

For this exercise, use the menu option.

1. Select File from the menu bar.
2. Select Open.

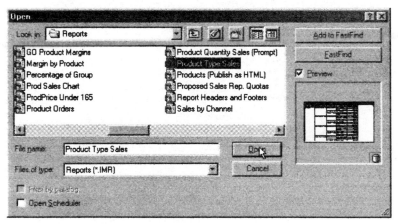

Figure 2.2   The Open dialog box.

3. Select the report: Product Type Sales.

4. Click Open.

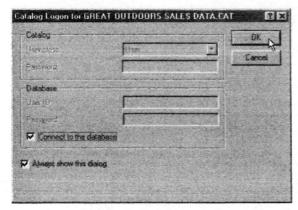

Figure 2.3
The Catalog.

The report tries to open and build the report, but Impromptu needs to know which Catalog to use, as shown in Figure 2.3. This concept is explained in the next section.

5. Click OK on the Catalog dialog box.

The report then runs and returns the results.

And the Results Are...

Congratulations! You just ran your first Impromptu report (see Figure 2.4).

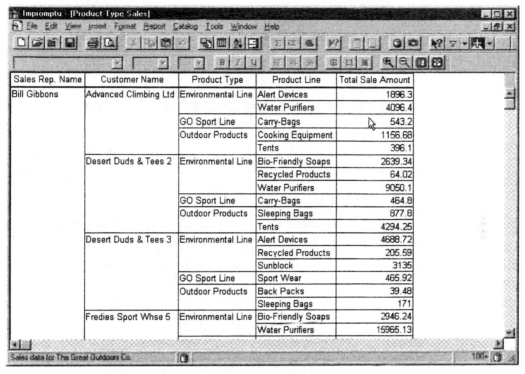

Figure 2.4   The Product Type Sales report.

What Just Happened?

In the few seconds that it took for the report to run, several things happened behind the scenes in Impromptu. This section discusses some of the inner workings of Impromptu.

At a High Level

When you opened the report in the last example, several things happened. First, the report looked for something called a Catalog. In the example, when you first opened Impromptu, you did just that—opened Impromptu, nothing else. By default, No Catalog immediately opens when you open Impromptu. So when you opened this report, you really needed to log on to the Catalog used to build this report. Luckily, you don't have to remember which Catalog was used or where it was stored; that information is stored in the report.

Once you logged on to the Catalog, Impromptu gleaned several key pieces of information from this Catalog. For now, the most important piece of information is which database to connect to. Once connected, Impromptu then requested information from the database, retrieved the data, and performed any additional steps and calculations. Finally,

Impromptu displayed roughly the first 100 records as results for the report that you are looking at. All of that in a couple of seconds!

A Little Deeper

That's all well and good, but it sure leaves quite a few unanswered questions. For example, what is this Catalog you keep hearing about? The first time you open a report, Impromptu needs to know what database is used and where it is, so it can retrieve the data for the report. This what and where information on the database is stored in the report. The report never stores the data itself, just the information on what is to be retrieved from the database and how that data is to be displayed. The actual connecting to the database is stored in something called a Catalog.

The Catalog concept works like the old card catalogs in libraries, or like a filing cabinet used in offices. You use the Catalog to look up columns you wish to use in a report. The Catalog is organized with folders to group common columns. Inside the Catalog, the critical information of where a database is and how Impromptu finds the data inside the database for the reports to be populated is stored.

The Impromptu administrator develops the Catalog. The administrator sets up the relationships for all of the data elements in the database and configures the display of the Catalog so users can more efficiently build reports. The Catalog also has its own logon as well as a database logon. This feature enables Impromptu administrators to allow different user groups to access different parts of the same Catalog, as well as different data.

Simply put, Impromptu needs to use the Catalog to retrieve the specific database used for the report's results. That is why you will see the Catalog logon box every time you open Impromptu and run a report—Impromptu is trying to connect to a database.

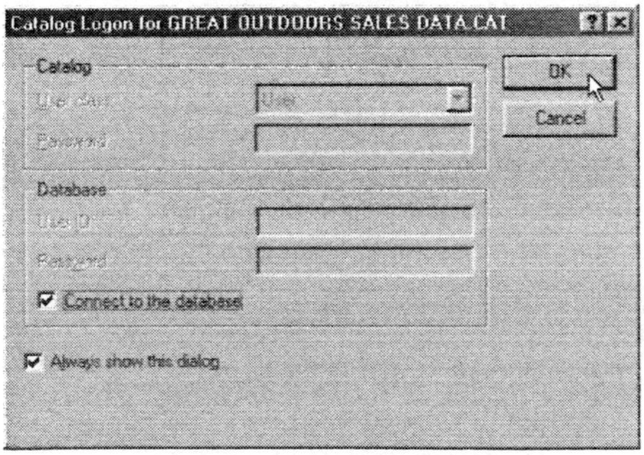

Figure 2.5
Catalog logon box.

And Deeper Still

Databases are very complex storage structures for valuable corporate information. They are kept on expensive machines and are hidden behind locked doors and passwords over the networks. Also, programmers and database administrators are highly trained technical people who know the languages used for extracting data from these databases.

Figure 2.6   An example of a computer room.

In order for Impromptu to allow a nontechnical person, a report developer, to look at items from a database and build reports, it had to have a simple way for users to view and select pieces of information from a database. These pieces of information are stored as columns, and these columns relate to the columns that are stored in database tables.

This separation of database columns and Catalog columns allows the Impromptu administrator to do the following:

1. Label otherwise confusing database column names in more user-friendly, business functional terms.
2. Organize the Catalog columns to make sense to the report developer and report consumer.
3. Group items not in the database tradition form. Report developers and report consumers can select columns from the Catalog regardless of which table in the database the column comes from.

The Catalog stores all that information. An important note: the Catalog does not have to contain every single column from every table in the database. The Impromptu administrator can control the Catalog to include only the columns needed for report developers and consumers to perform their reporting needs.

So, taking this a step further, the report developer may want to build a report using four columns. Each of these columns is stored in different tables. For you to retrieve the right pieces of information from the database, each table has to be matched up with the correct row level information or "joined" together for the results to be accurate. Joining tables can become very complicated very quickly because databases have become so complex in how they store information, as Figure 2.7 shows.

This leads to another terrific service that the Catalog provides for the report developer. When the Impromptu administrator creates the Catalog, he creates joins from table to table and stores that information in the Catalog. All the report developer has to do is choose which column to use for any given report; Impromptu refers back to the Catalog to determine what tables to use, understands how they are joined together, and creates and sends an intelligent request to the database for results. When getting these columns from a Catalog, the report developer just selects the necessary columns, and Impromptu does the rest.

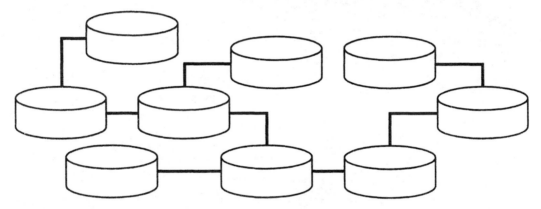

Figure 2.7 A database with tables drawn as cylinders in an ERD (entity-relationship diagram).

How This Affects the Report Developer/Consumer

The Catalog eliminates the need for you to worry about all that join stuff, table stuff, and abbreviations. When you look at a Catalog, you are looking at columns with short descriptions you are familiar with. These columns are organized in a way you want to see them, not how they are stored in some database.

As a report consumer and/or developer, you do not need to worry about connecting to your database. When you installed Impromptu, it made sure you had everything you need to connect to any database. If you initially run into problems trying to run a report against your database, you should get in touch with your database administrator.

Looking at the Report

Now that you have opened your first report, let's take a look at how the report interacts with the Catalog. As you learn more about Impromptu, you will see that there are several pieces that make up a report. This section focused on the relationship between the Catalog and the report itself.

While your report is open:

1. Click the Report menu option.
2. Select Query... to open the Query Dialog Box.

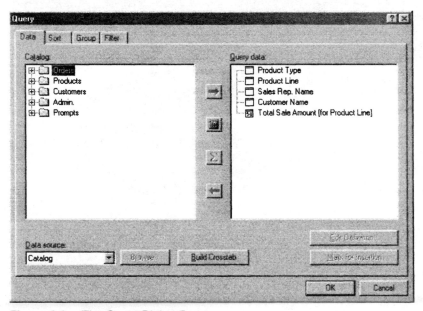

Figure 2.8   The Query Dialog Box.

What you are seeing is the Query Dialog Box (QDB). The QDB contains the contents of the report, but it also provides a view of the Catalog. For a report developer, this is the main place to view a Catalog—the report environment you will be encountering the QDB the most.

The QDB is divided into several tabs, with each tab serving a purpose for the report. Throughout this book, you will discover how these tabs interact and relate to the development of a report. For this chapter, focus your attention on the first tab, the Data tab.

Query Data

The Data tab contains both the Catalog box and the Query box. The Catalog box is a portal
for the report to the database. From a report developer's standpoint, the Catalog box is just
an extension of the database. When a report developer wants to build a report or add columns
from the database to the report, the source is the Catalog and the destination is the report.

For each report, the destination or holding place for the columns coming from the Catalog to the report is the Query Data box. As you can see in Figure 2.9, the columns in the
Query Data box are the same columns shown on the report.

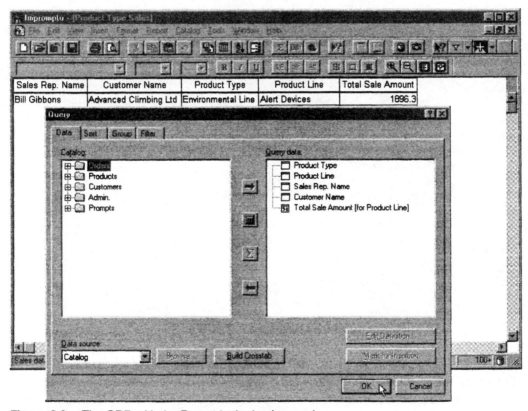

Figure 2.9   The QDB with the Report in the background.

The Catalog

Catalogs are the heart of every Impromptu environment within a company. The one place
where report developers get their columns to build reports is from the Catalog. When an
administrator develops a Catalog, great care is taken to provide an easy-to-use and under-
standable environment for the report developer.

The design of the Catalog—how folders are named and what columns should be where—is every bit as important as the reports themselves. Some companies have researched and conducted usability studies to determine the best possible way to construct Catalogs. This is a smart thing to do, because a well-constructed Catalog makes report building easier and, more important, quicker. In the QDB of Product Type Sales.imr, the Catalog on the left side of Figure 2.9 is the only thing the report developer needs to worry about when populating the report. Behind the scenes of the Catalog are all the ugly table definitions, joins stuff, and complexity. All the report developer has to do is select the items that represent data columns from a database to build a report.

In this specific Catalog, there are five folders. These contain a multitude of items representing the building blocks of reports.

Note

Catalogs can contain any number of folders. I've worked with Catalogs that contain hundreds of folders. The limit is some large number not worth remembering, but what should be noted is that you should limit the number of folders to a list that is manageable by a report user, one not so large that the developer gets "lost in the Catalog."

The Catalog Components

Each Impromptu Catalog contains two essential components, Folders and Columns. In addition to these two required components, a Catalog can contain any combination of the five major component categories.

Folders. Folders are just organizers for the Catalog. They contain all of the other components of the Catalog, as well as additional folders. The additional folders allow information to be further categorized.

For example, in Figure 2.10, the Orders folder contains columns related to an order. This includes customer information, order detail line item information, and additional data that are further grouped into their own folders.

Note

What is really nice about this feature is that you do not have to know which column or data item belongs to which table (or file), or how to match up the tables (files) to each other to obtain the proper information. This takes all of the programming and table relationships out of your hands. You just have to use the columns from the Catalog to build your reports.

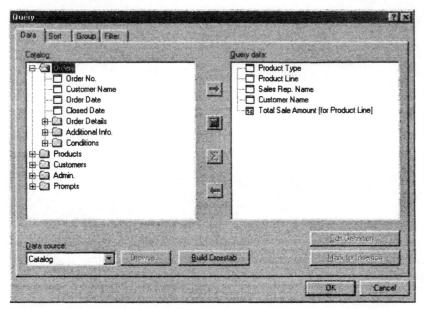

Figure 2.10   Expanded Catalog from QDB, showing the Orders folders.

Columns and Calculated Columns. The items you see in Figure 2.11 other than additional folders are Catalog Columns. These items identify columns (or fields) of data from the database. Catalog Columns, or columns for short, can represent data in a database in two ways:

1. As a straight representation of data (regular columns)
2. As a collection of columns and calculations of data in a database (Calculated Columns)

For example, let's assume your database has the Sales Rep Name broken out into two separate columns: one for the first name, and the other for the last. The Impromptu administrator can create a Calculated Column to show the full Sales Rep Name with one column in the Catalog. So, when you select the column Sales Rep Name, you will automatically get the full Sales Rep Name—you don't have to select the first name and last name separately. This is a simple example, but some advanced calculations can take 15 minutes to an hour to develop!

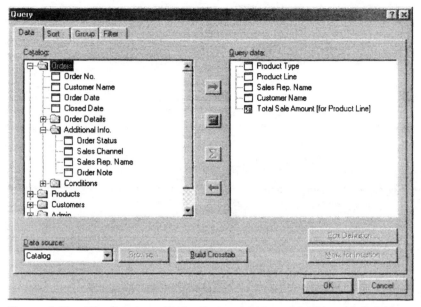

Figure 2.11 The Catalog with the Orders folder and Additional Info folder expanded.

Catalog Filters and Prompts. These items are discussed in later chapters.

Questions and Answers

At this point, you may have some questions about the information just covered.

Questions	Answers
Where are the data stored?	The data are always stored in the database. Data are never stored in an Impromptu IMR report.
Does Impromptu change the values inside the database?	No, Impromptu is a read-only reporting tool. That means you can only retrieve data from the database. You can never write information back to the database.
Do I need to have a Catalog?	Yes, that is the only way Impromptu can find and access the data for the report.
The Catalog in my company has no logon passwords for us. What do we do when we see the Catalog logon?	Simply click OK. You are actually a lucky individual because your Impromptu administrator has taken the time to set up a default for you so you don't have to remember yet another set of passwords.
Does that mean the report knows where the Catalog is stored?	Yes. When a report is saved, the report also stores the location of the Catalog used to build the report.

Questions	Answers
Do I have to logon to my Catalog every time I run a report?	No, once you connect to the Catalog, you can run as many reports that were developed using that Catalog as you want as long as the report retrieves data defined by that Catalog.
What if I have one report open and I open another report that needs a different Catalog?	Each Impromptu report contains a link to the Catalog it needs to retrieve data. If you have a report open and you want to view this new report that uses a different Catalog, Impromptu will close the first report, close the currently opened Catalog, and prompt you to logon to the new Catalog. Then it will run the new report.

Summary

At this point, you should be able to

- Open a report.
- Select and logon to the appropriate Catalog for the report.
- Identify and understand the elements of Impromptu's Catalog.

What was covered here is the foundation of information used in building and running every report in Impromptu. Each time you open a report and run it, the underlying steps outlined here are performed by Impromptu. You now can open reports and have a feel for what happens. In the next chapter, we take a closer look at the user interface and how to navigate around the report once it is open.

Of Desktops, Menus, and Toolbars

So far, so good. You have installed Impromptu, opened it, and opened your first report. The purpose of this chapter is to introduce both report developers and report consumers to the user interface, or "the report." You will use the "Customer Discount" report to become familiar with the features available.

This chapter covers these concepts in two sections:

1. The Impromptu user interface
2. The Impromptu report

Before We Begin

Before we start on these two pieces of information, open the Customer Discount report by following these steps:

1. Open Impromptu, if it is not already open.
2. Select File.Open.
3. Either double click the file "Customer Discount" or click to select it and then click Open.

   Impromptu will bring up the logon for the Catalog.

4. Click OK.

The report will open, retrieve data, and display the results.

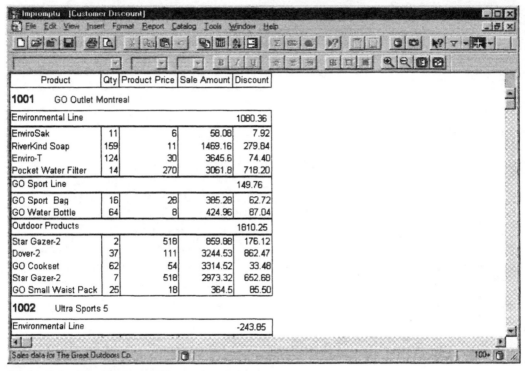

Figure 3.1 The Customer Discount report.

Question	Answer
How do I know if I am logged on to the right Catalog, or any Catalog for that matter?	Impromptu lets you know if you are logged onto a Catalog in the Status bar.

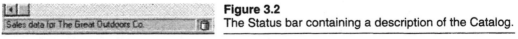

Figure 3.2
The Status bar containing a description of the Catalog.

The Status bar is covered in greater detail throughout this chapter, but to see whether you are logged on to any Catalog at all, look to the lower left of your window, as shown in Figure 3.2. This example shows a description of the Catalog.

The Impromptu User Interface

When you open the Customer Discount report, you will see the standard Impromptu graphical user interface. The graphical user interface, or GUI, is the same no matter what report you have open in Impromptu. You will always see the same basic elements. Impromptu's GUI, shown in Figure 3.3, is divided into four main parts: desktop, menu, toolbars, and Status bar. This section covers each in detail.

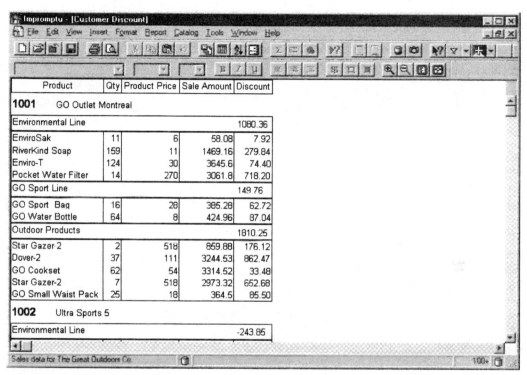

Figure 3.3   Impromptu with Customer Discount report open.

Desktop

The desktop, shown in Figure 3.4, is not only the location where the report is displayed, but it also provides a wealth of information about the report, from the data itself, to the report's appearance, and even down to the layout of the GUI. Additionally, the Impromptu GUI is a standard multidocument interface. That means you can open several reports at once.

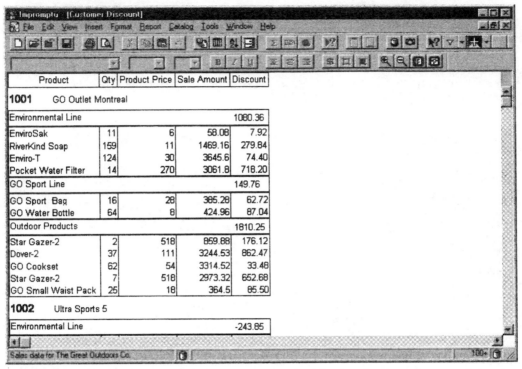

Product	Qty	Product Price	Sale Amount	Discount
1001 GO Outlet Montreal				
Environmental Line				1080.36
EnviroSak	11	6	58.08	7.92
RiverKind Soap	159	11	1469.16	279.84
Enviro-T	124	30	3645.6	74.40
Pocket Water Filter	14	270	3061.8	718.20
GO Sport Line				149.76
GO Sport Bag	16	28	385.28	62.72
GO Water Bottle	64	8	424.96	87.04
Outdoor Products				1810.25
Star Gazer-2	2	518	859.88	176.12
Dover-2	37	111	3244.53	862.47
GO Cookset	62	54	3314.52	33.48
Star Gazer-2	7	518	2973.32	652.68
GO Small Waist Pack	25	18	364.5	85.50
1002 Ultra Sports 5				
Environmental Line				-243.85

Figure 3.4   The Desktop, identifying tags for name of application: impromptu, name of report, window management buttons of upper right: min, max, and close. The report window has the same application buttons: min, max, and close.

Tip

New to Impromptu 6.0—you can open up several instances of Impromptu at the same time! All you have to do to run a second instance of Impromptu is start it the way you would the first time.

You will also find that Impromptu has taken advantage of the tooltip feature, as shown in Figure 3.5. As you move your cursor around the desktop and briefly hold the cursor over buttons, you will get a brief description of what each button does.

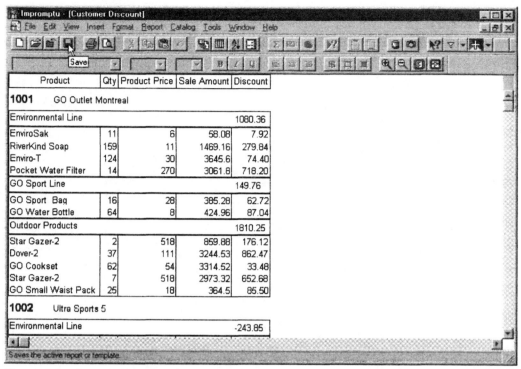

Figure 3.5   A tooltip identifying the Save button.

Menu

The menus in Impromptu work exactly the same as in other Windows applications. In the Impromptu GUI, there are 10 menus to assist you in your report development and viewing. A brief explanation of each menu follows.

File Menu

The file menu controls the report processing functions, such as opening a report, saving a report, and printing the report. Click the menu header to get a drop-down selection of items. The underlined letters on the menu, shown in Figure 3.6, identify quick keystrokes to access functions directly from the keyboard. For example, using the keyboard you can choose the File menu by holding down the Alt key and pressing the key for "F."

Tip

You can use the mouse to select File.Open to open a report, or you can choose the quick key-stroke combination of Ctrl+O, as shown in Figure 3.6. Each performs the same function.

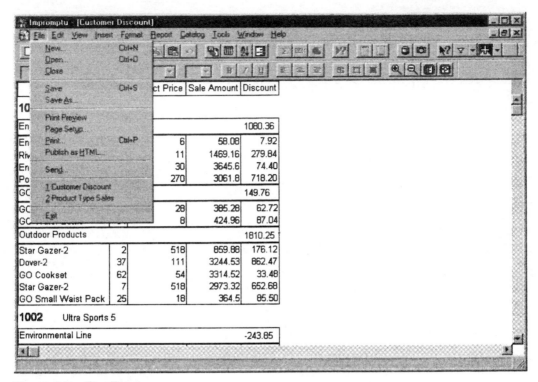

Figure 3.6   The File menu.

The "Send..." option allows you to send the report you have open to anyone via your e-mail. All you have to do is choose File.Send... and an e-mail window opens up with the report attached to the e-mail.

This is very useful, but be careful. Even though the report being sent does not contain data, always think twice before sending reports to someone outside your company.

Additionally, the "Publish as HTML..." option allows you to create the report as an HTML Web page. When selected, Impromptu retrieves all of the data for the report and creates a set of HTML pages to display the Impromptu report with a Web browser. This feature is helpful if you want others to see the report using just a Web browser.

Edit Menu

The Edit menu, shown in Figure 3.7, is used in the same way as Edit menus in other GUIs. They give the user easy commands and shortcuts to handle searching, copying, and pasting content from one place to another. The options available in this menu vary, depending on what portion of an Impromptu report is selected. It would take too long to describe each possible scenario here, so note that when you want to use a function in the Edit menu and you cannot choose it, then you probably have not accurately chosen something to perform that function on.

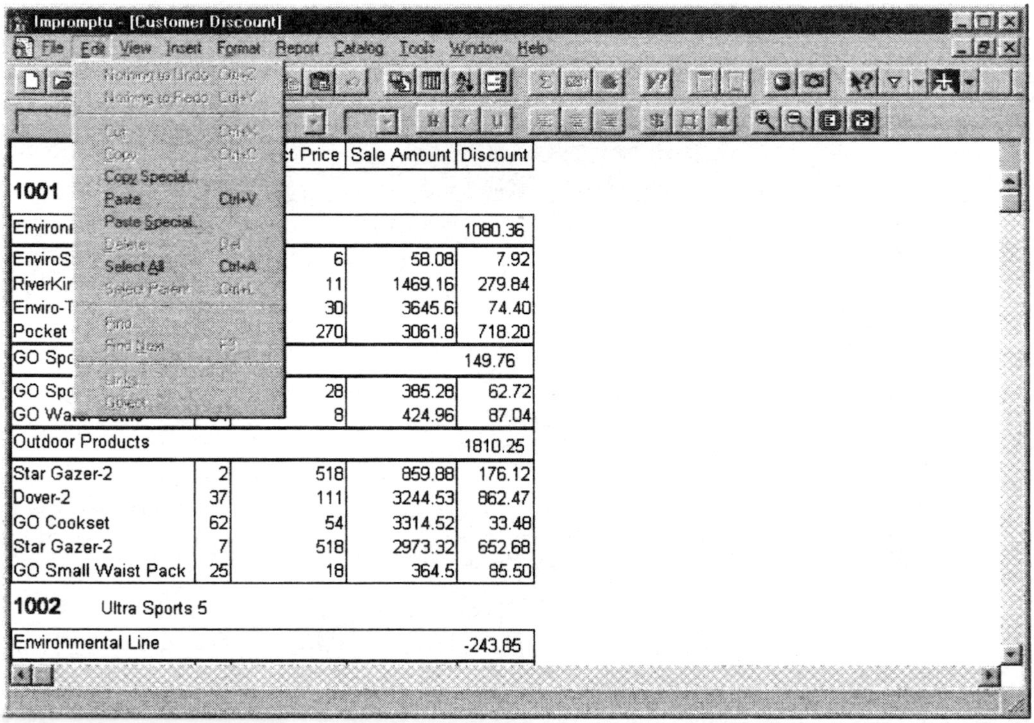

Figure 3.7   The Edit menu.

Included in the Edit menu are such familiar features as Cut/Copy/Paste, Select All (selects all items on screen), Select Parent, (to be described in chapter 11), Undo, Redo, Find, and Find Next.

Note

The grayed-out items in all of the menu lists are options that are not available for what the cursor has selected on the report at this time. When you have an item selected that makes sense for a grayed-out item, it will be black, allowing you to select it. This activated option is now enabled, whereas the grayed option is disabled.

View Menu

The View menu, shown in Figure 3.8, is the menu that controls the layout of Impromptu. In this menu, you can choose how to look at the report, control what toolbars to use (discussed later in this chapter), and decide whether or not you want to have a ruler display around the border of the report. Unlike the other menus, there are not any shortcut keys for the items in this menu. This is due to the frequency with which these functions are used. The functions in the View menu are those a report developer or a report consumer would not use too often, so it does not make sense to overload Impromptu with unnecessary functions.

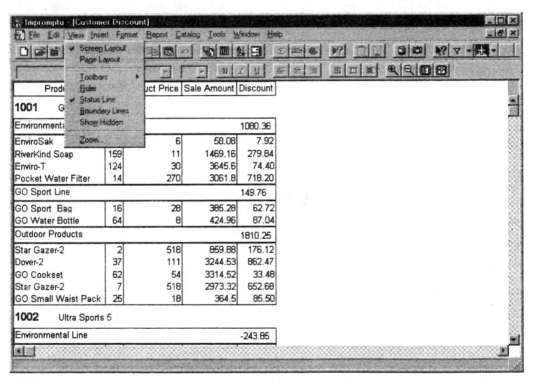

Figure 3.8   The View menu.

This menu enables you to view the ruler and status line. These options all help you to customize the viewing of the report area. Layout allows you to toggle between viewing styles. The current layout is Page layout. This is similar to the typical word processing application's Page layout. This is how the items look as if you were looking at a sheet of paper and/or if you were to print the report.

Insert Menu

The Insert menu, shown in Figure 3.9, allows report developers to insert items into the report. This menu opens the door to the types of reports and content you can add to a report. During the first few chapters, you are limited to the first couple of menu choices. In Chapter 11, the rest will be explained as you learn how to build dynamic reports.

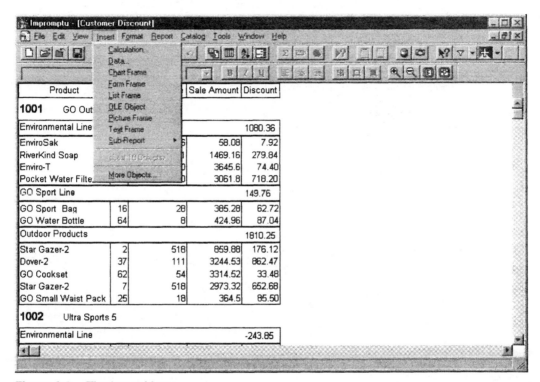

Figure 3.9   The Insert Menu.

This menu allows report developers to insert items into the report itself. Items can range from data columns to lines to page numbers. These items will be discussed in greater detail in Chapter 11.

Format Menu

The Format menu, shown in Figure 3.10, provides menu access to such functions as controlling the format, style, size, and properties of everything about the report. As you will see in further detail in Chapter 5, and later in Chapter 11, there are many things involved in formatting, and you will be able to format many parts of the report.

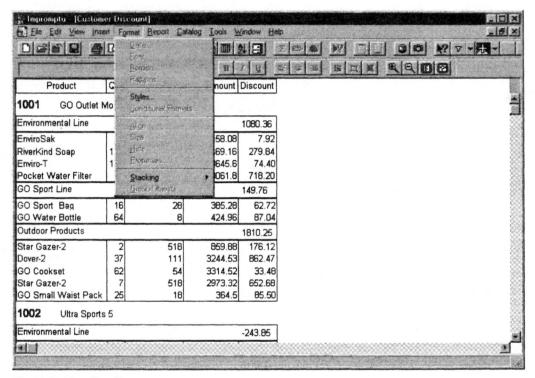

Figure 3.10   The Format menu.

Report Menu

The Report menu, shown in Figure 3.11, provides menu access to Query and other management tools for the report. The focus of this book is to address the reporting needs of report consumers and report developers, which includes the first five options on this menu. These features and functions are discussed throughout the upcoming chapters.

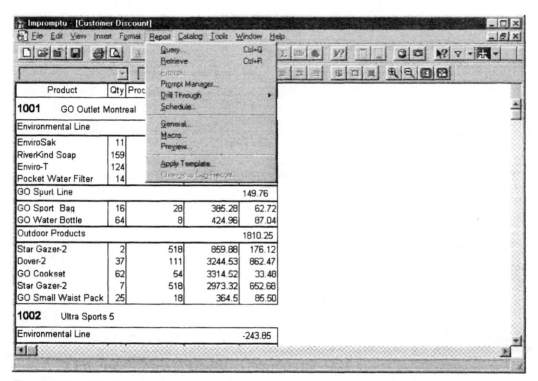

Figure 3.11   The Report menu.

Catalog Menu

The Catalog menu has two distinctly different lists. On one hand, there is the User version Catalog menu, as shown in Figure 3.12. This menu gives report developers and report consumers the ability to directly access and logon to a Catalog. The other version of the Catalog menu is the Administrator version, as shown in Figure 3.13. The administrator's Catalog menu allows the administrator to maintain the components in the Catalog and manage access to the database.

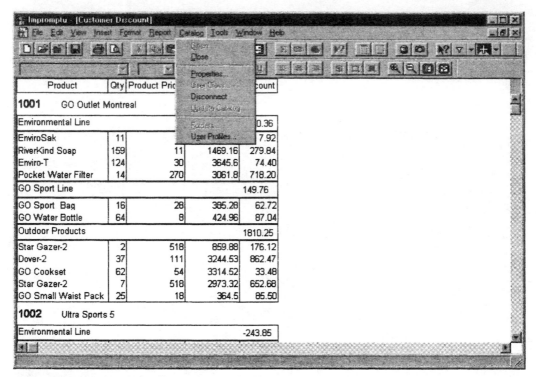

Figure 3.12   User version Catalog menu. The User version allows you to perform simple features such as opening and closing a Catalog.

Figure 3.13
Administrator version Catalog menu. The Administrator version gives the administrator the full capability to manage the Catalog. It is strongly recommended that one take the administrator's class before constructing a Catalog.

Tool Menu

The Tool menu, shown in Figure 3.14, is rarely used. This menu contains accessories to Impromptu such as the scheduling tool, the macro language editor, toolbar customization, Impromptu options, and database access configuration. As the need for using one of these functions arises during the course of the book, it is explained in complete detail.

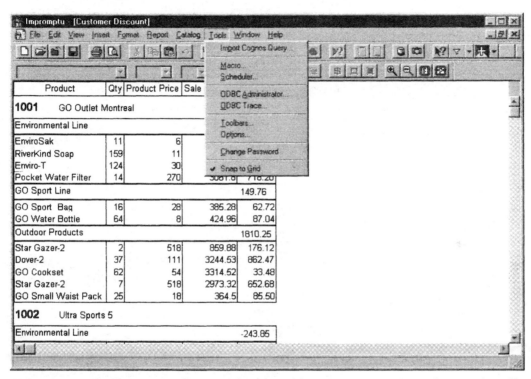

Figure 3.14   The Tools menu allows users to customize the buttons on the toolbars and modify Impromptu options.

Window Menu

The Window menu, shown in Figure 3.15, manages how the reports are displayed inside Impromptu. This menu acts just like other Window menus you have used in the past. When you have opened multiple reports within Impromptu, the Window menu lets you bring one specific report to the front.

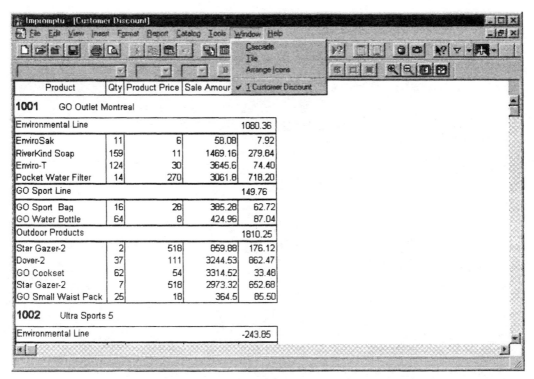

Figure 3.15   The Window menu allows users to arrange reports inside Impromptu in various ways. Also, if the reports are all maximized, users can select between multiple open reports.

Help Menu

The final menu is the Help menu, as shown in Figure 3.16. Impromptu provides help in two ways. One is the typical Contents and Index style Windows help. The second delivery system of help is the online books provided by Cognos. These books contain detailed explanations of all of the advanced features and functions needed to tackle the most challenging question.

The Help menu enables a user to obtain online help with Impromptu. It contains a documentation roadmap, a quick tour, and the traditional Help Contents and Index. Additionally, Cognos provides all of its books electronically through the Adobe Acrobat Reader utility. (This comes with the Impromptu CD and is recommended in the initial installation.)

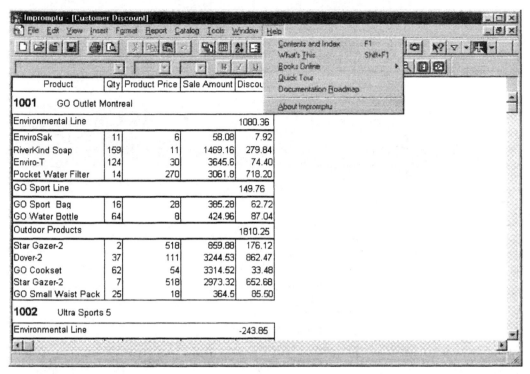

Figure 3.16   The Help menu.

Toolbars

The Impromptu reporting environment has been designed to be user friendly and graphical to make building and viewing reports easier for nontechnical people. The use of Menus appealed to users, but there were times when just clicking a button to do something was desired because of convenience and speed.

Therefore, three toolbars evolved to group common tasks together. These toolbars are Standard, Format, and Layout. From their titles alone, you can determine the general use for the buttons contained in them.

Tip

The buttons shown in the following toolbars are not the only buttons available. See the online Help for instructions on customizing your toolbars.

Standard Toolbar

The standard toolbar, shown in Figure 3.17, provides the basic functionality you would expect: Open, Close, Save, Print, Cut, Copy, and Paste. Each of these buttons uses the common icons that other Windows applications use.

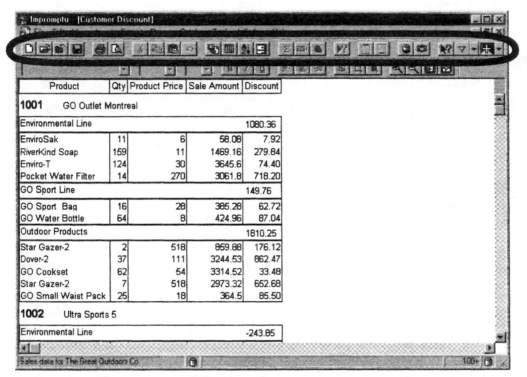

Figure 3.17   The Standard toolbar.

Format Toolbar

The format toolbar provides buttons to manage the format of the item you have selected, whether it is a text item, a number, a rectangular box, a column of data, or even a header.

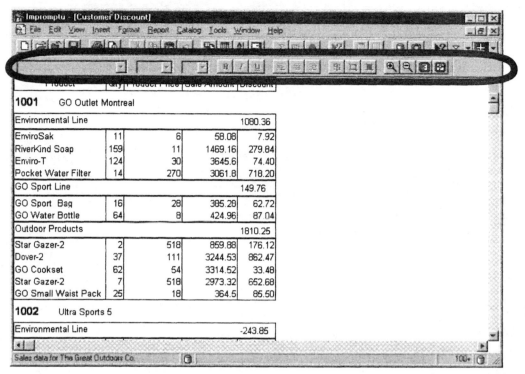

Figure 3.18 The Format toolbar.

Layout Toolbar

The layout toolbar, shown in Figure 3.19, allows for more advanced features within Impromptu. Here you are able to manipulate how the report layout is established, what is included, and how it is to be seen on the screen by the report writer and consumers.

Icons associated with items that can be placed on the report at various places are covered in Chapter 11. Also, you will find a group of icons that allow easy alignment of items on a report, as well as the Screen layout and Page layout.

Tip

When you install Impromptu, the default user interface does not include the Layout toolbar. Once you display the Layout toolbar and then close Impromptu, Impromptu remembers that you had it open previously; the next time you open Impromptu, the Layout toolbar will display. To add it, do the following:

1. *Select View from the menu bar.*
2. *Move the cursor down to Toolbars.*
3. *Move the cursor to the right to a Flyout menu, and then down to Layout.*

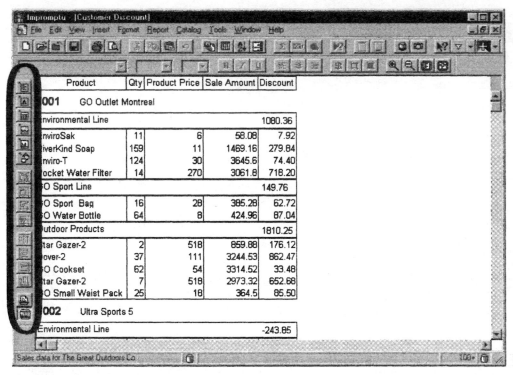

Figure 3.19   The Layout toolbar.

At this time, take a moment to move your cursor over each of the buttons and allow the tooltips to appear.

The Status Bar

With every report you build, Impromptu, in most cases, is making data requests to extremely powerful and complex databases. Impromptu takes care of 95% of the dirty work for you! The other 5% comes from knowing the GUI and constructing the report to your specifications. The Status bar gives you the information you need to make those reports.

The Status bar for Impromptu provides a wealth of information at a quick glance. From the Status bar, you can answer questions about your report such as:

- What Catalog am I connected to?
- Am I connected to a database?
- What have I selected inside the report?
- How many records have I received from the database?

The Status bar answers all of these questions. Granted, some of these questions are asked infrequently, such as the Catalog information. But others, such as determining what is selected on the screen, are extremely useful.

The Contents of the Status Bar

This section dissects the Status bar, as shown in Figure 3.20. We consider at each part of the Status bar to determine what it means, what you the report writer should look for, and how to use the information you see.

Basically, the Status bar is made up of five indicators:

1. Catalog description
2. Catalog connection status
3. Highlight identifier
4. Rows retrieved
5. Report Data source

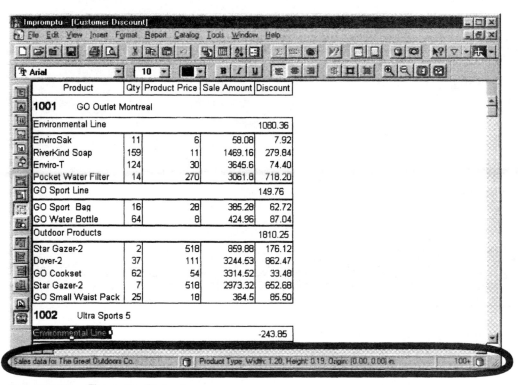

Figure 3.20   The entire Status bar.

Catalog Description

This is a description that the administrator manually types in to describe the Catalog. It helps the report developer identify which database or reporting environment she is working in. For example, an administrator may use the Catalog Description "Sales" for the sales Catalog.

Catalog Connection Status

The Catalog Connection Status indicator quickly lets the report writer know if Impromptu is connected to the database. This is either a yes, shown in Figure 3.21, or a no, shown in Figure 3.22. Being connected to the database is essential to displaying the information, the report.

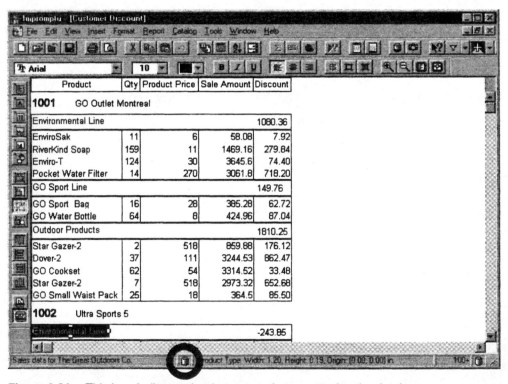

Figure 3.21   This icon indicates that Impromptu is connected to the database.

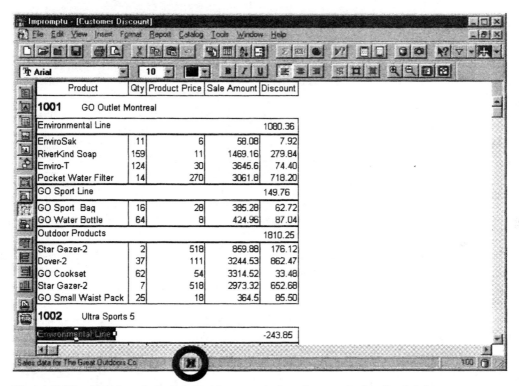

Figure 3.22   This icon indicates that Impromptu is not connected to the database.

Tip

To connect or disconnect a Catalog from a database, Select Catalog.Connect (or Disconnect).

Remember

When you initially logon to the Catalog, you are asked if you want to connect to the database. The default is always to connect to the database. Checking or unchecking this box will give the same results.

Question	*Answer*
Why would I ever want to disconnect from a database when I'm building or running a report? If the IMR file, the report, does not store any actual data, how am I going to see my report, my data, when I am not connected to the one thing, the database, that has the data?	You are correct in assuming that when you are not connected to a database, you get no data in your report. That does not mean that you cannot look at your report. You can still open the report and make changes to the appearance or the layout of the report, but you cannot see any results.
	For example, say you want to change a formatting component of one of the columns in a report, and the database is currently "down for repairs." Any attempts to run the report would result in frustration. Running the report while Impromptu is disconnected from the database enables you to modify the report without having to request data from the database. Later, when the database is working again, you can just attach to the database and run that report by retrieving data.

Tip

While connected to the database, to retrieve data from the database on demand, select Report. Retrieve.

Highlight Identifier

As a report writer, you will constantly be referring to this portion of the Status bar, because it tells you what you have selected on the report. As Figure 3.23 shows, a particular cell that has the value 1469.16 was clicked. By looking at just the value, you could guess that this is the Sale Amount for "RiverKind Soap." But with some reports, you want to be sure. To be sure, go to the Status bar, as shown in Figure 3.24.

Not only does the identifier tell you about the columns you have selected, but it will also tell you about the other "elements" of the report, such as height and width of the cell and its point of origin.

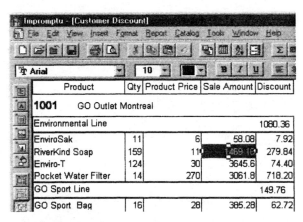

Figure 3.23   Impromptu report, with just the 1469.16 Cell highlighted.

Try This:

You probably have already clicked on an item in the report body—that is OK. Go ahead and click on a few more items in the report and notice the change with the Status bar and the toolbars. You have separate functionality for each item you have selected. The Status bar tells you what you have selected, and the toolbar allows you to select the proper buttons for the given object.

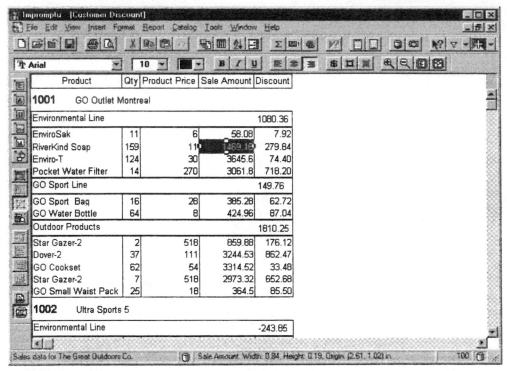

Figure 3.24   Impromptu report, with the 1469.16 cell highlighted and Status Bar shown.

The Esc Key

Question	Answer
I clicked on the wrong cell, and I clicked somewhere else on the report, and the whole darn report is now highlighted. How do I get out of this and what happened?	This is a very common question asked by nearly every report developer. Impromptu is a frame-based reporting environment. What that means is everything is a frame, from the cell you selected to the white space off to the side.
	We will explain this fully in Chapter 11. For now, to remove the improper selecting of a frame and clear the report of any selections/highlighting, press the Esc key.

Rows Retrieved

This is a very helpful, yet a very deceptive indicator if it is not properly explained. The number that you initially see in the sample report, shown in Figure 3.25, is the initial number of rows retrieved. That is all that this indicator identifies—the number of rows being retrieved from the database.

Sometimes, people interpret this number as the number of rows being displayed on the report. This is a common mistake.

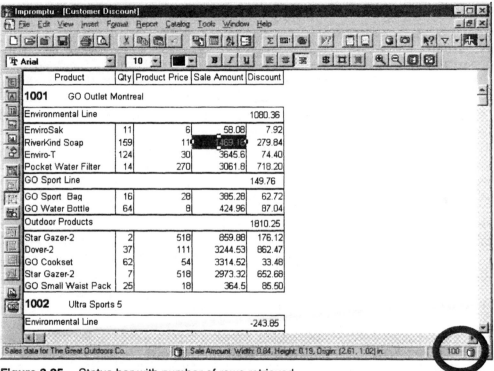

Figure 3.25   Status bar with number of rows retrieved.

What makes this tricky is how Impromptu works behind the scenes to get the results to the report. Impromptu takes the columns and other requirements of the report from the QDB and creates a request for data to display. These requests cannot always be processed quickly and efficiently. Sometimes the database has to pass information back to Impromptu in stages before the results can be shown. It is in these cases that this number becomes a little deceptive. This is further explained later in this chapter.

Report Data Source

The Report Data Source describes where the data that is populating the report come from. In the beginning of report building, you build your report against a database. Afterward, there are a couple of ways to "store" some of the data locally. This storing of data locally is mainly used as a temporary holding area for Impromptu to use when it needs to request data. The four Data Sources used by Impromptu are

- **Database.** This is the default and main source for reports in Impromptu. It contains live information constantly being retrieved when reports are run.
- **HotFile.** HotFiles are separate files from a database. They are used in conjunction with databases when not all the information necessary for a report is stored in the main database.
- **Snapshot.** A snapshot is a permanent local copy of the data used by the report. Snapshots are useful when a report needs to be viewed while the user is not connected to the database. For example, an Account Executive wants to show the report on his laptop to a client while at the client's office. The Account Executive is not connected to the database, so he would need a snapshot of the report to show the data.
- **Thumbnail.** A thumbnail is used to temporarily store a small amount of data locally while some minor modifications are made to the report or database. For example, a report developer is using a database that sometimes runs slowly to run an Impromptu report. The developer notices a few small changes to make to the report before printing. Instead of making each change and waiting for the database to return the information, the developer can create a thumbnail and view the changes more quickly.

The Two Parts of a Report

When you build an Impromptu report, you build one thing—the report. As a report developer in Impromptu, you do not have to worry about how many parts to the report there are, whether there is a query, or whatever. You just want to build and/or run a report.

The following is solely for informational purposes. It provides insight into why certain things happen when you run a report. So, instead of always wondering what is actually going on when you run a report, you will have an understanding of how the different elements of a report interact with Impromptu to deliver a report.

Each Impromptu report is made of two components: one is the query and the other is the layout of the results. This section discusses each component and how the two interact with each another.

The Query

Most users do not know SQL (Structural Query Language, pronounced Se-quel), the programming language used by technical people to extract information from databases. Because of Impromptu's friendly user interface, the Impromptu report developer and consumer do not have to know SQL. In fact, Impromptu is structured so users don't have to do any query programming at all.

When you take columns from a Catalog and add them to the report using the QDB, Impromptu is essentially building a query, one of those nasty SQL things. When you "run" the report, Impromptu sends the query off to the database to perform its job. The database then sends the data back to Impromptu. That happens first. After the data is received by Impromptu, Impromptu then takes that data, data from the results of the query, and makes any changes for the layout of the report.

More on the QDB

The QDB, shown in Figure 3.26, helps you build your query. With this, you select the columns you want in your report, filter in/out information, sort and group data, and tell what is to be displayed in the layout—all from this window and the four tabs within the User version. The Administrator version contains three additional tabs to perform expert, or black belt, reporting techniques.

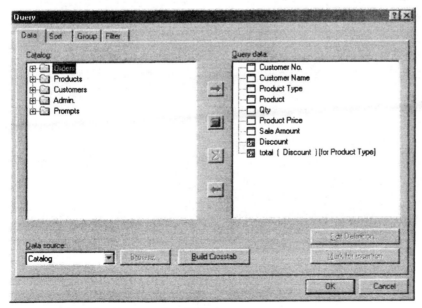

Figure 3.26   The User version QDB.

Data Tab.   The Data tab is where all of the action takes place. Here columns are added, created, modified, inserted, and removed. Functionality within the Data tab is discussed throughout this book. Specifically, the mechanics of the Data tab are discussed later in this chapter and in Chapter 4. For this chapter, we focus only on using the QDB to delete columns from the Query Data. In the next chapter, we discuss the finer points of the QDB.

Sort Tab.   The Sort tab lets the report developer choose how the report is sorted and in what order. This is discussed in Chapter 8.

Group Tab.   The Group tab has quite a few features stacked in it. Chapter 8 covers the essentials of grouping while Chapter 9—Summaries—contains additional information regarding the Group tab.

Filter Tab.   The Filter tab is used to exclude unwanted information from the report. This is discussed in Chapters 6 and 10.

Tip

Impromptu is just like any other Windows application; it provides several ways to perform one operation. The same holds true for accessing the QDB. You can access the QDB in three ways:

1. *By Menu: Use Report.Query.*
2. *By Toolbar: click the QDB button, as shown here:*
3. *By Desktop: press the Ctrl+Q combo.*

The Layout

The layout is what you see when the report is displayed on the screen. If you were to look inside a database, it would be extremely difficult to retrieve a simple "picture" of the information you are looking for. Most databases store only the necessary information, saving precious space. The database doesn't care what the layout looks like. The layout of the report gives the report consumer a clearer picture of the data.

One of the major advantages of using Impromptu is the powerful layout. Throughout this book, there are exercises, tips, and advice on getting the most out of the layout. For now, start with some basic concepts of viewing information in the Customer Discount report and begin to understand the impact of the placement of data in the report layout.

Moving Columns Around in the Layout

Impromptu's layout gives the user a great deal of flexibility in customizing a reporting view. After you ran the current report, you noticed that the columns and headers were displayed in a default manner. But as you already know, things change, especially reports and their requirements.

Simple Report Change.   Let's say you wanted to move the "Qty" column to the far right. With Impromptu, this is an easy task.

To move a column from one location to another, follow these simple steps:

1. Select a column by clicking on a cell in that column, as shown in Figure 3.27.
2. Click, hold, and drag that column to the new location, as shown in Figure 3.28.

Note

When you hold down the mouse button and move the cursor, a dotted line placeholder signifies the new location.

3. Let go of the mouse click, and it's done, as shown in Figure 3.29.

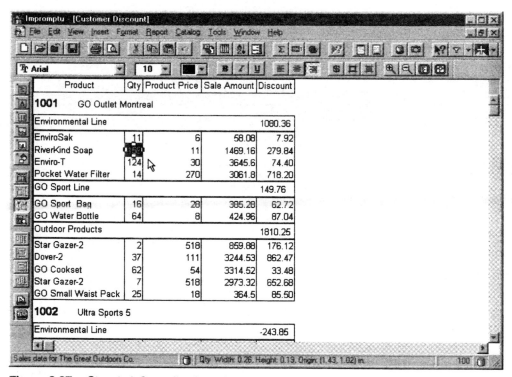

Figure 3.27   Step 1: A Qty cell selected.

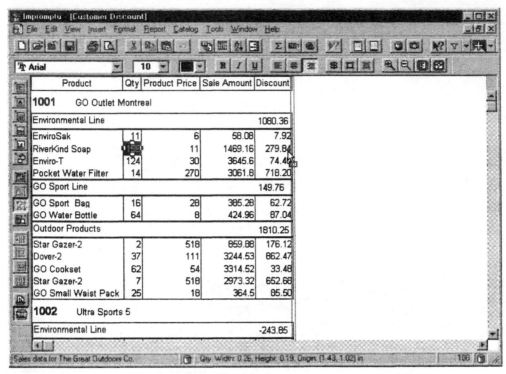

Figure 3.28   Step 2: The vertical dashed line representing where it's being moved to.

Note

You may notice that during step 2, the dotted line placeholder is vertical. You are also allowed to have this as horizontal. The horizontal placement indicates an advanced feature in Impromptu for creating Crosstab reports. Crosstabs are covered in Chapter 13.

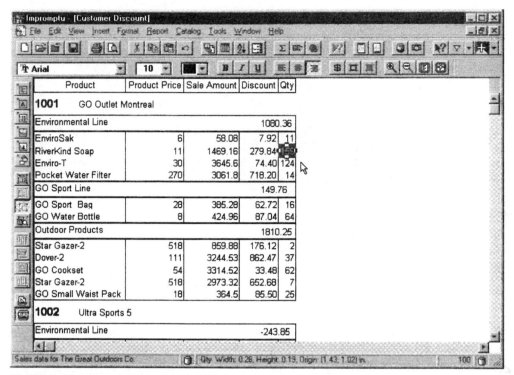

Figure 3.29 Step 3: Where the cursor was released, the column now rests.

The Undo

Question	Answer
Hey! I accidentally let go of the mouse button during the last step-by-step. What do I do now? Or I was doing something and... I don't know what happened, I just lost it!	Yes, these things happen all the time. That is why Impromptu has an Undo button (Figure 3.30): This button is nestled in the standard toolbar. The sky is not the limit. Keep in mind you only get 10 Undo's from the current point when editing a report.

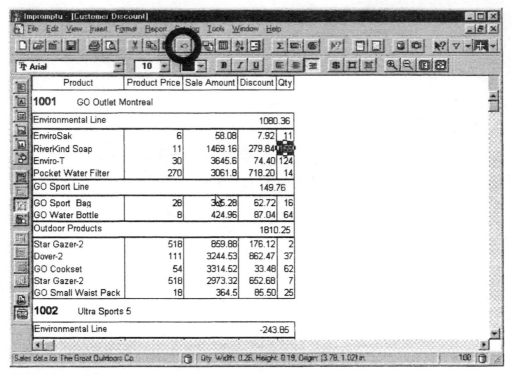

Figure 3.30   The Undo button.

When you hit the Undo button, there was a brief flicker of the Impromptu screen. Impromptu decided that it needed to requery for data before redisplaying because of the Undo.

Try This:

Try this new technique on a couple of columns by trying to duplicate the following manipulated version of the Customer Discount report:

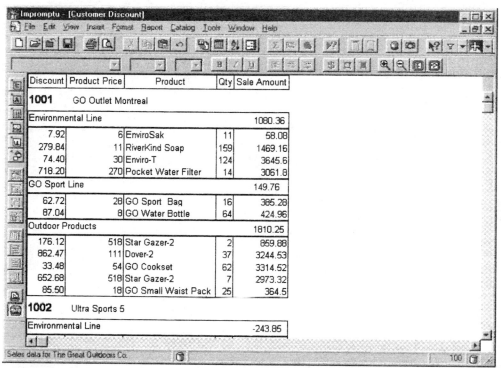

Figure 3.31   The Customer Discount report with the columns changed around.

This practice is a vital skill because the majority of report writing involves getting the report to look right for your boss.

Deleting Columns

There will come a time when you will want to delete a data column from the report. This is a simple and easy process. Never be afraid to delete a column from a report, because you are never going to mess something up on the database, nor are you going to lose or delete the data itself. The only thing you will do by deleting a column is to remove it from the report.

Deleting columns is as simple as moving columns in Impromptu. This example deletes the Qty column you just moved around a few minutes ago. To delete, follow these simple steps:

1. Click on one of the cells in the Qty column.
2. Press the Del key on your keyboard, and it's done.

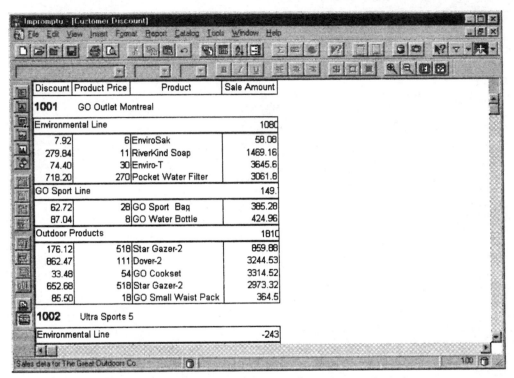

Figure 3.32   The Customer Discount report without Qty column selected.

Now, the Catch.   The column of data for Qty is no longer visible on the layout of the report. It is deleted. Right? Well, not exactly. You deleted the visible column of Qty, but this was in the layout of the report only. You cannot see it on the report, but the Qty column is still being brought back with all of the other columns that we are looking at. Why? In the last section, we talked about how the report is part query and part layout. When you delete the column in the layout, that is the only place it is deleted. It still exists as a column in the query part of the report. To delete the column from the report entirely, you need to go back to the QDB.

Back to the QDB.   One thing you'll notice immediately after opening the QDB is that the Qty column still exists on the right-hand side. This column on the right-hand side is the list of Query Data items. These are the columns requested from the database. Because you only deleted the column in the layout, it still is being brought back during the query phase. Is that bad? No, you can leave as many columns in the Query Data box as you like. But, the more you leave in there, the more crowded and congested it gets.

To remove the Qty column from the query, follow these steps:

1. On the QDB, select the Data tab.
2. Click the Qty column in the Query Data box on the right.
3. Press the Del key on the keyboard.

You can also use the left arrow.

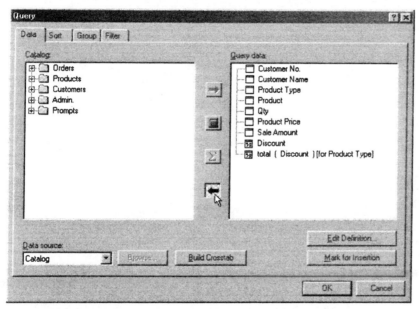

Figure 3.33   The QDB, Deleting the Qty column with the left arrow.

4. Press OK to run the report.

Now the QTY column is gone from the layout and the query. We cover more of the QDB in the next chapter.

Summary

At this point, you should be able to

- Recognize and navigate the Impromptu interface.
- Understand the two stages of building a report in Impromptu.
- Move and delete data columns from the layout view.
- Use the Undo functionality.
- Employ the basic functionality of the Query Data Box aka the QDB.

Impromptu is an easy-to-use tool. It has been engineered to provide easy navigation throughout the report. As the tool developed over the years, many improvements have been added to make it even more simple and powerful.

Creating New Reports

You've loaded Impromptu, opened a previously built
report, and navigated around "the report." This chapter explains how you build a report
from scratch. Here, you will learn the steps necessary to build a basic report and learn about
other important features available to you when you create a report.

Do not be discouraged by the number of questions you will have at the end of this
chapter, just look forward to learning the answers in the upcoming chapters.

This chapter will teach you how to

- Review the different reporting templates.
- Use Impromptu templates to create a report.
- View the report you created in different on-screen layouts.
- Save the report for later viewing.

Creating a New Report

As in most Windows applications, there are multiple ways to do something in Impromptu.
Even though each method ends with the same result, each one has its own advantages.

Impromptu offers three different ways to create a new report:

1. Select File.New from the menu bar.
2. Click the New Report button on the toolbar.
3. Use the keystroke combination of Ctrl+N.

When you create a new report using options 1 or 3, the system displays the New Report
dialog box. From here, you can choose one of the seven types of report templates that

Impromptu provides. The default template is the Simple List. These two methods are used when the report user does not want to build a report using the standard template. Options 1 and 3 provide the user with the flexibility to choose different types of reporting styles.

If you create a new report using option 2, the system launches the Report Wizard, which walks you step by step through the process of creating a basic report. We do not cover the Report Wizard because it is so simple to use; compared with building a report manually, the Report Wizard provides no real advantages. Most people who use the Report Wizard are completely new to Impromptu and have not seen how easy it is to build a report without it. Feel free to give option 2, the Report Wizard, a try and then return to this chapter when you are finished.

Question	Answer
Does the toolbar button always have to launch the Create Report Wizard?	No. The system default is to launch the wizard, but you can change this so that Impromptu uses the default template instead by following these steps:

    1. Select Tools from the menu bar.

    2. Select Options.

    3. Go to the General tab.

    4. At the bottom, de-select the Use the Report Wizard checkbox.

Now Impromptu will launch the default template as the report format.

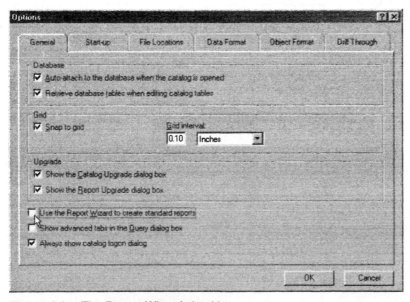

Figure 4.1   The Report Wizard checkbox.

A Word About Templates

Impromptu comes with seven predefined report templates that can help you create reports quickly and efficiently. The templates are installed regardless of how little you choose to install when you load Impromptu. Even if you choose to load just the application, these templates load and are stored on the drive where you installed Impromptu. If you chose to do this, you will not be able to follow some of the examples the book uses.

To find these templates, look in:

```
<(drive you installed Impromptu on)...\Cognos\cer1\samples\
impromptu\templates\standard
```

Several templates contain placeholders to assist you in determining what data columns are to be used. Later, when you become comfortable with building reports, you can create templates and either include placeholders or not—it is optional.

The following section describes the templates provided by Impromptu and provides a view of the QDB for each:

Available Templates

Template Name	Description
Simple List	The Simple List, shown in Figure 4.2, is the default report template. This template provides a report shell in the format of a simple row-by-row list. You will use this template the most.

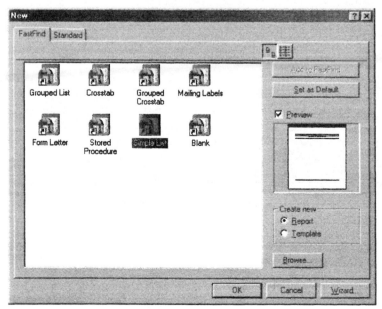

Figure 4.2
The Simple List report template.

Template Name	Description
Grouped List	This template, shown in Figure 4.3, is an extension of the default report. When you open this template, the Query Data box already contains a column. This one column is a placeholder that forces you to provide at least a data column from the Catalog and use that column for grouping within the report. To use a placeholder, just click, hold, and drag a column from the Catalog to the placeholder. Certain placeholders are type specific. For example, a numeric placeholder will not accept a string such as a customer name; it accepts only numbers.

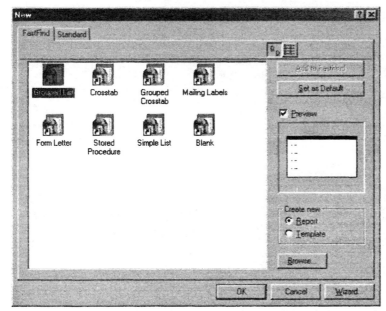

Figure 4.3
The Grouped List template.

Form Letter	This template, shown in Figure 4.4, showcases the flexibility of the reporting environment in concert with database retrieval. The template provides placeholders to select the address information from the Catalog and create a full-page letter, one page for each address you want to print and mail.
Mailing Labels	A report can achieve many different objectives. Think of mailing labels as a uniquely formatted report. When you want a mailing list, you use this template, shown in Figure 4.5, for an initial mailing label report format. The selection requirements are the name and address, and the output is a 2×5 list of mailing labels. You just select columns from your Catalog and place them in the corresponding placeholder.

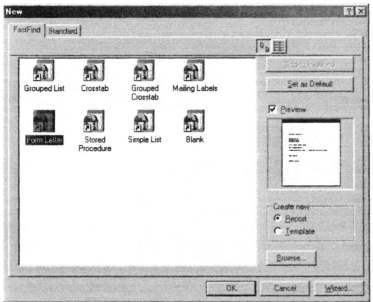

Figure 4.4
The Form Letter
template.

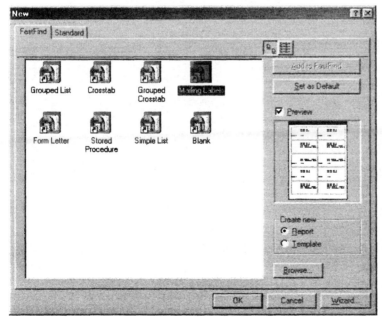

Figure 4.5
The Mailing Label
template.

Template Name	Description
Blank	This template, shown in Figure 4.6, is a "clean sheet of paper." You can retrieve data, but the layout of the report is a blank page. You have to build the report from scratch. You can create any combination of objects to generate this completely customized report. Use this template primarily for advanced, viewable reports using combinations of charts and scrollable lists. Chapter 11 describes how to build reports using this template.
Crosstab	The Crosstab template, shown in Figure 4.7, lets you create complex reports. You populate row and column data "items" and identify a measure for intersection. The row items appear as row headers on the report, and the column items appear as Column Headers. The intersections will be the calculation of the sum of that row and column. For example, say you wanted to see all your sales reps' quantity totals by Product Line. You could have Sales Rep Names as rows and Product Lines as columns, and the cell detail would be quantity sold. This will be covered extensively in Chapter 13.
Grouped Crosstab	An extension to Crosstabs, this report template, shown in Figure 4.8, takes the row-and-column concept of a crosstab report and provides you with the ability to have an additional row. This same functionality is permitted in the basic Crosstab Report, but this template provides a placeholder for a grouped column.

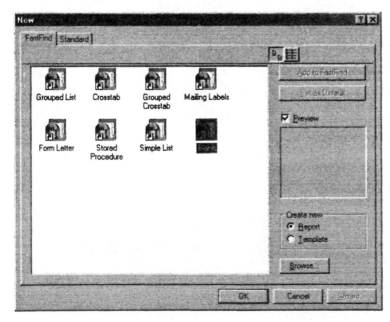

Figure 4.6
The Blank report template.

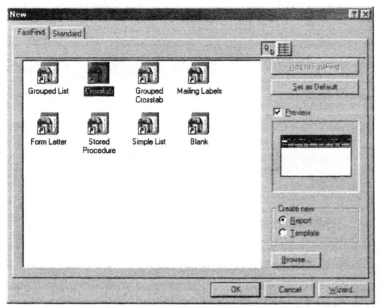

Figure 4.7
The Crosstab
report template.

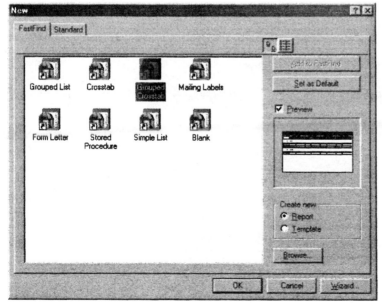

Figure 4.8
The Grouped Crosstab
report template.

Template Name	Description
Stored Procedure	A stored procedure is an SQL statement designed to extract data from certain tables within a database. This template is not discussed here. This is an advanced topic reserved for database professionals with experience in both database administration and Impromptu administration.

Let's Create a Report

The following exercise takes you, from start to finish, through building a very basic and raw report. The goal of the exercise is not to impress you with flashy content or colorful graphics. Its purpose is to take you through the essentials of building a report.

To build a report, a report developer generally needs a goal, a set of instructions, some directions, and some sort of report requirements. Throughout this book, as you build exercise-oriented reports, you will be provided with a sense of what to look for when obtaining or gathering report requirements. In some instances, you will start with what a typical user would want, and you will be provided with some insight or analysis to enable you to translate those requirements to make sense within Impromptu.

In some cases to further illustrate a concept, you will be provided "changes" to the original report requirements. Changing report requirements is inevitable. People will always change their minds, especially once they see what they get when they open their first Impromptu report.

Report Requirement

Your Boss: *Can you give me a simple list report that just shows the following columns from the database:*

- *Order No.*
- *Customer Name*
- *Order Date*
- *Sale Amount*

Analysis

This seems pretty straightforward. Your boss wants a basic report that contains the columns listed above.

Steps to Create a New Report

First select a template.

1. Select File.New from the menu bar.
2. Choose the template you will be using most: "Simple List," as shown in Figure 4.9.
3. Click OK.

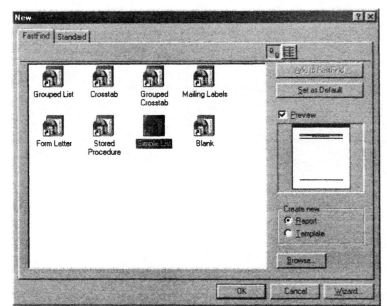

Figure 4.9
The Simple List report
template highlighted.

4. On the left side, in the Catalog box, expand the Order folder.
5. Select (double click) the Order No. column.
6. Select the Customer Name column.
7. Select the Order Date column.

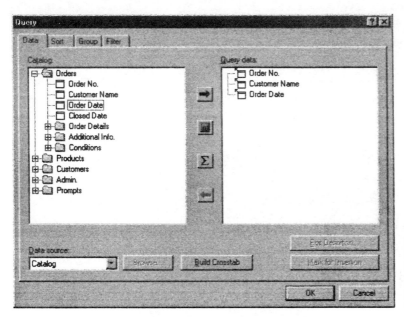

Figure 4.10
QDB with expanded
Order folders with sev-
eral columns moved to
the Query Data Box.

8. From the Catalog box, expand the Order Details folder.
9. Select the Sale Amount column.

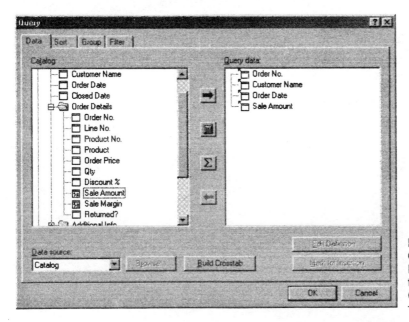

Figure 4.11
QDB with Order
Details expanded and
the columns moved to
Query Data box.

Before We Run the Report...

There are just a few more things to cover before you click the OK button to launch the report. The Query Data box is loaded with functionality that frequently goes unnoticed. Taking the time now to explain the details will give you a clear understanding and a foundation for knowing what's going on when you build your own reports in the future.

There are two things to discuss: the order of the columns you add to a report and the concept of marking the column for insertion into the report. These two topics are the most unassuming features in Impromptu, but they are two key ingredients to the success of the product.

The Order of Columns

When you select a Catalog column in the report, its destination is the Query Data box. This box depicts everything that comes from the database and is applied to the query portion of the report, whether it is a column or a calculation. Remember from the last chapter, where you learned about the two parts to every report. Here you are building the first part. You are creating the extracted list to be retrieved from the database.

The important point here is the order in which you retrieve columns. The order the columns appear will be the order, from left to right, that they appear on the simple list. Easy enough? Almost. This holds true for the initial query request, when you create the query for the first time. Afterward, the order of columns in the Query Data box does not affect the order of the viewable report at all.

Is this a big deal? No, not really. In Chapter 2, we talked about how you can think of Impromptu as a two-part report generator. The first part is considered the request of columns from the database. The second part is the WYSIWYG, the visual part of the report, the part that everyone sees and cares about.

WYSIWYG stands for "What You See Is What You Get," pronounced wizzy-wig.

So, when you build a new report for the first time, the report requests the columns in a certain order, the order of the Query Data box. Then, Impromptu displays them in that order. After that first request, you can move columns around on the screen, as we did in Chapter 2. This does not affect the order of the Query Data box.

Marking Items for Insertion

When you first add columns to the Query Data box, you will notice that there is a little arrow pointing up and to the left, as shown in Figure 4.11. This indicates that this column is "Marked for Insertion," meaning you are flagging this column to be included in the second part of the report, the WYSISYG part of the report.

Also, take a look at the lower right portion of the QDB's Data tab. There is a button that is grayed-out or disabled when no Query Data items are selected. This button is the Mark for Insertion button, as shown in Figure 4.12. When you select, for example, the Order No. column, the button becomes enabled, as shown in Figure 4.13.

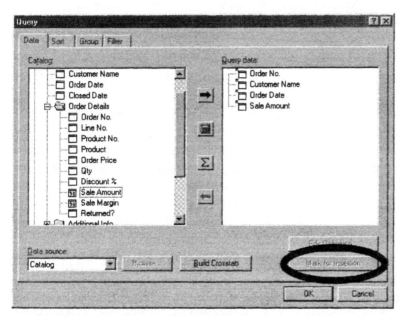

Figure 4.12
The Mark for
Insertion button.

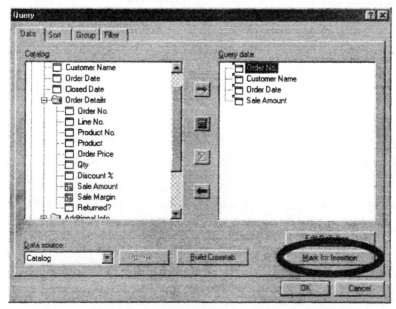

Figure 4.13
The enabled Mark
for Insertion button.

Go ahead and select a column in your report, then click the Mark for Insertion button. Notice that the arrow disappears for the Order No. column, as shown in Figure 4.14. What does that mean? Since the column is still in the QDB, it is still being retrieved from the database, but the column will not be displayed. Go ahead and press the button again; notice that the arrow comes back.

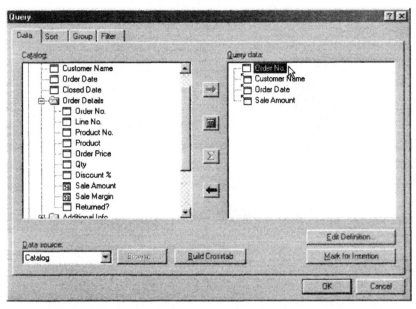

Figure 4.14   A column un-Marked for Insertion.

Running the Report

OK, OK, I know you have been wanting to press the OK button, but let's double-check to make sure we will be seeing the same results. The Query Data column I will be using to "run" my report is shown in Figure 4.15.

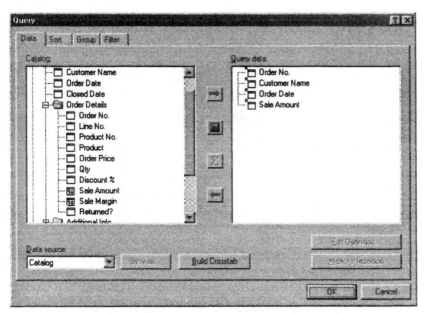

Figure 4.15   Full picture of the QDB Data tab.

10. Now, click OK to run the report.

And the Results Are...

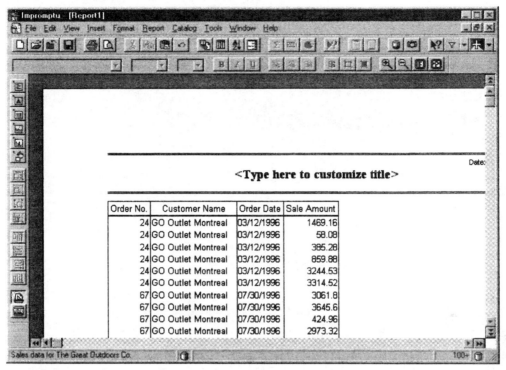

Figure 4.16   The new report results, shown in a simple list style.

Question	Answer
Wait a minute! Did I just see a fish swimming back and forth at the bottom of the screen?	Yes, when the report runs and queries for data, a little fish named Gil, swims back and forth in the right side of the Status bar, as shown in Figure 4.17. He's the little indicator that Impromptu is building your report.

Figure 4.17   Picture of Gil.

Remember the Status Bar?

Remember that the Status bar contains many tidbits of valuable information. Now that a new report has run, it is a great time to review just what the Status bar has.

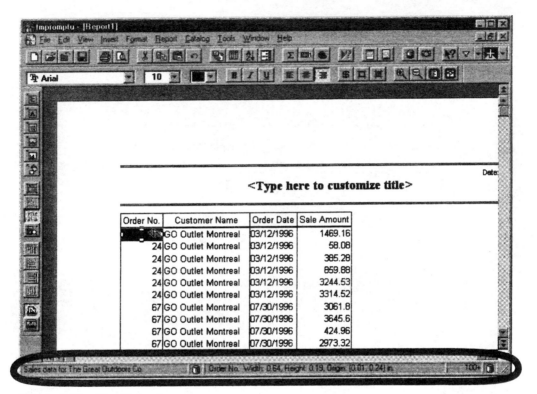

Figure 4.18   The Status bar.

Status Bar Portion	Description
The Catalog Description	At the far left is a short text description of the Catalog. The Catalog administer entered this.
Middle Drum	The middle drum determines whether there is a connection to the database. If there is a connection, you will see the drum. If Impromptu is not connected to the database, there will be a red x over the drum.
Field Identification Zone	This area describes the item or object you have selected in the report. Included in this description are the dimensions and the location of the objects. These objects include such reporting items as columns, rows, headers, and footers.

Status Bar Portion	Description
Report Retrieval Count	The total number of rows retrieved from the database. Remember, do not rely on this number as a counting figure. The Impromptu reporting tool sometimes has to split functionality between the database and the desktop.
Drum on the Right	This drum indicates the source of the data. It can be a drum, which is the database; a camera for a snapshot of data; or a drum ½ blue indicating a thumbnail or small sample of data that is stored locally on a desktop computer.

Viewing the Report

Once the report has run and data is returned and displayed, you will most likely be looking at the report in a Page layout format like the one in Figure 4.19. This is identical to the Page layout view as seen in other Windows applications such as Microsoft Word. The gray space around the white background provides an estimate of size and scale of the report and gives the impression that you are looking at the report as though it is on a sheet of paper.

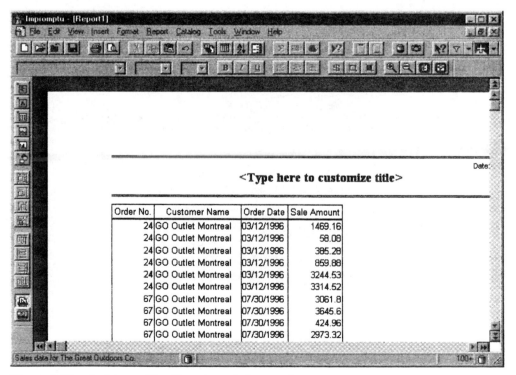

Figure 4.19   A picture of the Page layout of a report.

Alternatively, you can view a report just to examine the data (Figure 4.20). This view is called Screen Layout, and the report displays only the data, hiding the header area and the gray space around the edges.

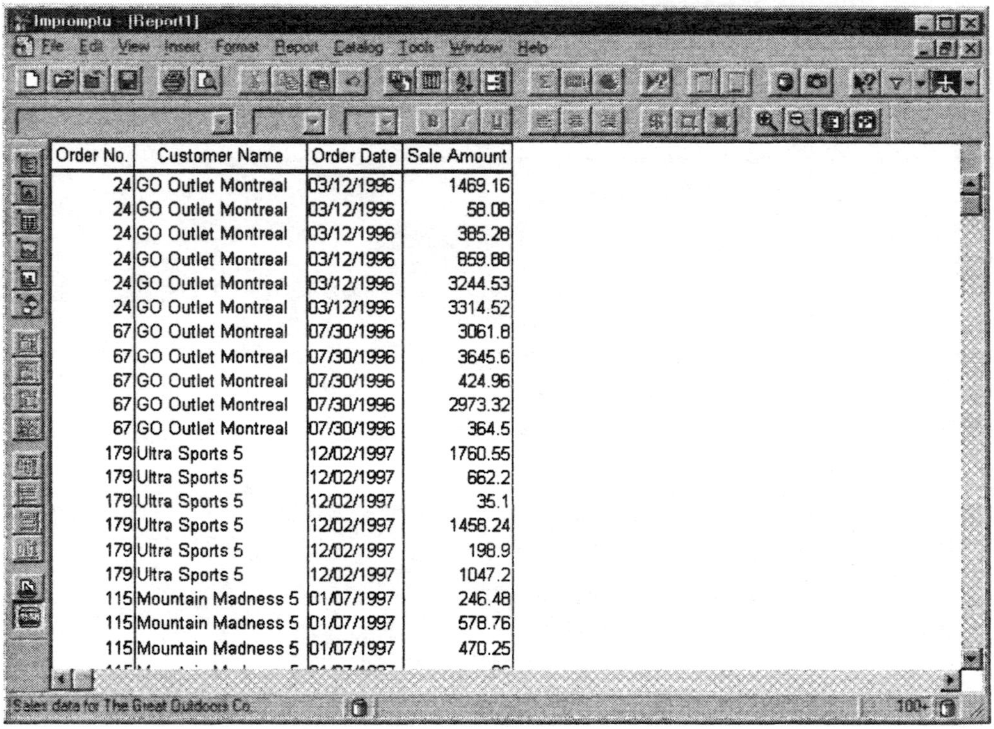

Order No.	Customer Name	Order Date	Sale Amount
24	GO Outlet Montreal	03/12/1996	1469.16
24	GO Outlet Montreal	03/12/1996	58.08
24	GO Outlet Montreal	03/12/1996	385.28
24	GO Outlet Montreal	03/12/1996	859.88
24	GO Outlet Montreal	03/12/1996	3244.53
24	GO Outlet Montreal	03/12/1996	3314.52
67	GO Outlet Montreal	07/30/1996	3061.8
67	GO Outlet Montreal	07/30/1996	3645.6
67	GO Outlet Montreal	07/30/1996	424.96
67	GO Outlet Montreal	07/30/1996	2973.32
67	GO Outlet Montreal	07/30/1996	364.5
179	Ultra Sports 5	12/02/1997	1760.55
179	Ultra Sports 5	12/02/1997	662.2
179	Ultra Sports 5	12/02/1997	35.1
179	Ultra Sports 5	12/02/1997	1458.24
179	Ultra Sports 5	12/02/1997	198.9
179	Ultra Sports 5	12/02/1997	1047.2
115	Mountain Madness 5	01/07/1997	246.48
115	Mountain Madness 5	01/07/1997	578.76
115	Mountain Madness 5	01/07/1997	470.25

Figure 4.20 A picture of the Screen layout of a report.

There are two ways to toggle between these two views:

1. Select the Screen layout button on the toolbar.
2. Select the appropriate option from under the View menu.

The advantages of using a Page layout are that you get a clear view of how the report is going to look when it is printed. You also get the ability to view how much information you can put on one page width, as well as the formatting of the headings and footings. The disadvantages are just the opposite. The Page layout view may not show all of the columns selected because they may not all fit the width of one page. This leads to pages of mistakes when printing.

Saving the Report

Saving the report is just as vital as building the report. You can save an Impromptu report at any time during the building process. Saving a report that is still in the development stages is done the same way a report is saved a final time for report consumers to view it. All Impromptu reports are saved using the same file extension: IMR, standing for IMpromptu Report.

As a default, Impromptu essentially saves three main pieces of information in each IMR:

1. Catalog information—which Catalog and where it is.
2. The query needed to access the data from the database.
3. The layout of the report, the WYSIWYG design.

These three components are needed to run the report at a later date. As a default, Impromptu does not save any data from the report. If you want to save the report, follow these steps:

1. Select File.Save As, as shown in Figure 4.21.
2. Navigate to the directory where you would like to save the report.
3. For now, keep the name as "Report 1" and the "Save as Type" as an IMR.
4. Click Save.

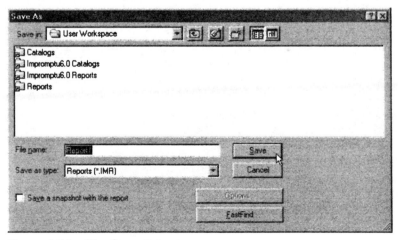

Figure 4.21   The Save dialog box.

What Was Just Saved?

Remember, Impromptu reports do not store the data; they only store the query and the layout. More specifically, Impromptu saves the report layout, which Catalog the report needs, and what columns need to be retrieved from the database, as well as other functionality such as how the report developed and used. This is covered in later chapters.

Different "Save As" Formats

The default "Save As" type in Impromptu is the IMR, but if you want to save the information in some other format, Impromptu gives you several options. With each one of these options, you get the raw data from the query. None of the fancy formatting that you can do in Impromptu flows through to the extracts.

The following table lists some of the potential extract formats.

Format	Description
IMT	This is called an Impromptu Template. It saves the visual layout only. The query portion does not get saved.
IMS	This is called a HotFile. Impromptu uses HotFiles to transfer a result of a query to be used in other queries. For example, say you have a database that contains sales information, and you had details of customers in another database. Impromptu lets you save the information you want from the customer database, store it as a HotFile, and use it with a query in the sales database. This is an advanced topic beyond the scope of the book. For further instruction contact Cognos for an advanced training class.
DAT	Saves in a format that allows PowerPlay, another Cognos product, the ability to read the data.
DBF	Stores the results from the Impromptu query as a single dBase file. The dBase file is a simple version of a local database structure easily read by other applications such as Excel and Lotus.
CSV	CSV stands for Comma Separated Value file. Selecting this format will give the user the ability to open this report in a number of other applications. Under the Options button, Impromptu provides all the CSV format options to choose from in setting up the output format.
XLS	There are now two ways to save data to Excel, one being a strict datadump to Excel. The other way is saving a formatted version.
WK1	The preferred format of Lotus 1-2-3.
PDF	This is another new feature for Impromptu 6.0. This option allows you to create an Adobe Acrobat file, known as a PDF. This format is an excellent way to display reports and keep the rendering—how it looks from one computer to another—intact.
TXT	This is another popular format, similar to CSV. This stands for "Text file," and that is all it is, a text extract of the reports column content.

Format	Description
SQL	SQL is a common language used by databases. In a technical installation of Impromptu, there may be Database Administrators who want to see the basic commands Impromptu is sending to the database. They would save a report as an SQL file to be able to view what Impromptu is sending to the database.
IQD	This file format is specifically used by other Cognos Products called PowerPlay and Cognos Query (Web reporting).

You can change the report directory to the one that suits your needs. As a precautionary measure, always store your IMR files on a network directory. Most companies have a scheduled process that backs up those directories. Contact your network administration group for details on what is backed up.

Tip

Changing the Template Layout

The templates that come with Impromptu are designed to display data simply and efficiently in Page layout. Sometimes, however, you may want to view a report differently from the beginning. You will find that Impromptu templates are easy to change.

One way to look at reports while in the development process is to look at the report in Screen layout. Since you may find yourself changing the simple list report you use to create reports to the Screen layout, you may create your own template of a simple list report that shows the report as a Screen layout instead of a Page layout. Let's try an exercise that demonstrates the flexibility of the templates.

The following steps change the default Simple List template from a Page layout to a Screen layout:

1. Select File.New from the menu.
2. Select the Simple List template. (This is the link to the actual report.)
3. Click OK. (This opens a new report. You'll be saving it as a new template in a few steps.)
4. You do not want any columns in your new template. So, do not select any while the QDB is open. Click OK to "run" the empty report (Figure 4.22).

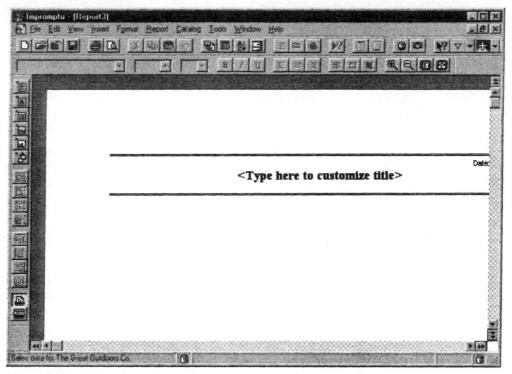

Figure 4.22   The empty report result.

Now you have a report without any columns. You can modify the report as much as you like. For example, you could set up standard headers and footers using your company's logo. For this exercise, just change the layout from Page view to Screen view:

5. Select View.Screen Layout from the menu (Figure 4.23).

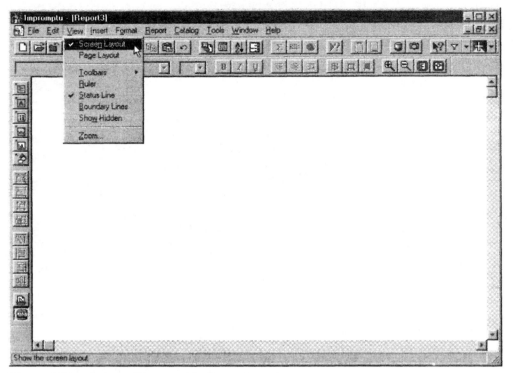

Figure 4.23 A view of the report in Screen layout.

The following are the steps to save the new Screen layout template:

6. Select "File.Save As."
7. Type a unique name. For this book, you could choose to name it "Chapter 4—template."
8. Choose "Save as Type": IMT from the dropdown (Figure 4.24).
9. Close the new template.

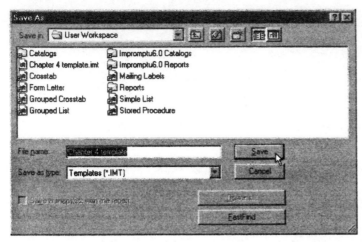

Figure 4.24
I always give the new
template a unique name.

Now that you have created this new template, if you want to make it the default template, you have to select it as your new default. Here's how:

1. Select File.New.
2. Single click on the new shortcut, as shown in Figure 4.25.
3. Click the "Set as Default" button, and you have your new template as the default report template.

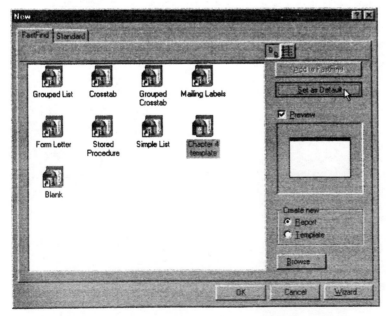

Figure 4.25
The new template is now
my default template.

Saving Exercises

Each chapter covers features of Impromptu using a report developed in that chapter. You may save those reports when you complete the exercise or at any time during the exercise. It is not required to save any report. Each report is self-contained within its chapter.

Summary

At this point, you should be able to

- Create a new report from scratch, using the templates provided with Impromptu.
- View a report in at least two ways.
- Run a report.
- Save a report in a different format.
- Create a template of a report to use repeatedly.

This thorough explanation will pay big dividends when you start building reports against your own data. Use this and the following chapters wisely. Their sole intent is to teach you how to do certain things in Impromptu, not how to build report x against a sample database.

Formatting a Report

Creating the initial report is the first part in building a report. In the preceding chapter, we created a basic report using the Catalog and got a good idea of what it takes for Impromptu to get the data on the screen

This chapter takes a closer look at formatting the report to make it look presentable. Some of you have already yielded to the temptation of doing a little bit on your own. That's perfectly fine. The chapter takes an in-depth look at the major formatting options available through Impromptu and explains why certain things happen when you format the report.

This chapter discusses each portion of formatting and describes the different ways to perform similar formatting functions. Throughout the chapter, step-by-step instructions and visual examples are provided so that you can refer to these examples as reference points when you build your own reports.

Once these concepts have been learned, you will immediately apply these basic formatting features to a Report Header. You will learn

- The basics of formatting options
- Formatting strategies for both individual cells and multiple columns
- The basics of report headers, and customizing them with formatting

Before We Begin

Before we begin, let's open the Customer Discount report. If you already have it open from the last chapter, I recommend closing it and reopening it to follow along with the visual examples.

To open it, follow these steps:

1. Open Impromptu, if it is not already open.
2. Select File.Open.
3. Either double click the file "Customer Discount," or click to select it and then click Open.
4. Impromptu will bring up the logon for the Catalog.
5. Click OK.

The report will open, retrieve data, and display the results.

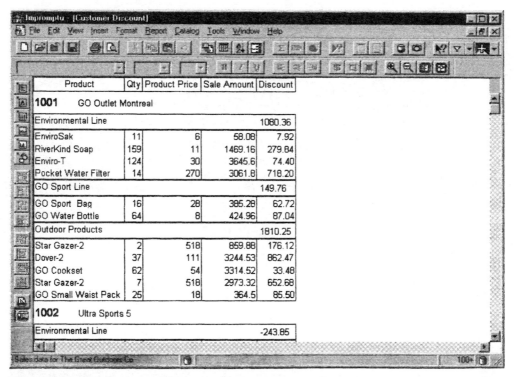

Figure 5.1   The Customer Discount report.

Different Ways to Format a Report

Changing how something looks is one of the most commonly performed tasks in building a report. One user wants to see the data with decimals, some other person likes to see the month in the three letter abbreviation, and the "Boss" wants to see the reports only in a certain font and size.

These are the challenges that report developers face daily, and Impromptu has made a sometimes grueling or tedious task easier. Buttons on a toolbar may seem trivial, but the time and effort they save amount to a tremendous advantage for report developers and consumers.

There are several ways to format your report:

1. Use the toolbar.
2. Use the right mouse button.
3. Use the format menu option.

The following sections show how to effectively use each of these methods. There is no right way or wrong way to format your report. You have to experiment to find what works best for you. You may find that a combination of these methods makes the formatting process more efficient.

Using the Toolbar

One of the biggest misconceptions about Impromptu involves the way formatting information on the report affects the underlying database. Remember, Impromptu does not change the data in the database. When you change the formatting of a column of data, you are not changing the data itself, just how it's represented on the screen.

One of the easiest methods for changing the way data is displayed is to use buttons on the Format toolbar. Using this option is simple: you select the data you want formatted, point to the toolbar formatting button, and click. All of the frequently used formatting features you would expect from Windows are available in buttons on the Format toolbar. All you need to know is what to click when you want to format something.

Basically, the toolbar buttons work the same in Impromptu as they do in other GUI applications.

Try This:

1. Click on a cell in the Sale Amount column of data.
2. Click on the **$** button.

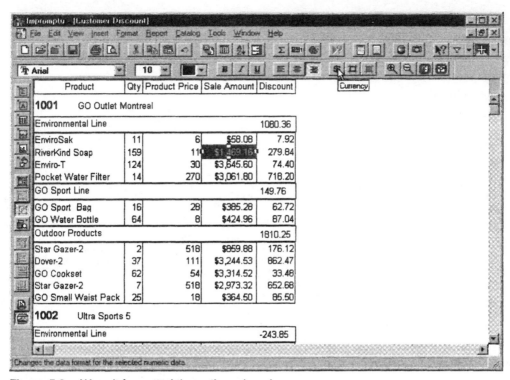

Figure 5.2   Wow, it formatted the entire column!

The rest of the toolbar buttons work in a similar fashion. The buttons provided on the Format toolbar by Impromptu are those most commonly used.

Note

Spreadsheet programs have many features and are very powerful analysis tools. Impromptu is not, and has never claimed to be, a spreadsheet tool. The initial confusion sets in when you first look at an Impromptu list report, particularly in a Screen layout. It looks a lot like a spreadsheet with the grid-like layout of the data. This is where the similarities begin and end. The big difference you need to remember with Impromptu is that although in a simple list report layout you may select (click) on a particular cell, the movements of that cell represent the entire column—for example, the Sale Amount you brought in on your new report.

Now that you have used one toolbar button to format data, take a look at what options you have with the toolbar. You can break the toolbar functionality into several categories. But for now, focus on the two categories that help you quickly format your report: Fonts and Borders Formatting.

Font Formatting

Icon	Name	Description
𝕋 Arial ▾	Font	Allows user to select font desired for selected column.
10 ▾	Font Size	Changes the selected columns to the new font size.
■ ▾	Font Color	Changes the selected columns to the new color.
B *I* <u>U</u>	Bold, Italics, Underline	Changes the selected columns to the desired effect.

Border and Pattern Formatting

Icon	Name	Description
▫	Borders	Changes the current border to default border layout.
▦	Pattern	Modifies the background pattern to default pattern.

Note

Remember, when you select one cell in a report, you are selecting the entire column. Also, if you do not see formatting that you want to do represented on the toolbar, that does not mean you cannot do the formatting. There are other ways to format columns, like the right click and the Menu Bar. Also, if you still do not see a formatting topic discussed here, that is because it has been categorized under a different subject. For example, say you wanted the product description in the Customer Discount report to be right justified, instead of left justified. That does not fall under the Formatting category; instead we need to discuss the properties of the item on which you want to do that type of formatting. This process is discussed in Chapter 11.

Right Click Approach

The next way to make formatting changes to your report is by using the right click technique common to other GUI applications. Either click to select the cell/column or just point the cursor to the cell/column you wish to make formatting changes to and press the right mouse button, as shown in Figure 5.3. Next, move the cursor down the option list to the word Format.

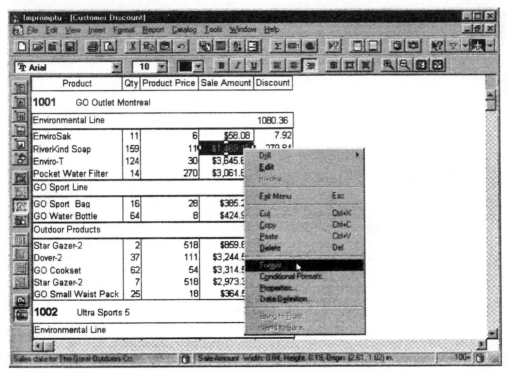

Figure 5.3   The selection you are using in this chapter is Format. The rest of the options will be explained throughout the book.

Once you select the Format option, the Format Dialog box will appear, as shown in Figure 5.4. The Format Dialog box contains all of the features found on the toolbar and adds a few more selections.

All of the formatting features are stored within this dialog box. The box groups like formatting features into four tabs. Take a look at the formatting features tab by tab.

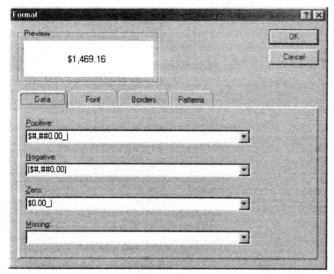

Figure 5.4
The Format dialog box.

Data Tab

The first tab is the Data tab. Within this tab, you can modify how the column you selected is viewed on the report. This tab is an interactive tab. This means that once you select an option or change a selection, the rest of the tab changes to accommodate the selection immediately.

For example, on the Format Dialog box you just opened, the report initiated with a default of "General" selected for the Positive selection, as shown in Figure 5.5. This is the

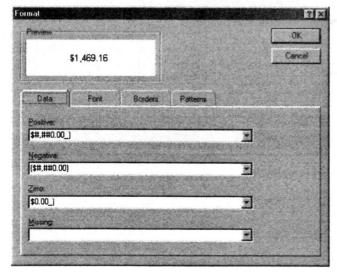

Figure 5.5
The Data tab of the Format box.

default way Impromptu displays numbers. The following figure shows some of the other options available.

Impromptu allows you to customize any of the default data format settings. This and many other features are available to be customized in the Options box, as you saw earlier when you turned off the Report Wizard from the General tab.

To change Data format defaults, follow these simple steps:

1. *From the Menu, select Tools.Options.*
2. *Choose the Data Format tab.*
3. *Select the specific Data Type. For now, choose the "Date" Data Type.*
4. *Change the "Normal" dropdown boxes to the right to: "mm/dd/yyyy".*

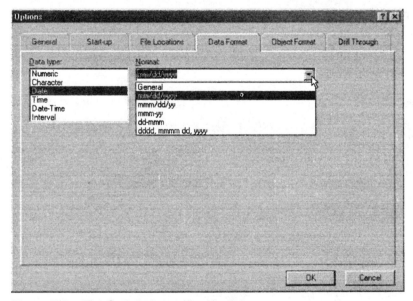

Figure 5.6   The Options box with selection.

5. *Click OK, to keep the new format.*

Font Tab

The next tab is the Font tab, as shown in Figure 5.7. Here, you can modify the column's font, style, and size. Additionally, you can select the underline and strikethrough options. When you select a different option, such as changing the font size, you see a preview in the Preview window at the top.

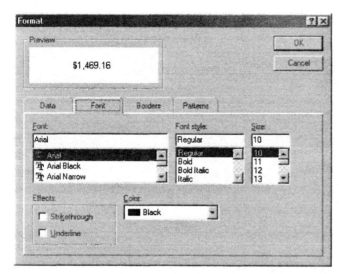

Figure 5.7
The Font tab.

Borders Tab

The third tab is the Borders tab, as shown in Figure 5.8. This tab allows you to modify the border of the entire column; it gives you the ability to modify any combination of bor-

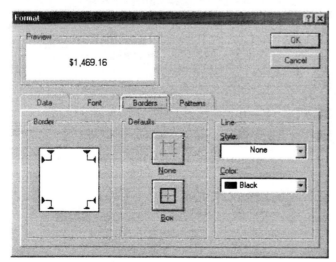

Figure 5.8
The Borders tab.

ders for each cell of a column. The border you select here will be reflected on each cell of that column on each line of the report.

The default, as seen in the Borders section of the Borders tab, is set to nothing. At this point, Impromptu allows you to make changes to all the borders. Also, each side is preselected when you enter this tab. This is noted by the black triangles pointing inward to each border of the working area example cell.

You have a choice of two defaults:

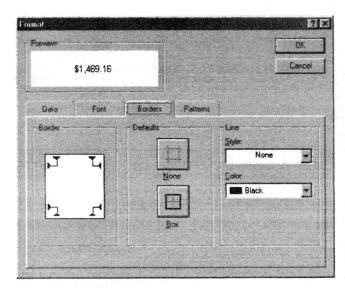

Figure 5.9
The defaults in Borders tab.

1. **None:** This selection provides no additional bordering around the cells.
2. **Box:** This selection, as Figure 5.10 shows, provides a box around each cell for that column.

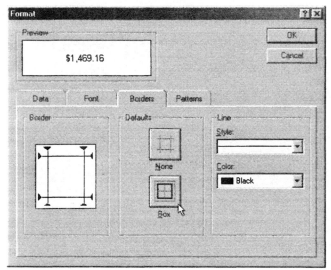

Figure 5.10
The report with formatting
accomplished.

The line section of this tab allows you to select a specific line style and color for the border.

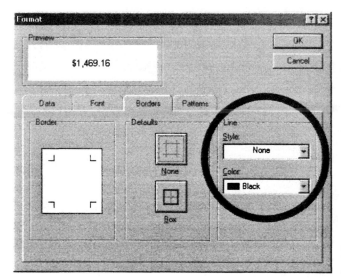

Figure 5.11
The Line section from Border tab.

Selecting the dropdown list, gives you a peek at what line combinations are available.

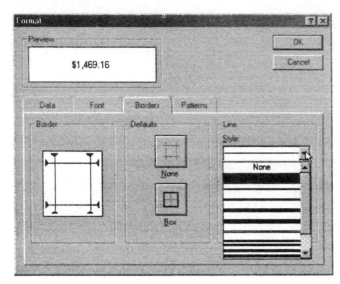

Figure 5.12
The line dropdown options.

Patterns Tab

The final format tab is the Patterns tab, as shown in Figure 5.13. The tab selections here also feed into the preview after each option is selected. The ability to type this into the preview is a nice feature that keeps you from having to select a pattern and then return to the report to see how it looks.

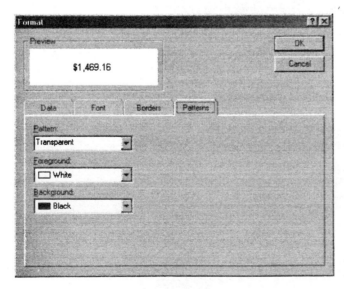

Figure 5.13
The Patterns tab.

The default selection for any pattern is Transparent. You can choose a pattern that blends together the foreground and background colors. Additionally, you can choose either of the colors, both foreground and background.

Format Menu Approach

So far, you have formatted by using the toolbar and by right clicking. The last way is by using the Menu bar, as shown in Figure 5.14. There are many options available from the menu, but this chapter focuses on the four options available for formatting. These four options are familiar because they are the four tabs just discussed from the Right Click section. So, really there are no surprises with the Menu—you just have to see how to use it.

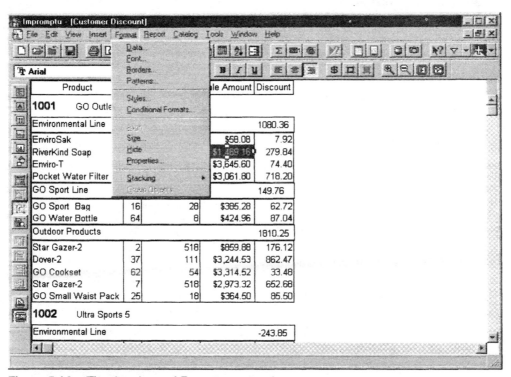

Figure 5.14   The dropdown of Format menu option.

Each of the first four selections from the Format Menu takes you directly to the tab within the Format Dialog box.

Formatting Strategies

There are many different ways to go about formatting your report.

Overall Theme

You should have an overall plan of attack for how you want your report to look before you start formatting each column. The initial theme should be a shared vision between the report developer and the report consumer. The report developer needs to be involved for two reasons: (1) because he is going to be doing most of the formatting, and (2) because the report developer has a general idea of what the company standards are for report form and layout. The report consumer needs to be involved in the design of a theme because she will end up seeing the report on a regular basis.

The format of the report, or its theme, is initially developed during the gathering of the report requirements. This part is generally simple if the company has strict standards for reports. But it can be pretty elaborate if the report consumer has specific needs.

Report developers should pay attention to the consumer's formatting needs. Take extra time when you are gathering the reporting requirements to ask them if they have a preference as to font, size, and borders. Remember, whether they admit it or not, they judge a report by how it looks and then determine how successful that report is, not whether the results are right. The report consumer expects correct results in a report. The theme can take on a life of its own and sometimes overshadow the actual content of the report, so be careful.

Multitasking Formats

Another formatting strategy is multitasking of formatting. This is a tactical approach to formatting a report, a real time saver.

Making changes to a selected column is effective, but you may want to change multiple columns at once to be efficient. Impromptu allows you to do this by clicking and dragging. This is a concept known as lassoing items, or using a mouse to select multiple columns at once.

1. Click and hold the mouse button down on a selected cell/column.
2. Drag to show a dotted box and surround the columns you want.

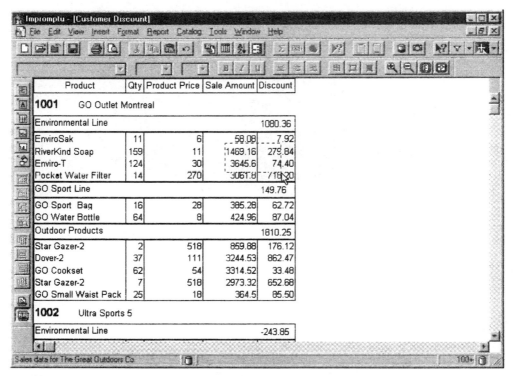

Figure 5.15   A view of the report with dotted lasso around two columns.

This dotted box determines what items are selected. Every item that the dotted line touches gets selected. Letting go of the mouse button causes Impromptu to highlight the selected cells.

3. Release the mouse button to finish (Figure 5.16).

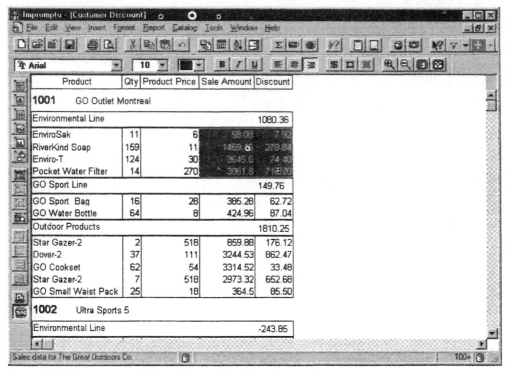

Figure 5.16   After the mouse button was let go: darkened cells.

As explained earlier in the chapter, when you selected a single cell and formatted it, you formatted the entire column. The same holds true here for multiple columns. Highlighting the specific cells in the column for both the Sale Amount column and the Discount column allows you to format both columns. With these columns selected, you can format the two columns using any one of the three approaches. For example, pressing the Currency button will format both columns as currency.

Note

Any previously written report will have its own data type formats. For example, assume you built a report with no decimals, and now you change the default to include decimals. When you open up the old report, you will not see decimals until you change the data type. If you add another column that is a numeric data type, you will see decimals.

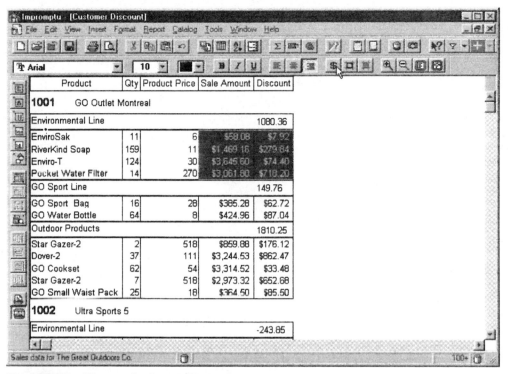

Figure 5.17 The result of pressing the Currency button.

Do not set your default numeric to currency unless the majority of your numeric data columns are currency. Impromptu is not choosy—when you tell it to make all numeric data types currency, it will. This will include non-currency numbers such as order numbers, quantities, and some items like Part Numbers, which may technically be numbers in your database; logically, however, they are used as text fields.

Conditional Formats

The type of formatting you have applied so far in this chapter has been static. That is, if you bold a cell, then the format change applies to the entire column of data. But, what if you wanted to change the format of particular cells in a column based on some defined condition?

This is addressed by using a feature called Conditional Formatting. Conditional Formatting allows a report developer to apply a set of rules or a condition to a column or columns and, based on the results of those rules, apply a particular format or style to that column or columns.

This next section examines how you can extend the use of formatting and apply Conditional Formatting. For the following exercise, assume that a report requirement has been obtained, and use the analysis.

Analysis

You need to apply a Conditional Format to the Customer Discount report's Discount data column. The condition to apply here is one already developed in the Catalog, called "Sales Closed Late." When the condition holds true, format the column using a predefined format—a style.

Do not worry if this analysis seems cloudy; there are new terms used that are explained in the step-by-step.

Steps to Apply Conditional Formatting

1. With the Customer Discount report open, select any cell in the Discount column.
2. Right Click, and choose "Conditional Formats...".

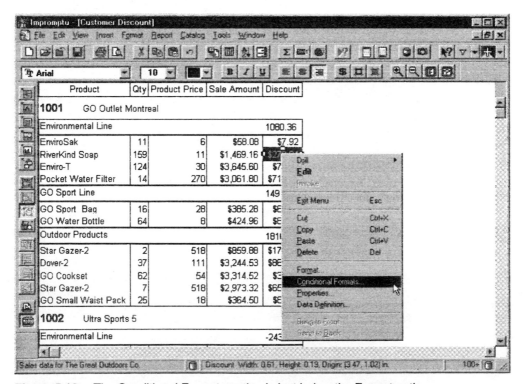

Figure 5.18   The Conditional Formats option is just below the Format option.

The Conditional Formats window, shown in Figure 5.19, is where conditions are applied to defined styles. It is also the place where you can create conditions and styles. These manually created conditions require additional knowledge, found in Chapter 6. Chapter 6 revisits this report to apply a manual Conditional Format.

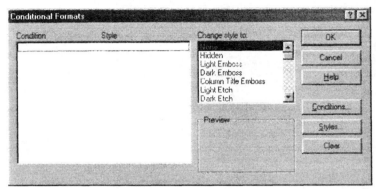

Figure 5.19
The Conditional Formats window.

The Styles button allows you to both modify the predefined styles provided by Impromptu and create your own styles. These styles can be applied not only as formats through Conditional Formatting but also directly to a column.

3. From the Conditional Formats window, choose Conditions.

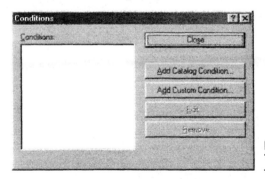

Figure 5.20
The Conditions window.

The Conditions window allows you to add as many Catalog or custom conditions to this report as you want. Additional maintenance buttons are available to remove unwanted conditions or edit custom conditions.

4. Choose Add Catalog Condition (Figure 5.21).

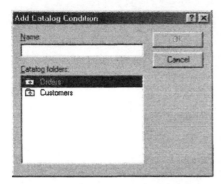

Figure 5.21
The Add Catalog Condition window.

5. Expand the Order Folder.

6. Expand the Conditions Folder.

7. Select the Sales Closed Late condition.

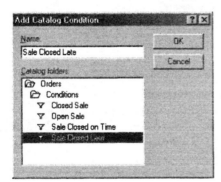

Figure 5.22
The expanded Catalog folders and selected condition.

The Catalog folder is a view of the full Catalog you have seen in the QDB. The only items that are available in this window are conditions, so the only folders you see are those that contain conditions.

8. Click OK.

9. Click Close. This takes the chosen condition and places it in the Conditional Formats... window (Figure 5.23).

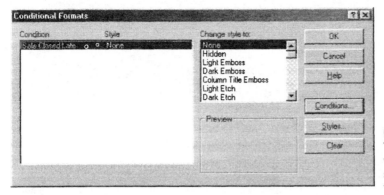

Figure 5.23
The Conditional Formats window, with a default style of "none."

10. Select the "Dark Emboss" style from the "Change Style to:" box.

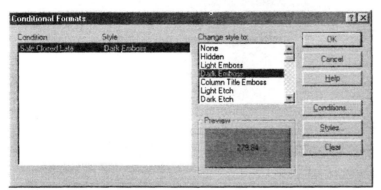

Figure 5.24
Completed Conditional Formats window.

In the future, you can click the Style button and create your own style. But for this exercise, using one of the predefined styles is fine.

11. Click OK to run the report.

And the Results Are...

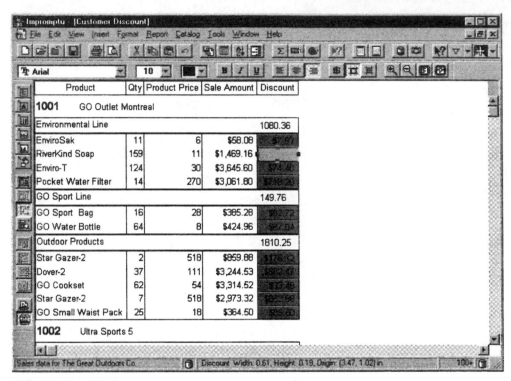

Figure 5.25   The Report results.

Tip

To apply a style directly to a report,
1. *Choose a cell or column.*
2. *Select Format.Styles (Figure 5.26).*

Figure 5.26
The Style window.

3. *Choose a style.*
4. *Click Apply.*

In the Style window, you can add a personal style or edit an existing one. The styles you add or edit remain with Impromptu, so you can use your personal styles from one report to the next.

Notice that the report has to run again. That is because there is new logic involved: the condition you just applied.

To use your own reports, here are the basic steps to apply a Conditional Format to a column:

1. *Select the column.*
2. *Select Conditional Formats.*
3. *Choose a condition in the Condition window, this involves either:*
   a. *Adding a Catalog Condition.*
   b. *Adding a Custom Condition (Custom Conditions require applying knowledge learned in Chapter 6).*
4. *Back in the Conditional Format window, with the condition you just selected or created, either:*
   a. *Choose a previously defined style to apply from the "Change to Style:" box.*
   b. *Create a style, using the Styles button, and apply it to the condition.*
5. *Click OK.*

Basics on Headers

This section takes a beginning look at formatting headers. This section will cover the page header of the report and describe the Column Headers of a List report. Footers will be introduced in Chapter 9.

To take a good look at headers, let's open up the Product Type Sales report from Chapter 3 again.

1. Select File.Open.
2. Choose "Product Type Sales."
3. Click OK.

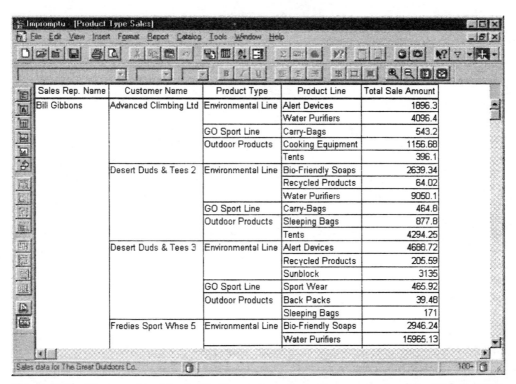

Sales Rep. Name	Customer Name	Product Type	Product Line	Total Sale Amount
Bill Gibbons	Advanced Climbing Ltd	Environmental Line	Alert Devices	1896.3
			Water Purifiers	4096.4
		GO Sport Line	Carry-Bags	543.2
		Outdoor Products	Cooking Equipment	1156.68
			Tents	396.1
	Desert Duds & Tees 2	Environmental Line	Bio-Friendly Soaps	2639.34
			Recycled Products	64.02
			Water Purifiers	9050.1
		GO Sport Line	Carry-Bags	464.8
		Outdoor Products	Sleeping Bags	877.8
			Tents	4294.25
	Desert Duds & Tees 3	Environmental Line	Alert Devices	4688.72
			Recycled Products	205.59
			Sunblock	3135
		GO Sport Line	Sport Wear	465.92
		Outdoor Products	Back Packs	39.48
			Sleeping Bags	171
	Fredies Sport Whse 5	Environmental Line	Bio-Friendly Soaps	2946.24
			Water Purifiers	15965.13

Figure 5.27   The report is defaulted in Screen layout, where you cannot see the Page header.

Change the layout from screen to page: Select View.Page layout (Figure 5.28).

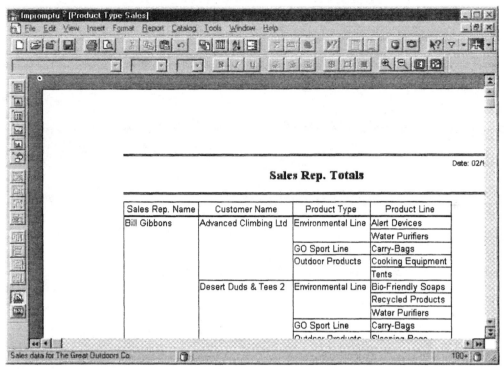

Figure 5.28 The report results in Page layout.

Report Page Header

The Page Header for this report, shown highlighted in Figure 5.29, can encompass a number of items. Chapter 11 covers including additional items in the header; this chapter considers only the basic formatting.

Using the right click approach discussed previously, you can see different items to format. You can format anything in the Page Header, from the entire highlighted area down to the date in the upper right corner.

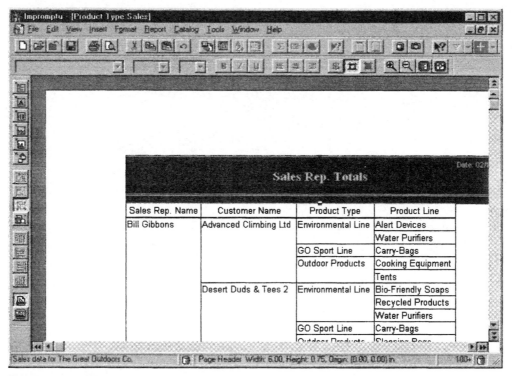

Figure 5.29   The Page header: highlighted.

For example, let's see what format options are available when you select the title of the report:

1. Single click anywhere on the title "Sales Rep. Totals." This selects the title of the report (Figure 5.30).

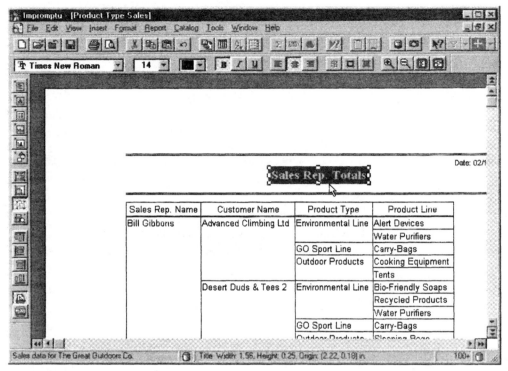

Figure 5.30 The highlighted title.

2. Right click and select Format.

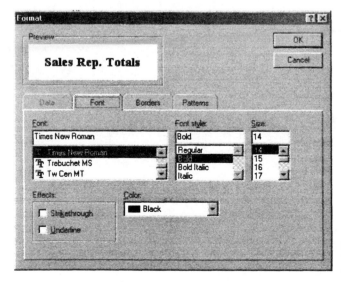

Figure 5.31
The Format box.

Notice that three out of the four tabs are darkened, or enabled. Impromptu does not permit any changes to the Data tab. Why? The title of the report does not represent a data column; therefore, there is no data from a database to be formatted. The Data tab-like formatting is done when the report developer enters the title.

If you have a moment, go ahead and do this small exercise for a few more items in the Page Header. This will make you comfortable with what can be modified.

Column Headers

Impromptu gives you a head start in formatting your report when you select a simple list report template. Impromptu takes the name of the column from the Catalog and applies it to the Column Header in the report.

The first time a report is created, Impromptu uses the name of the query data column from the Catalog and applies it to the visual part of the report. After that, you can make changes to the Column Header, and Impromptu will keep the modifications to the column you made.

Let's take a look at the Column Headers for the Product Type Sales report. To see all of the Column Headers in the single layout, let's go back to Screen layout:

• Select View.Screen Layout (Figure 5.32).

The Column Headers can be changed either one at a time, or all at once. The following two sections describe how to make Column Header changes and, more important, when you would want to do them one by one and when you would want to do them all at once.

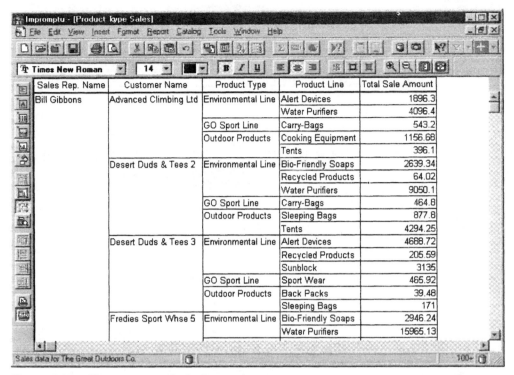

Figure 5.32   The report results in Screen layout.

Changing the Column Headers: One by One

You generally want to make single column changes when you are customizing how just one Column Header looks. Impromptu allows you to format the individual Column Header using the formatting features available for the columns of the report. This means you can apply any of the three formatting approaches you learned with the cells and columns to the Column Headers. To illustrate this point, let's format the Column Header.

Make the Customer Name Column Header bold.

1. Single click on the Customer Name Column Header.
2. Click the Bold button on the toolbar (Figure 5.33).

Additionally, you can format any Column Header using the other two approaches.

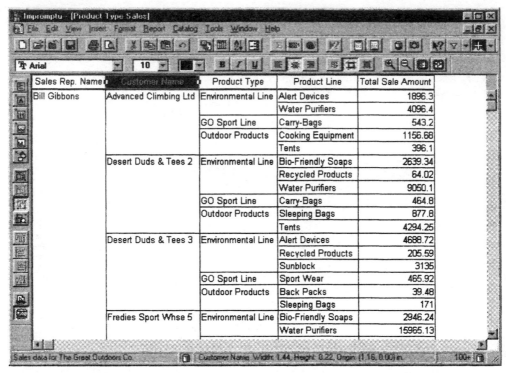

Figure 5.33   The Customer Name is bolded.

In addition to making formatting changes to Column Headers, you can control the text being displayed in the Column Headers. Since Column Headers are stored inside the report as visual markers, they are not required to match the column name in the Catalog once they have been used in the report. This means you can change the text of them to say anything.

Take the following report requirement and apply the Column Header text change to the Product Type Sales report.

Report Requirement

You found out that the report consumer does not want to see the Column Header for Customer Name read "Customer Name." Instead, she just wants to see the word Customer.

Analysis

This requirement asks us to change one specific column: "Customer Name" should read "Customer."

Steps to Change a Column Header

1. Move the cursor to the center of the Customer Name Column Header.
2. Double click.

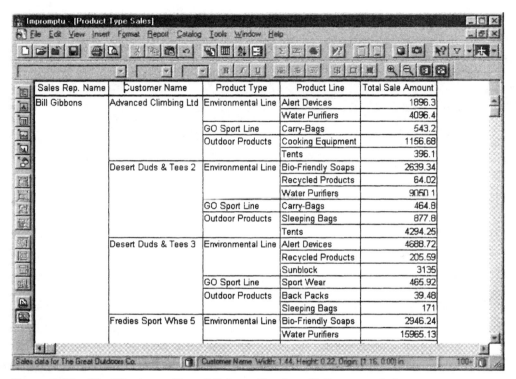

Figure 5.34   The "Customer Name" Column Header with the cursor in it.

3. Move the cursor to the right of "Name."
4. Using the delete key, delete "Name."
5. Hit the Esc key.

And the Results Are...

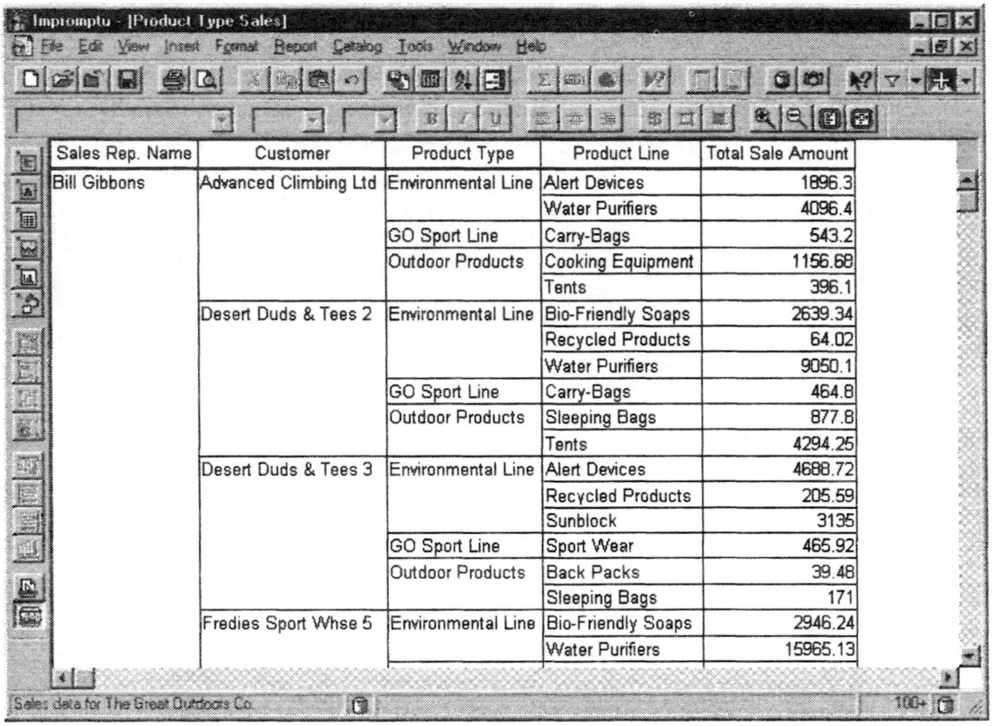

Sales Rep. Name	Customer	Product Type	Product Line	Total Sale Amount
Bill Gibbons	Advanced Climbing Ltd	Environmental Line	Alert Devices	1896.3
			Water Purifiers	4096.4
		GO Sport Line	Carry-Bags	543.2
		Outdoor Products	Cooking Equipment	1156.68
			Tents	396.1
	Desert Duds & Tees 2	Environmental Line	Bio-Friendly Soaps	2639.34
			Recycled Products	64.02
			Water Purifiers	9050.1
		GO Sport Line	Carry-Bags	464.8
		Outdoor Products	Sleeping Bags	877.8
			Tents	4294.25
	Desert Duds & Tees 3	Environmental Line	Alert Devices	4688.72
			Recycled Products	205.59
			Sunblock	3135
		GO Sport Line	Sport Wear	465.92
		Outdoor Products	Back Packs	39.48
			Sleeping Bags	171
	Fredies Sport Whse 5	Environmental Line	Bio-Friendly Soaps	2946.24
			Water Purifiers	15965.13

Figure 5.35 The header with just the word "Customer".

That last step may seem counterintuitive, but whatever you type, the header keeps, so you do not have to press Enter. Pressing Enter will only create another line in this header.

Note

This changed the Column Header only. The name of the column, as it is known in the QDB, did not change. To see this, open the QDB (Figure 5.35).

This is perfectly fine in Impromptu. Impromptu will remember that the "Customer Name" column goes under the "Customer" Column Header. Remember, if you ever want to double check to see what the data column name is, select a cell and look at the Status bar.

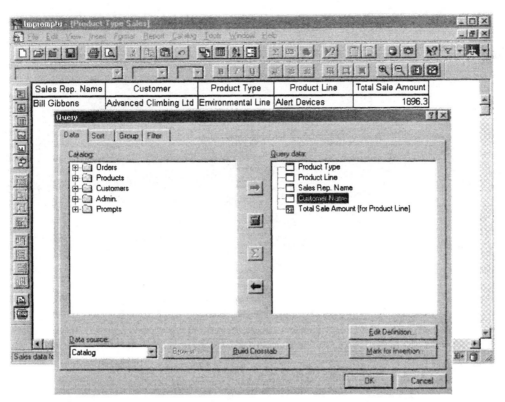

Figure 5.36 As you can see, the column name "Customer Name" remained the same in the QDB, while the Column Header is different.

All this single clicking and double clicking can be a nightmare. So, if you think you double clicked wrong at any time, just hit the Esc key, which removes focus from the report layout, and try again.

The following is what the Column Header looks like when you do not correctly double click:

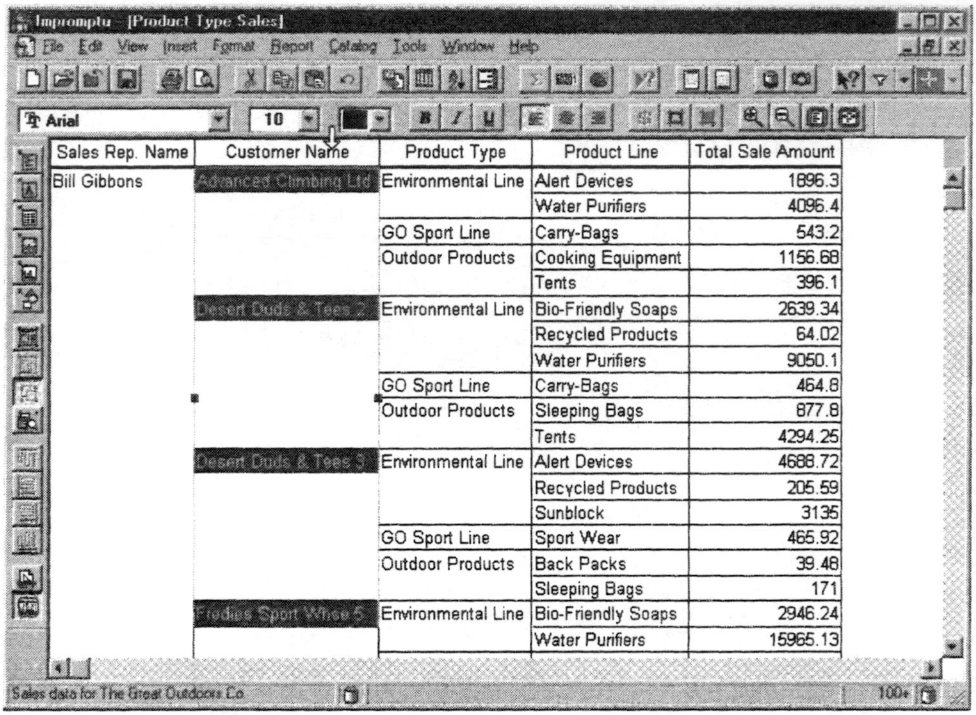

Figure 5.37   The entire column is selected, and notice the cursor is an odd arrow pointing down. This arrow indicates that Impromptu is ready to select the entire column, which is what happened in this case.

Changing the Column Headers: All at Once

When you have the same change to make to all the Column Headers, you can make format changes to all of them at the same time instead of changing one format Column Header and then the next, and so on. This is a really useful timesaving feature.

The following steps walk you through one way of making format changes to the Column Headers all at once.

1. Move the mouse to the far left side of the leftmost Column Header until the cursor changes to the one shown in Figure 5.38.

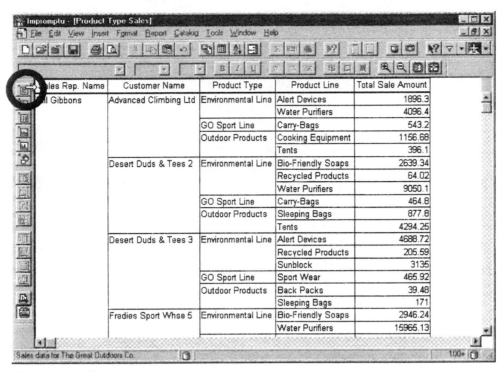

Figure 5.38   The right pointing arrow.

2. Click the left mouse button, which selects the entire group of Column Headers (Figure 5.39).

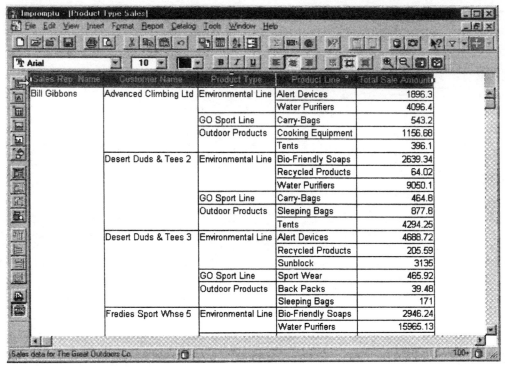

Figure 5.39 A whole row of Column Headers selected.

Then you can choose the desired formatting options using any approach discussed earlier in this chapter.

Summary

At this point, you should be able to

* Use three different options to format your report.
* Modify a basic Report Header and Column Header.

We now have a good understanding of the basic concepts of formatting the appearance of our reports. From this chapter, you were able to build on the report from the previous chapter by making its numbers show their decimal features and by formatting Column Headers to match your reporting requirements. The next part of the book, Part 2, shows how to customize the report to deliver real business value.

Fundamental Reporting Concepts

Looking back at the previous five chapters, you have indeed come a long way. The level of detail back in these chapters will pay big dividends as you move forward to becoming a proficient report developer. This does not mean that only report developers can read on. There are many report consumers who possess the skills found in the upcoming chapters. Often the best report developers evolve from efficient report consumers.

The second part of Impromptu Startup covers intermediate to advanced concepts in report building. The object of these chapters is to take report development to the next level. These chapters answer the majority of the questions you had after you started to become empowered—those questions you were starting to ask as far back as Chapter 2, and even more in Chapter 4. With the content in the following four chapters, you can master 80% of all reporting skills.

Filtering

Chapter 6 covers a critical function for building a report: filtering. The concept of filtering out information comes naturally. You and I do it everyday. For example, when I read the Sunday paper, I read only the Sports section. First, I retrieve the paper, then I pull out the Sports section, and finally I walk over to the kitchen counter and look at the headlines. This entire process can apply directly to running a report. The "retrieve the paper from the curb" equates to Impromptu retrieving data from a database. Pulling out the Sports section equates to filtering out information I don't want. And reading the headlines at the kitchen counter is equivalent to viewing the specific information in a report.

This chapter instructs you how to perform filtering. It covers the different ways to perform filtering, the different types of filters, and how to change them if you change your mind about a filter you applied. It is then up to you to apply these skills to your own data and reports.

Specifically this chapter covers the following information:

- Using the toolbar to filter reports
- Using the QDB to filter reports
- Changing your Filter Definitions

Before We Begin

Before you start learning about all this filter stuff, create a new report. If you already have Impromptu open along with some reports from the last chapter, I recommend closing those reports to have a clean start. Many times, as you become more efficient, you will find yourself opening up more and more reports at once.

The report that you are about to create will be used to demonstrate the concepts of filtering and will be used throughout this chapter.

1. Click the New button.

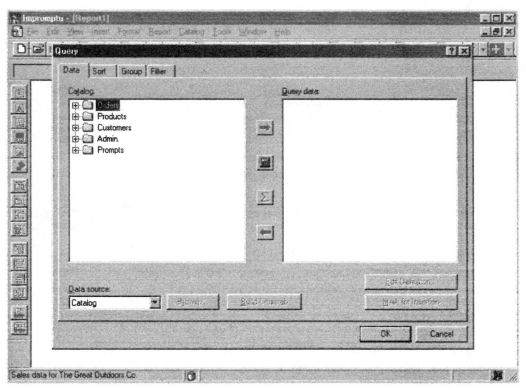

Figure 6.1   This creates a new report using the default template. The default template you set up in Chapter 4.

2. Expand the Orders folder, and select the Customer Name column.
3. Expand the Orders Detail folder.
4. Select the Product, Order Price, Qty, Discount %, and Sale Amount (Figure 6.2).
5. Click OK (Figure 6.3).

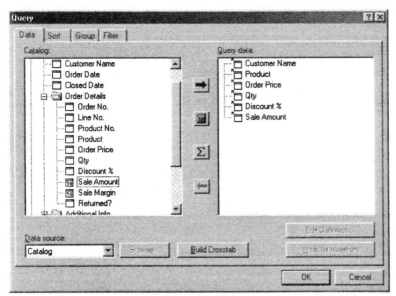

Figure 6.2
The QDB with
the Order Detail
folder open.

Customer Name	Product	Order Price	Qty	Discount %	Sale Amount
GO Outlet Montreal	Star Gazer-2	518	2	17	859.88
GO Outlet Montreal	Dover-2	111	37	21	3244.53
GO Outlet Montreal	GO Cookset	54	62	1	3314.52
GO Outlet Montreal	GO Sport Bag	28	16	14	385.28
GO Outlet Montreal	EnviroSak	6	11	12	58.08
GO Outlet Montreal	RiverKind Soap	11	159	16	1469.16
GO Outlet Montreal	Star Gazer-2	518	7	18	2973.32
GO Outlet Montreal	GO Small Waist Pack	18	25	19	364.5
GO Outlet Montreal	GO Water Bottle	8	64	17	424.96
GO Outlet Montreal	Enviro-T	30	124	2	3645.6
GO Outlet Montreal	Pocket Water Filter	270	14	19	3061.8
Ultra Sports 5	Dover-2	117	2	15	198.9
Ultra Sports 5	GO Camp Kettle	22	56	15	1047.2
Ultra Sports 5	GO Sport Bag	31	48	2	1458.24
Ultra Sports 5	Pocket U.V. Alerter	10	77	14	662.2
Ultra Sports 5	Enviro-Kit	13	3	10	35.1
Ultra Sports 5	RiverKind Shampoo	11	165	3	1760.55
Mountain Madness 5	Star Lite	193	10	24	1466.8
Mountain Madness 5	GO Large Waist Pack	25	2	25	37.5
Mountain Madness 5	GO Water Bottle	8	16	25	96

Sales data for The Great Outdoors Co.

Figure 6.3   The report results.

Filtering Reports

As with previous topics covered in this book, there is more than one way to perform a filter in Impromptu. To start, we will discuss simple filtering concepts. Then, as you become more comfortable, I will show the other ways to add filters.

This section covers the following information:

- The basics of filtering
- Multiple filtering
- Dropdown Filtering
- Using the Filter Definition box

The Basics of Filtering

Conceptually, when you filter a report, you can think of the filtering process as either including or excluding certain information. If you wanted to show a report that displayed only a certain product, you would want to *include only* that product. Another way to describe the same filtering requirement is to *exclude all* of the items except that one product. At this level, it is just a manner of semantics.

This is filtering at its lowest level of complexity—a simple comparison between a selected cell and a data value using the "equal" filter operand. There are several filter operands available in performing filters, but for the basics, we will concentrate on the easiest one, the equal sign. In the basic point and click filtering that you will be doing, the only option available is the equal sign.

Before you can create complex filters in Impromptu reports, you need to understand the basics. This section provides the base functional understanding of performing a filter on a report. First, I will walk you through one simple filter, and I will explain what happened.

The first and most convenient way to perform basic filtering is by using the Filter button on the toolbar.

Steps to Create a Filter

1. Select any "GO Sport Bag" cell from the Product column.

Customer Name	Product	Order Price	Qty	Discount %	Sale Amount
GO Outlet Montreal	Star Gazer-2	518	2	17	859.88
GO Outlet Montreal	Dover-2	111	37	21	3244.53
GO Outlet Montreal	GO Cookset	54	62	1	3314.52
GO Outlet Montreal	GO Sport Bag	28	16	14	385.28
GO Outlet Montreal	EnviroSak	6	11	12	58.08
GO Outlet Montreal	RiverKind Soap	11	159	16	1469.16
GO Outlet Montreal	Star Gazer-2	518	7	18	2973.32
GO Outlet Montreal	GO Small Waist Pack	18	25	19	364.5
GO Outlet Montreal	GO Water Bottle	8	64	17	424.96
GO Outlet Montreal	Enviro-T	30	124	2	3645.6
GO Outlet Montreal	Pocket Water Filter	270	14	19	3061.8
Ultra Sports 5	Dover-2	117	2	15	198.9
Ultra Sports 5	GO Camp Kettle	22	56	15	1047.2
Ultra Sports 5	GO Sport Bag	31	48	2	1458.24
Ultra Sports 5	Pocket U.V. Alerter	10	77	14	662.2
Ultra Sports 5	Enviro-Kit	13	3	10	35.1
Ultra Sports 5	RiverKind Shampoo	11	165	3	1760.55
Mountain Madness 5	Star Lite	193	10	24	1466.8
Mountain Madness 5	GO Large Waist Pack	25	2	25	37.5
Mountain Madness 5	GO Water Bottle	8	16	25	96

Figure 6.4 The selected cell in report.

2. Click the toolbar button with the yellow funnel. This is the Filter button.

Figure 6.5 The Filter button, with cursor over it.

> **Note**
>
> *The entire Filter button is both the yellow cylinder and the black triangle to the right of it. The black arrow gives you access to the advanced features that we will get to further on. For now, let's just use the Filter button and see what it does.*

And the Results Are...

Customer Name	Product	Order Price	Qty	Discount %	Sale Amount
Mountain Madness 3	GO Sport Bag	28	80	16	1881.6
OutBack Pty 2	GO Sport Bag	28	16	12	394.24
GO Outlet Montreal	GO Sport Bag	28	16	14	385.28
Pro Form Supplies 4	GO Sport Bag	28	48	22	1048.32
Tregoran AB 1	GO Sport Bag	28	32	11	797.44
Lookout Below Ltd	GO Sport Bag	28	32	18	734.72
123 Fitness PTE Ltd	GO Sport Bag	28	16	12	394.24
Juan's Sports 3	GO Sport Bag	28	64	4	1720.32
Pro Form Supplies 4	GO Sport Bag	28	64	15	1523.2
Vacation Central 4	GO Sport Bag	31	64	15	1686.4
Vacation Central 3	GO Sport Bag	31	32	17	823.36
OutBack Pty 2	GO Sport Bag	31	16	11	441.44
Ultra Sports 1	GO Sport Bag	31	80	9	2256.8
Tregoran AB 1	GO Sport Bag	31	48	15	1264.8
Supras Camping Supplies 2	GO Sport Bag	31	48	24	1130.88
Botanechi K.K. 1	GO Sport Bag	31	80	7	2306.4
Ultra Sports 5	GO Sport Bag	31	48	2	1458.24
Mountain Madness 2	GO Sport Bag	31	64	21	1567.36
OutBack Pty 4	GO Sport Bag	31	16	7	461.28
Mountain Madness 5	GO Sport Bag	31	64	4	1904.64

Figure 6.6   The results of the filter.

Congratulations! You just filtered on the "GO Sport Bag" report, as shown in Figure 6.6. What you are now looking at is a report that displays who bought "GO Sport Bag," how many were bought (Qty), the price, the discount applied (Discount %), and the final sale amount (Sale Amount). What we also can learn from this report is that not many customers who bought "GO Sport Bag."

What did Impromptu just do? When you initially built the report, Impromptu took your selected columns and formulated a request, the first part of a report—the query—and sent it to the database for the results. When you filtered on a certain aspect of the report,

Impromptu had to refine the query. So with a change to the query, Impromptu had to send the query to the database, and the returned results are displayed for you to view.

Multiple Filters

Impromptu also allows for the report developer to perform multiple filters on any given report. What this means is you can perform one filter, as you just did in the preceding exercise, and then, based on those results, perform another filter. What Impromptu does at that point is take the new filter, the second one entered, add that to the query, and send it off to the database. Logically, you can think of it as once a row of data/information passes through the first filter, it then has to pass through the second filter to be valid information to return to Impromptu.

The order in which you enter filters is extremely important to the outcome of the report. The second filter entered is the second filter performed. This sequencing of filters is carried on for as long as you add filters to the report. Impromptu does have a ceiling number of filters you can add to any given report (around 127 filters).

For the next example, let's consider what we want to do with a reporting requirement.

Report Requirement

Boss: *This report looks better just showing the "GO Sport Bag," but can you also filter on the customer: "Pro Form Supplies 4"?*

Analysis

The reporting requirements still provide a clear path to what you need, but you do not have to decipher cryptic requests at this point. The requirement the boss has requested is to add another filter to the one you have already processed: Customer Name = "Pro Form Supplies 4"

Steps to Add Another Filter

For this exercise, you want to filter on "Pro Form Supplies 4" in addition to "GO Sport Bag."

1. Select a cell that contains "Pro Form Supplies 4" from the report (Figure 6.7).
2. Click the Filter button again.

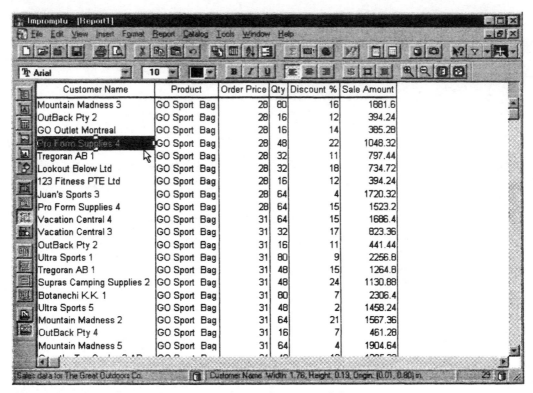

Customer Name	Product	Order Price	Qty	Discount %	Sale Amount
Mountain Madness 3	GO Sport Bag	28	80	16	1881.6
OutBack Pty 2	GO Sport Bag	28	16	12	394.24
GO Outlet Montreal	GO Sport Bag	28	16	14	385.28
Pro Form Supplies 4	GO Sport Bag	28	48	22	1048.32
Tregoran AB 1	GO Sport Bag	28	32	11	797.44
Lookout Below Ltd	GO Sport Bag	28	32	18	734.72
123 Fitness PTE Ltd	GO Sport Bag	28	16	12	394.24
Juan's Sports 3	GO Sport Bag	28	64	4	1720.32
Pro Form Supplies 4	GO Sport Bag	28	64	15	1523.2
Vacation Central 4	GO Sport Bag	31	64	15	1686.4
Vacation Central 3	GO Sport Bag	31	32	17	823.36
OutBack Pty 2	GO Sport Bag	31	16	11	441.44
Ultra Sports 1	GO Sport Bag	31	80	9	2256.8
Tregoran AB 1	GO Sport Bag	31	48	15	1264.8
Supras Camping Supplies 2	GO Sport Bag	31	48	24	1130.88
Botanechi K.K. 1	GO Sport Bag	31	80	7	2306.4
Ultra Sports 5	GO Sport Bag	31	48	2	1458.24
Mountain Madness 2	GO Sport Bag	31	64	21	1567.36
OutBack Pty 4	GO Sport Bag	31	16	7	461.28
Mountain Madness 5	GO Sport Bag	31	64	4	1904.64

Figure 6.7   The report showing the "Pro Form Suppliers 4" data.

And the Results Are...

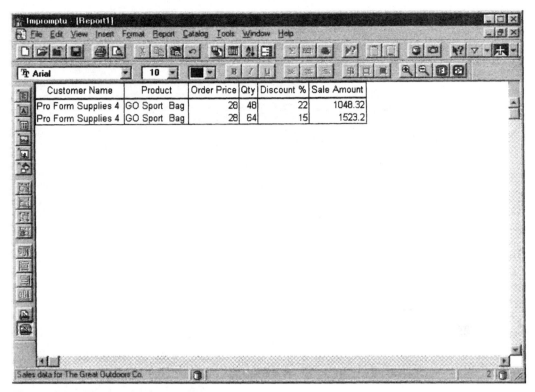

Figure 6.8   The result of latest filter.

The "Pro Form Supplies 4" company ordered a "GO Sport Bag" twice. What you also see is that one order was discounted at 22% and the other at 15%. With this one feature of Impromptu, you can discover information in your database that you may not have expected.

Leaving the subject of filters, momentarily, this is a perfect time to discuss expanding a report. What you see in the exercise is one company getting two different discounts. That is perfectly normal, it happens all the time, but what appears to be just a little odd is that the smaller quantity has the larger discount.

To further explore this feature, let's try to determine why there might have been different discounts.

Try This:

1. Click on the QLB button.
2. Expand the Orders folder from the Catalog side.
3. Select the Order Date column.
4. Press OK.

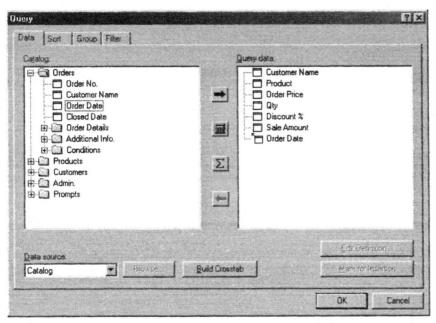

Figure 6.9   The report results with the inserted Order Date column.

As you see in Figure 6.10, the Order Date for these two orders is different. This helps explain why you have differences in the Discount %: there may have been different discounting programs offered by sales from one year to the next.

Clean Up

Having the ability to undo previous actions in Impromptu is a valuable feature.

The next section covers more advanced toolbar filtering features. To prepare for this, let's clean up what we just did in the previous exercises by using the Undo button, as shown in Figure 6.10. Click the Undo button twice to return our report to the original state, or three times if you walked through the Tip.

Now, you are ready to perform the next set of exercises.

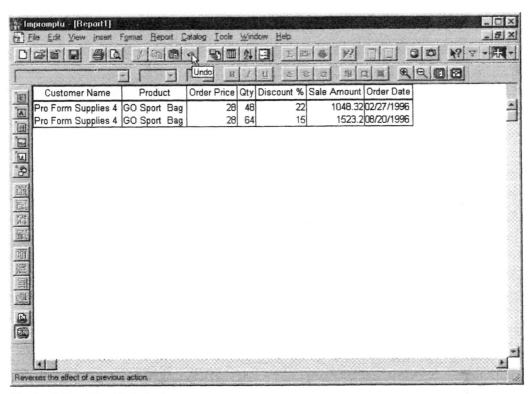

Figure 6.10 The Undo button.

Dropdown Filtering

Dropdown Filtering is an extension of the push-button filtering that you performed in the previous section. The dropdown ability comes from the down arrow to the right of the filter funnel. The combination of a selected cell and a pressed arrow opens the filtering capabilities to more than just an equivalent comparison. Impromptu allows a report developer to perform a number of different filtering comparisons.

This section first covers the basic functionality of performing a basic Dropdown Filter. The next step is to discover the full potential of Dropdown Filtering. This simple enhancement provides a world of opportunity to control the results of the report right from the report layout.

Basic Dropdown Filtering

In short, Dropdown Filtering allows you to expand past the "equals to" barrier with a click of the button. Now, you can use comparisons such as "greater than" and "less than or equal to." Before we dive into the different things you can do, let's repeat the simple filter from the last section using a Dropdown Filter.

Try This:

1. Select the "GO Sport Bag" cell again.
2. Click the dropdown arrow immediately to the right of the yellow funnel.

Keep the mouse button pressed.

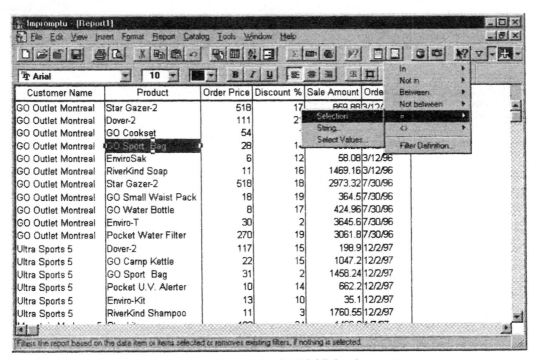

Figure 6.11   The dropdown arrow with the selection highlighted.

3. Move the mouse down to the equals operand.
4. Move the cursor over the word Selection. This means you wish to use the cell you have selected in this filter.

You should end up with the same result as you did after the very first filter (Figure 6.12).

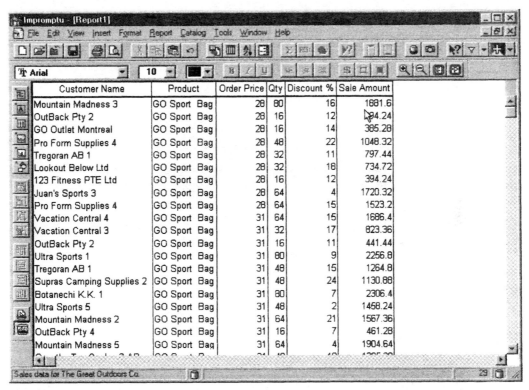

Figure 6.12 The results of the recent filter.

The Dropdown Filter operand list is sensitive to what you have selected on the report. The dropdown list above is available for string columns and columns that contain letters, numbers, and any other characters.

Additional operands are available for numeric columns, columns that contain only numbers.

Basic Dropdown Filtering: Multiple Filters

The whole notion of multiple filters discussed in the previous section applies to Dropdown Filters as well. You can add additional filters using the Dropdown Filter, regular point and click filters, or any combination you prefer. Additionally, the same principles apply in Dropdown Filtering as they do in point and click filtering. When you add another filter, it falls in line and is applied after the first filter.

Use the Dropdown Filter to perform a second filter. Instead of doing the same second filter here as you did in the last section, let's use the abilities of the Dropdown Filter to answer the following request:

Reporting Requirement

Show me the orders for "GO Sport Bag" that had a Discount % greater than 15%.

Analysis

In order to answer it, break down this question into two filters. One we already did: show just the "GO Sport Bag" orders. For the second half, we need an additional filter to see only the orders that had a Discount % greater than 15%.

Steps to Perform a Dropdown Filter

1. Select a cell in the Discount % column that has 15 as the discount. The first row that has this is the one with customer "Pro Form Supplies 4." You may have to scroll down to see this row of information.
2. Click the Dropdown Filter arrow, keeping the mouse button pressed.
3. Move the mouse down to the ">" operand.
4. Move the cursor over the word Selection (Figure 6.13), and let go of the mouse button.

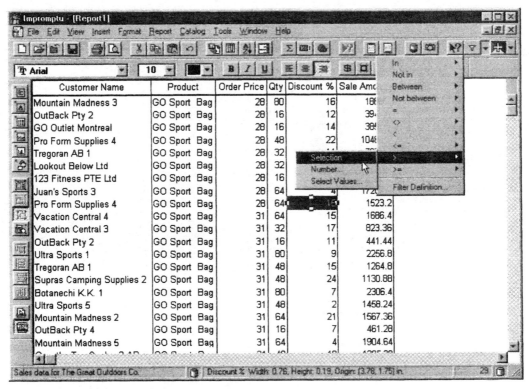

Figure 6.13   The Flyout of the Dropdown Filter.

And the Results Are...

The result is a report (Figure 6.14) showing all of the orders for the "GO Sport Bag" that had a Discount % over 15.

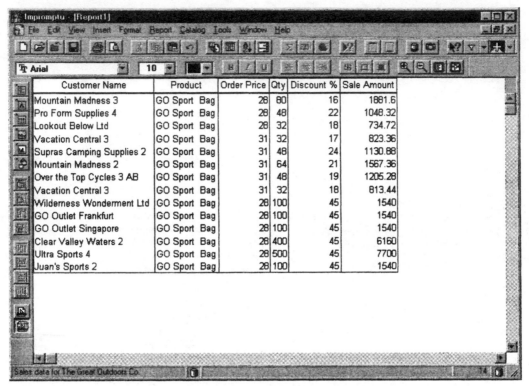

Figure 6.14   The report result of Dropdown Filtering.

Clean Up

Remove the latest filtering you just did by clicking the Undo button twice, once for the last filter: Discount % > 15, and another time for the first filter: Product = "GO Sporting Bag."

Other Dropdown Filtering Options

In addition to using the selection in Dropdown Filtering, two other options are available when creating Dropdown Filters: a specific value and Select Value. In demonstrating these options, the typical report requirements and analysis are waived to get to the heart of how to perform them.

A Specific Value

The specific value option allows you to type in your own value. When you have a string selected, Impromptu allows you to type in your own string value. Likewise, when you have a number or date selected, you will be able to type in your own number or date. It is a flexible option that changes based on what cell you select in the report.

Try This:

1. Select the first Discount % cell value: 17.
2. Select the Dropdown Filter from the toolbar.
3. Select the ">" operand.
4. Select the "Number…" option.

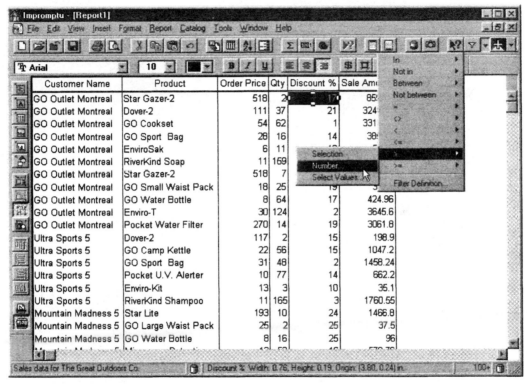

Figure 6.15   The Dropdown Filter, with the "Number…" option selected.

5. With the Enter Value window open, type in 20.

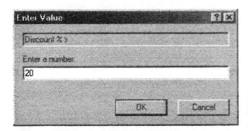

Figure 6.16
The Enter Value box.

6. Select the OK button.

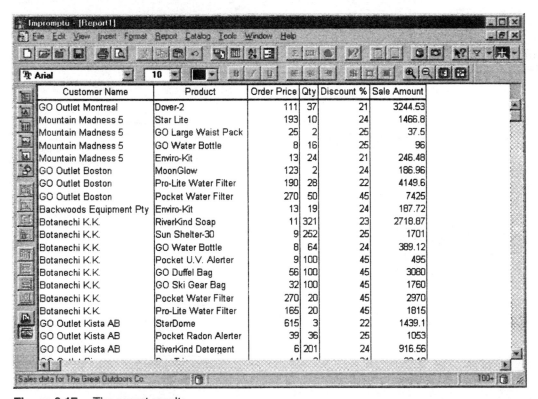

Figure 6.17   The report results.

Select Values

The Select Values option is just that—it allows you to choose real values that come directly from the database. When you use this option, Impromptu retrieves up to the first 100 unique values from that column in the database. So, the list that you have to choose from is that of actual data values stored in the database. This ensures that the data you are using in the filter will match the data from the database. Then, based on which operand you select, you are able to choose one or more items from the database.

If you choose the "=" operand, you are allowed to choose one value to complete the equation (Figure 6.18).

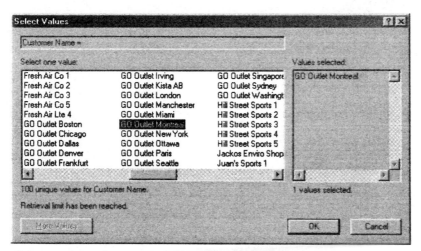

Figure 6.18 A Select Values box for an "=" operand and one Customer Name selected.

If you select a different operand, such as the "Between" operand, you are required to select two values to complete that equation.

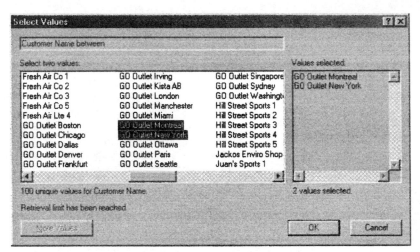

Figure 6.19   A Select Values box for a "Between" operand and Two Customer Names selected.

Note

To keep up with the exercises and be able to follow along with the figures, keep the filter from the past exercise, Discount % > 20. This is used in a later section.

Try This:

1. Select the first Customer Name: "GO Outlet Montreal."
2. Select the Dropdown Filter arrow.
3. Select the "between" operand.
4. Select the "Select Values" option (Figure 6.20).
5. The Select Values dialog box appears (Figure 6.21).

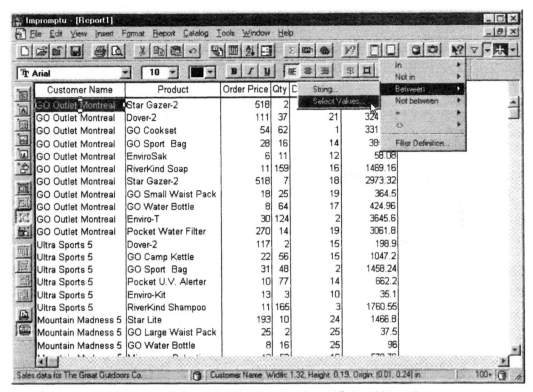

Figure 6.20   The Dropdown Filter selecting "Between" and "Select Values."

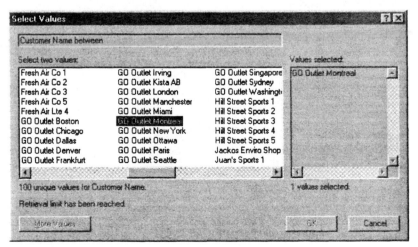

Figure 6.21   The Select Values dialog box, with initial Customer Name selected.

Depending on what you initially selected, the dialog box will take you directly to what you selected. In this example, Impromptu defaults to the cell you selected. Now you are required to select two items to complete the formula. Note that initially the OK button is disabled. This is because the exact values are not selected to complete the formula. If you select too many, then the OK button will stay disabled.

6. To complete the formula, select the first value: Desert Duds & Tees 1.

7. Hold down the Ctrl key and select Desert Duds & Tees 8.

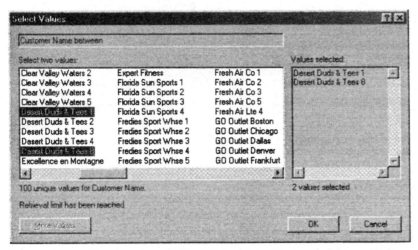

Figure 6.22 The completed Select Values box. Notice, once two values have been selected, the OK button is enabled.

8. Click OK (Figure 6.23).

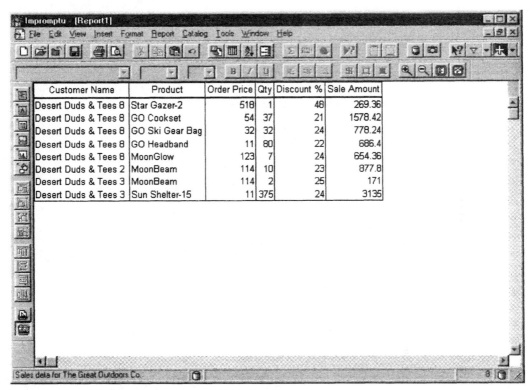

Figure 6.23 The report results, showing all Desert Duds & Tees companies sales.

This will enable us to see all of the Desert Duds & Tees customers and their product orders that also meet the Discount % > 20 filter.

Note

There are many variations of filtering available through the Dropdown Filter. Unfortunately, we cannot go through an exercise for every variation. The following tables provide a basis for what each variation of filter operands is and when you should use it.

String Operands

Table 6.1 applies to string values, those columns that contain both numeric and alphabetic characters.

Table 6.1

For String Columns	Explanation	When to Use
In	When using the "In" clause, any number of string cells that are selected are used to filter on the result coming back.	When you have multiple string expressions you wish to select and filter on at once.
Not In	The "Not In" is the exact opposite of the "In" clause. This filters out string expressions selected.	This feature is used primarily when the number you wish to filter out is smaller than the number you wish to keep.
Between	This is similar to the "In" clause, but instead of an uncorrelated group of strings, this can select an alphabetically ordered group by selecting a starting and ending point. Note that, the starting and ending points are included.	This is used with strings mainly when quickly selecting a range of data items. For example, you have a seven-character product number that starts with an "S," and you want the "SD"s through "SM"s.
Not Between	Like the "Not In," the "Not Between" performs exactly the same way. This excludes items selected and used here.	Used when you have a smaller ordered amount to be excluded from a report.
=	When you want to select the particular item.	Primarily used when you want to quickly filter one string expression.
<>	This works the opposite of "=". Selecting an item and using "not equals to" eliminates it from the report.	This is used to quickly remove an item from a report.

Numeric/Date/Date-Time Operands

Table 6.2 applies to Numeric, Date, and Date-Time columns.

Table 6.2

For Numeric and Date Columns	Explanation	When to Use
In	Used to include in a report specific numeric values	When you want to select a couple and include them in a report
Not In	Used to do the exact opposite of the "In" clause	Used when the group to be excluded is smaller than the group to be included.
Between	This is similar to the range function in MS Excel. It selects a group of numeric values in a sequence. For example, "Between (1 and 10)" will result in a set from 1 to 10, inclusive.	Used when you want to grab a quick group of values that is ordered together. The key here is having a defined beginning and end. When you don't have either of these two, you would be better off using the greater-than, less-than criteria below.
Not Between	This excludes the criteria selected in the range of values.	Used to view the other values. For example, you know that a certain series of product numbers are very profitable, and you want to see what the others look like.
=	This finds all values that match the criteria exactly.	Used when you have one specific value.
<>	This finds all of the values that are not equal to the value selected.	Used when you want to quickly eliminate a value.
<	Returns values less than the defined selection.	Used when you have a defined value at one end of a range, but do not have another defining end point.
<=	Returns values that are less than and equal to the defined selection.	Used when you have a defined value at one end of a range, but do not have another defining end point.
>	Returns values that are greater than the defined selection.	Used when you have a defined value at one end of a range, but do not have another defining end point.
>=	Returns values that are greater than or equal to the defined values.	Used when you have a defined value at one end of a range, but do not have another defining end point.

Using the Filter Definition Box

There is one more option from the Dropdown Filter selection—the Filter Definition box.

The Filter Definition takes us to the QDB's Filter tab, where you can construct any Filter Definition you like. It is available at the bottom of every Dropdown Filter option. It is also the default selection when there is no other option available. As seen below, if nothing on the report is selected, you will get at least one option.

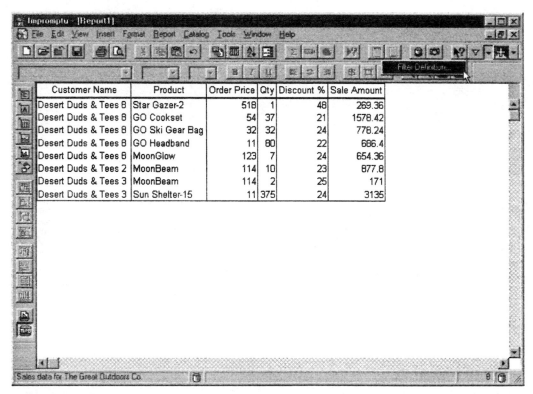

Figure 6.24   When nothing is selected on a report, the Dropdown on the Filter button shows just "Filter Definition."

With nothing selected on the report (if something is selected, hit the Esc key), do the following:

1. Select the Dropdown Filter arrow.
2. Choose "Filter Definition" (Figure 6.25).

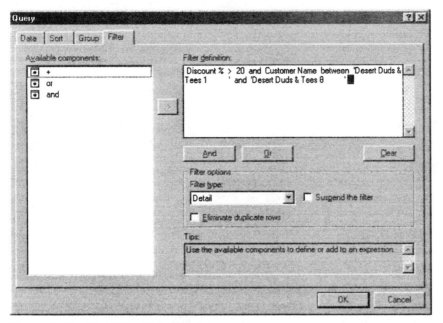

Figure 6.25 The Filter Definition box.

This is what the Filter Definition looks like. The Filter Definition resides within the Filter tab of the QDB. If you stop and think about it for a second, that makes perfect sense. The QDB stores all of the pertinent information for retrieving the values from the database. It makes sense that when you are asking for a refined subset of data, the requirements of the filter are stored with the other components of the report. As you can see from Figure 6.25, there are several new components to become familiar with. These will be the heart of our conversation in the next section.

Filters in the QDB

This begins the advanced part of working with filters. Until now, you have been using the toolbar to apply your filter logic to the report. The filters built using the Filter button and Dropdown Filters are applied to the overall Filter Definition; this is where they are stored. So, when you go in to work on the Filter Definition for a report and you have applied a filter already, you will see all the Filter Definitions, regardless of how they were built.

The Filter tab in the QDB is where I go to perform these complex Filter Definitions. There are certain instances, certain report requirements that will require you to custom develop a filter. This section breaks down the Filter tab to the following three parts:

- Taking a look at components of the Filter tab of the current report, which the Filter Definition built from the last section
- Creating a Filter Definition from scratch
- Making a modification to the recently created Filter Definition

Looking Around in the Filter Tab

The Filter tab is something we have not looked at so far. It is the first in a series of three tabs to be discussed in the upcoming chapters. The Filter tab contains several key components that are designed to ease the Filter Definition development. This section begins by taking a quick tour of the tab, identifying each component, and describing how it works with the rest.

To provide a good example of an existing Filter Definition, we will keep using the report you built at the beginning of this chapter. The filters you just applied will reside in the Filter Definition box.

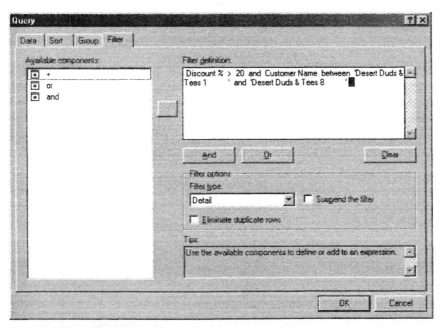

Figure 6.26   The current Filter tab of the report.

Filter Definition

The first thing that draws your attention when you look at the Filter tab is the Filter Definition. The Filter Definition box contains the heart of the filter. It is where all of the filtering work is displayed.

If you do not have the Filter tab left open from the last section,

    1. Select Report.Query.
    2. Click on the Filter tab.

What you see in the Filter Definition are comparison equations. When you selected a column and performed a point and click filter, Impromptu sent to the query a filter arranged like this:

```
(Column name of the cell you selected) = (the value you want)
```

The next comparison you performed was added on to the original, using the "and" operand. We will get into the "and" operand later, but for now, realize that it lets Impromptu know that both filters *must* be satisfied in order for the value to be returned.

Note

The entry and navigation of the Filter Definition box is common to all Impromptu definition boxes. The next section covers specifically how to navigate with the cursor. There are several definition boxes throughout Impromptu that are discussed in ensuing chapters, all similar in basic functionality even though they serve different purposes.

Filter Option Group

The Filter Option group, shown in Figure 6.27, is an area that provides additional filtering capabilities. By default, the filter type dropdown box is set to "Detail." This indicates that the Filter Definition shown above it is for the detail level records. The other option is "Summary," which allows you to create a Filter Definition for the summary part of the query. Creating filters for summaries is an advanced topic, where an intricate report request will demand using a summary filter.

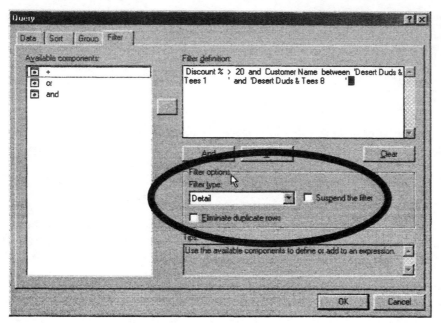

Figure 6.27   The Filter Option group.

There are two additional checkboxes that relate in functionality to filter options. They are:

- **Eliminate Duplicate Rows.** "Eliminate duplicate rows" is a special filter command that Impromptu incorporates into the query to the database. What the request does is to allow only one unique row of data to be returned to the report at a time. For example, if you were to build a report that had a query requesting just customer name and Sales Rep Name, you may get multiple rows of the same sales rep and customer, depending on how the database returned the data. With the Eliminate Duplicate Rows filter on, you will receive from the database one Sales Rep Name and customer combination, with no duplicates.

- **Suspend the Filter.** When this box is checked, Impromptu does not use the filter in the query to the database. This is helpful when you want to "turn off" the filter briefly, see the results, and then return to the filter. To use the filter again, just uncheck the box.

Tips Box

The Tips box, shown in Figure 6.28, gives you hints as to what you the report developer can do with what you have selected in the Filter Definition box or the available components toolbox. If your cursor falls on items requiring instructions, the Tips box will assist you by displaying a tip on how to use the item. Also, if you have a problem in the definition for any reason, the Tips box suggest an answer.

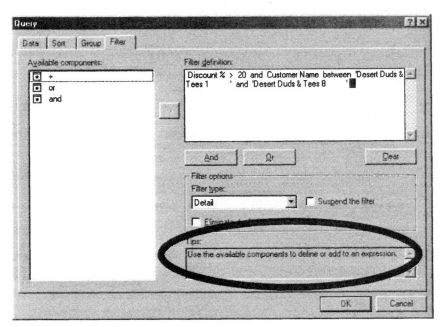

Figure 6.28   The Tips box.

Available Component Toolbox

The Available Component Toolbox contains all of the building blocks for building the Filter Definition. This toolbox concept is used throughout Impromptu in conjunction with the various definition boxes.

First, let's look at the existing definition. In doing this, we will cover a few things. First, we discover how to navigate in and around the definition box. Then, we learn how to use the Available Components Toolbox. Additionally, we learn how to work with the "and" and the "or" operands. Finally, we discuss how the things we did earlier in the chapter translate into what we see here.

The quickest way to learn navigate in the definition box is to jump right. What you initially see is the definition and the cursor at the end of the definition, which is highlighted, as shown in Figure 6.29.

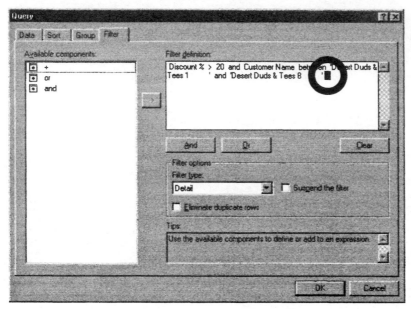

Figure 6.29
The Filter Definition
cursor or token.

Initially, the cursor is where the focus of the dialog box is. To change the focus, click on the first part of the definition: "Discount %."

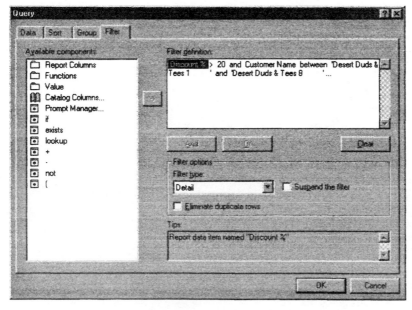

Figure 6.30
The item selected
in the Filter Defini-
tion is the column
Discount %.

As the focus of the cursor in the definition box changes, something else changes significantly—the Available Components Toolbox.

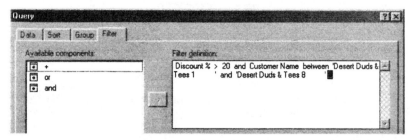

Figure 6.31   The Available Components Toolbox before the cursor move.

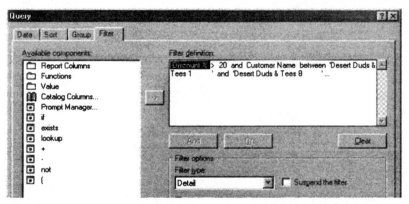

Figure 6.32   The Available Components Toolbox after the cursor move.

The Available Components Toolbox content changes based on the placement of the cursor in the Filter Definition. Each part of the toolbox is covered in more detail later, but for now it is important to know that the toolbox is sensitive to where the cursor is in the definition of the filter.

Question	Answer
Why are all those spaces in place after the text in "Desert Duds & Tees 1 "?	All those spaces at the end are a result of how that value is stored in the database. The database that we are using for our examples has the products stored in a fixed-length string field. That means that whatever is stored in that column is what is stored, and if something does not take up the entire space provided, the database will "fill" the value in with spaces at the end.
	In our example here, this Customer Name value is "Desert Duds & Tees 1 "; the ten spaces at the end complete the 30 characters required.

Logical Operands

The next component is a special one. In our example, it is an "and" component. This, and the "or" component, are both logical operands. The purpose of these two components is to logically tie an expression together.

"Ands"

The first comparison in your example report filters the report to show only rows that have a Discount % greater than 20, as shown in Figure 6.33. The next comparison, in Fig-

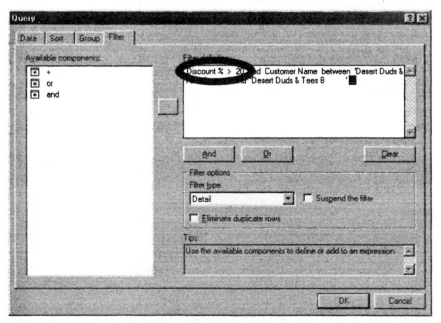

Figure 6.33   The first filter.

ure 6.34, is a little tricky. It restricts the Customer Name to the ones between "Desert Duds & Tees 1" and "Desert Duds & Tees 8." This gives a potential for Desert Duds & Tees 2 through 8 to return from the database. The use of "and" here, however, is not as an independent operand; it is part of the Between filter.

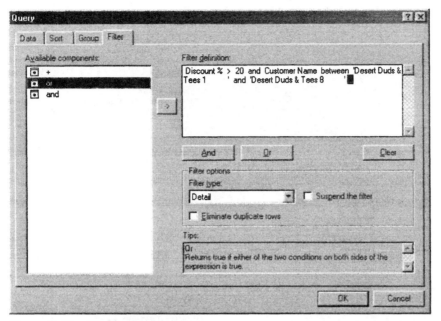

Figure 6.34   The second filter.

What ties these two separate filters together is the "and," and this means that *both* conditions have to be satisfied in order for that particular record to be retrieved.

"Ors"

Ors work a little differently. An "or" means that you can have either filter be satisfied for that particular row to be sent back from the database to the report. This provides a lot more flexibility in building combination filters when *either* filter can be true for data to be returned.

The following example takes you through changing the logical operand from "and" to "or" in the example report you have been working with.

Try This:

In this exercise, you are going to change the current Filter Definition and see the ramifications of using the "or" instead of the "and."

With the Filter tab open:

1. Click on the first "and."

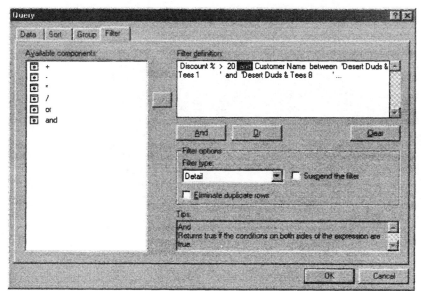

Figure 6.35
The Filter tab with
the first "and"
selected.

2. Click the "or" button beneath the Filter Definition box.

The intermediate result in the Filter Definition box should look like the following:

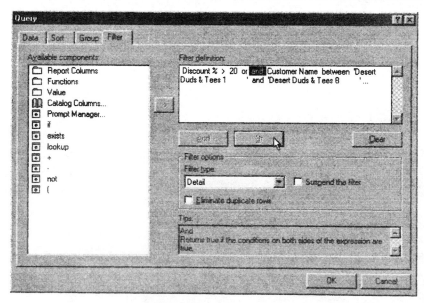

Figure 6.36
The Filter tab with
both "and" and
"or" next to one
another.

Now, you have two logical operands next to each other. That doesn't make any sense! To prove this, go ahead and click the OK button. If your computer has sound, you heard a beep, and the Filter tab changed to this:

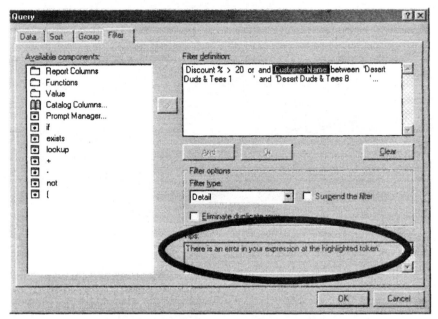

Figure 6.37   The Filter tab with the error message on the bottom.

The Tips box tells you that there is an error at the highlighted token. But what this really means is that something directly to the left of the "token," the cursor, does not make sense or is not technically right.

Try This:

You can resolve your operand problem in two ways:

1. If the cursor is on the "Customer Name" label, hit the Backspace key on your keyboard.

Note

This deletes the token to the left of the cursor, thus removing the unwanted "and" operand. This works if your cursor is on the item to the right of what you want to delete.

2. Click on the "and" operand and hit the Delete key on the keyboard. This deleted the token the cursor resides on.

After either option, the Filter Definition box looks like this:

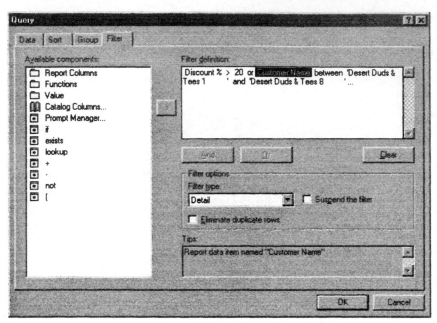

Figure 6.38   The Filter tab, with Customer Name highlighted.

3. Click OK (Figure 6.39).

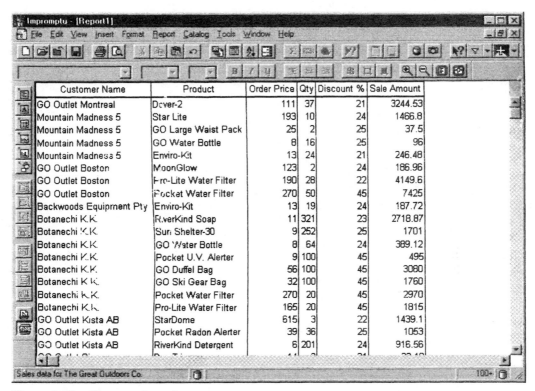

Figure 6.39 The report results.

There is now a combination of results: there are many of companies, all of which have passed the filter: Discount % > 20. And, there are all the Desert Duds & Tees companies, complying with the second filter, regardless of their Discount %. This is the result of the "or" logical operand.

Creating a Filter in the QDB Filter Tab

You will often find yourself building a report from scratch, and you will think to yourself, "I don't want all of the data. I just want Product X." Or, you may be writing a report at the beginning of the month when the database is always slow, and you think, "Hey, the report I'm using always takes a long time to run this time each month. I don't want to wait for all of the data to come down from the database just so I can just filter click on Product X." In either of these cases, you will find yourself wanting to build a filter from scratch.

First, continue to use the report you have been working with this entire chapter. To build a new Filter Definition from scratch, you must remove all the filtering you have done up to now.

There is a quick way to undo all of the filters. If you have nothing highlighted on your report, you can press the Filter button, and you will be prompted with the following message:

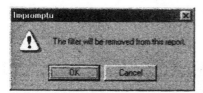

Figure 6.40
The Impromptu Filter warning box.

The message informs you that if you hit OK, you will remove all of your filters. This is a great shortcut, but it can be dangerous; once done, your filters are gone.

Creating a Filter

There are three ways to get to the Filter tab:

1. Hold the Ctrl key down and press the Filter button.

This option is similar to the way just mentioned to quickly clear the Filter Definition box. If you hold down the Ctrl key on the keyboard and press the Filter button, you will be taken directly to the Filter tab in the QDB.

2. Choose the Dropdown Filter·arrow.

This also takes you to the Filter tab in the QDB.

3. Go to the QDB.

You might have noticed that when you first create a report in the QDB, there is a Filter tab. The Filter tab is an integral part of the report and is available from the beginning. Before you even click OK for the first time, you have the ability to just select the Filter tab and create an initial Filter Definition. Anytime during the report-building process, you have the ability to modify the Filter tab.

Creating a Filter from Scratch

Note

If you have something already in your Filter Definition box, select the Clear button (Figure 6.41).

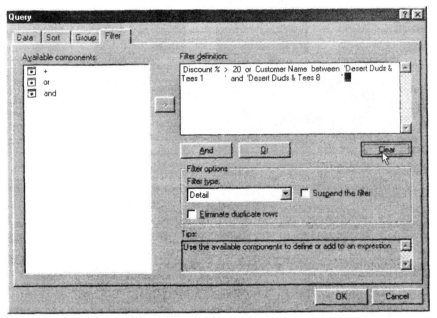

Figure 6.41   A used Filter tab before the cursor pushes the Clear button.

Adding items into the Filter Definition is a simple process. In the Available Components Toolbox, just select what you want from the list. A single click identifies either the object for the filter, or identifies a folder containing a group of items. To move an item from the Available Component Toolbox to the Filter Definition box, either double click that item or, once it is selected, press the right arrow separating the Available Component Toolbox from the Filter Definition.

Before you starting building filters from scratch, a few more items within the Available Components Toolkit should be explained (Figure 6.42).

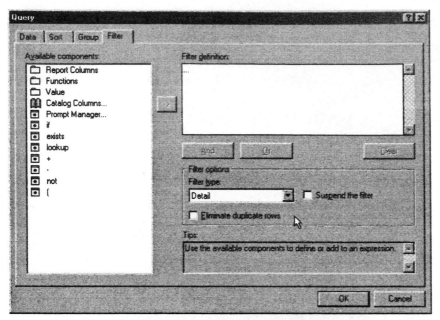

Figure 6.42   The base Available Components Toolbox.

Report Columns.   Report Columns is a folder containing all of the columns that have been selected for the report. This contains all of the columns from the Query box back in the Data tab, both straight from the Catalog and calculated.

Also, as the report column is displayed in other definition boxes, the Report Columns show only the columns applicable to what is needed in the definition box.

Functions.   Functions contain formulas and calculation extensions supplied by Impromptu. Functions are covered in detail in Chapter 7.

Value.   This folder contains components that allow report builders to type values directly into the Filter Definition. This is the only way you can type anything into this definition or any others. The following table provides a description of each data value type you can encounter in Impromptu.

Table 6.3

Data Value Types	Description
String	String values consist of alphanumeric combinations used to compare against data values in string columns from the database.
Numeric	Numeric values are used for both comparisons with numeric columns from the Catalog and manually entered values.
Date	Used to compare Date and Date-Time columns in the Catalog.
Time	Used to compare Date and Date-Time columns in the Catalog.
Date-time	Used to compare Date and Date-Time columns in the Catalog.
Interval	Used to compare Date and Date-Time columns in the Catalog.

Question	Answer
Why can't we type everything in directly?	On one hand, it would be great to be able to just type in an entire Filter Definition. You could type exactly what you wanted, quickly and efficiently.
	On the other hand, typing everything in would require Impromptu to debug and check every character, much as a programming language debugs a program a programmer develops.
	This is why Impromptu does not allow the report builder to type everything directly in. This would greatly degrade the speed and effectiveness of report generation. As you become more proficient, you will be bouncing in and out of the QDB, changing filters, adding calculations, and more.

Catalog Columns. Don't have the column in your report that you want to use in a filter? No problem. The Catalog Columns works like a the Report Columns folder in that you double click on it, and a Catalog Column selection window pops up. You get a separate window to navigate through the entire Catalog to select the column you want to add to the filter. Yes, you can have a column from the Catalog in your Filter Definition that does not appear in the Query box from the Data tab (Figure 6.43).

Inside the Catalog Columns you see the same folders you saw in the QDB Data tab's Catalog selection box. Here, the Catalog box is also sensitive to where the cursor is. If you are working in the definition and you are working with dates, the Catalog shows only the folders that contain date columns and shows only columns/Catalog calculations that are date columns.

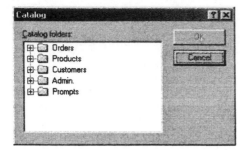

Figure 6.43
The Catalog Column from the
Available Components Toolbox.

Prompt Manager.   The Prompt Manager contains an environment where users can build selective prompts that allow them to select a value to be inserted into a filter. Prompts are covered in Chapter 10.

Additional Items.   These components are available to the definition box to provide additional features for specific purposes. The following table describes each of these and where you would apply them to a definition.

Table 6.4

Component	Description
If … Then … Else…	The If component is part of a powerful combination of If … Then … Else…, which is explained in Chapter 7.
Exists	Exists checks a dataset (an Impromptu Report that obtains values when called by a dataset) to see if values coming into this report match those from the dataset.
Lookup	This allows you to evaluate a value from the database and apply a specific value of your choice. For example, if you wanted to use lookup to convert country codes coming from a database to values, it would look like this:
	Lookup (country code) in ('01' -> 'USA', '02' -> 'Canada') default (country code)
	Country Code 01 will display as USA, and 02 will display as Canada, while the rest would just default to the country code from the database.
+, −, /, *	These are the available arithmetic operations.
Not	This reverses a logical expression. For example, if you wanted to filter on all the country codes not equal to 01, the filter would look like this:
	Not Country Code = '01'
(…)	You first see the Open parenthesis "(", and once you select it, you will be able to select the Close parenthesis ")". This is used in the explanation of the If… Then… Else… in Chapter 7.

Report Requirement

Your boss: Show the sales with a discount greater than or equal to 15%.

Analysis

Every time you get a request, it is always worth the time to analyze it. This gives you a chance to think through the request and follow up with any questions before you implement the answer. Here, this requirement is looking for is a filter. The key components are the phrase "discount," "greater than or equal to," and "15%." You can turn that into the filter: Discount % >= 15.

Steps to Build a Filter in the Filter Tab

1. Open the QDB.
2. Select the Filter tab.
3. Double click the "Reports Column."
4. Double click the "Discount %" column.

Remember

Every time you select something into the Filter Definition, the Available Component Toolbox changes.

5. Double click the '>='.
6. Double click on the blue Number token.
7. Type in the number 15 (Figure 6.44).
8. Click OK.

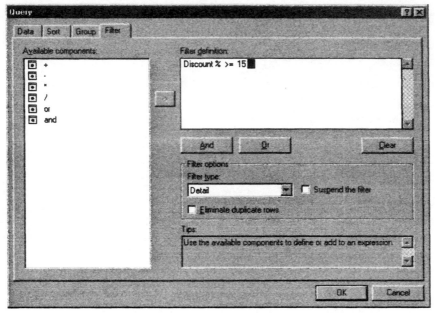

Figure 6.44   The completed Filter Definition.

And the Results Are...

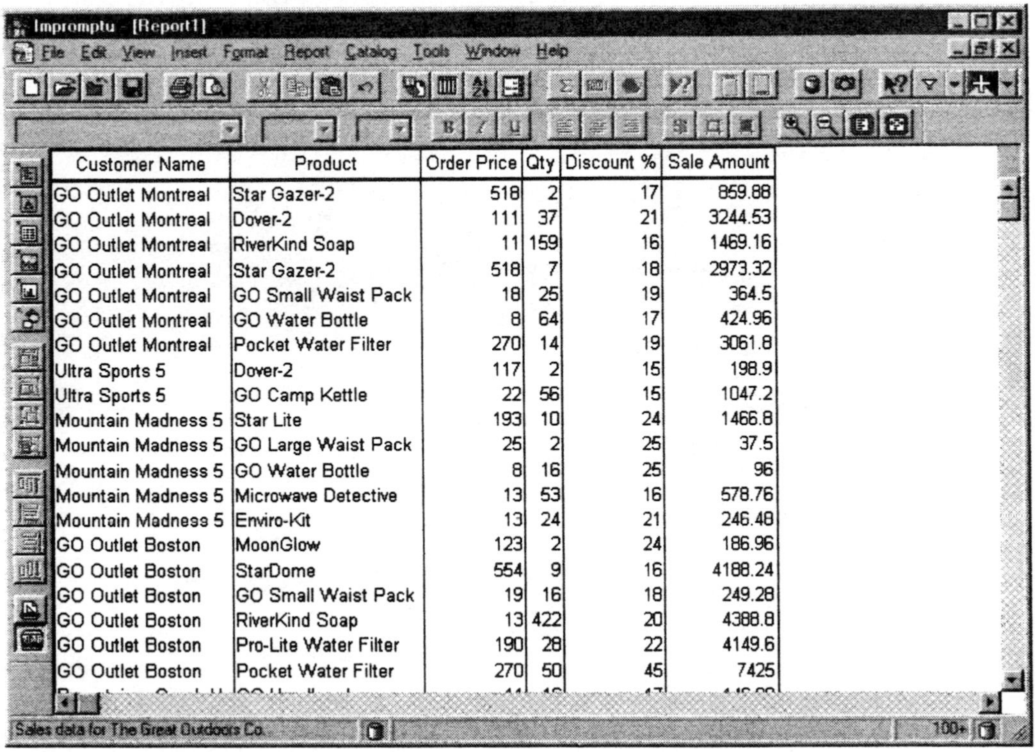

Customer Name	Product	Order Price	Qty	Discount %	Sale Amount
GO Outlet Montreal	Star Gazer-2	518	2	17	859.88
GO Outlet Montreal	Dover-2	111	37	21	3244.53
GO Outlet Montreal	RiverKind Soap	11	159	16	1469.16
GO Outlet Montreal	Star Gazer-2	518	7	18	2973.32
GO Outlet Montreal	GO Small Waist Pack	18	25	19	364.5
GO Outlet Montreal	GO Water Bottle	8	64	17	424.96
GO Outlet Montreal	Pocket Water Filter	270	14	19	3061.8
Ultra Sports 5	Dover-2	117	2	15	198.9
Ultra Sports 5	GO Camp Kettle	22	56	15	1047.2
Mountain Madness 5	Star Lite	193	10	24	1466.8
Mountain Madness 5	GO Large Waist Pack	25	2	25	37.5
Mountain Madness 5	GO Water Bottle	8	16	25	96
Mountain Madness 5	Microwave Detective	13	53	16	578.76
Mountain Madness 5	Enviro-Kit	13	24	21	246.48
GO Outlet Boston	MoonGlow	123	2	24	186.96
GO Outlet Boston	StarDome	554	9	16	4188.24
GO Outlet Boston	GO Small Waist Pack	19	16	18	249.28
GO Outlet Boston	RiverKind Soap	13	422	20	4388.8
GO Outlet Boston	Pro-Lite Water Filter	190	28	22	4149.6
GO Outlet Boston	Pocket Water Filter	270	50	45	7425

Figure 6.45 The result of your first filter.

Note

Typing in numbers, words, etc, is a great way to specifically enter what you want into a report. One special technique you can use is to press the Enter when you are done typing in a number. This guarantees that when you're done typing, the cursor in the Filter Definition moves to the next item. This is critical, because if you forget to finish the typing and double click to bring in the next component, it will be misplaced to the left of the type-in field.

Tip

In the previous chapter, you used a Catalog Filter to create a Conditional Format. This Catalog Filter can be used anywhere you would normally apply a filter. This means that in addition to using the Catalog Filter in the Conditional Formats, you can use it in the Filter tab as well. A Catalog Filter is simply a filter defined by the administrator.

To use a Catalog Filter in a Filter Definition is easy:

1. In a clear Filter Definition, double click on the Catalog Column as you would to select a column.
2. Expand the Orders folder and then the Conditions folder.

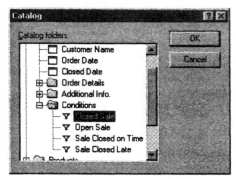

Figure 6.46
Choosing the condition from the Catalog.

3. Select Closed Sale and click OK. This places the condition in the Filter Definition, and that is all you need. Everything is contained in the label; you just select it (Figure 6.47).
4. Click OK to Run.

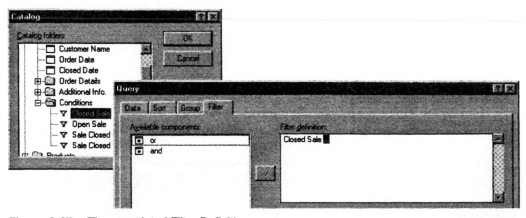

Figure 6.47   The completed Filter Definition.

And the Results Are...

Customer Name	Product	Order Price	Qty	Discount %	Sale Amount
GO Outlet Montreal	Star Gazer-2	518	2	17	859.88
GO Outlet Montreal	Dover-2	111	37	21	3244.53
GO Outlet Montreal	GO Cookset	54	62	1	3314.52
GO Outlet Montreal	GO Sport Bag	28	16	14	385.28
GO Outlet Montreal	EnviroSak	6	11	12	58.08
GO Outlet Montreal	RiverKind Soap	11	159	16	1469.16
GO Outlet Montreal	Star Gazer-2	518	7	18	2973.32
GO Outlet Montreal	GO Small Waist Pack	18	25	19	364.5
GO Outlet Montreal	GO Water Bottle	8	64	17	424.96
GO Outlet Montreal	Enviro-T	30	124	2	3645.6
GO Outlet Montreal	Pocket Water Filter	270	14	19	3061.8
Ultra Sports 5	Dover-2	117	2	15	198.9
Ultra Sports 5	GO Camp Kettle	22	56	15	1047.2
Ultra Sports 5	GO Sport Bag	31	48	2	1458.24
Ultra Sports 5	Pocket U.V. Alerter	10	77	14	662.2
Ultra Sports 5	Enviro-Kit	13	3	10	35.1
Ultra Sports 5	RiverKind Shampoo	11	165	3	1760.55
Mountain Madness 5	Star Lite	193	10	24	1466.8
Mountain Madness 5	GO Large Waist Pack	25	2	25	37.5
Mountain Madness 5	GO Water Bottle	8	16	25	96

Sales data for The Great Outdoors Co.

Figure 6.48   The results, just as if you had defined the filter yourself.

Filters stored in the Catalog should be reserved for either commonly used filters or extremely complicated and/or long filters. Otherwise, everybody would want all of his or her filters in the Catalog, and it would get overloaded quickly.

Changing Filters

In the real world, you don't just pick a filter and stay with it for the life of the report. You change it as often as you like. In the following section, we change the Filter Definition a few times to get some practice.

Changing the Number in the Filter

One such change that occurs frequently can be related to the example you just did. In that filter, you selected Discount % >= 15. Many times you can get report requirements from users and even have them sign off on the report requirements. The minute you show them the report to review the request, they inevitably want to make changes. With that said, let's walk through one of those scenarios.

Report Requirement

Boss: *Hmm, 15% did not quite give me the picture I was hoping for. Could you make that 10%? Thanks!*

Analysis

Yes, it can and usually does happen to everyone: a last-minute change. Such changes can infuriate report developers and kill project deadlines; even so, the needs of the users come first. They want us to change the value in the filter from 15% to 10%

Steps to Change a Filter

1. Open the QDB.
2. Select the Filter tab.
3. Click between the 1 and the 5 in the Filter Definition; this ensures that you are in the middle of the type-in value (Figure 6.49).

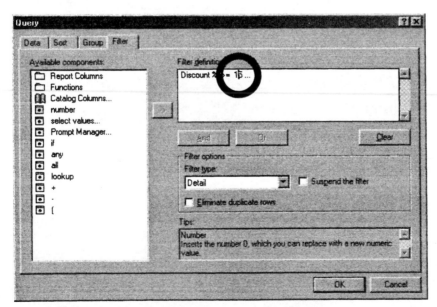

Figure 6.49   The cursor placed between the two numbers.

4. Use the Delete key to the erase the 5, and then type 0 (Figure 6.50).

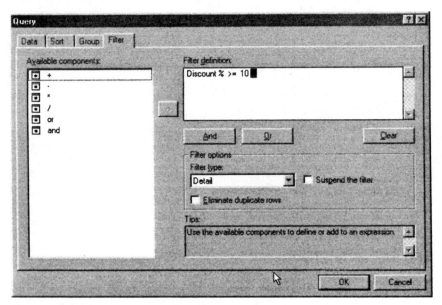

Figure 6.50   The changed value.

5. Press Enter.
6. Click OK.

And the Results Are...

	Customer Name	Product	Order Price	Qty	Discount %	Sale Amount
	GO Outlet Montreal	Star Gazer-2	518	2	17	859.88
	GO Outlet Montreal	Dover-2	111	37	21	3244.53
	GO Outlet Montreal	GO Sport Bag	28	16	14	385.28
	GO Outlet Montreal	EnviroSak	6	11	12	58.08
	GO Outlet Montreal	RiverKind Soap	11	159	16	1469.16
	GO Outlet Montreal	Star Gazer-2	518	7	18	2973.32
	GO Outlet Montreal	GO Small Waist Pack	18	25	19	364.5
	GO Outlet Montreal	GO Water Bottle	8	64	17	424.96
	GO Outlet Montreal	Pocket Water Filter	270	14	19	3061.8
	Ultra Sports 5	Dover-2	117	2	15	198.9
	Ultra Sports 5	GO Camp Kettle	22	56	15	1047.2
	Ultra Sports 5	Pocket U.V. Alerter	10	77	14	662.2
	Ultra Sports 5	Enviro-Kit	13	3	10	35.1
	Mountain Madness 5	Star Lite	193	10	24	1466.8
	Mountain Madness 5	GO Large Waist Pack	25	2	25	37.5
	Mountain Madness 5	GO Water Bottle	8	16	25	96
	Mountain Madness 5	Microwave Detective	13	53	16	578.76
	Mountain Madness 5	Enviro-Kit	13	24	21	246.48
	Mountain Madness 5	MoonBeam	114	1	11	101.46
	Mountain Madness 5	Pack n' Hike	138	1	11	122.82

Figure 6.51 The resulting report.

Adding a Part to the Filter

Let's create a filter that accomplishes the following:

Report Requirement

You can see that there are many sales that have greater than 10% discounts. Now, keeping just that filter, let's see the sales for the product "GO Sport Bag"?

Analysis

It takes two things to turn this requirement into a plan of action:

- Looking at the requirements
- Having an understanding of the current filter

The requirements are asking for a filter: Products = "GO Sport Bag." The next step is having an understanding and applying the new requirement to the current Filter Definition.

The current filter already has the Discount %>= 10 and another filter. Looking back at the requirement, you can see that the new filter requirement is an addition (an "and" operand) to just the first filter in the current Filter Definition. This is an important evaluation because it determines what you keep as well as whether you use an "and" or an "or" between the current Filter Definition and the new filter.

Steps to Add a Part to a Filter

1. Open the QDB.
2. Click on the Filter tab.
3. With the cursor at the end of the current Filter Definition, either double click on the "and" component in the toolbox, or click the "and" button below the Filter Definition box.
4. Expand the Reports folder.
5. Double click on the Product column to insert it in the Filter Definition.
6. Double click on "=".
7. Double click on Select Values.

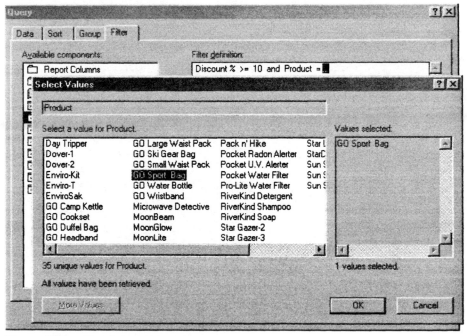

Figure 6.52 The Select Values box.

Note

The Select Values option queries the database for up to the first 100 unique values. The results are then displayed on the Select Values selection box. Here you are able to select as many units as needed to finish the selection. In our example, we need only one value selected to be able to return to the Filter tab.

Your administrator will be able to increase that number if so desired. This should be done by the Cognos administrator because it is not as simple as changing a number in a file. Increasing this number can affect the database, your desktop computer's performance, and the network around you.

Note

Notice how there are spaces associated with the value we selected. The good part is that you didn't have to type them in!

Question	Answer
Can I copy a filter from one report and paste it into a new report?	Yes. Impromptu allows you to highlight a section in the Filter Definition and paste it into another report's Filter Definition.

8. Select "GO Sport Bag;" the values selected box now contains "GO Sport Bag," and the OK button is now enabled.

9. Click OK; the new filter added to the Filter Definition is shown (Figure 6.53).

10. Click OK.

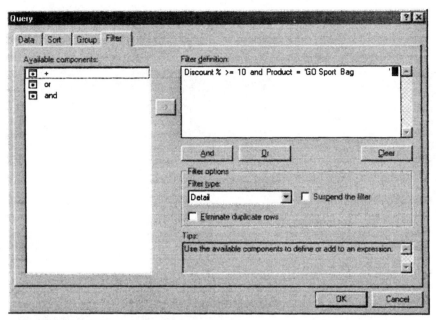

Figure 6.53   The completed Filter Definition.

And the Results Are...

Customer Name	Product	Order Price	Qty	Discount %	Sale Amount
Mountain Madness 3	GO Sport Bag	28	80	16	1881.6
OutBack Pty 2	GO Sport Bag	28	16	12	394.24
GO Outlet Montreal	GO Sport Bag	28	16	14	385.28
Pro Form Supplies 4	GO Sport Bag	28	48	22	1048.32
Tregoran AB 1	GO Sport Bag	28	32	11	797.44
Lookout Below Ltd	GO Sport Bag	28	32	18	734.72
123 Fitness PTE Ltd	GO Sport Bag	28	16	12	394.24
Pro Form Supplies 4	GO Sport Bag	28	64	15	1523.2
Vacation Central 4	GO Sport Bag	31	64	15	1686.4
Vacation Central 3	GO Sport Bag	31	32	17	823.36
OutBack Pty 2	GO Sport Bag	31	16	11	441.44
Tregoran AB 1	GO Sport Bag	31	48	15	1264.8
Supras Camping Supplies 2	GO Sport Bag	31	48	24	1130.88
Mountain Madness 2	GO Sport Bag	31	64	21	1567.36
Over the Top Cycles 3 AB	GO Sport Bag	31	48	19	1205.28
Vacation Central 3	GO Sport Bag	31	32	18	813.44
Wilderness Wonderment Ltd	GO Sport Bag	28	100	45	1540
GO Outlet Frankfurt	GO Sport Bag	28	100	45	1540
GO Outlet Singapore	GO Sport Bag	28	100	45	1540
Clear Valley Waters 2	GO Sport Bag	28	400	45	6160

Figure 6.54   The report results. Note the result set is only 22 records. That means there are 22 "GO Sport Bag" sales that had a Discount over 10%.

This exercise illustrated the topics covered in this chapter while providing something new. From this exercise alone, an entire book could be written exploring different methodologies applied to filtering. Use this, and build your own skills.

Summary

The main points we learned from this chapter are:

1. How to Point and Click filter a report
2. How to filter using the QDB
3. How to change filters once we create them

For those of you who are scratching your head and thinking about sticking with being a report consumer, my advice is, "hang in there." Walk away from this chapter for a day or two, come back, and browse through it again. These chapters are not for the faint of heart, but the topics are do-able. Be patient; it takes time to understand these concepts.

For those who think to themselves "But, how do I do this... or that...," this is the perfect time for you to try to do some of those reports. The best advice I can provide at this time, outside of "read on," is to experiment with your environment. Try, fail a couple times, and learn from those initial efforts. You will only get better, be able to answer your questions, and become more comfortable with Impromptu and filters.

Calculations and Functions

Calculations and functions have enough in common that it makes sense to discuss them in the same chapter. Both calculations and functions are simple enough that you can develop intricate and complicated ones in no time. You will be amazed not only at the calculations you can perform, but also at the places where you will be able to use them throughout the report.

This chapter instructs you in the fundamentals of creating calculations and functions. We discuss some interesting alterations you can do with these. Then it will be your turn to apply these skills to your own data and reports.

This chapter covers the following topics:

- Basic calculations
- Complex calculations
- Different uses for calculations
- Function basics
- Multiple and nested functions
- Places to use functions

Before We Begin

Before you start creating all these wonderful calculations and functions, let's create a new report. Once again, if you already have a couple of reports open, close them for a clean start.

1. Click the New report button.
2. With the QDB open, expand the Orders folder.

3. Expand the Additional Info folder.

4. Select the Sales Rep Name.

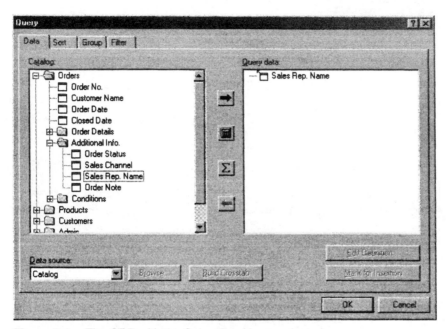

Figure 7.1   The QDB with the Sales Rep Name selected.

5. Expand the Orders Detail folder.

6. Select the remaining columns for this report, as shown in Figure 7.2:

   • Product

   • Order Price

   • Qty

   • Discount %

   • Sale Amount

7. Click OK (Figure 7.3).

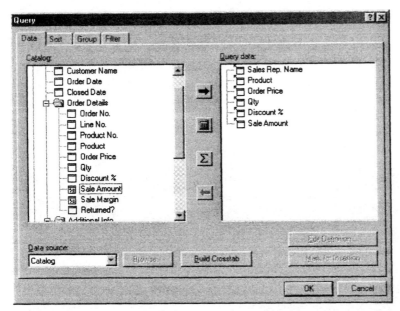

Figure 7.2
The completed QDB.

Sales Rep. Name	Product	Order Price	Qty	Discount %	Sale Amount
Bjorn Flertjan	Sun Shelter-8	6	247	7	1378.26
Bjorn Flertjan	Sun Shelter-15	9	617	21	4386.87
Bjorn Flertjan	Star Gazer-2	518	1	16	435.12
Bjorn Flertjan	StarDome	615	3	22	1439.1
Bjorn Flertjan	Day Tripper	14	7	18	80.36
Bjorn Flertjan	GO Duffel Bag	56	48	14	2311.68
Bjorn Flertjan	Pocket Radon Alerter	39	36	25	1053
Bjorn Flertjan	Sun Shelter-15	9	378	2	3333.96
Bjorn Flertjan	Star Lite	165	34	19	4544.1
Bjorn Flertjan	Star Gazer-3	555	10	24	4218
Bjorn Flertjan	StarDome	615	4	3	2386.2
Bjorn Flertjan	GO Sport Bag	28	32	11	797.44
Bjorn Flertjan	Pocket Radon Alerter	39	24	1	926.64
Bjorn Flertjan	EnviroSak	6	36	18	177.12
Bjorn Flertjan	StarDome	615	7	1	4261.95
Bjorn Flertjan	MoonGlow	129	19	8	2254.92
Bjorn Flertjan	Dover-1	65	73	14	4080.7
Bjorn Flertjan	GO Wristband	8	48	20	307.2
Bjorn Flertjan	RiverKind Detergent	6	201	24	916.56
Bjorn Flertjan	Pocket Water Filter	270	14	6	3553.2

Sales data for The Great Outdoors Co.

Figure 7.3   The report results.

Basic Calculations

A critical strength of Impromptu is its ability to provide an environment where users can easily develop reports and build calculations. Basic calculations start with what you might expect: simple math. We take one number and add, subtract, multiply, and/or divide by another number.

There are two ways to insert a calculation into a report:

1. Via the Menu bar: Insert.Calculation

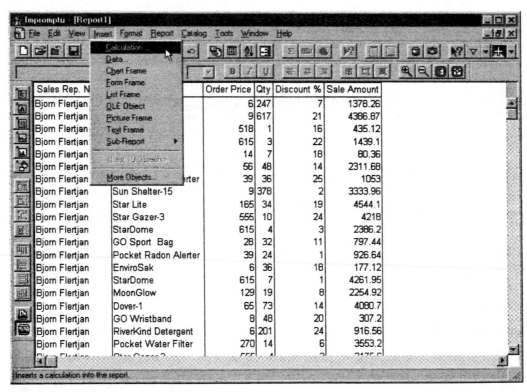

Figure 7.4   The Insert.Calculation.

2. Via the QDB Data tab: Calculate button

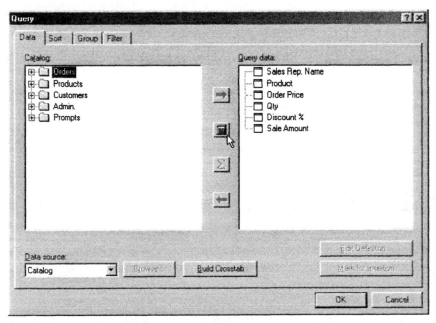

Figure 7.5   The Calculate button.

First: A Basic Calculation

For our first calculation, let's figure out the full price for all the quantities ordered. To do this, we have to create a calculation in our new report.

Note

*Because these basic calculations are relatively simple, I will bypass the **Report Requirements** and **Analysis** to speed up the process of getting you to the information. When it makes sense to bring in the requirement and analysis, I will.*

Steps to Create a Calculation

1. From the menu bar, select Insert.Calculation.
2. You can now move the cursor around the report. This marker, along with the dashed line, lets you know where the inserted column will reside.

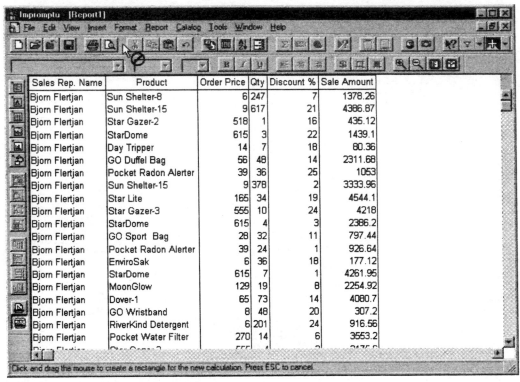

Sales Rep. Name	Product	Order Price	Qty	Discount %	Sale Amount
Bjorn Flertjan	Sun Shelter-8	6	247	7	1378.26
Bjorn Flertjan	Sun Shelter-15	9	617	21	4386.87
Bjorn Flertjan	Star Gazer-2	518	1	16	435.12
Bjorn Flertjan	StarDome	615	3	22	1439.1
Bjorn Flertjan	Day Tripper	14	7	18	80.36
Bjorn Flertjan	GO Duffel Bag	56	48	14	2311.68
Bjorn Flertjan	Pocket Radon Alerter	39	36	25	1053
Bjorn Flertjan	Sun Shelter-15	9	378	2	3333.96
Bjorn Flertjan	Star Lite	165	34	19	4544.1
Bjorn Flertjan	Star Gazer-3	555	10	24	4218
Bjorn Flertjan	StarDome	615	4	3	2386.2
Bjorn Flertjan	GO Sport Bag	28	32	11	797.44
Bjorn Flertjan	Pocket Radon Alerter	39	24	1	926.64
Bjorn Flertjan	EnviroSak	6	36	18	177.12
Bjorn Flertjan	StarDome	615	7	1	4261.95
Bjorn Flertjan	MoonGlow	129	19	8	2254.92
Bjorn Flertjan	Dover-1	65	73	14	4080.7
Bjorn Flertjan	GO Wristband	8	48	20	307.2
Bjorn Flertjan	RiverKind Detergent	6	201	24	916.56
Bjorn Flertjan	Pocket Water Filter	270	14	6	3553.2

Click and drag the mouse to create a rectangle for the new calculation. Press ESC to cancel.

Figure 7.6   Initially, the cursor changes to this symbol. This indicates you cannot place the Calculation where the mouse is pointing.

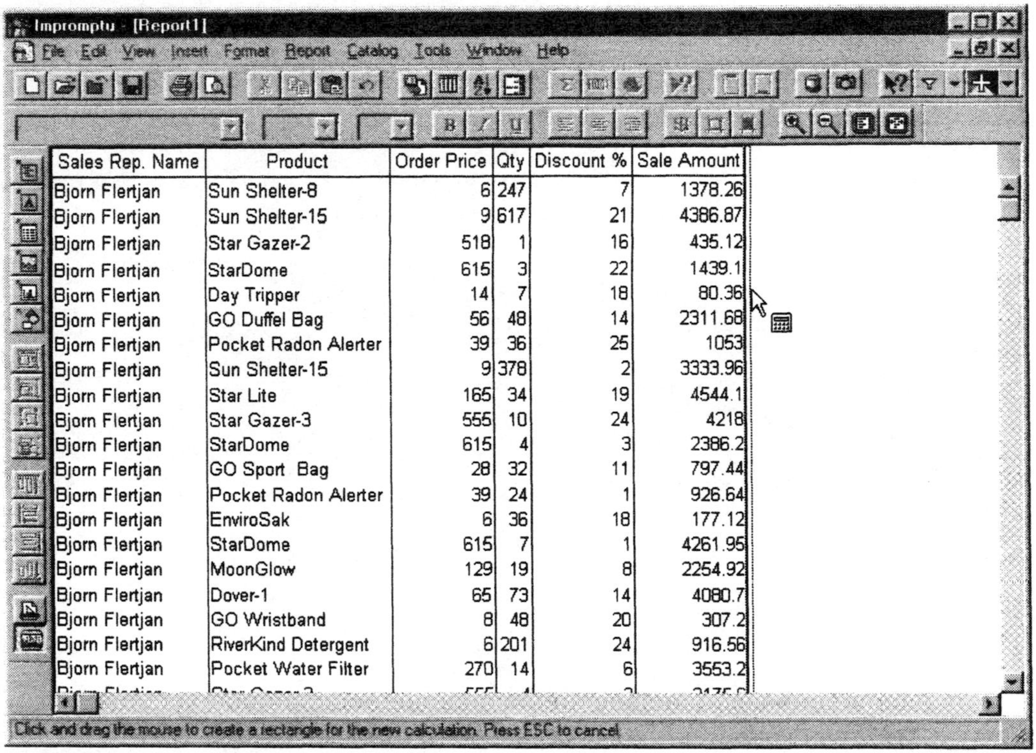

Sales Rep. Name	Product	Order Price	Qty	Discount %	Sale Amount
Bjorn Flertjan	Sun Shelter-8	6	247	7	1378.26
Bjorn Flertjan	Sun Shelter-15	9	617	21	4386.87
Bjorn Flertjan	Star Gazer-2	518	1	16	435.12
Bjorn Flertjan	StarDome	615	3	22	1439.1
Bjorn Flertjan	Day Tripper	14	7	18	80.36
Bjorn Flertjan	GO Duffel Bag	56	48	14	2311.68
Bjorn Flertjan	Pocket Radon Alerter	39	36	25	1053
Bjorn Flertjan	Sun Shelter-15	9	378	2	3333.96
Bjorn Flertjan	Star Lite	165	34	19	4544.1
Bjorn Flertjan	Star Gazer-3	555	10	24	4218
Bjorn Flertjan	StarDome	615	4	3	2386.2
Bjorn Flertjan	GO Sport Bag	28	32	11	797.44
Bjorn Flertjan	Pocket Radon Alerter	39	24	1	926.64
Bjorn Flertjan	EnviroSak	6	36	18	177.12
Bjorn Flertjan	StarDome	615	7	1	4261.95
Bjorn Flertjan	MoonGlow	129	19	8	2254.92
Bjorn Flertjan	Dover-1	65	73	14	4080.7
Bjorn Flertjan	GO Wristband	8	48	20	307.2
Bjorn Flertjan	RiverKind Detergent	6	201	24	916.56
Bjorn Flertjan	Pocket Water Filter	270	14	6	3553.2

Figure 7.7   The cursor has changed to indicate the new activity, and the marker indicates the destination of the calculation.

3. When you have the column where you want it, click the left mouse button.

The dialog box you see in Figure 7.8, looks a lot like the Filter Definition box. The Calculation Definition box uses the same style as the Filter tab, and is used by many other definition boxes throughout Impromptu. This is a way to promote consistency from one area of Impromptu to another. The only difference between the Calculation and the Filter is that here the box is called the Expression, and in the Filter it is called the Definition.

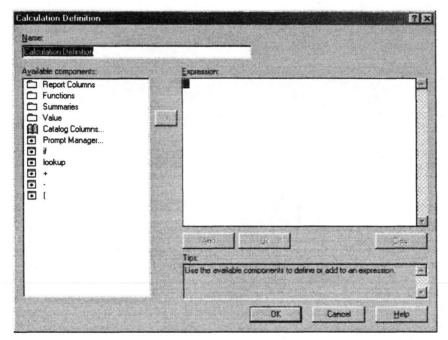

Figure 7.8   The Calculation Definition window.

4. The first thing that is highlighted is the name. Name this column "Full Price" by typing this into the Name box.

Next, use the Available Components Toolbox to assemble or create the calculation expression. The Available Components Toolbox is exactly the same as the one used in the preceding chapter, so you should be fairly comfortable with navigating and using it.

5. Expand the Report Columns.
6. Select the Order Price by double clicking on it.

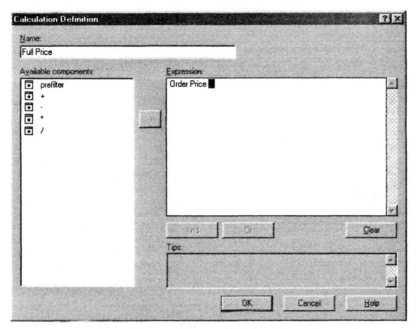

Figure 7.9
The selected Order price with new Available Components Toolbox view.

7. Since the Available Components have changed, use the newly visible multiply symbol "*" to select that for the expression (Figure 7.10).

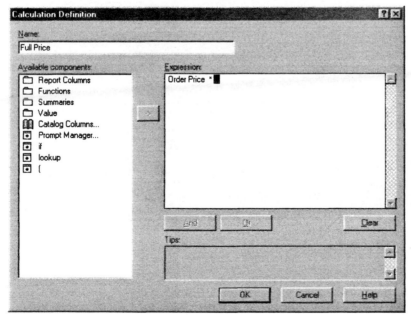

Figure 7.10
The Filter Definition including the * and with a new Available Components Toolbox view.

8. Expand the Reports Folder.

9. Select the Qty column, and add it to the calculation (Figure 7.11).

10. Click OK.

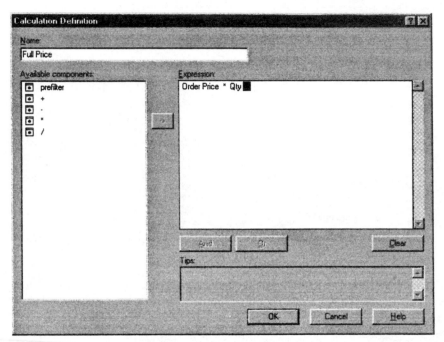

Figure 7.11   The completed Calculation Definition.

Adding this calculation changes the query initially built by Impromptu. So when there is a change to the query, Impromptu has to rerun the query.

And the Results Are...

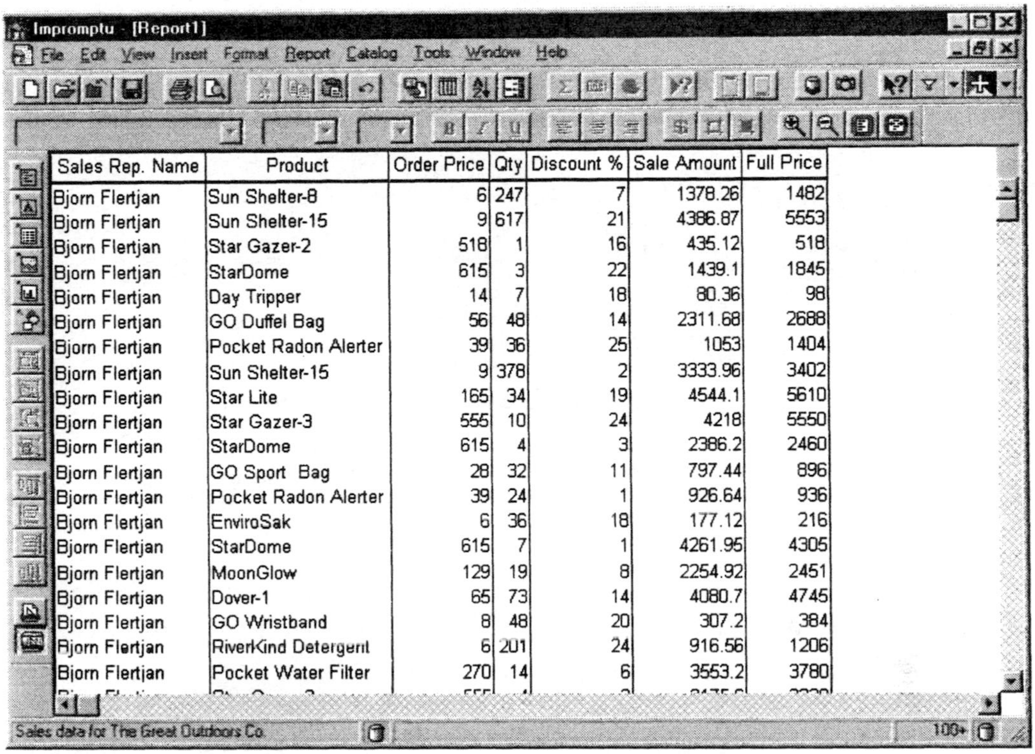

Sales Rep. Name	Product	Order Price	Qty	Discount %	Sale Amount	Full Price
Bjorn Flertjan	Sun Shelter-8	6	247	7	1378.26	1482
Bjorn Flertjan	Sun Shelter-15	9	617	21	4386.87	5553
Bjorn Flertjan	Star Gazer-2	518	1	16	435.12	518
Bjorn Flertjan	StarDome	615	3	22	1439.1	1845
Bjorn Flertjan	Day Tripper	14	7	18	80.36	98
Bjorn Flertjan	GO Duffel Bag	56	48	14	2311.68	2688
Bjorn Flertjan	Pocket Radon Alerter	39	36	25	1053	1404
Bjorn Flertjan	Sun Shelter-15	9	378	2	3333.96	3402
Bjorn Flertjan	Star Lite	165	34	19	4544.1	5610
Bjorn Flertjan	Star Gazer-3	555	10	24	4218	5550
Bjorn Flertjan	StarDome	615	4	3	2386.2	2460
Bjorn Flertjan	GO Sport Bag	28	32	11	797.44	896
Bjorn Flertjan	Pocket Radon Alerter	39	24	1	926.64	936
Bjorn Flertjan	EnviroSak	6	36	18	177.12	216
Bjorn Flertjan	StarDome	615	7	1	4261.95	4305
Bjorn Flertjan	MoonGlow	129	19	8	2254.92	2451
Bjorn Flertjan	Dover-1	65	73	14	4080.7	4745
Bjorn Flertjan	GO Wristband	8	48	20	307.2	384
Bjorn Flertjan	RiverKind Detergent	6	201	24	916.56	1206
Bjorn Flertjan	Pocket Water Filter	270	14	6	3553.2	3780

Figure 7.12 The report results.

Surprisingly simple, right? Actually, that is all there is to calculations, in their most basic form. This is the foundation for building more complicated calculations. The following sections take this basic concept and apply it to several different scenarios and even use data types other than numbers.

Complex Calculations

Simple calculations are easy, but can Impromptu do complex calculations? The answer is an overwhelming Yes.

The example you will use is creating a new calculation called Profit Margin. Now, profit margin is not what most people would call a difficult calculation, but it uses elements required by complex calculations.

Steps to Create a Complex Calculation

1. Open the QDB, and choose the Data tab if it is not already selected.
2. Between the Catalog box and the Query Data box, select the button with a small calculator on it.

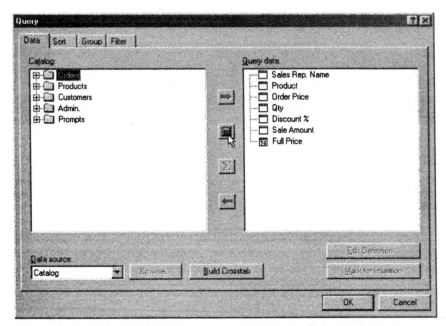

Figure 7.13   The QDB with the cursor pointing to the Calculate button.

3. Give this calculation the name Profit Margin.

   Here's the formula for this calculation:

   $$\frac{(\text{Order Price} - \text{Product Cost})}{\text{Cost}}$$

If you do not need the step-by-step, try building this calculation by looking at the finished product in Figure 7.15.

4. To start things off in the expression, you need an Open parenthesis "(". Double click on it from the Available Components Toolbox.

5. Expand the Reports Folder.

6. Select the Order Price column.

7. Select the Minus icon "–".

8. Open the Catalog Columns… folder.

9. Expand the Products folder.

10. Expand the Price and Cost folder.

11. Select Product Cost and click OK.

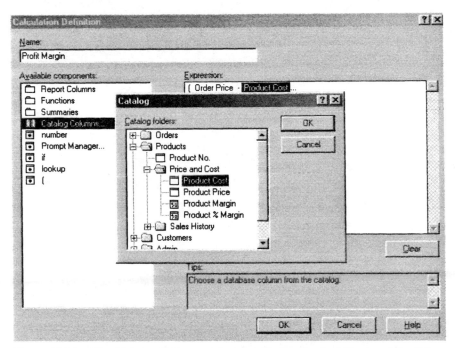

Figure 7.14   The Catalog Columns window with the Product Cost and the Filter Definition in the background showing where the Product Cost will end up.

12. Close the parenthesis that you first added in step 4 by double clicking on it.

Note

You do not have to worry about learning where things are in this Catalog. You won't be writing reports for your company with it. When you get back to your office and work with your own Catalog, you will become familiar with them after a little exploring.

13. Select the "/" divide operand.

    To finish this off, add the final column.

14. Expand the Reports Folders.
15. Select Order Price (Figure 7.15).
16. Click OK.

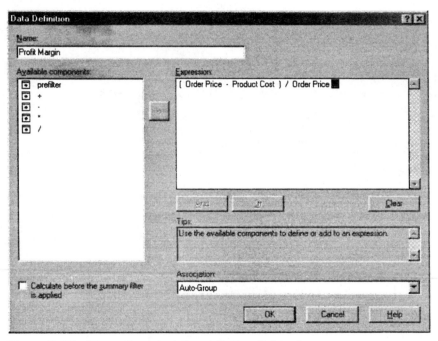

Figure 7.15   The entire calculation definition, finished.

And the Results Are...

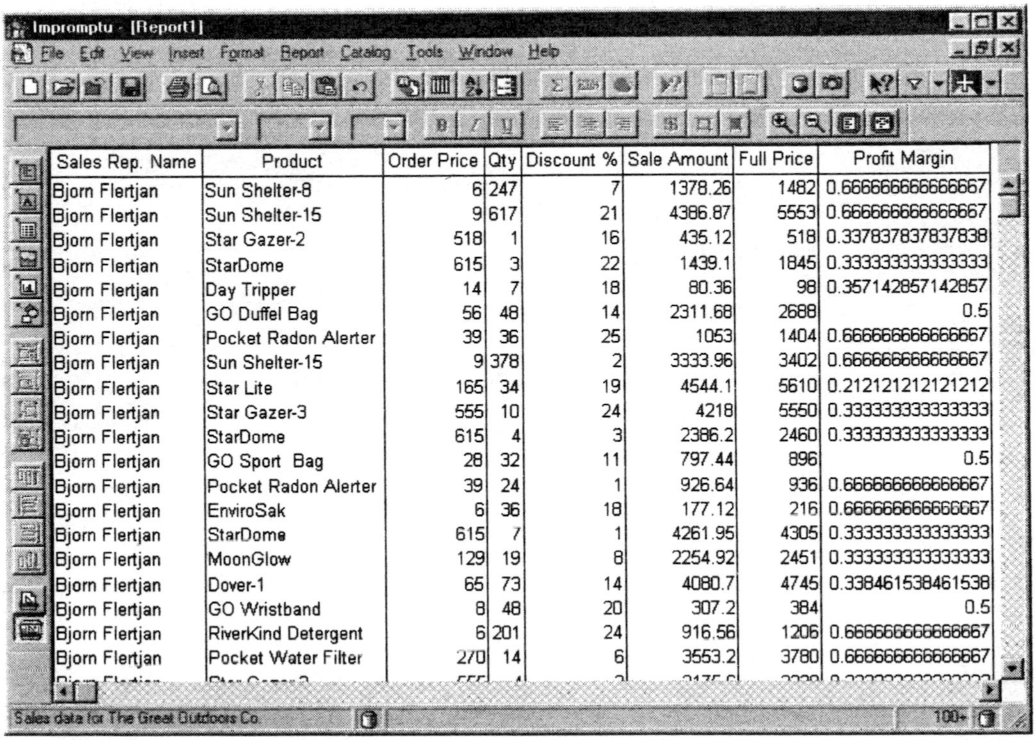

Sales Rep. Name	Product	Order Price	Qty	Discount %	Sale Amount	Full Price	Profit Margin
Bjorn Flertjan	Sun Shelter-8	6	247	7	1378.26	1482	0.666666666666667
Bjorn Flertjan	Sun Shelter-15	9	617	21	4386.87	5553	0.666666666666667
Bjorn Flertjan	Star Gazer-2	518	1	16	435.12	518	0.337837837837838
Bjorn Flertjan	StarDome	615	3	22	1439.1	1845	0.333333333333333
Bjorn Flertjan	Day Tripper	14	7	18	80.36	98	0.357142857142857
Bjorn Flertjan	GO Duffel Bag	56	48	14	2311.68	2688	0.5
Bjorn Flertjan	Pocket Radon Alerter	39	36	25	1053	1404	0.666666666666667
Bjorn Flertjan	Sun Shelter-15	9	378	2	3333.96	3402	0.666666666666667
Bjorn Flertjan	Star Lite	165	34	19	4544.1	5610	0.212121212121212
Bjorn Flertjan	Star Gazer-3	555	10	24	4218	5550	0.333333333333333
Bjorn Flertjan	StarDome	615	4	3	2386.2	2460	0.333333333333333
Bjorn Flertjan	GO Sport Bag	28	32	11	797.44	896	0.5
Bjorn Flertjan	Pocket Radon Alerter	39	24	1	926.64	936	0.666666666666667
Bjorn Flertjan	EnviroSak	6	36	18	177.12	216	0.666666666666667
Bjorn Flertjan	StarDome	615	7	1	4261.95	4305	0.333333333333333
Bjorn Flertjan	MoonGlow	129	19	8	2254.92	2451	0.333333333333333
Bjorn Flertjan	Dover-1	65	73	14	4080.7	4745	0.338461538461538
Bjorn Flertjan	GO Wristband	8	48	20	307.2	384	0.5
Bjorn Flertjan	RiverKind Detergent	6	201	24	916.56	1206	0.666666666666667
Bjorn Flertjan	Pocket Water Filter	270	14	6	3553.2	3780	0.666666666666667

Figure 7.16 The report results.

You added a column, so Impromptu had to rerun the query. This new calculation contains Catalog Columns that were not even in the original query, but that's OK.

Now, correct the format of this newly calculated column to make it look like the following:

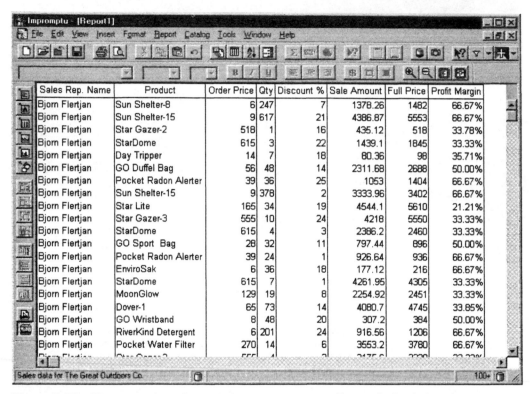

Figure 7.17   The new column formatted as a percentage with two decimal places.

Hint

Refer back to the Format chapter.

Question	Answer
Can I copy a calculation from one column and paste it into a new column?	Yes. This works just like the cut/copy/paste feature available in the Filter Definition. You highlight a section of the Data Definition Expression and paste it into another Expression. This works even between the Filter Definition and the Expression. You can copy a section from one and paste it into another.

A Calculated Column Without a Calculation

What? How can a calculated column not be a calculation? This calculated column is a combination of a filter concept and a calculated column concept applied to an "if... then... else..." statement.

Using the If... Then... Else can be thought of as having two phases to it. The first is the comparison, the If phase. This is where the filter concept comes into effect. Here you build a comparison, where the outcome is either true or false. The result then directs Impromptu to the specific portion of second phase.

The second phase applies a value to this column, the Then portion. When an If phase is evaluated as false, the Else portion is applied.

The best way to understand it is to walk through an example, showing you how to build it and describing what it does. Then you can take the concept and apply it to your reporting needs.

Steps to Create an "If" Calculation

1. Open the QDB and choose the Data tab if it is not already selected.
2. Select the Calculation button.
3. Give this a name: Sale Size.
4. Select the "If" component.

Note

The component displayed as just the "IF" in the Available Components Toolbox, and when you selected it, the expression placed both the "IF" and an open parenthesis. This is a helper feature provided by Impromptu to save you from making extra selections when you build this expression.

5. Expand the Report Columns folder.
6. Select the Sale Amount column.
7. Select the > operand.
8. Select the blue Number component.
9. Type in 1000, then hit either Enter or the right arrow key to move out of the type-in area (Figure 7.18).
10. Close the parenthesis.

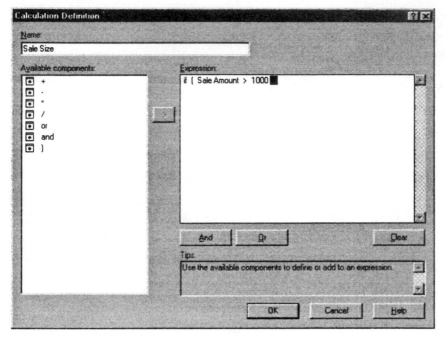

Figure 7.18   Check point.

Hey, Impromptu already added the "Then" component? Yes, this is another nice, click-saving feature Impromptu provides for you. Now, this takes you directly into building the second phase. Here is where a little thought and planning should take place. Remember how the Then portion is a true comparison. The result of the Then section will be what is displayed when the comparison is true, so put a value in for a true result.

11. Select the Value folder.
12. Select the String component, type "Large Sale," space included, then arrow right to move the cursor out of the type-in area.
13. End the Then portion with a closed parenthesis (Figure 7.19).

Impromptu helped you out again. It added the Else portion. The else is a unique portion. Here you can choose to provide a value to the finished calculated column or you can choose Null. The Null option will return absolutely nothing to the column when the If comparison is a false result. Additionally, you can also start another If... Then... Else... statement. In this example, add a value to the false result.

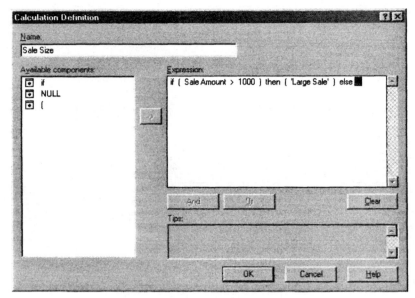

Figure 7.19
Check point.

14. Select the open parenthesis.

15. Select the String component, type "Small Sale," space included, then arrow right to move the cursor out of the type-in area.

16. Close the parenthesis.

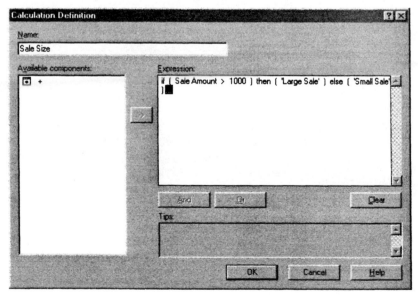

Figure 7.20
The calculation is complete!

17. Click OK to close the Calculation.

18. Click OK to run the report.

And the Results Are...

Sales Rep. Name	Product	Order Price	Qty	Discount %	Sale Amount	Full Price	Profit Margin	Sale Size
Bjorn Flertjan	Sun Shelter-8	6	247	7	1378.26	1482	66.67%	Large Sale
Bjorn Flertjan	Sun Shelter-15	9	617	21	4386.87	5553	66.67%	Large Sale
Bjorn Flertjan	Star Gazer-2	518	1	16	435.12	518	33.78%	Small Sale
Bjorn Flertjan	StarDome	615	3	22	1439.1	1845	33.33%	Large Sale
Bjorn Flertjan	Day Tripper	14	7	18	80.36	98	35.71%	Small Sale
Bjorn Flertjan	GO Duffel Bag	56	48	14	2311.68	2688	50.00%	Large Sale
Bjorn Flertjan	Pocket Radon Alerter	39	36	25	1053	1404	66.67%	Large Sale
Bjorn Flertjan	Sun Shelter-15	9	378	2	3333.96	3402	66.67%	Large Sale
Bjorn Flertjan	Star Lite	165	34	19	4544.1	5610	21.21%	Large Sale
Bjorn Flertjan	Star Gazer-3	555	10	24	4218	5550	33.33%	Large Sale
Bjorn Flertjan	StarDome	615	4	3	2386.2	2460	33.33%	Large Sale
Bjorn Flertjan	GO Sport Bag	28	32	11	797.44	896	50.00%	Small Sale
Bjorn Flertjan	Pocket Radon Alerter	39	24	1	926.64	936	66.67%	Small Sale
Bjorn Flertjan	EnviroSak	6	36	18	177.12	216	66.67%	Small Sale
Bjorn Flertjan	StarDome	615	7	1	4261.95	4305	33.33%	Large Sale
Bjorn Flertjan	MoonGlow	129	19	8	2254.92	2451	33.33%	Large Sale
Bjorn Flertjan	Dover-1	65	73	14	4080.7	4745	33.85%	Large Sale
Bjorn Flertjan	GO Wristband	8	48	20	307.2	384	50.00%	Small Sale
Bjorn Flertjan	RiverKind Detergent	6	201	24	916.56	1206	66.67%	Small Sale
Bjorn Flertjan	Pocket Water Filter	270	14	6	3553.2	3780	66.67%	Large Sale

Figure 7.21   The report results.

The use of the If... Then... Else... calculated column is an extremely useful feature. This opens the door for a great deal to be done with calculated columns. When you try your own, instead of just typing in a value in the Then portion, create a calculation there as well.

Finally, Calculations for Strings

In addition to performing calculations on numeric values, Impromptu has the ability to perform simple calculations to string values as well. Huh? I know, you cannot take a string like "GO Sport Bag" and divide it by a Sales Rep Name and get the customer name. But, the calculations that you can do with strings are things like joining two string values together. This is described as adding them together. For example, if you take two separate columns, like first name and last name, and join or "add" them together, you can get a whole name.

The following example shows you how to "add" both City and State string columns together.

Steps to Add String Columns Together

1. Open the QDB, and choose the Data tab if it is not already selected.
2. Between the Catalog box and the Query Data box, select the button with a small calculator on it.

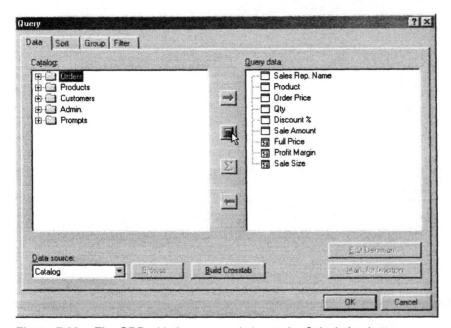

Figure 7.22   The QDB with the cusor pointing to the Calculation button.

3. Name this calculation: "City, State." This column will show where the sale took place.

Note

Since you have not yet brought either of these two fields into your report, you have to get them from the Catalog Columns... folder.

4. Double click on Catalog Columns.
5. Expand the Customers folder.

6. Expand Customer Sites folder.

7. Expand the Address folder.

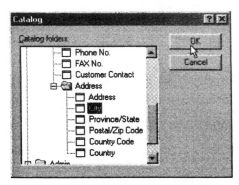

Figure 7.23
The Catalog Columns.

8. Select City. This takes you back to the Calculation Definition window.

9. Select the "+" operand.

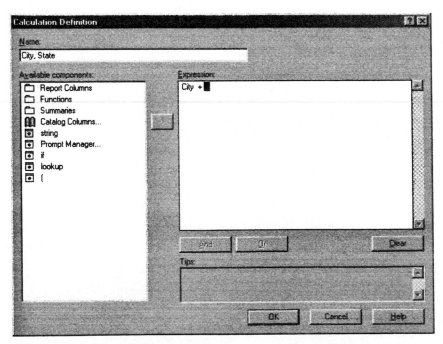

Figure 7.24   Check point.

10. Go back to the Catalog to get the State column.

11. Double click on Catalog Column.

12. Expand the Customers folder.

13. Expand Customer Sites folder.

14. Expand the Address folder.

15. Select Province/State to complete the calculation expression.

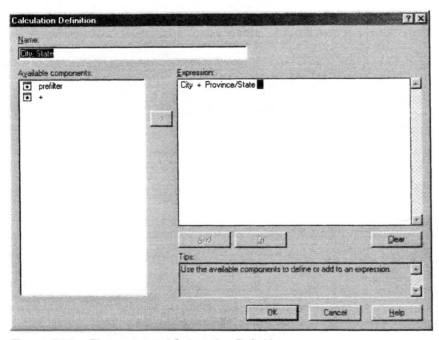

Figure 7.25 The completed Calculation Definition.

16. Click OK (Figure 7.26).

17. Click OK.

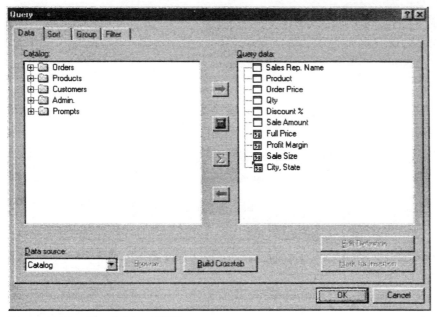

Figure 7.26   The finished QDB.

And the Results Are...

	Sales Rep. Name	Product	Order Price	Qty	Discount %	Sale Amount	Full Price	Profit Margin	Sale Size	City, State	
	Henri LeDuc	Star Gazer-2	518	2	17	859.88	1036	33.78%	Small Sale	Montreal	Quebec
	Henri LeDuc	Dover-2	111	37	21	3244.53	4107	33.33%	Large Sale	Montreal	Quebec
	Henri LeDuc	GO Cookset	54	62	1	3314.52	3348	33.33%	Large Sale	Montreal	Quebec
	Henri LeDuc	GO Sport Bag	28	16	14	385.28	448	50.00%	Small Sale	Montreal	Quebec
	Henri LeDuc	EnviroSak	6	11	12	58.08	66	66.67%	Small Sale	Montreal	Quebec
	Henri LeDuc	RiverKind Soap	11	159	16	1469.16	1749	63.64%	Large Sale	Montreal	Quebec
	Henri LeDuc	Star Gazer-2	518	7	18	2973.32	3626	33.78%	Large Sale	Montreal	Quebec
	Henri LeDuc	GO Small Waist Pack	18	25	19	364.5	450	33.33%	Small Sale	Montreal	Quebec
	Henri LeDuc	GO Water Bottle	8	64	17	424.96	512	50.00%	Small Sale	Montreal	Quebec
	Henri LeDuc	Enviro-T	30	124	2	3645.6	3720	66.67%	Large Sale	Montreal	Quebec
	Henri LeDuc	Pocket Water Filter	270	14	19	3061.8	3780	66.67%	Large Sale	Montreal	Quebec
	Greg Torson	Dover-2	117	2	15	198.9	234	36.75%	Small Sale	Boston	Massachusetts
	Greg Torson	GO Camp Kettle	22	56	15	1047.2	1232	36.36%	Large Sale	Boston	Massachusetts
	Greg Torson	GO Sport Bag	31	48	2	1458.24	1488	54.84%	Large Sale	Boston	Massachusetts
	Greg Torson	Pocket U.V. Alerter	10	77	14	662.2	770	70.00%	Small Sale	Boston	Massachusetts
	Greg Torson	Enviro-Kit	13	3	10	35.1	39	69.23%	Small Sale	Boston	Massachusetts
	Greg Torson	RiverKind Shampoo	11	165	3	1760.55	1815	72.73%	Large Sale	Boston	Massachusetts
	Dave Mustaine	MoonBeam	114	1	11	101.46	114	29.82%	Small Sale	San Francisco	California
	Dave Mustaine	Pack n' Hike	138	1	11	122.82	138	36.23%	Small Sale	San Francisco	California
	Dave Mustaine	GO Sport Bag	31	64	4	1904.64	1984	54.84%	Large Sale	San Francisco	California

Sales data for The Great Outdoors Co.

Figure 7.27   The completed report.

Well, it worked. But, it does not look all that attractive. There are spaces between city and state, which will not be acceptable to the user who requested this column. To resolve the unattractive layout, you need to apply a few functions to this calculation.

Question	Answer
I don't see any City, State column. Where did it go? Did it not take? Did I do something wrong?	No, if you are in the Page layout and you do not see the column, that's OK. Impromptu is doing what it is supposed to do. If there is not room on the current page for a column, Impromptu by default creates a page 1a, which is actually to the right of the page you are looking at right now. Think of this as laying a multiple-page report on a table—you would have one right below the other until you ran out of room. Some people even take multiple-page reports and tape them together. For you to see all of the information, you would need another piece of paper to the right of page 1 to have the row information match. That is what Impromptu did. So, to see the column, you can do one of two things.

1. Click on the double arrow pointing right, in the bottom right-hand corner of Impromptu.

2. View the report in Screen layout. It is for this reason alone that you may find it easier to have a default report in the Screen layout.

Functions

Functions are critical to understand in order to successfully build complex reports. Functions are required by many reports, simply because databases cannot store every variation of a data value. Its job is to just store values. Functions provide you with the means to perform variations to the data to fit your specific reporting needs. Like calculations, functions are not limited to use with certain data types; there are also functions in Impromptu to use with any form of data.

As you can see from the previous section, calculations offer a valuable set of features. But they alone do not offer all the features you need to construct the reports you need. Functions provide those features along with flexibility.

Impromptu has developed quite an arsenal of functions. Each function is equipped with a tool tip to provide users a real-time quick reference to what the function will do, the syntax of the function, and what is needed to perform it. This section covers how to use a function, how to apply functions to both columns and calculated columns, and how to put a function within a function.

First, A Basic Function

Before we solve the entire world's problems with functions and more precisely the problem we are having with that City, State calculated column, let's go over the basics of using functions.

There are a few simple rules to follow while building functions. First, you are allowed to mix functions only with the appropriate columns. This means Impromptu inherently does not permit you to build a function like this:

> Month (Product)

Here, the month function requires the expression inside the parenthesis to be a Date.

Question	Answer
What is the difference between an expression and a column?	An expression is a combination of values whether it is a calculated group of strings or a mathematical formula. The expression represents the entire effort that you are trying to do.
	A column is a subset of an expression. It can be the entire expression or one part of an expression. From the above example, if done correctly, the function should read something like this:
	Month (Order Date)
	where Order Date is both a column from the Catalog and the correct expression needed to perform the Month function.

Expressions come in five distinct varieties. When using functions, the tool-tip area describes what expressions are required to complete that particular function.

Since there are so many functions, and since a function can apply only to certain types of data in columns and calculation expressions, Impromptu gives you only what you can apply to a calculation. The Available Components Toolbox comes in handy, because it allows you to apply the correct function only on the basis of where your cursor is in the report. So, when you expand the Functions Folder, you can choose only a function expression that applies to a specific data type that you are working with in the definition.

Table 7.1 lists function expressions and descriptions:

Table 7.1

Function Expression	Description
String	String expressions can be applied to any free-form combination of numbers, letters, and characters. They can range from: Product "GO Sleeping Bag" Serial Number: EKM90999 to even what appears to be a number: Part Number: 15604 The above is an example of a database storing a series of numbers as a string data column. This is done in a database because there is no useful way to perform calculations on a part number. Generally, there is no need to divide a part number by cost. This just does not make sense.
Numeric	Numeric expressions are decimal numbers. When stored in a database, a numeric column is stored with a defined number of decimal places. When using numeric expressions in functions, you are allowed to use decimals, but you don't have to. You can use just an integer value.
Integer	Integer expressions are identical to numeric expressions, with the exception that Integers do not carry decimals with them. Some functions require integers exclusively. If you end up trying to stick a decimal in there, the function will not know how to handle it and will "try" to interpret it. The results generally are not something you want to share with and/or explain to your boss.
Date	A Date expression represents a calendar date. (Now that we're over the Y2K scare, it is good to know that Impromptu is Y2K compliant.) The Date expression is in the format of YYYY-MM-DD Y=Year M=Month D=Day
Date Time	A Date Time expression is an extension of the date expression. It represents a complete picture of when, by storing a date, and a particular time, down to the thousandths of a second: YYYY-MM-DD HH:NN:SS:TTT HH = Hour NN = Minute SS = Second TTT = Thousandth of a second

Function Expression	Description
Interval	An Interval is the difference in days, hours, minutes, seconds, and thousandths of a second from two points (Date or Date Time) in time. These functions are extremely valuable in manufacturing environments where shift analysis and production run analysis are critical.

To become more familiar with functions, create a calculated column that shows just the month number of the Order Date for each record.

Steps to Create a Basic Function

Using the report we have worked with for the entire chapter, open the QDB and select the Calculation button.

1. Name this new column: Order Month.
2. Double click on Functions.

Notice all of the functions are sorted alphabetically; when you single click on a function, the tool tip populates with a syntax layout and a brief description.

3. Scroll down to the Month function and double click on it.

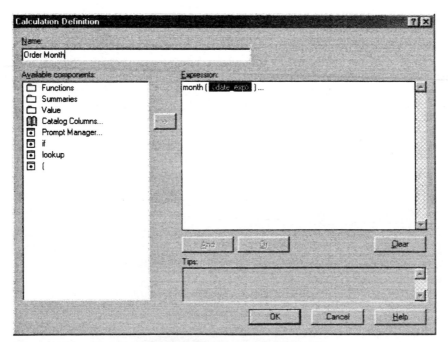

Figure 7.28 The Calculation definition with Month function.

This is how it works for using every function. When you insert a function into the definition, Impromptu inserts the function and puts a placeholder for an expression. The placeholder describes what the function requires for it to work.

Since you do not have the Order Date column in the report, you cannot get it from the Reports Folder; you have to go fishing in the Catalog.

4. Double click on the Catalog column.
5. Expand the Orders folder.

Remember, the only columns you can use for the Month function are Date columns.

6. Double click on Order Date, and notice how the Order Date column neatly fits into the parenthesis (Figure 7.29).
7. Click OK to complete the calculation.
8. Click OK to run the report.

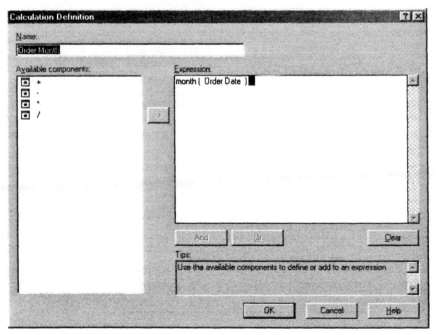

Figure 7.29   The finished month function.

And the Results Are...

Sale Amount	Full Price	Profit Margin	Sale Size	City, State		Order Month
859.88	1036	33.78%	Small Sale	Montreal	Quebec	3
3244.53	4107	33.33%	Large Sale	Montreal	Quebec	3
3314.52	3348	33.33%	Large Sale	Montreal	Quebec	3
385.28	448	50.00%	Small Sale	Montreal	Quebec	3
58.08	66	66.67%	Small Sale	Montreal	Quebec	3
1469.16	1749	63.64%	Large Sale	Montreal	Quebec	3
2973.32	3626	33.78%	Large Sale	Montreal	Quebec	7
364.5	450	33.33%	Small Sale	Montreal	Quebec	7
424.96	512	50.00%	Small Sale	Montreal	Quebec	7
3645.6	3720	66.67%	Large Sale	Montreal	Quebec	7
3061.8	3780	66.67%	Large Sale	Montreal	Quebec	7
198.9	234	36.75%	Small Sale	Boston	Massachusetts	12
1047.2	1232	36.36%	Large Sale	Boston	Massachusetts	12
1458.24	1488	54.84%	Large Sale	Boston	Massachusetts	12
662.2	770	70.00%	Small Sale	Boston	Massachusetts	12
35.1	39	69.23%	Small Sale	Boston	Massachusetts	12
1760.55	1815	72.73%	Large Sale	Boston	Massachusetts	12
101.46	114	29.82%	Small Sale	San Francisco	California	12
122.82	138	36.23%	Small Sale	San Francisco	California	12
1904.64	1984	54.84%	Large Sale	San Francisco	California	12

Figure 7.30 The report results. Notice how the report results had to be shifted to the right to view the new column.

Applying a Function to an Existing Calculated Column

Now that you have worked through the example, let's apply this newfound knowledge to the City, State problem. As you may recall, you created a calculated column for the report grouping the City and State columns from the Catalog. When you did though, you did not realize that the City column stored extra spaces at the end of each city in the database. So, you need to fix this. Our goal is to remove the spaces for both columns and add a comma between City and State.

We need to make it go from this:

Montreal   Quebec

To this:

Montreal, Quebec

We fix this by using a string function that will remove those extra spaces. Normally, in these situations, you would browse around in the Functions folders looking at the tool tips to find a function that will do what you want. For this exercise, I will direct you to the specific functions we need.

Tip

As in the previous exercise, we took a closer look at the function list. Now, let's dig a little deeper. You might have noticed that the blue boxes to the left of the name of each function are not all the same, as shown in Figure 7.31.

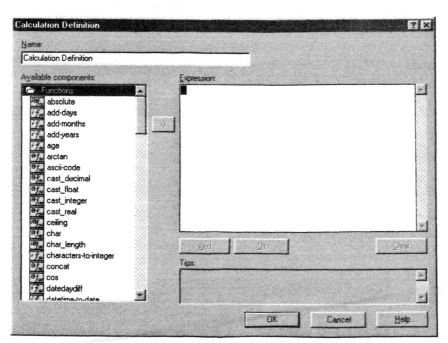

Figure 7.31 A blue function button. The 'i' means it is an Impromptu function, and the drum means it is a database function.

Question	Answer
What is the difference between an Impromptu function and a database function?	**Impromptu Function.** An Impromptu function is one that can be performed by Impromptu locally on your desktop.
	Database Function. A database function is one that can be done back in the dusty old server room on the machine where the database sits.
	If a function has **both indicators**, it can be done either on the desktop or in the database. If it has only one or the other, then that is the only place where it can be done.

Follow these steps to apply a function to a column:

1. Open the QDB Data tab.
2. Highlight the City, State calculated column.
3. Click the button below Edit Definition.

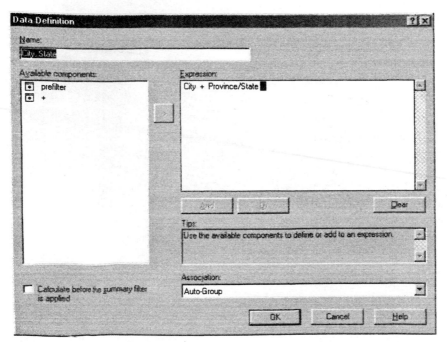

Figure 7.32   The Data Definition.

You did create this with a Calculation Definition, but since it is now firmly placed in the query, Impromptu refers to it like any other column, whether it is calculated or not, as a part of the query. The *Data* Definition window works exactly the same as the *Calculation* Definition window.

Step 1: Adding the Comma

The Name of the column should come up highlighted.

1. Click on the Province/State column in the definition window.

   In the Available Components Toolbox, the options appear for a String data column.

2. Double click the blue String component.
3. Type: ",", no spaces.
4. Press Enter. This will move the cursor to the right highlighting the Province/State column.

   There is a "+" between the City and the ",". Now you need to add a "+" between the "," and the State.

5. Double click on the "+" from Available Components Toolbox.

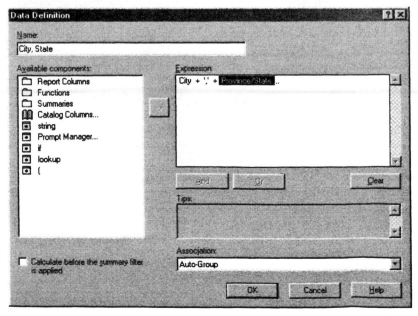

Figure 7.33
The Data Definition with the comma and the plus sign added.

Step 2: Removing Spaces from the State Column

6. While you are still making changes to this calculated column, select the City column in the expression.

7. Double click the Functions folder.

8. Note there are a bunch of functions—functions for numeric columns, date columns, all kinds. Isn't Impromptu supposed to be sensitive to where the cursor is and display only the functions available to what the cursor has selected, which is a string column? Yes, Impromptu is sensitive, but the first column of the expression is the lone exception. Here Impromptu has to allow the report developer the ability to select anything. This takes precedence over the narrow focus of helping to weed out unnecessary functions. Scroll down and double click the function called "Trim-Trailing," which removes trailing spaces to a string.

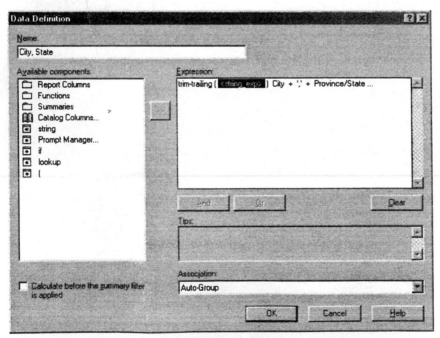

Figure 7.34   The Data definition with trim-trailing and placeholder.

Question	Answer
I thought that since City is a string, it would just drop the City column right in.	Unfortunately, and fortunately, Impromptu does not think of that this way. From Impromptu's perspective: "The report developer is in the middle of a definition, and she is adding a function. I better do just that, add everything, placeholder included." So, Impromptu does. It may not make sense at first and may seem a little frustrating, but this is there to protect us and give flexibility.

So, how do you fix it? You can do this and also take advantage of where the cursor in the definition is. With the cursor on the placeholder "<string exp>",

9. Hit the delete key twice.

This removes both the placeholder and the closing parenthesis, but it moves the City column where you want it. You now just have to repair the function by adding the closing parenthesis.

10. Either click on the "+" token or, using the keyboard, hit the arrow right key one stroke.

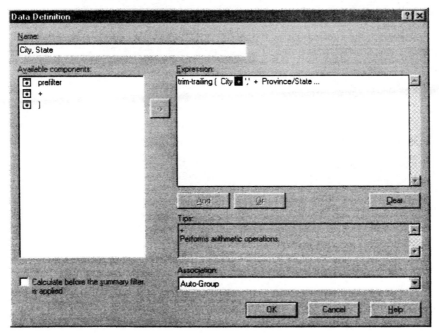

Figure 7.35
Checkpoint.

11. Since you moved the cursor, Impromptu changes your Available Components and gives you what you want.

12. Double click on the close parenthesis (Figure 7.36).

13. Click OK to close the Data Definition window.

14. Click OK to run the report.

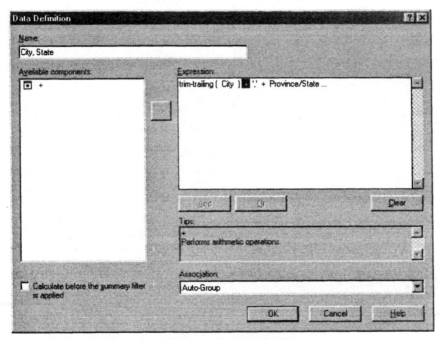

Figure 7.36   The finished definition with embedded function.

And the Results Are...

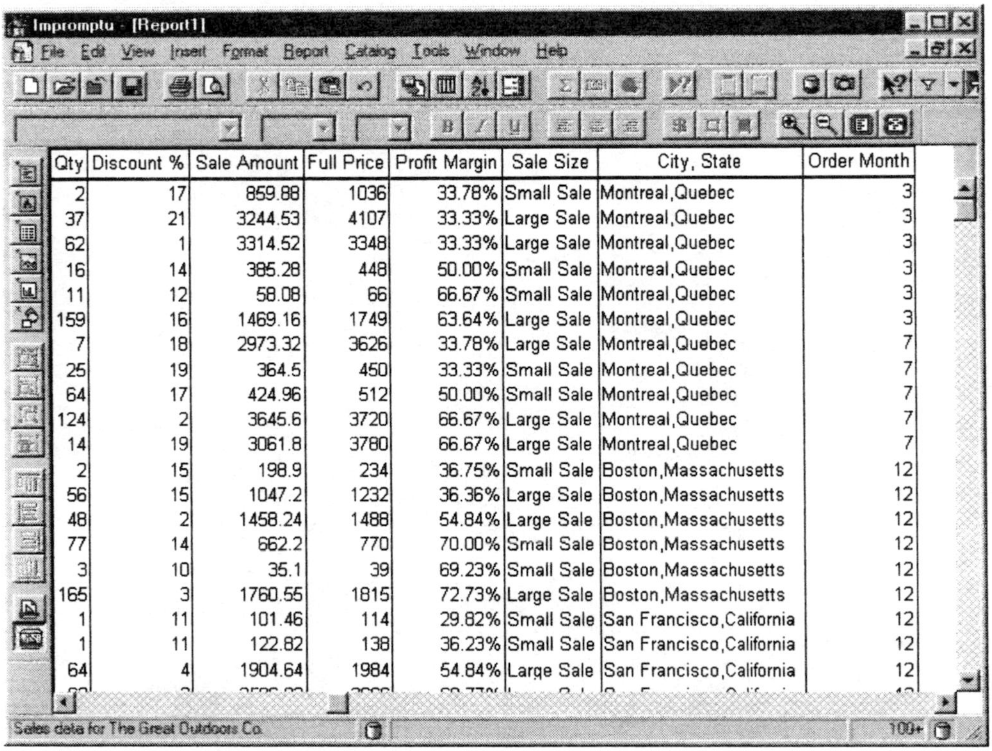

Figure 7.37   This looks good, except that there is no space between the comma and the Province/State.

Part 3: Add a Space Before the State

I had you run the report for two reasons: one, to let you see what you have done so far, and two, to experience the iterative process of building and customizing a report. I could have easily told you to add the space after you typed the comma a few steps ago, but the value of getting the experience of doing something, looking it over, and going back to make additional changes will be clear when you write your own reports. Simulating that with these exercises will make you more comfortable when you start building your own reports.

Now add the space after the comma.

1. Open the QDB.
2. Click on the City, State column.
3. Click Edit Definition.

4. In the expression, click just a hair to the right of the comma. See Figure 7.38. If you were not able to get it, and the cursor landed to the left or right, just use the appropriate arrow key to line up the cursor (Figure 7.38).

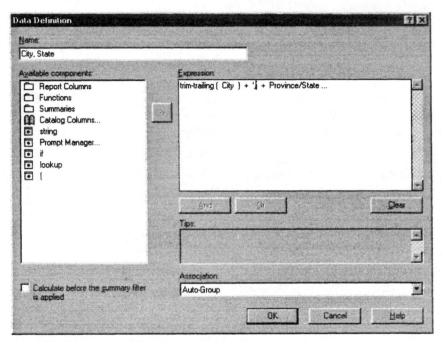

Figure 7.38   This is where we are going to add the space.

5. Press the space bar once.

6. Click OK on the Data Definition window.

7. Click OK on the QDB, and the report runs again.

And the Results Are...

Qty	Discount %	Sale Amount	Full Price	Profit Margin	Sale Size	City, State	Order Month
2	17	859.88	1036	33.78%	Small Sale	Montreal, Quebec	3
37	21	3244.53	4107	33.33%	Large Sale	Montreal, Quebec	3
62	1	3314.52	3348	33.33%	Large Sale	Montreal, Quebec	3
16	14	385.28	448	50.00%	Small Sale	Montreal, Quebec	3
11	12	58.08	66	66.67%	Small Sale	Montreal, Quebec	3
159	16	1469.16	1749	63.64%	Large Sale	Montreal, Quebec	3
7	18	2973.32	3626	33.78%	Large Sale	Montreal, Quebec	7
25	19	364.5	450	33.33%	Small Sale	Montreal, Quebec	7
64	17	424.96	512	50.00%	Small Sale	Montreal, Quebec	7
124	2	3645.6	3720	66.67%	Large Sale	Montreal, Quebec	7
14	19	3061.8	3780	66.67%	Large Sale	Montreal, Quebec	7
2	15	198.9	234	36.75%	Small Sale	Boston, Massachusetts	12
56	15	1047.2	1232	36.36%	Large Sale	Boston, Massachusetts	12
48	2	1458.24	1488	54.84%	Large Sale	Boston, Massachusetts	12
77	14	662.2	770	70.00%	Small Sale	Boston, Massachusetts	12
3	10	35.1	39	69.23%	Small Sale	Boston, Massachusetts	12
165	3	1760.55	1815	72.73%	Large Sale	Boston, Massachusetts	12
1	11	101.46	114	29.82%	Small Sale	San Francisco, California	12
1	11	122.82	138	36.23%	Small Sale	San Francisco, California	12
64	4	1904.64	1984	54.84%	Large Sale	San Francisco, California	12

Figure 7.39   This looks a little better with the space added.

Multiple and Nesting Functions

You have created calculated columns, created calculated columns with functions, and applied multiple functions to calculated columns. Now there's nesting. Nesting is the concept of applying a function within a function.

For example, you can use a function in Impromptu to retrieve the computer's date and time. In this case, the function is called Today(). It does not require any additional expressions to make it work. It just returns the date to the definition requesting it. If you were to want to find just the month of today to show as its own column on a report to visually compare it with the Order Date, then you would have to use a function within a function, and it would look something like this:

    Month (Today ())

where the expression required for the Month function is supplied by the Today() function.

Let's build a new column applying this technique.

Steps to Create a Nested Function

1. Either open the QDB and add a calculation or use the menu Insert.Calculation.
2. Name this calculated column "Current Month."
3. Expand the Function folder.
4. Select the Month function.

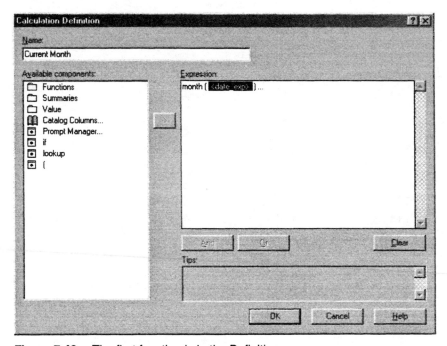

Figure 7.40   The first function is in the Definition.

5. Expand the Function folder. Notice how few options there are now. That is because you are working only with functions that work with date expressions.
6. Select the Today() function (Figure 7.41).
7. Click OK.
8. If you used the QDB, click OK again to run the report.

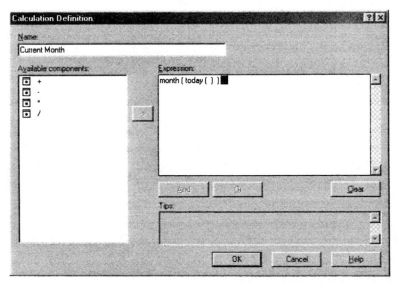

Figure 7.41
The completed nested function.

And the Results Are...

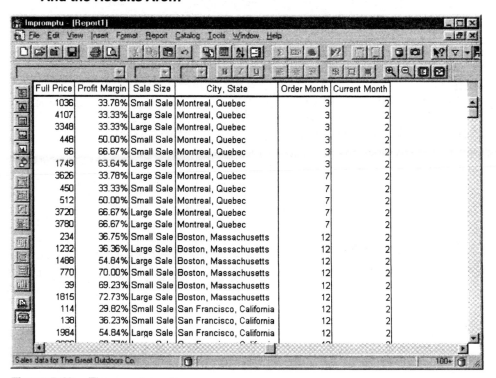

Figure 7.42 The report results.

Note

When you add a calculation in the QDB, Impromptu automatically places that new column at the end of the report.

Other Uses

As you have seen in this chapter, calculations and functions are an extremely valuable asset to Impromptu. You have mixed and matched them and even nested them. But where else can you use them?

Remember the chapter on filters? In the Filter tab, there was an Available Components Toolbox. That was the first time you saw the toolbox. That had a multitude of features and options in it, one of which is Functions. Yes, you can apply all that we have learned here with calculations and functions back to the Filter tab to create wonderfully complex filters.

Let's build a filter using a function. The filter will look like this: Closed Date < Today. In the past, when you built Filters, you added the column from Catalog then you added a value. It is no different here with Functions. The Catalog Column is Closed Date, and the Value is the function Today().

Steps to Build a Filter with a Function

In the report you have been using, go to the Filter tab.

1. Open the QDB and select the Filter tab.

Since the Closed Date is not in your original query, you need to get it from the Catalog.

2. Double Click "Catalog Columns…".
3. Expand the Order Folder.
4. Select the Closed Date, and click OK to return it to the definition.
5. Select the '<' operand.
6. Expand the Functions folder.
7. Select the Today function (Figure 7.43).
8. Click OK, to run the report.

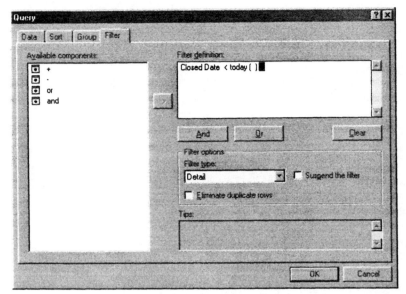

Figure 7.43
The completed filter, using the Today( ) function.

And the Results Are...

Sales Rep. Name	Product	Order Price	Qty	Discount %	Sale Amount	Full Price	Profit Margin
Henri LeDuc	Star Gazer-2	518	2	17	859.88	1036	33.78%
Henri LeDuc	Dover-2	111	37	21	3244.53	4107	33.33%
Henri LeDuc	GO Cookset	54	62	1	3314.52	3348	33.33%
Henri LeDuc	GO Sport Bag	28	16	14	385.28	448	50.00%
Henri LeDuc	EnviroSak	6	11	12	58.08	66	66.67%
Henri LeDuc	RiverKind Soap	11	159	16	1469.16	1749	63.64%
Henri LeDuc	Star Gazer-2	518	7	18	2973.32	3626	33.78%
Henri LeDuc	GO Small Waist Pack	18	25	19	364.5	450	33.33%
Henri LeDuc	GO Water Bottle	8	64	17	424.96	512	50.00%
Henri LeDuc	Enviro-T	30	124	2	3645.6	3720	66.67%
Henri LeDuc	Pocket Water Filter	270	14	19	3061.8	3780	66.67%
Greg Torson	Dover-2	117	2	15	198.9	234	36.75%
Greg Torson	GO Camp Kettle	22	56	15	1047.2	1232	36.36%
Greg Torson	GO Sport Bag	31	48	2	1458.24	1488	54.84%
Greg Torson	Pocket U.V. Alerter	10	77	14	662.2	770	70.00%
Greg Torson	Enviro-Kit	13	3	10	35.1	39	69.23%
Greg Torson	RiverKind Shampoo	11	165	3	1760.55	1815	72.73%
Dave Mustaine	MoonBeam	114	1	11	101.46	114	29.82%
Dave Mustaine	Pack n' Hike	138	1	11	122.82	138	36.23%
Dave Mustaine	GO Sport Bag	31	64	4	1904.64	1984	54.84%

Sales data for The Great Outdoors Co.

Figure 7.44 The report results.

Now, with that said, the possibilities are endless. You can do virtually anything you wanted in the Filter Definition now. Once you get back to your Catalog, you will be able do reports with filtering like these:

- Closed Date > Today(): to find order close dates improperly entered.
- Month(Closed Date) = Month(Today()): to find all closed orders within this month.
- Closed Date >= Add_Months(Today(), -3): to find all the orders closed within the past three months.

Summary

In this chapter we covered the following:

- How to create a calculation.
- How to create a function.
- How to integrate a function within a calculation.
- Review of how to apply functions to filters.

I encourage you to experiment with different calculations and functions. But remember, check your results. That is something that Impromptu will not do for you.

Sorting and Grouping

Chapter 8 is another chapter that double-dips and presents two different topics together. This is a little different from the other chapters, because the topics of sorting and grouping are so closely related. Each topic is such a valuable asset to Impromptu and your report development that they complete the final two tabs in the QDB.

Additionally, this chapter should be read before you work with the next chapter. The material learned here lays a foundation for what you can do and what Impromptu does with summaries, which is covered in the next chapter. So, not only does this chapter have quality content, but the impact of this material also reaches to the next chapter.

When you create a report, you are looking either at a detailed list or at a summarized report. Either way, you will want to organize your information in some manner to better understand the report. Sorting and grouping both help you as a report developer to better organize the information in the report. The past chapters have covered topics that have helped you either include or exclude information from a report. Once the information has come back, sorting and grouping help you organize how it is displayed.

This chapter covers:

- Point and Click Sorting
- Sorting in QDB
- Point and Click Grouping
- How they work together
- Associations: pseudo grouping

Before We Begin

You must create the following report to participate in the exercises described throughout this chapter. Again, if you already have a few reports open, I recommend closing them for a clean start.

With Impromptu Open, and using the Great Outdoors Catalog, create a simple list report, following these steps:

1. Expand the Admin folder and then the Branch folder.
2. Select the Branch Code.
3. Select the Branch.
4. From the root of the Catalog, expand the Order folder.
5. Expand the Additional Info. Folder.
6. Select the Sales Rep Name.
7. Select the Sales Channel.
8. Expand the Order Details folder.
9. Select: Product, Qty, and Sale Amount.

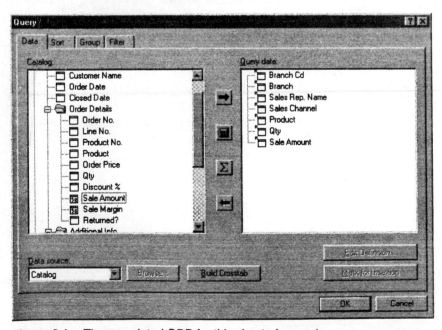

Figure 8.1   The completed QDB for this chapter's report.

10. Click OK to run the report.

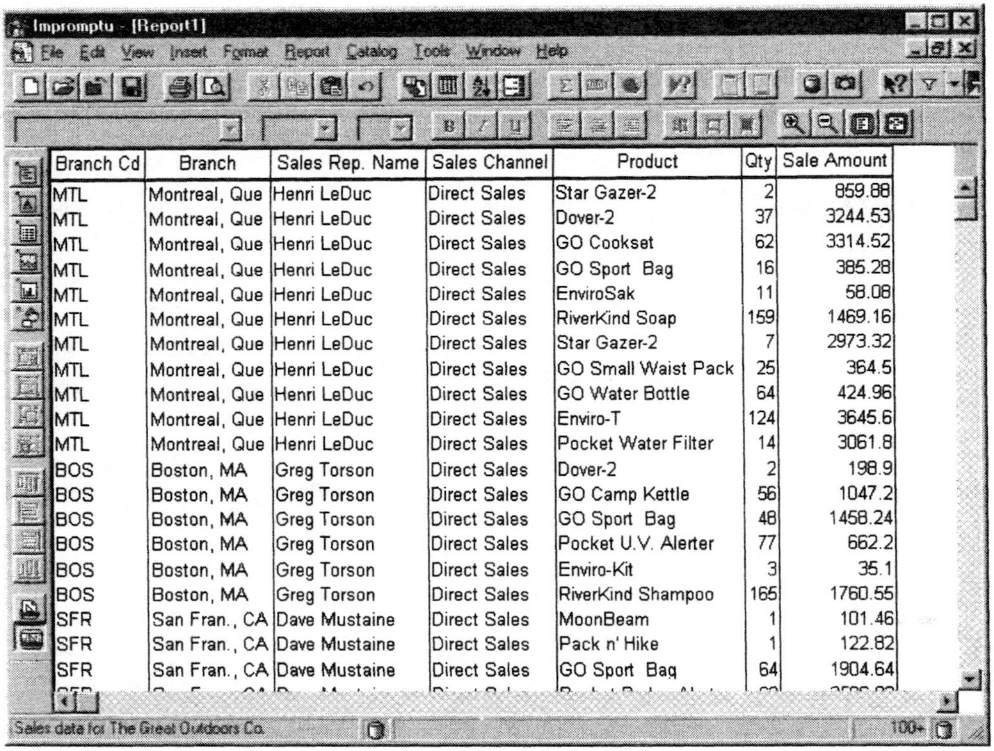

Figure 8.2   The returned report in Screen layout.

Sorting

Sorting is a very simple concept. Information that does not have a sequential order is organized in either an ascending or a descending order. This concept is applied to any data type. A sort on a date data column performs exactly the same way as a sort on a string data column.

This section describes how to specifically perform sorts, and explores different uses and techniques. There are two basic ways to sort the data to your liking: one is the point and click method, the other is by using the QDB.

Point and Click Sorting

Point and Click sorting is a quick and efficient way to do a simple, yet useful task. Simple because it does not require a great deal of effort to sort a column on the report developer's part, but useful because it is something that will have to be done in one report or the next.

Your First Sort

Your first sort will be fairly straightforward, with no need for analysis of the Report Requirement.

Report Requirement

Boss: *I want this report sorted by our Products, so I can see every sale for each product, without having to hunt and peck from page to page.*

Analysis

This is a simple request for a sort on the Product column.

Steps to Sort a Column

1. Click on any cell in the column for Product.
2. Click the sort button.

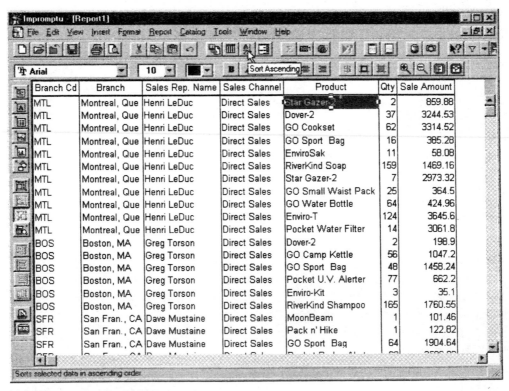

Figure 8.3   The Sort button.

And the Results Are...

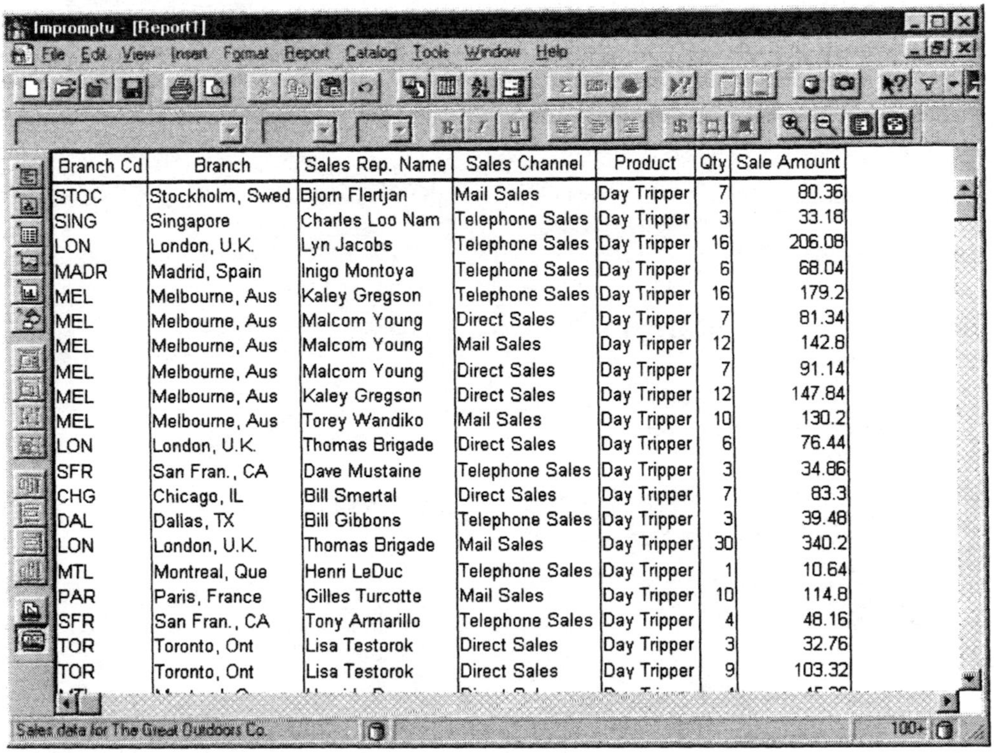

Figure 8.4 The newly sorted report.

When you selected the ascending sort, Impromptu had to rerun the query and retrieve a different first 100 rows. Also note that the newly sorted report kept the integrity of each row of data. Because of the sort command, the row of data that supports the first cell in the Product column moved from wherever it was in the report to the same row as the newly organized "Day Tripper" cell.

Onward and Upward

Yet another Report Requirement:

Report Requirement

Boss: *Well, that looks better, but why are the branches all spread around? I see a London up at the top and one down at the bottom. Fix that, and I think you may have something.*

This is typical. Once you show report consumers a solution to a reporting requirement, they always want more. There are always additional changes.

Analysis

What the boss above is requesting is a sort within a sort, or a nested sort. Remember nesting of functions from the previous chapter when you put a function inside another function? Well, nesting in the sorting world applies to the order in which items are sorted, or the sort order.

In our example, the boss liked the first sort. What the boss did not like though was how this affected the rest of the report layout. The new sorting resulted in something he did not expect. So the boss made another request to sort the Branches. This, too, is easy enough.

Steps to Add Additional Sorts

1. Click on any cell in the Branch column.
2. Click the Sort button.

And the Results Are...

Branch Cd	Branch	Sales Rep. Name	Sales Channel	Product	Qty	Sale Amount
CHG	Chicago, IL	Bill Smertal	Direct Sales	Day Tripper	7	83.3
DAL	Dallas, TX	Bill Gibbons	Telephone Sales	Day Tripper	3	39.48
LON	London, U.K.	Lyn Jacobs	Telephone Sales	Day Tripper	16	206.08
LON	London, U.K.	Thomas Brigade	Direct Sales	Day Tripper	6	76.44
LON	London, U.K.	Thomas Brigade	Mail Sales	Day Tripper	30	340.2
LON	London, U.K.	Thomas Brigade	Telephone Sales	Day Tripper	1	11.2
LON	London, U.K.	Lyn Jacobs	Telephone Sales	Day Tripper	12	166.32
MADR	Madrid, Spain	Inigo Montoya	Telephone Sales	Day Tripper	6	68.04
MEL	Melbourne, Aus	Kaley Gregson	Telephone Sales	Day Tripper	16	179.2
MEL	Melbourne, Aus	Malcom Young	Direct Sales	Day Tripper	7	81.34
MEL	Melbourne, Aus	Malcom Young	Mail Sales	Day Tripper	12	142.8
MEL	Melbourne, Aus	Malcom Young	Direct Sales	Day Tripper	7	91.14
MEL	Melbourne, Aus	Kaley Gregson	Direct Sales	Day Tripper	12	147.84
MEL	Melbourne, Aus	Torey Wandiko	Mail Sales	Day Tripper	10	130.2
MTL	Montreal, Que	Henri LeDuc	Telephone Sales	Day Tripper	1	10.64
MTL	Montreal, Que	Henri LeDuc	Direct Sales	Day Tripper	4	45.36
PAR	Paris, France	Gilles Turcotte	Mail Sales	Day Tripper	10	114.8
SFR	San Fran., CA	Dave Mustaine	Telephone Sales	Day Tripper	3	34.86
SFR	San Fran., CA	Tony Armarillo	Telephone Sales	Day Tripper	4	48.16
SING	Singapore	Charles Loo Nam	Telephone Sales	Day Tripper	3	33.18

Figure 8.5   The newly sorted report.

Easy enough? A new request prompted Impromptu to run the report again. Now, the report first sorts the Products column, then it sorts the Branch column.

You can sort as much as you like; every time you add a sort, you add it to the bottom of the sort order, and it gets done after the others are performed. There is a theoretical limit to how many sorts can be performed, but what is notable here is that the more sorts you add to a report, the longer it may take to run. Sorting is done at either the database or on your computer. Sorting is a fairly intensive process, one that requires processing power and disk space. Most sorting requests can be done with no problem, but when sorts start to stack up 8 to 20 deep, performance will lag; this makes other users and database administrators (also commonly known as a DBA) not very happy. You will end up with a slow report and, possibly, a very unhappy DBA.

Sorting in the QDB

This leads us to the next area where sorting can be performed, in the QDB. In the QDB, we have all the features that there are in the Point and Click, and more. In the QDB, you can sort on any column in the query. You can also control the sort order. In the QDB, you can remove a sort on a column if you choose not to sort on it anymore. You can even sort on query data columns that are used in the Query but do not show on the WYSISYG layout.

The Sort Tab

The sort tab provides you, the report developer, with a lot of flexibility to manage how the report is sorted. In it, you can control what columns are sorted; whether a column is sorted ascending, descending, or not sorted at all; and the sort order of the columns. To illustrate, here is another report requirement.

Report Requirement

Boss: *The last report you did looked good. Sorry for making so many changes, but after looking at this report, I really want to see the items listed first by Branch, then by Sales Rep Name, then by Product.*

Analysis

This request is best performed using the Sort tab. The request added another column to be sorted, and reordered the columns to be ordered. The new order is:

1. Branch
2. Sales Rep Name
3. Product

Steps to Add and Reorder Sorts

The following steps will do this while at the same time introducing you to the Sort tab in the QDB.

1. Open the QDB, and click on the Sort tab.

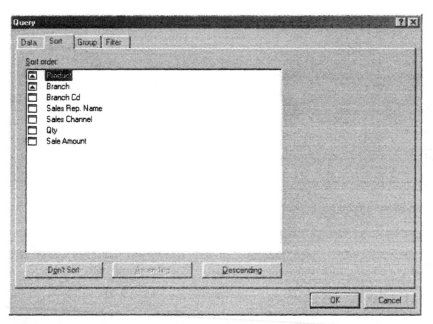

Figure 8.6   The Sort tab in the QDB.

Table 8.1	
Feature	*Description*
Don't Sort	This button removes a sort request from a column.
Ascending	The Ascending button sorts a column by lowest to highest. Lowest to highest in a string sort means sort this column alphabetically. I always remember the "A" in Ascending really means alphabetically.
Descending	Sorts a column the opposite way as Ascending. This is Z to A alphabetically, and with numeric columns this is a highest to lowest sort.

2. Click on the Branch column.

Note

The up arrow is a visual indicator that this column is an ascending sort. Notice the buttons available for the Branch column; you have a choice of not sorting the column or changing the direction of the sort.

3. Click and drag the Branch column up to hover over the sorted Product column, as shown in Figure 8.7

Note

Some mouse settings are a little tricky. If click and drag doesn't seem to be working for you, you may have to use the mouse a little differently.

Try This:

- Click and let go of the mouse button to select the column.
- Click and drag the column.

Sometimes mouse speed settings are temperamental.

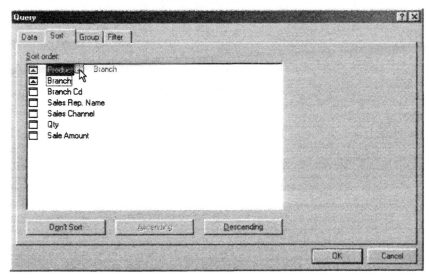

Figure 8.7
The report result with the Branch column first.

4. Release the mouse button. This reorders the sort, and the Branch is now the first column sorted.

   Next is to add the new sort, the Sales Rep Name sort, and place it in the right order.

5. Click on the Sales Rep Name.
6. Click the Ascending button.
7. Click and drag the sorted Sales Rep Name column until it is hovering over Product column and let go.

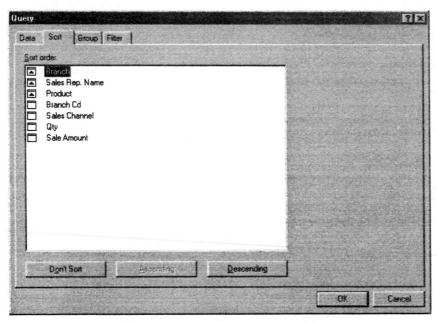

Figure 8.8   Now the sort order meets the requirements.

8. Click OK to run the report.

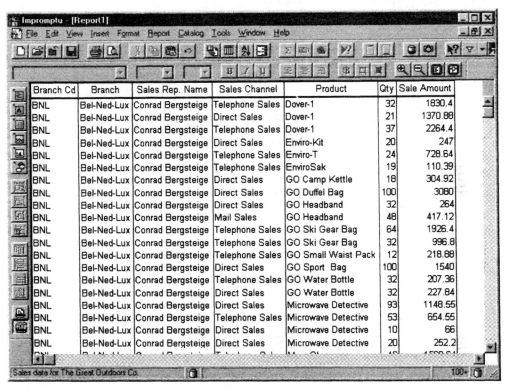

Figure 8.9   The report with new sort strategy.

Removing a Sort

Removing individual sorts are just as easy as applying new sorts in the QDB. Say you wanted to see what the report looked like without sorting on Product. Just remove that sort using the QDB.

Steps to Remove a Sort

1. Open the QDB.
2. Click on the Sort tab.
3. Click on the Product Column.
4. Click the Don't Sort button (Figure 8.10).
5. Click OK to run the report.

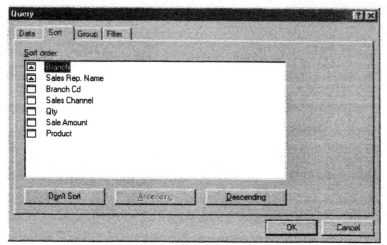

Figure 8.10
After the column is unsorted, it is dropped to the bottom of the sort list. This does not change how the column is displayed or anything else about the column or the report. The Product column is just not sorted any more.

And the Results Are...

Branch Cd	Branch	Sales Rep. Name	Sales Channel	Product	Qty	Sale Amount
BNL	Bel-Ned-Lux	Conrad Bergsteige	Telephone Sales	MoonGlow	16	1568.64
BNL	Bel-Ned-Lux	Conrad Bergsteige	Telephone Sales	Pack n' Hike	4	503.04
BNL	Bel-Ned-Lux	Conrad Bergsteige	Telephone Sales	Dover-1	32	1830.4
BNL	Bel-Ned-Lux	Conrad Bergsteige	Telephone Sales	GO Water Bottle	32	207.36
BNL	Bel-Ned-Lux	Conrad Bergsteige	Telephone Sales	Sun Shelter-8	504	2540.16
BNL	Bel-Ned-Lux	Conrad Bergsteige	Direct Sales	Star Gazer-3	7	3080
BNL	Bel-Ned-Lux	Conrad Bergsteige	Direct Sales	Dover-1	21	1370.88
BNL	Bel-Ned-Lux	Conrad Bergsteige	Direct Sales	GO Water Bottle	32	227.84
BNL	Bel-Ned-Lux	Conrad Bergsteige	Direct Sales	Microwave Detective	93	1148.55
BNL	Bel-Ned-Lux	Conrad Bergsteige	Direct Sales	Sun Shelter-8	136	799.68
BNL	Bel-Ned-Lux	Conrad Bergsteige	Direct Sales	Sun Shelter-15	198	2134.44
BNL	Bel-Ned-Lux	Conrad Bergsteige	Telephone Sales	Star Gazer-3	16	6320
BNL	Bel-Ned-Lux	Conrad Bergsteige	Telephone Sales	GO Small Waist Pack	12	218.88
BNL	Bel-Ned-Lux	Conrad Bergsteige	Telephone Sales	GO Ski Gear Bag	64	1926.4
BNL	Bel-Ned-Lux	Conrad Bergsteige	Telephone Sales	Microwave Detective	53	654.55
BNL	Bel-Ned-Lux	Conrad Bergsteige	Telephone Sales	EnviroSak	19	110.39
BNL	Bel-Ned-Lux	Conrad Bergsteige	Telephone Sales	RiverKind Detergent	332	2523.2
BNL	Bel-Ned-Lux	Conrad Bergsteige	Direct Sales	Pocket U.V. Alerter	4	19.8
BNL	Bel-Ned-Lux	Conrad Bergsteige	Direct Sales	Microwave Detective	10	66
BNL	Bel-Ned-Lux	Conrad Bergsteige	Direct Sales	Pocket Radon Alerter	100	2145

Sales data for The Great Outdoors Co.

Figure 8.11   Same report, but the Products are not sorted.

Moving unsorted columns around does nothing. Impromptu won't even let you do it, because it doesn't make sense to change the sort order on an item that is not even being sorted.

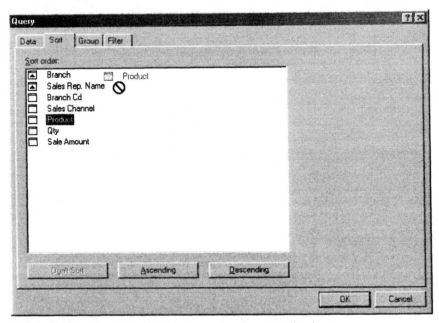

Figure 8.12   Example of trying to move an unsorted column.

Additional Things You Can Do with the Sort Tab

Additionally, while inside the Sort tab, you can perform other Windows navigational techniques. You can utilize the multiselect feature of Windows. For example, when you want to sort on multiple columns and they already are in the hierarchical order you want, all you have to do is either hold down the Ctrl key to select random items, or hold down the Shift key to select a group of items.

Clean Up

Before we go on to the next section on grouping, let's clean up the report we built at the beginning of the chapter. This means you should remove all of the sorting that we have done over the last couple pages. To do this, I will show you a trick in Impromptu.

Tip

Here's the trick, when nothing is selected (remember from Chapter 3, the Esc Key), on the report layout, do the following:

1. Press the Sort Key (Figure 8.13).

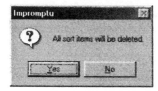

Figure 8.13
The "All sort items will be deleted"
message box pops up.

2. Click OK.

And the Results Are...

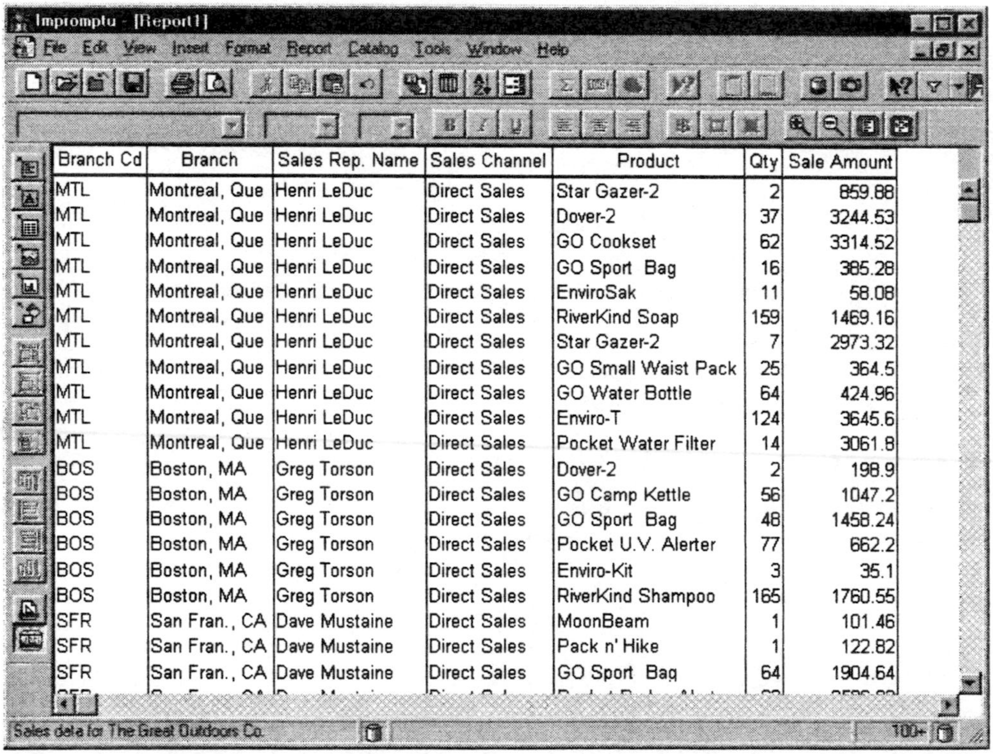

Branch Cd	Branch	Sales Rep. Name	Sales Channel	Product	Qty	Sale Amount
MTL	Montreal, Que	Henri LeDuc	Direct Sales	Star Gazer-2	2	859.88
MTL	Montreal, Que	Henri LeDuc	Direct Sales	Dover-2	37	3244.53
MTL	Montreal, Que	Henri LeDuc	Direct Sales	GO Cookset	62	3314.52
MTL	Montreal, Que	Henri LeDuc	Direct Sales	GO Sport Bag	16	385.28
MTL	Montreal, Que	Henri LeDuc	Direct Sales	EnviroSak	11	58.08
MTL	Montreal, Que	Henri LeDuc	Direct Sales	RiverKind Soap	159	1469.16
MTL	Montreal, Que	Henri LeDuc	Direct Sales	Star Gazer-2	7	2973.32
MTL	Montreal, Que	Henri LeDuc	Direct Sales	GO Small Waist Pack	25	364.5
MTL	Montreal, Que	Henri LeDuc	Direct Sales	GO Water Bottle	64	424.96
MTL	Montreal, Que	Henri LeDuc	Direct Sales	Enviro-T	124	3645.6
MTL	Montreal, Que	Henri LeDuc	Direct Sales	Pocket Water Filter	14	3061.8
BOS	Boston, MA	Greg Torson	Direct Sales	Dover-2	2	198.9
BOS	Boston, MA	Greg Torson	Direct Sales	GO Camp Kettle	56	1047.2
BOS	Boston, MA	Greg Torson	Direct Sales	GO Sport Bag	48	1458.24
BOS	Boston, MA	Greg Torson	Direct Sales	Pocket U.V. Alerter	77	662.2
BOS	Boston, MA	Greg Torson	Direct Sales	Enviro-Kit	3	35.1
BOS	Boston, MA	Greg Torson	Direct Sales	RiverKind Shampoo	165	1760.55
SFR	San Fran., CA	Dave Mustaine	Direct Sales	MoonBeam	1	101.46
SFR	San Fran., CA	Dave Mustaine	Direct Sales	Pack n' Hike	1	122.82
SFR	San Fran., CA	Dave Mustaine	Direct Sales	GO Sport Bag	64	1904.64

Sales data for The Great Outdoors Co.

Figure 8.14   The report that is unsorted.

I know, it doesn't look that different from before, but doing this ensures us that there is nothing sorted.

Tip

This trick applies to the following toolbar buttons:

- *Sort*
- *Filter*
- *Group*

Grouping

Grouping is another powerful feature available to report developers in Impromptu. This is for such groups as values in a column. For example, in the section above, you sorted by Product. The first product you saw was "Day Tripper." There was one "Day Tripper" after another. Did you need to see every instance of the word "Day Tripper," row after row? No, not really. You could have just seen it once, and that would have been enough. Seeing just one occurrence of a series of values is what grouping does for you.

Grouping really needs two things to happen for it to function. First, a grouping request sorts the column ascending. Then, like column values are grouped together, and only the first occurrence of a new value is displayed.

Question	Answer
So, does that mean I don't have to use the Sort button if I want to both Sort and Group?	Correct. The Group button does both. You don't have to use the Sort button at all.
	One note: The Group button has precedence over any other sorted item, except for other grouped items. That means if you have several items sorted in a report and you then decide to group on another column, that newly grouped column will become the highest sorted item.

Just as in sorting, there are two ways to perform this task:

1. Point and click using the toolbar.
2. Use the QDB, Group tab.

In addition to learning how to perform groupings, a concept called Associations will be introduced. Associations complement groupings in many ways. This final section will introduce associations and prepare you for the next chapter on Summaries.

Point and Click Grouping

First let's perform some groupings on this report using the basic way, pointing and clicking. This uses the toolbar icon for grouping. To perform this, select a cell in a column and click the Group button. Next, the report is rerun, meaning that a new query is generated by Impromptu and passed off to the database. Once the results of the query are returned, Impromptu displays the results on the screen.

Now that you have a general understanding of what a Group does to the report visually, let's do one. With the report that you have open, we will answer the following report requirement.

Report Requirement

Boss: *I would like to see this report grouped by Product.*

Analysis

Not really too much to analyze here. The requirements are pretty much spelled out by the request. The Product column needs to be grouped.

Follow these instructions:

1. Click on any cell in the Product column.
2. Click the Group button.

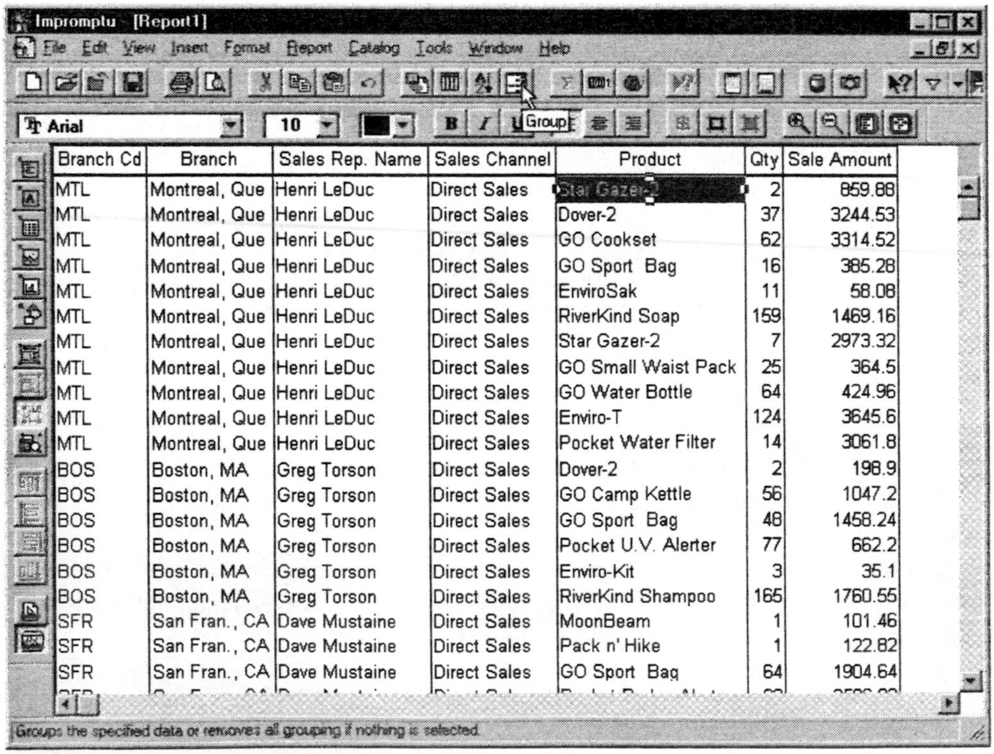

Figure 8.15   The Group button.

And the Results Are...

Branch Cd	Branch	Sales Rep. Name	Sales Channel	Product	Qty	Sale Amount
STOC	Stockholm, Swed	Bjorn Flertjan	Mail Sales	Day Tripper	7	80.36
SING	Singapore	Charles Loo Nam	Telephone Sales		3	33.18
LON	London, U.K.	Lyn Jacobs	Telephone Sales		16	206.08
MADR	Madrid, Spain	Inigo Montoya	Telephone Sales		6	68.04
MEL	Melbourne, Aus	Kaley Gregson	Telephone Sales		16	179.2
MEL	Melbourne, Aus	Malcom Young	Direct Sales		7	81.34
MEL	Melbourne, Aus	Malcom Young	Mail Sales		12	142.8
MEL	Melbourne, Aus	Malcom Young	Direct Sales		7	91.14
MEL	Melbourne, Aus	Kaley Gregson	Direct Sales		12	147.84
MEL	Melbourne, Aus	Torey Wandiko	Mail Sales		10	130.2
LON	London, U.K.	Thomas Brigade	Direct Sales		6	76.44
SFR	San Fran., CA	Dave Mustaine	Telephone Sales		3	34.86
CHG	Chicago, IL	Bill Smertal	Direct Sales		7	83.3
DAL	Dallas, TX	Bill Gibbons	Telephone Sales		3	39.48
LON	London, U.K.	Thomas Brigade	Mail Sales		30	340.2
MTL	Montreal, Que	Henri LeDuc	Telephone Sales		1	10.64
PAR	Paris, France	Gilles Turcotte	Mail Sales		10	114.8
SFR	San Fran., CA	Tony Armarillo	Telephone Sales		4	48.16
TOR	Toronto, Ont	Lisa Testorok	Direct Sales		3	32.76
TOR	Toronto, Ont	Lisa Testorok	Direct Sales		9	103.32

Sales data for The Great Outdoors Co.

Figure 8.16   The report results.

Notice all of the extra space below the first occurrence of Day Tripper. This is just one of the many benefits to grouping in Impromptu. When there is a new product, Impromptu draws a line between the new product and the last row of the previous product.

That was Easy, Let's Do Another:

Report Requirement

Boss: *Could you group the Sales Channel too?*

Analysis

This just asks to group the Sales Channel column as well.

Steps to Group a Column

1. Click on any cell in the Sales Channel column.
2. Click the Group button.

And the Results Are...

Branch Cd	Branch	Sales Rep. Name	Sales Channel	Product	Qty	Sale Amount
MEL	Melbourne, Aus	Malcom Young	Direct Sales	Day Tripper	7	81.34
MEL	Melbourne, Aus	Malcom Young			7	91.14
MEL	Melbourne, Aus	Kaley Gregson			12	147.84
LON	London, U.K.	Thomas Brigade			6	76.44
CHG	Chicago, IL	Bill Smertal			7	83.3
TOR	Toronto, Ont	Lisa Testorok			3	32.76
TOR	Toronto, Ont	Lisa Testorok			9	103.32
MTL	Montreal, Que	Henri LeDuc			4	45.36
STOC	Stockholm, Swed	Bjorn Flertjan	Mail Sales		7	80.36
MEL	Melbourne, Aus	Malcom Young			12	142.8
MEL	Melbourne, Aus	Torey Wandiko			10	130.2
LON	London, U.K.	Thomas Brigade			30	340.2
PAR	Paris, France	Gilles Turcotte			10	114.8
SING	Singapore	Charles Loo Nam	Telephone Sales		3	33.18
LON	London, U.K.	Lyn Jacobs			16	206.08
MADR	Madrid, Spain	Inigo Montoya			6	68.04
MEL	Melbourne, Aus	Kaley Gregson			16	179.2
SFR	San Fran., CA	Dave Mustaine			3	34.86
DAL	Dallas, TX	Bill Gibbons			3	39.48
MTL	Montreal, Que	Henri LeDuc			1	10.64

Figure 8.17   The report result. The new second group is secondary to the initial Product grouping. Note the extra line dividing the groups—this line shows up when printing.

The latest grouping is performed directly after the first. The Sales Channels are grouped based on the finish of the first grouping of Product. Yes, the order concept that applied to sorting applies here as well. When the report was run this time, the first grouping happened, and then the second grouping occurred.

Grouping with the QDB

Grouping is the final tab yet to be discussed in the QDB. Here, you can group and ungroup columns just the way you sorted and unsorted columns in the Sort tab. This is where the similarities end. The Group function itself has several components to it.

The entire concept of grouping is a very powerful feature provided by Impromptu, and there are some subtle nuances that, if used well, make it as valuable as any other feature in Impromptu. Now that you have the swing of things, take a look at the Group tab in the QDB.

1. Open the QDB.
2. Click on the Group tab.

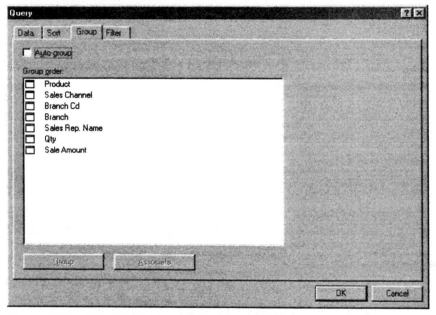

Figure 8.18 The QDB Group tab. The grouped columns are identified by a solid bar across the top of the column icon. Note that the order is the same as the order selected.

Inside the Group tab, you will notice that there is a column for each column in the Query Data. This means if you wanted to, you could group on each and every column, even the ones that make no sense, like Sale Amount. At the top of the tab, there is a checkbox labeled Auto-group. This feature is discussed in the next chapter because it ties directly to adding summary columns into a report.

At this time, this report has two columns grouped. The two columns, Product and Sales Channel, are identified by solid, black bands across the top of their column icons.

Group Order

As in the Sort tab, you can move grouped columns up and down in order in the Group tab. Changing the order of grouped columns in a report changes the entire focus of the report.

For example, the report in which you have grouped the two columns has a product focus. That is because the product column was the first column grouped; then the sales channel was grouped. So, when a Product Manager looks at the report, she will be looking at how a product was sold within different sales channels. If you were to flip the group order around on just these two columns, you would change the report drastically. The report now has a sales channel focus. The report would be geared to a different user, a sales channel manager. He would look at the report and see within a specific sales channel, how the Qty and Sale Amount columns were sold. This shows just how dynamic grouping is. Here you have one report, but depending on the grouping order, you have two different reports for two different audiences.

What is so compelling is how quickly this report, or any, can change focus.

Steps to Reorder the Grouped Columns

1. Open the QDB and select the Group tab.
2. Click on Product to select it.
3. Click again, hold the mouse button down, and drag the Product column until it appears to be hovering over the Sales Channel column. You know you are there when the Sales Channel column is highlighted (turns blue) (Figure 8.19 and Figure 8.20).
4. Click OK and run the report.

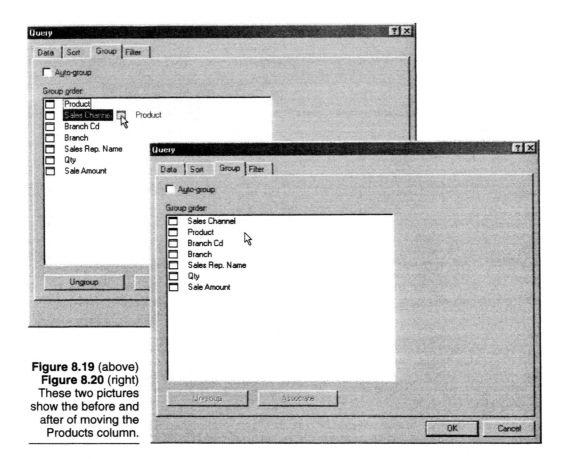

Figure 8.19 (above)
Figure 8.20 (right)
These two pictures
show the before and
after of moving the
Products column.

And the Results Are...

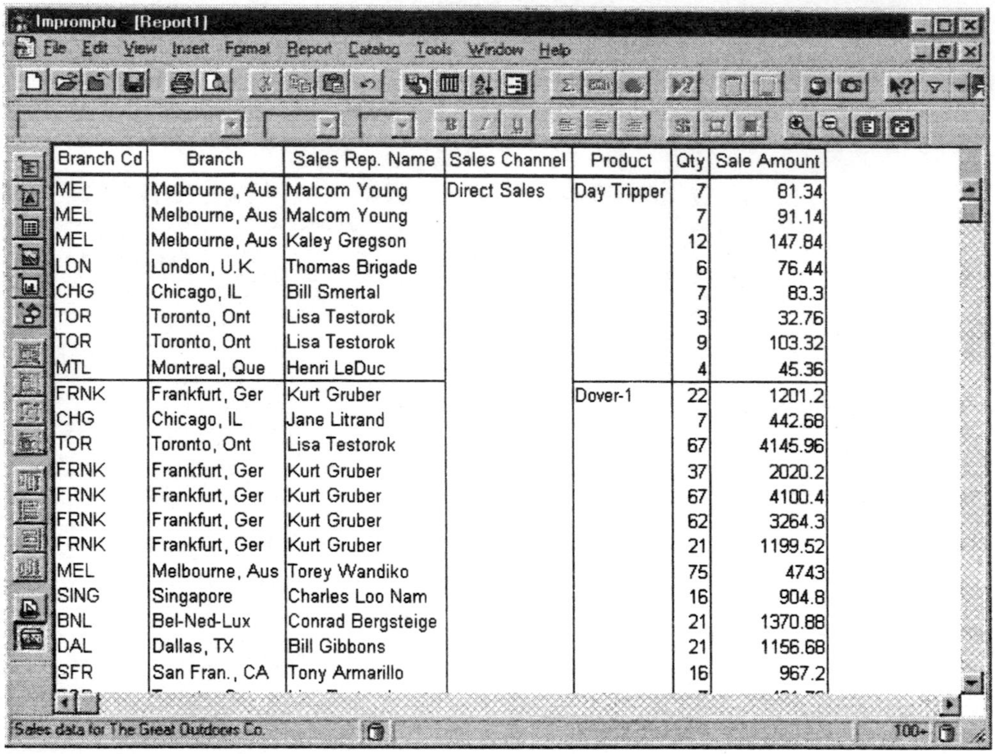

Branch Cd	Branch	Sales Rep. Name	Sales Channel	Product	Qty	Sale Amount
MEL	Melbourne, Aus	Malcom Young	Direct Sales	Day Tripper	7	81.34
MEL	Melbourne, Aus	Malcom Young			7	91.14
MEL	Melbourne, Aus	Kaley Gregson			12	147.84
LON	London, U.K.	Thomas Brigade			6	76.44
CHG	Chicago, IL	Bill Smertal			7	83.3
TOR	Toronto, Ont	Lisa Testorok			3	32.76
TOR	Toronto, Ont	Lisa Testorok			9	103.32
MTL	Montreal, Que	Henri LeDuc			4	45.36
FRNK	Frankfurt, Ger	Kurt Gruber		Dover-1	22	1201.2
CHG	Chicago, IL	Jane Litrand			7	442.68
TOR	Toronto, Ont	Lisa Testorok			67	4145.96
FRNK	Frankfurt, Ger	Kurt Gruber			37	2020.2
FRNK	Frankfurt, Ger	Kurt Gruber			67	4100.4
FRNK	Frankfurt, Ger	Kurt Gruber			62	3264.3
FRNK	Frankfurt, Ger	Kurt Gruber			21	1199.52
MEL	Melbourne, Aus	Torey Wandiko			75	4743
SING	Singapore	Charles Loo Nam			16	904.8
BNL	Bel-Ned-Lux	Conrad Bergsteige			21	1370.88
DAL	Dallas, TX	Bill Gibbons			21	1156.68
SFR	San Fran., CA	Tony Armarillo			16	967.2

Figure 8.21 The report results with the new group order.

New Groupings

Inside the Group tab, you are also able to group additional columns and remove a group request from a column. This is done with one button, the Group/Ungroup button. Depending on whether the button is grouped or ungrouped, the Group button will reverse the grouping status.

Report Requirement

Boss: *In addition to the two previous groupings, further break down and group the report by Branch.*

Analysis

This requirement asks you to add another grouping to the other two groupings you have. It asks you to group on the Branch Column. But you have two, a Branch and a Branch Code; which one applies? For our example, choose the Branch, which happens to be the description.

Steps to Add Additional Groups

1. Open the QDB and click over to the Group tab:
2. Click on the Branch.
3. Click the Group button at the bottom.

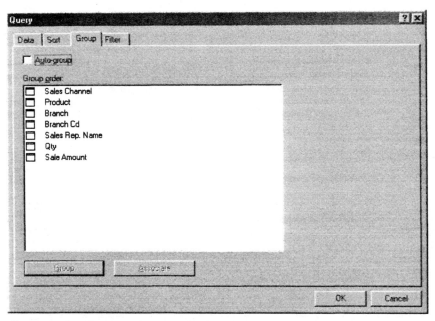

Figure 8.22 The new Group falls behind the previous two groupings.

4. Click OK and run the report.

And the Results Are...

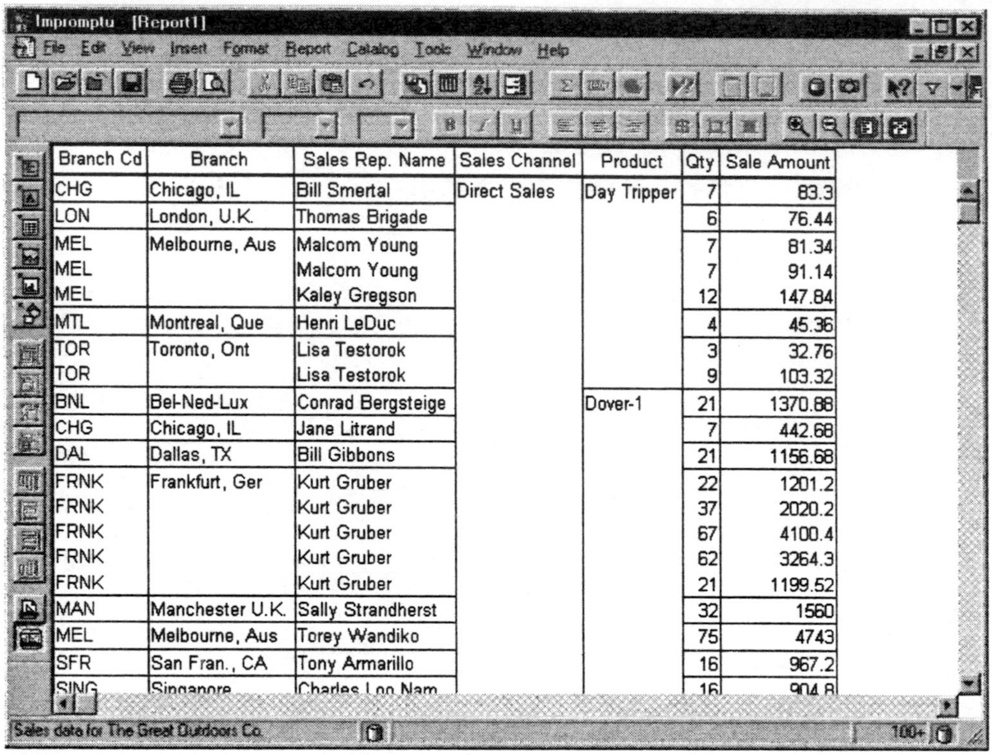

Branch Cd	Branch	Sales Rep. Name	Sales Channel	Product	Qty	Sale Amount
CHG	Chicago, IL	Bill Smertal	Direct Sales	Day Tripper	7	83.3
LON	London, U.K.	Thomas Brigade			6	76.44
MEL	Melbourne, Aus	Malcom Young			7	81.34
MEL		Malcom Young			7	91.14
MEL		Kaley Gregson			12	147.84
MTL	Montreal, Que	Henri LeDuc			4	45.36
TOR	Toronto, Ont	Lisa Testorok			3	32.76
TOR		Lisa Testorok			9	103.32
BNL	Bel-Ned-Lux	Conrad Bergsteige		Dover-1	21	1370.88
CHG	Chicago, IL	Jane Litrand			7	442.68
DAL	Dallas, TX	Bill Gibbons			21	1156.68
FRNK	Frankfurt, Ger	Kurt Gruber			22	1201.2
FRNK		Kurt Gruber			37	2020.2
FRNK		Kurt Gruber			67	4100.4
FRNK		Kurt Gruber			62	3264.3
FRNK		Kurt Gruber			21	1199.52
MAN	Manchester U.K.	Sally Strandherst			32	1560
MEL	Melbourne, Aus	Torey Wandiko			75	4743
SFR	San Fran., CA	Tony Armarillo			16	967.2
SING	Singapore	Charles Loo Nam			16	904.8

Figure 8.23 The finished report with new grouping added.

The report is further broken down by Branch. Although this may not be the best looking report, it fulfilled the requirements.

Associations

So far, you have learned how to group, ungroup, and change the order of grouped columns. Next, we need to investigate that little button on the Group tab called "Associate." Associations are a special feature related to grouping in Impromptu. Cognos created this feature because report developers need to perform grouping of like capabilities on columns that have a one-to-one relationship with an already grouped column. By making this association, Impromptu does not send an additional group request to the database like a typical group request. Instead, like a grouping request, an association request tells Impromptu to eliminate the extra cells on the report. Impromptu performs this locally, so the overhead of sending an extra group request back to the database for processing is avoided.

Grouping, like sorting, can become very intensive for a database when a report requests to group on more and more columns. Also, there are times when a group request does not add any value.

For example, say a sales report has a country code and a country description, and these two columns have an inherent one-to-one relationship—for every country code there is only one description:

Code	Description	Sale Amount
A1	Australia	45.00
A1	Australia	30.00
B1	Belgium	90.00
B2	Brazil	15.00
B2	Brazil	30.00
B2	Brazil	45.00
B2	Brazil	100.00
B2	Brazil	15.00

Next, a grouping is performed on the Description column. The resulting report would look like this:

Code	Description	Sale Amount
A1	Australia	45.00
A1		30.00
B1	Belgium	90.00
B2	Brazil	15.00
B2		30.00
B2		45.00
B2		100.00
B2		15.00

The report consumer does not want to see all of these Codes because it defeats the purpose of performing the initial grouping of the description. So, you can either group the Code column, or associate the Code column with the description column. By associating, the same results are displayed as if the report had performed a grouping on the Code column. But by performing an association, the report is not asking the database to perform any additional, unnecessary work. The results would be as follows:

Code	Description	Sale Amount
A1	Australia	45.00
		30.00
B1	Belgium	90.00
B2	Brazil	15.00
		30.00
		45.00
		100.00
		15.00

This "grouping like capability" is best defined by an example.

Report Requirement

Boss: *I like having the Branch Code on the report, but could you group on that so I don't have to see these multiple MEL's when I only see one Melbourne, Australia.*

Analysis

Here is a very common business requirement. It is a request to do something directly (grouping), while we, as report developers, know that there is a better way of doing it while delivering the same results. Instead of unnecessarily grouping on an item that has a one-to-one relationship, you can use the Associate button in the Group tab.

Steps to Associate a Column

1. Open the QDB.
2. Select the Group tab.
3. Click on the Branch Code.
4. Click the Associate button (Figure 8.24).

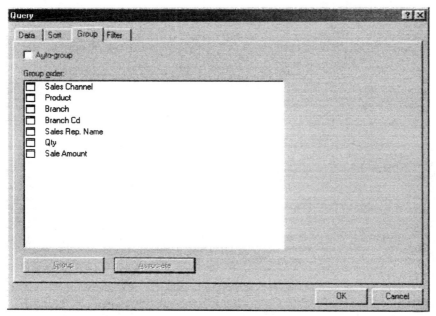

Figure 8.24   Notice how on our newly associated column, Branch Cd, has a halfway filled heading. This is to let us know that this column is associated, and not grouped.

5. Click OK to run the report (Figure 8.25).

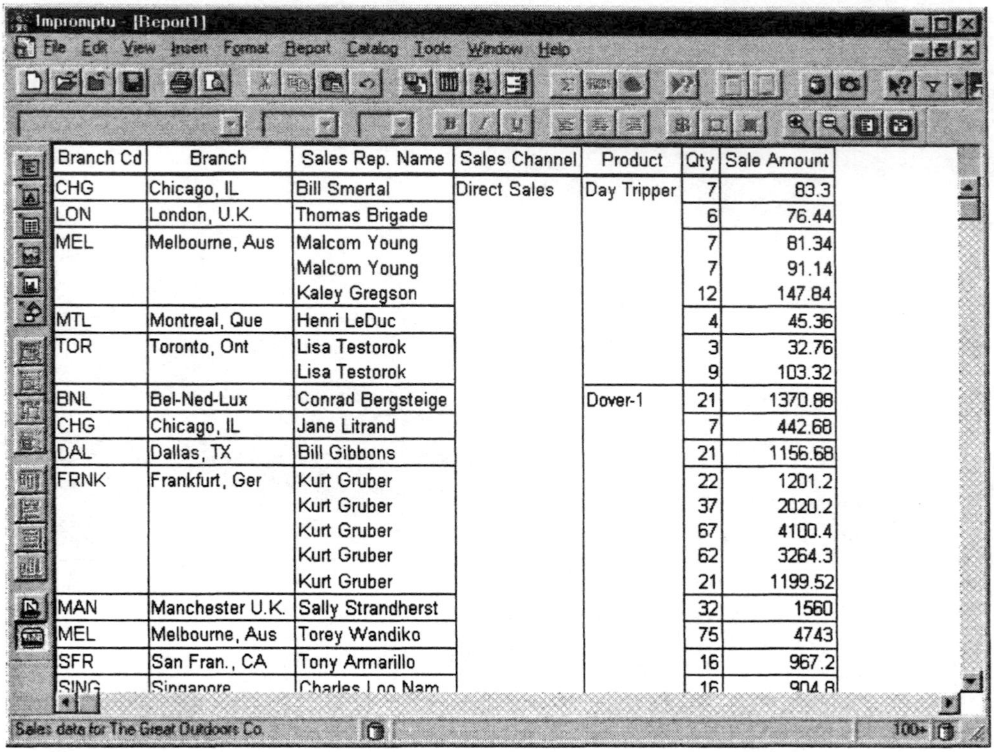

Branch Cd	Branch	Sales Rep. Name	Sales Channel	Product	Qty	Sale Amount
CHG	Chicago, IL	Bill Smertal	Direct Sales	Day Tripper	7	83.3
LON	London, U.K.	Thomas Brigade			6	76.44
MEL	Melbourne, Aus	Malcom Young			7	81.34
		Malcom Young			7	91.14
		Kaley Gregson			12	147.84
MTL	Montreal, Que	Henri LeDuc			4	45.36
TOR	Toronto, Ont	Lisa Testorok			3	32.76
		Lisa Testorok			9	103.32
BNL	Bel-Ned-Lux	Conrad Bergsteige		Dover-1	21	1370.88
CHG	Chicago, IL	Jane Litrand			7	442.68
DAL	Dallas, TX	Bill Gibbons			21	1156.68
FRNK	Frankfurt, Ger	Kurt Gruber			22	1201.2
		Kurt Gruber			37	2020.2
		Kurt Gruber			67	4100.4
		Kurt Gruber			62	3264.3
		Kurt Gruber			21	1199.52
MAN	Manchester U.K.	Sally Strandherst			32	1560
MEL	Melbourne, Aus	Torey Wandiko			75	4743
SFR	San Fran., CA	Tony Armarillo			16	967.2
SING	Singapore	Charles Loo Nam			16	904.8

Figure 8.25 The report results.

Congratulations, you have performed your first association! This is just the beginning though. As is shown in the next chapter, there is more to associations than meets the eye.

Tips

Here are some things to keep in mind when navigating around in the Group tab and doing associations:

- **Associate a column to any other column.** Just like sorts and groups, you can click and move associated columns up and down the list of grouped columns.
- **Associate a column only to a grouped column.** For example, moving a column to the bottom of the Group list where there may be ungrouped columns will not work. Impromptu does not allow this.
- Additionally, **you can also ungroup an item and then associate it to a grouped column.**
- And, as you might have guessed, **you can un-associate a column altogether.**

Be Careful!

It is extremely important to remember that associations are used only in situations where a column is related to another grouped column by a one-to-one relationship. If this criterion is not met, and a column is associated to a grouped column that does not have a one-to-one relationship, then unreliable results can be and most times will be displayed on the report.

To show the importance of how information can be incorrectly displayed, let's go through an example of a wrong use of an association. *I strongly urge you to not just skip over this section; this is where seeing is really believing.* And, as a report developer, the only way to identify reporting results is to see how many different things are done, whether those are correct or incorrect.

In this example, we will mistakenly associate the Branch Code to the Sales Channel. The results, we know, are wrong. But, what is important to see here is that when wrong results are returned by Impromptu, there are no flashing lights, no buzzing sounds, no indicators whatsoever. Impromptu's job is to return the results you asked for. It does not evaluate what you ask it to do and decide that you really should not do something because it may not look right.

Steps Involved in an Improper Association:

1. Open the QDB.
2. Select the Group tab.
3. Click on the associated Branch Code column.
4. Click and drag that column up until the Sales Channel column is highlighted, then let go of the cursor button.

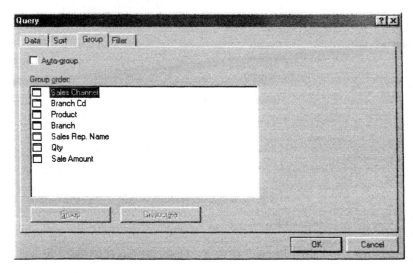

Figure 8.26
The Group tab with the Sales Channel column highlighted.

5. Click OK to run the report.

And the Results Are...

Branch Cd	Branch	Sales Rep. Name	Sales Channel	Product	Qty	Sale Amount
CHG	Chicago, IL	Bill Smertal	Direct Sales	Day Tripper	7	83.3
	London, U.K.	Thomas Brigade			6	76.44
	Melbourne, Aus	Malcom Young			7	81.34
		Malcom Young			7	91.14
		Kaley Gregson			12	147.84
	Montreal, Que	Henri LeDuc			4	45.36
	Toronto, Ont	Lisa Testorok			3	32.76
		Lisa Testorok			9	103.32
	Bel-Ned-Lux	Conrad Bergsteige		Dover-1	21	1370.88
	Chicago, IL	Jane Litrand			7	442.68
	Dallas, TX	Bill Gibbons			21	1156.68
	Frankfurt, Ger	Kurt Gruber			22	1201.2
		Kurt Gruber			37	2020.2
		Kurt Gruber			67	4100.4
		Kurt Gruber			62	3264.3
		Kurt Gruber			21	1199.52
	Manchester U.K.	Sally Strandherst			32	1560
	Melbourne, Aus	Torey Wandiko			75	4743
	San Fran., CA	Tony Armarillo			16	967.2
	Singapore	Charles Loo Nam			16	904.8

Sales data for The Great Outdoors Co.

Figure 8.27   The report results with the incorrectly displayed CHG branch code for items in London, which is actually in the UK Branch.

By just looking at the report, you can see that this doesn't look right. The first Branch Code you see is CHG, and then you don't see another until the next Sales Channel, which is around 700 records later. This is an extremely obvious example of a misuse of associations. Others may not be as noticeable.

Summary

A few key things to remember:

1. How to sort columns in a report.
2. How to group columns.
3. Grouping takes precedence over sorting.
4. Associations are an alternative for additional groupings.

Remember, Associations are tricky animals to tame. This will take some practice and experience. Don't be discouraged if the process does not just click in your mind right away.

CHAPTER 9

Totals and Summaries

This chapter explains the concepts of totals and summaries with Impromptu. As you are beginning to imagine, there are many different ways to create summaries and totals in Impromptu. And, as you have become more and more familiar with Impromptu, it is becoming more clear that many of the concepts of report building have interdependencies. Totals and summaries apply the knowledge of groupings and associations to understand and appreciate how summaries work.

Technically, there is a difference between totaling and summaries. When you think about it, a total is simply a type of summary. Every total performed in Impromptu or anywhere, using any tool for that matter, is a summary. So, when you are talking to a person you are writing a report for and they say they want a total here, here, and here, you can translate that into Impromptu by thinking summary here, here, and here.

This chapter will cover:

- Point and click totaling
- How summaries interact with the report
- Moving summaries around the report layout
- Different ways of inserting summaries
- Creating summaries at the beginning of the report

Totals and Summaries and Reporting

Totals and summaries were broken out into a separate chapter for two reasons. First, the grouping needed to be explained in the preceding chapter. Grouping plays a large role in some of the totaling features available to you in Impromptu. Impromptu has taken years of research and customer feedback on how people want to perform summaries and totals in their reports, and it has automated certain steps to save the report developer time. Throughout this chapter, we will uncover what those steps are, understand why they're done, learn how to take advantage of them, and learn how to undo them if you do not want to use them.

Second, summaries are considered a separate function within Impromptu. As you might have noticed earlier, in the QDB and in the Available Components Toolbox, there are separate areas specifically for summaries. Since summaries are separate, special functions, it is wise to learn the basics of summaries before trying to apply them.

Before We Begin

First let's create a report to work with throughout the chapter. In the past few chapters, I have thrown a little variety at you by creating different reports. For this chapter, let's use the same report we used last chapter for sorting and grouping.

With Impromptu open, and using the Great Outdoors Catalog provided by the original installation of Impromptu, create a Simple List report:

1. Expand the Admin folder, and then the Branch folder.
2. Double click on Branch Code.
3. Double click on Branch.
4. Expand Order folder.
5. Expand the Additional Info. folder.

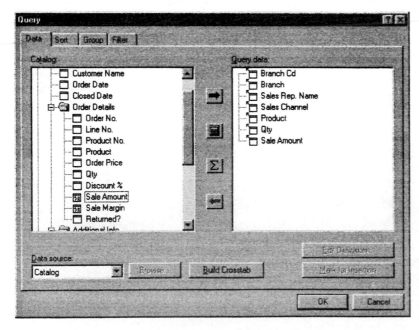

Figure 9.1
The completed
QDB.

6. Double click on Sales Rep Name.

7. Double click on Sales Channel.

8. Expand the Order Details folder.

9. Double click on Product, Qty, and Sale Amount (Figure 9.1).

10. Click OK to run the report.

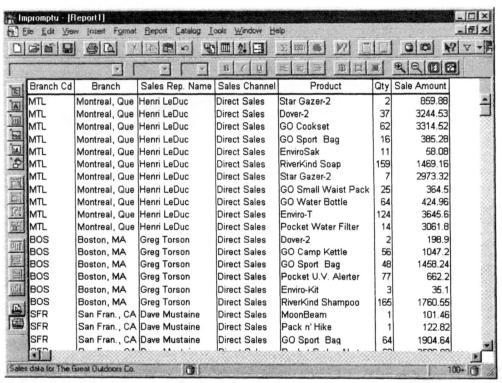

Figure 9.2   The report results in Screen layout.

Point, Click, and Total

When you create a report, you are looking either for a detailed list or a summarized report. Either way, you are organizing your information in some manner to better understand the report. When you start out with a detailed list report and you want to add some summaries to it, Impromptu provides that functionality from the toolbar.

Report Requirement

Boss: *I want the report you just developed to have a total sale amount for the entire report.*

Analysis

The boss wants a total of the Sale Amount for the entire report.

Steps to Create a Summary

With the report open,

1. Click on any cell in the Sale Amount column.
2. Click the Total button.

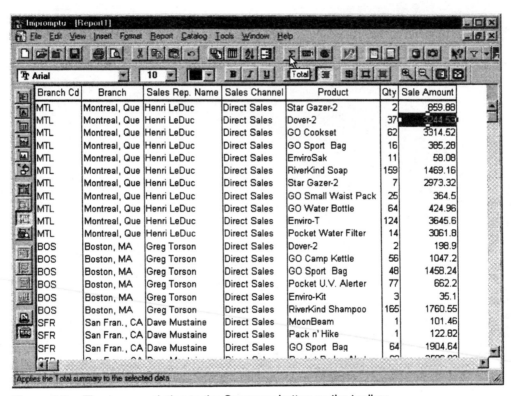

Figure 9.3   The cursor pointing to the Summary button on the toolbar.

Note

The little fish will swim in the Status bar for about 1.5 seconds, and you see the report.

And the Results Are...

Branch Cd	Branch	Sales Rep. Name	Sales Channel	Product	Qty	Sale Amount
MTL	Montreal, Que	Henri LeDuc	Direct Sales	Star Gazer-2	2	859.88
MTL	Montreal, Que	Henri LeDuc	Direct Sales	Dover-2	37	244.55
MTL	Montreal, Que	Henri LeDuc	Direct Sales	GO Cookset	62	3314.52
MTL	Montreal, Que	Henri LeDuc	Direct Sales	GO Sport Bag	16	385.28
MTL	Montreal, Que	Henri LeDuc	Direct Sales	EnviroSak	11	58.08
MTL	Montreal, Que	Henri LeDuc	Direct Sales	RiverKind Soap	159	1469.16
MTL	Montreal, Que	Henri LeDuc	Direct Sales	Star Gazer-2	7	2973.32
MTL	Montreal, Que	Henri LeDuc	Direct Sales	GO Small Waist Pack	25	364.5
MTL	Montreal, Que	Henri LeDuc	Direct Sales	GO Water Bottle	64	424.96
MTL	Montreal, Que	Henri LeDuc	Direct Sales	Enviro-T	124	3645.6
MTL	Montreal, Que	Henri LeDuc	Direct Sales	Pocket Water Filter	14	3061.8
BOS	Boston, MA	Greg Torson	Direct Sales	Dover-2	2	198.9
BOS	Boston, MA	Greg Torson	Direct Sales	GO Camp Kettle	56	1047.2
BOS	Boston, MA	Greg Torson	Direct Sales	GO Sport Bag	48	1458.24
BOS	Boston, MA	Greg Torson	Direct Sales	Pocket U.V. Alerter	77	662.2
BOS	Boston, MA	Greg Torson	Direct Sales	Enviro-Kit	3	35.1
BOS	Boston, MA	Greg Torson	Direct Sales	RiverKind Shampoo	165	1760.55
SFR	San Fran., CA	Dave Mustaine	Direct Sales	MoonBeam	1	101.46
SFR	San Fran., CA	Dave Mustaine	Direct Sales	Pack n' Hike	1	122.82
SFR	San Fran., CA	Dave Mustaine	Direct Sales	GO Sport Bag	64	1904.64

Figure 9.4 "I think the report ran, but, where is the total?"

Where Is the Total?

Wait a minute. There were only two steps. You clicked on the total button. But, what happened to the total? Did it work? Is Impromptu broken? Where did it go?

Those were just some of the thoughts I had the first time I did a point and click total, so I know what you might be thinking right now. Here's what just happened. When you clicked on the column and totaled on it, Impromptu did a few things; it

1. Checked to see if you had any columns grouped.
2. Created a summary of the column to be totaled for every column that had a group.
3. Created a summary of the column to be totaled for the entire report.
4. Placed the summary at the appropriate group level.
5. Placed the summary at the end of the report, for the report total.

Now, let's look at these steps with our report:

Summary Step	Our Report
Checked to see if you either had any columns grouped	No previously grouped columns
Created a summary of the Sale Amount column for every column that had a group	Since there were no grouped columns, no extra summaries were created
Created a summary of the column to be totaled for the entire report.	A total was built for the entire report
Placed the summary at the appropriate group level.	Since there were no grouped columns, and no extra summaries developed, no group level summaries needed to be placed
Placed the summary at the end of the report, for the report total	The report total was placed at the end of the report

This means you will find the total you just built at the bottom of the report. Scroll down to the bottom of the report to find the total displayed beneath the Sale Amount column.

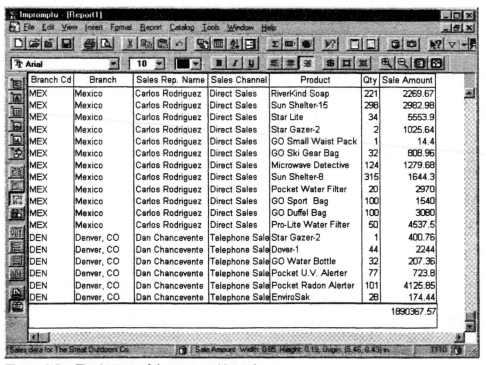

Branch Cd	Branch	Sales Rep. Name	Sales Channel	Product	Qty	Sale Amount
MEX	Mexico	Carlos Rodriguez	Direct Sales	RiverKind Soap	221	2269.67
MEX	Mexico	Carlos Rodriguez	Direct Sales	Sun Shelter-15	298	2982.98
MEX	Mexico	Carlos Rodriguez	Direct Sales	Star Lite	34	5553.9
MEX	Mexico	Carlos Rodriguez	Direct Sales	Star Gazer-2	2	1025.64
MEX	Mexico	Carlos Rodriguez	Direct Sales	GO Small Waist Pack	1	14.4
MEX	Mexico	Carlos Rodriguez	Direct Sales	GO Ski Gear Bag	32	808.96
MEX	Mexico	Carlos Rodriguez	Direct Sales	Microwave Detective	124	1279.68
MEX	Mexico	Carlos Rodriguez	Direct Sales	Sun Shelter-8	315	1644.3
MEX	Mexico	Carlos Rodriguez	Direct Sales	Pocket Water Filter	20	2970
MEX	Mexico	Carlos Rodriguez	Direct Sales	GO Sport Bag	100	1540
MEX	Mexico	Carlos Rodriguez	Direct Sales	GO Duffel Bag	100	3080
MEX	Mexico	Carlos Rodriguez	Direct Sales	Pro-Lite Water Filter	50	4537.5
DEN	Denver, CO	Dan Chancevente	Telephone Sale	Star Gazer-2	1	400.76
DEN	Denver, CO	Dan Chancevente	Telephone Sale	Dover-1	44	2244
DEN	Denver, CO	Dan Chancevente	Telephone Sale	GO Water Bottle	32	207.36
DEN	Denver, CO	Dan Chancevente	Telephone Sale	Pocket U.V. Alerter	77	723.8
DEN	Denver, CO	Dan Chancevente	Telephone Sale	Pocket Radon Alerter	101	4125.85
DEN	Denver, CO	Dan Chancevente	Telephone Sale	EnviroSak	28	174.44
						1890367.57

Figure 9.5   The bottom of the report with total.

Impromptu inserted the total for the entire report at the bottom, but in this new box. The new box is a footer for the entire list report. Impromptu inserted this into the display of the report because it needed a place to put the total.

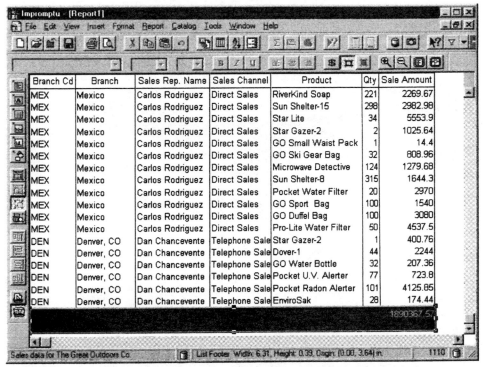

Figure 9.6   This new List footer is automatically placed in the report layout.

Question	Answer
Why does the program pause every so often while I'm scrolling to the bottom of the report?	Remember when we ran our first report, and we discussed how Impromptu brought back the first 100 or so records? At the time of initially running the report, that is all the rows that Impromptu brought back. If you wanted to see more (scroll down), Impromptu has to fetch more records from the database. This is where the pause comes from; Impromptu was retrieving more data from the database.

Totals in the QDB

How It Looks in the QDB...

Before we move on to more complex summaries, look at how this appears in the QDB.

- Open the QDB.

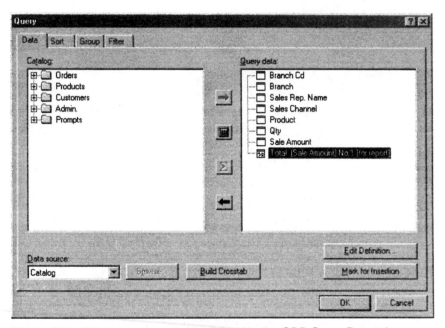

Figure 9.7   The new column is highlighted in the QDB Query Data tab.

When you create a total, even by the push of a button, Impromptu needs to keep track of that new column, and does so in the Query Data box. It has the calculated icon next to it, because technically, the summary is just a calculated column in the query.

Data Tab

The new summary appears in the Data tab because it is a new column in the query. This is because when you created it, Impromptu had to store it and give you the ability to modify it in the future. Also, the new summary column is part of the query that is sent to the database.

The summary column draws its name *Total (Sale Amount) No. 1 [for report]* from what it is, a *Total* of the *Sale Amount* column. Since the *Total* is essentially a function, albeit a special function, Impromptu must wrap parentheses around it. The *No. 1* is inserted by

Impromptu to order the new total because in Impromptu, there can be any number of additional totals that could be generated by the toolbar. This ensures a unique name for each. At the end, the *[for report]* means that this calculation is generated at the *report* level.

Sort Tab

Select the Sort tab next. Notice that the new Total column has a spot on the Sort list. Although it may not make any sense to have the ability to sort on a total right now, trust me; someday, you will go into this tab, expect it to be there, and sort it, without even thinking twice.

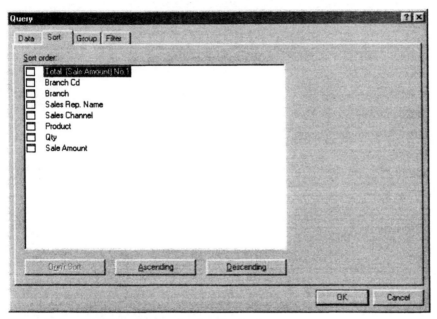

Figure 9.8   The Sort tab showing the Total column.

Group Tab

Now, select the Group tab. Here we see something interesting. The total we just created is associated to... nothing. But, wasn't it the rule that you only associate a column to a grouped column. In our report, there is nothing grouped. This is the lone exception to the rule—when you are dealing with a summary, you can associate it to the entire report. What this means is that you will see the column only once instead of once for every row (Figure 9.9).

Also in the grouped tab, you can see that the Total column icon has not only a half black bar, but also a red splat mark that is new. This indicates that the association is automatic, one generated by Impromptu when you selected the Total button on the toolbar. We will explain the usefulness of this subsequently.

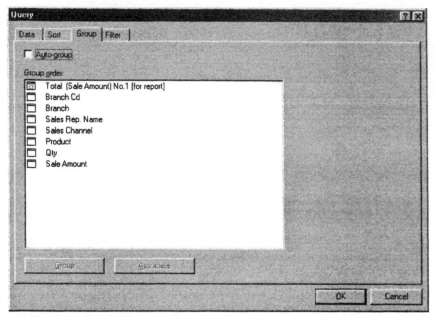

Figure 9.9   Remember look in the [for....] to see exactly what something is being associated with.

Let's Do Another One

Now that you have a general understanding of how the point and click total works, let's do another one to see how it works when we have done some grouping before we total. To set this exercise up, let's use the following requirement:

Report Requirement

Boss: *Well, the total is nice, but I don't want that total. What I really want to see is the Sale Amount totaled first by Sales Channel, then by Sales Rep Name, then finally, by Product.*

Analysis

Wow, in this one little sentence, the requirements turn out to be:

- Group Sales Channel.
- Group Sales Rep.
- Group the Product.
- Total Sale Amount for Sales Channel.
- Total Sale Amount for Sales Rep Name.
- Total Product.

Initially, this seems to be about an hour's worth of work, but really this can be done in a few minutes. When you have multiple tasks embedded in a request like this one, it is always best to break them up into logical groups. So, breaking this up into steps makes it look like this:

1. Remove the first total.
2. Group the columns.
3. Make the totals.

Step 1: Remove the First Total

Looking back at the requirements, the boss did not want the original total we built. So, the following erases the first total:

1. Open the QDB.
2. Select the Data tab.
3. Click on the Total (Sale Amount) No. 1 [for report] column.
4. Either press the Delete key or click the Remove button.

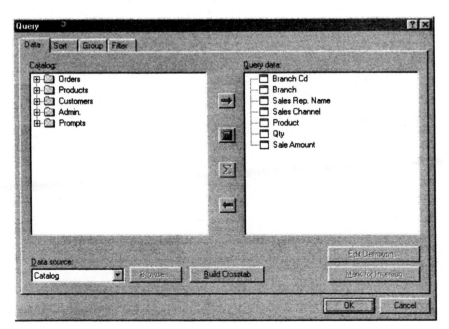

Figure 9.10 The QDB Query Data tab without the total column.

This removes the column from the Query Data box, as well as any reference in other tabs. To see the results, look at the Sort tab and the Group tab.

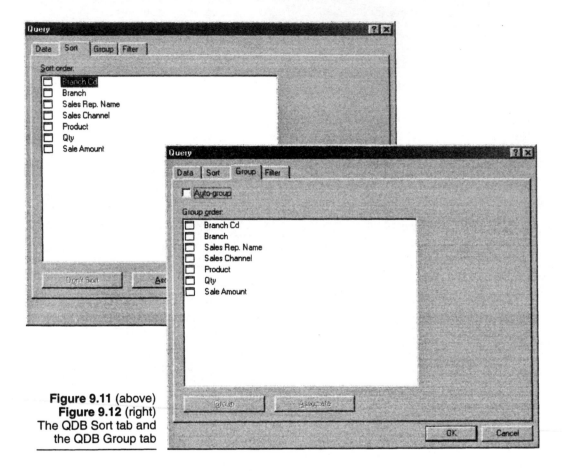

Figure 9.11 (above)
Figure 9.12 (right)
The QDB Sort tab and
the QDB Group tab

5. Click OK to run the report.

Running the report does not change its initial appearance; it just removes the total from both the query and the layout.

Step 2: Group and Order the Report Columns

The next part involves grouping the right columns in the right order. Follow the following sequence to properly group the report:

1. Open the QDB.
2. Select the Group tab.

3. Click the Sales Channel column.

4. Click the Group button.

5. Click the Sales Rep Name column.

6. Click the Group button.

7. Click the Product column.

8. Click the Group button.

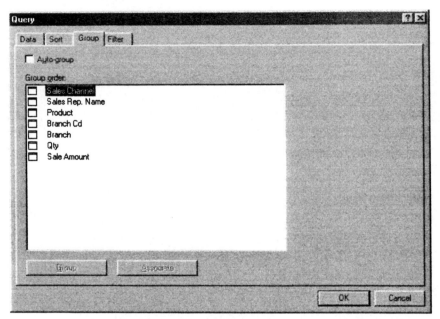

Figure 9.13 The QDB Group tab. Remember the order here dictates the order in which columns get grouped.

9. Click OK to run the report (Figure 9.14).

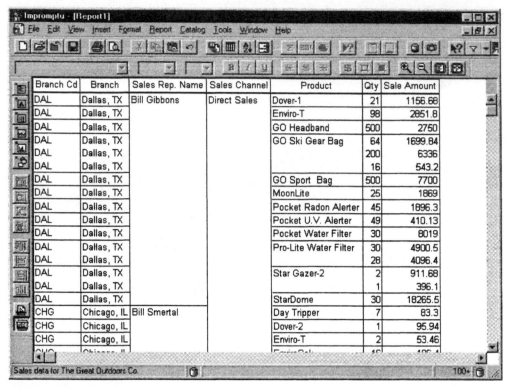

Figure 9.14   The report results, with grouping.

Tip

Here is something I always do when I'm building reports and I group a column in the middle of the layout. I move the columns to the order that they are grouped from left to right, as shown in Figure 9.15.

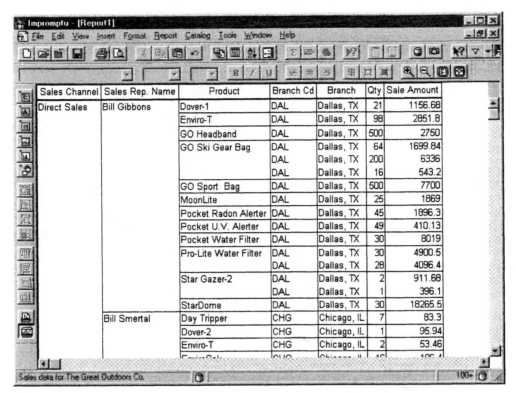

Figure 9.15   The report results in the ordering of the grouped columns.

Step 3: Create the Total

Finally, the totaling! This next step seems like will involve a lot of clicking. Well, not exactly. What you will find is that Impromptu will take the grouping you just did into consideration when you perform the point and click total.

From the report layout

1. Click on any cell in the Sale Amount column.
2. Click on the Total button.

And the Results Are...

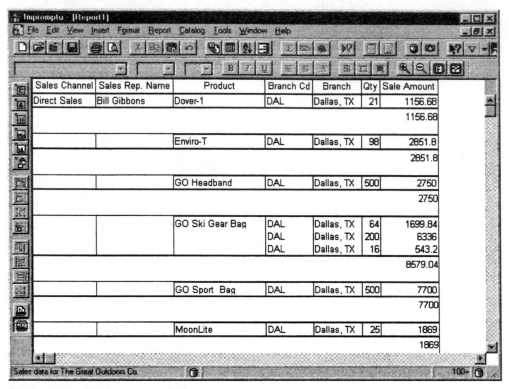

Figure 9.16   The report results.

Impromptu created a Product total and inserted it in a new footer. This time, it inserted a footer tied to the Product.

But Wait! There's More!

Now, granted, totaling the Products was pretty nice, but let's scroll down to the next breaking point, a different Sales Rep Name: "Bill Smertal." There are two totals and two footers, as shown in Figure 9.17. Why?

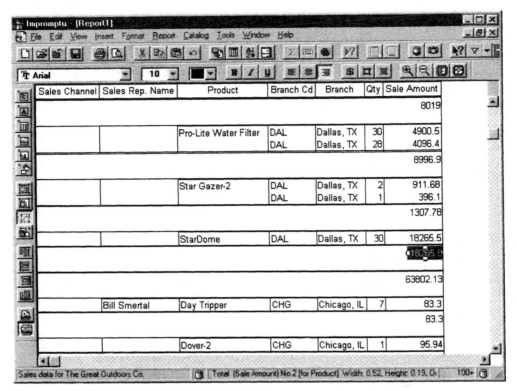

Figure 9.17   The new section and the Status bar.

The first, smaller number is fairly easy to figure out. The number 18265.5 is the same as the detail Sale Amount for the product Star Dome row, so this is a total for the Product.

To find out what the second, larger number is, use the Status bar.

1. Click on the larger number, 63802.13.
2. Look at the Status bar (Figure 9.18).

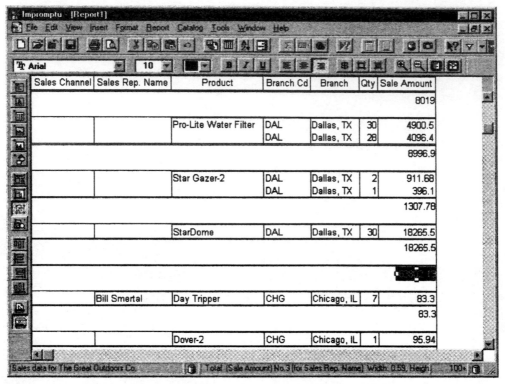

Figure 9.18 This is yet another column created automatically by the Total button. This one is generated for the Sales Rep, see the [for Sales Rep], in the Status bar. This is the total for all the products for this Sales Rep Name.

In fact, when there are columns grouped as you had them, and you select a column and total it, Impromptu creates summaries for each level of grouping. This is the automatic feature we talked about earlier. To see the extent of this, let's take a look at the QDB to see what Impromptu did when you pressed the Total button.

1. Open the QDB.
2. Select the Data tab (Figure 9.19).

Impromptu created each of these columns for the total request. Each is for one of the levels of grouping in the report. Two things separate their names: (1) the numbering and (2) what they are "for."

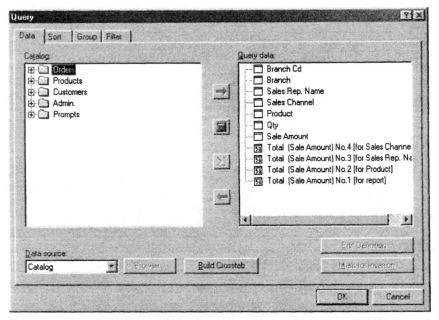

Figure 9.19   The QDB Data tab. There are four new calculated columns.

3. Click over to the Sort tab (Figure 9.20).

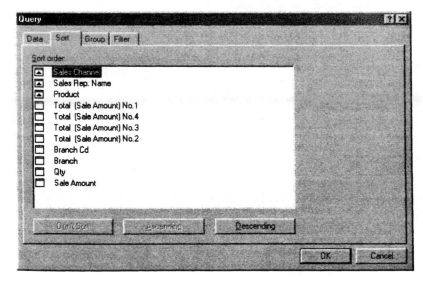

Figure 9.20
The QDB Sort tab.

These sorts are done during the grouping performed earlier. Additionally, the totals are displayed in the Sort tab because they are treated just like other columns in a query.

4. Click the Group tab.

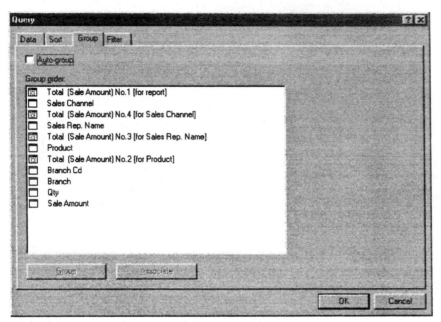

Figure 9.21   The QDB Group tab.

Remember when we did our first total and it gave a total for the entire report. Even though we have groupings, Impromptu still gives us a total for the entire report. Each of the grouped columns has a total "associated" with it. Associated means here that the summarized column is directly related to the grouped column it is beneath. Also note that each of the totals has the red splat, signifying this was done automatically.

Smart Summaries

Since we are here looking at a fairly advanced report, let's take a minute to further explore the automatic properties of the totals we just created. Impromptu does create these calculated columns and drop them onto the report only to be left there. When you click and total, you get a flexible total. This "calculated column" can be treated like any other item in the Impromptu layout. Here are a couple examples of what you can do with these columns:

Moving Smart Summary

First, you can move any total anywhere on the report. To see what happens, move the Product total to a column and see the results.

Try This:

1. While looking at the report, click on the first Product total.

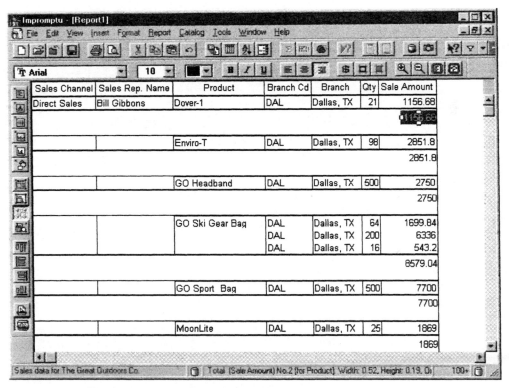

Figure 9.22   The first total is highlighted.

2. Click and drag the column to the right of the Sale Amount Column and let go.

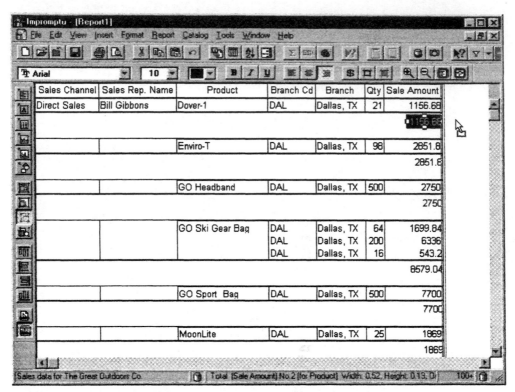

Figure 9.23   The dashed line shows where the column will be placed before the mouse button is let go.

This reruns the report because even though you view it as a change to the same column, Impromptu does not discriminate. If there is a change, Impromptu reruns the query.

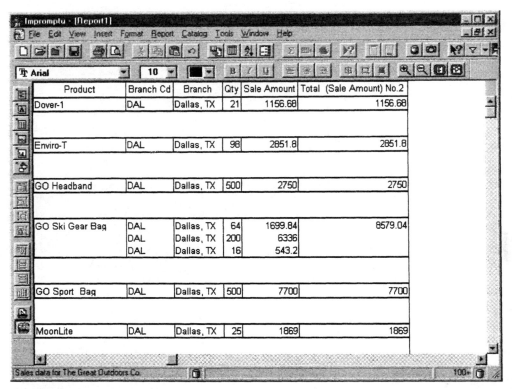

Figure 9.24 The report results.

- *The name "Total (Sale Amount) No. 2" is now the Column Header.*
- *The Product footer still remains on the report layout.*
- *Most important, down a few rows in the report, the "GO Ski Gear Bag" total matches the sum of all of the four items. It displays the total only on the first line.*

In fact, everything is OK. The result of just moving the total to the column position creates a different place for Impromptu to associate it. So, Impromptu did exactly what we asked it to; it moved the total column from one spot on the report to another.

Clean Up

- Undo the last step by clicking the Undo button.

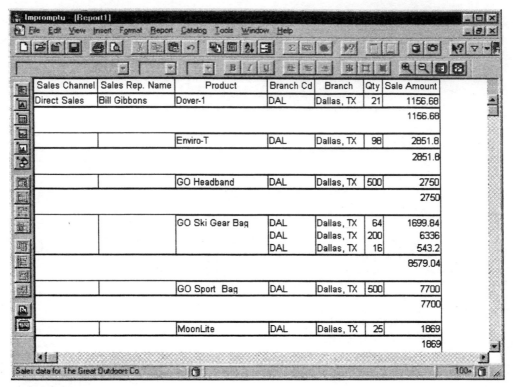

Figure 9.25   The report returned to the results before the column was moved.

Another Smart Summary Move

Now let's try something else. In this exercise, take the Product total and, instead of making it a column, move it from the Product footer to another footer, the Sales Rep footer.

Try This:

1. While viewing the Screen layout, scroll down anywhere from 10 to 15 clicks of the down arrow until you see the Sales Rep footer and Total.

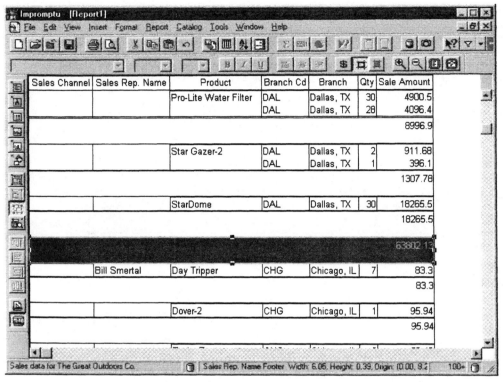

Figure 9.26   The report results with the Sales Rep Name footer highlighted.

2. Click on any Product Total.

3. Click, drag, and drop the Product Total down next to the Sales Rep total (Figure 9.27).

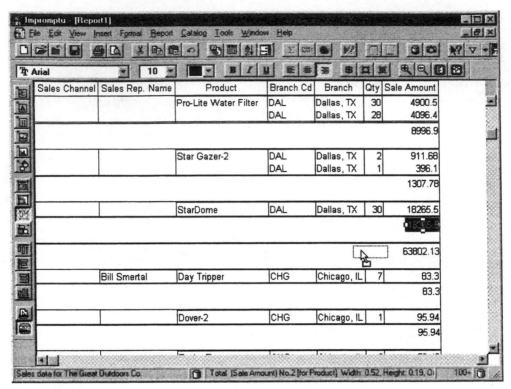

Figure 9.27   The dotted line is where I'm going to drop the Product Total.

Now, Impromptu runs the report again, and the totals recalculate, because there has been a change. When it finishes:

4. Scroll back down to that same spot to see what exactly changed.
5. Click on the total we just moved and see what the Status bar reads (Figure 9.28):
6. Open the QDB's Data tab to see how this is reflected in the QDB (Figure 9.29).

Note

There are Total No. 2 and Total No. 3, and both have the "for" clause of [for Sales Rep Name].

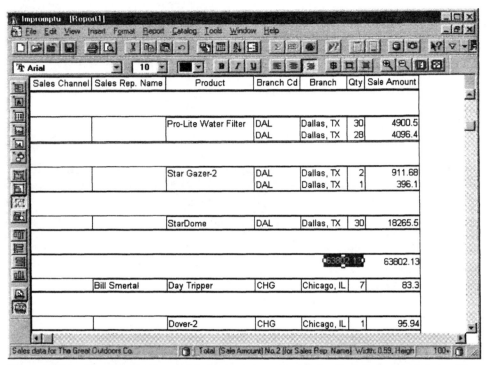

Figure 9.28 The two Totals are identical and next to each other. Note, that this is still Total No. 2, but look at the "for" clause, instead of Product; it is now Sales Rep Name.

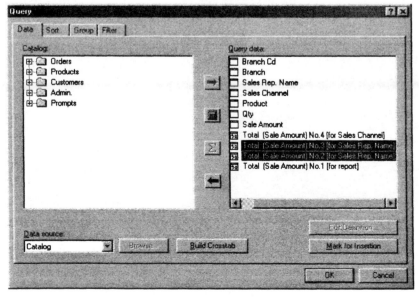

Figure 9.29
The Data tab with the two totals highlighted.

Question	Answer
With the only thing separating the No.2 and No. 3 totals from above, is it possible to have two columns in my query that have the exact same name and the exact same definition, and each shown separately on the report?	Yes, once you bring a column into the query or even build one, Impromptu remembers the initial name. That way, when you change the name in the query or even change the Column Header, Impromptu still remembers what it is. This does get a little confusing because even on the layout, you can see two of the exact same columns.

Now by looking at the Group tab, notice that there are two columns associated with the one Sales Rep Name column.

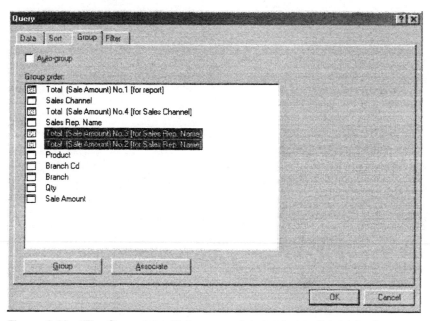

Figure 9.30 The Group tab with two associated columns (totals) for the one Sales Rep Name column.

This is due to the "Smart" features of this summary. This total takes into consideration where it is on the layout of the report, and then the total is calculated. Since it is "in" a different section—the Sales Rep Name footer as opposed to the Product Footer—it changes the totaling that it generates from being a total for the Product to a total for the Sales Rep Name.

Move Without Smart Summary

There will come a time when you build a smart summary and you do not want it to retain the smart properties; you just want it to be a total. You would like to move the column to another area of the report and have it retain the group and summary relationship. You can remove the smart summary feature from any column.

Try This:

1. Open the QDB.
2. Select the Group tab.
3. Select the Total (Sale Amount) No. 3 associated column.
4. Click the Associate button.

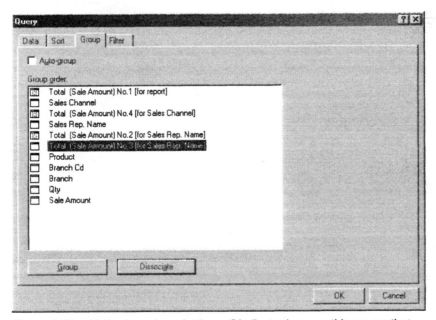

Figure 9.31   Notice how the splat "smart" indicator is gone, this means that the column is not dependent on where it lies in the report.

5. Click OK to run the report.

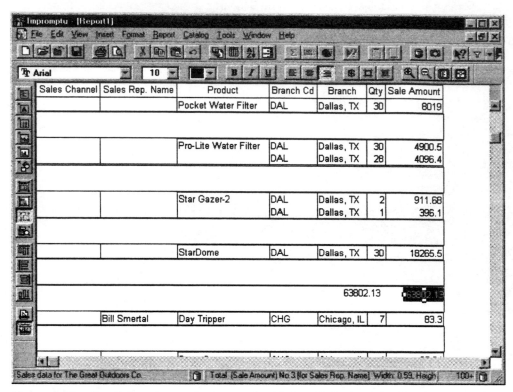

Figure 9.32   Scroll down to see the two totals side by side in the Sales Rep Name footer.

Now, move this total to a column position with the following steps:

6. Select the same column you just converted to a normal.
7. Click and drag it down until the vertical dashed line appears to the right of Sale Amount and let go.

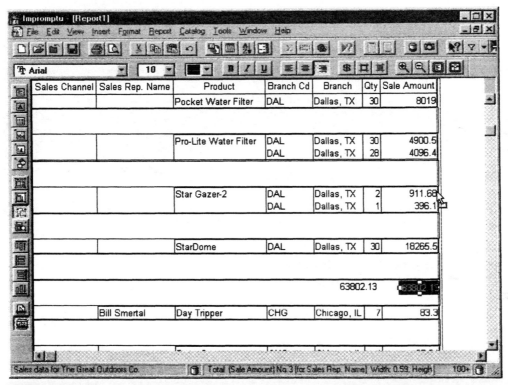

Figure 9.33   The dashed lines for the Product column indicated the moved column.

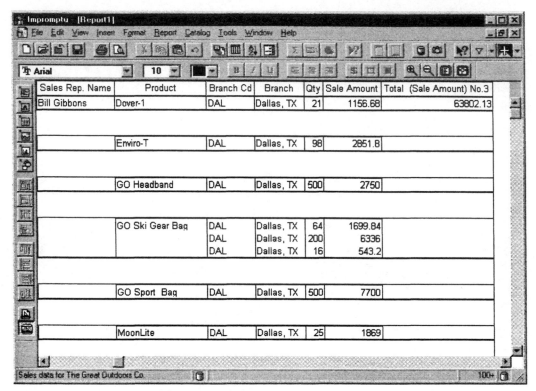

Figure 9.34   The report results show the Sales Rep Name total next to the detail Sale Amount column.

Question	Answer
Back in chapter 5, I learned how to include headers into our reports. Now that we know about totals, can I create a header and put a total in it?	"You really shouldn't, *but*, sometimes you can." That means, technically, yes, you can create a header for any given column and move a total into that area.
	The "but" comes into play when Impromptu has to do it. When Impromptu requests data from the database to populate the report, it generally takes the first 100 or so rows and uses them to populate the screen. By moving a total up to a header, you may be asking Impromptu to grab many rows to populate that one cell. This can do several undesirable things; it can
	1. Slow down the database.
	2. Make Impromptu take a long time to process the query and the report.
	What I advise people to do is try it. If the report takes too long to run, there are many things that could be wrong, and for this report, it may or may not be worth investigating. But you will not know until you try.

Tip

If you ever run into a situation where Impromptu seems like it has been "running forever," or if you did something that caused Impromptu to run the report, you can stop Impromptu from running the query by pressing the Esc key. This lets Impromptu know that you want the query request to stop.

Word of advice: sometimes it may take a few seconds for Impromptu to realize that you hit the Esc key. Impromptu may be waiting to hear back from the database, or it may be busy working on something. Don't worry, it will receive the Esc key request, and it will stop the query if the database you are using permits. So hitting several times out of frustration will not do you any good.

A Final Word on Associations

The final topic we need to cover before we are completed with the basics of Totaling is the one last piece on Associations. Impromptu provides report developers with the ability to change associations several different ways, a couple of which we have done. The following section discusses the other way of associating columns—by using the Data Definition box.

Ways We Know

One way of changing a column's association is by moving it around the report. Impromptu provides you with the ability to manipulate the way it automatically associates (Smart Summaries) to the new position in the layout of the report. This changes what the total is *for* and its association.

The other way we know of changing a column's association is with the QDB's Group tab. Here you can create associations, move them around from one grouped column to another, and even remove associations you do not want. You did this in the last chapter when you associated the Branch Code to the Branch.

A New Way to Associate

The last way to manipulate a column's association is by directly changing it through that column's Data Definition. Inside the definition of every column is a dropdown box to allow a report developer to associate this column to a grouped column.

Take a moment to look at some definitions in the current report.

Try This:

1. Open the QDB.
2. Select the first total column, Total (Sale Amount) No. 4.
3. Click the 'Edit Definition...' button.

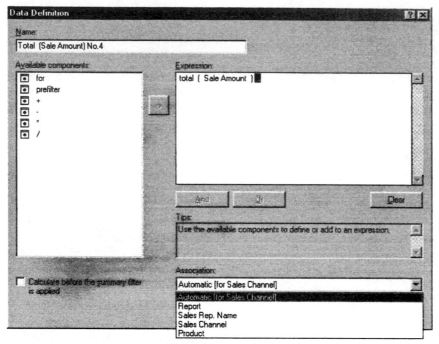

Figure 9.35   The Data Definition box for Total (Sale Amount) No. 4. This is originally an Automatic association for Sales Channel.

Note

Initially, the box contains Automatic (our smart summary at work), and when you open the drop-down, you can select any column that has been grouped as well as associate this total for the entire "Report." Changing the association dropdown from Automatic to another grouped column removes the automatic feature of this total.

4. Select Report from the Association dropdown.
5. Click OK to return to the QDB (Figure 9.36).

Selecting this makes this column a grand total for the entire report.

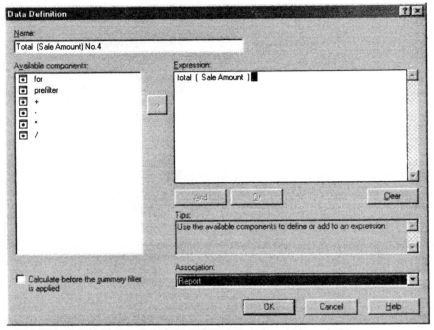

Figure 9.36   The new association for Total (Sale Amount) No. 4.

Tip

Using the right click on a column, you can go directly to the Data Definition. While looking at the report layout,

1. *Right click on any Total (Sale Amount).*
2. *From the Flyout menu, select the Data Definition... selection.*

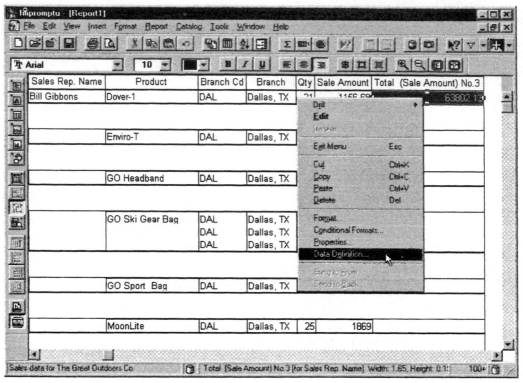

Figure 9.37   The Flyout to select the Data definition.

Not Just Totals

Associating columns applies to other columns as well. In the report you have been using, these include the Qty, Sale Amount, Branch, and Branch Code columns. Each of these columns has the Associations dropdown in its Data Definitions, which means they can be associated as well. Initially these columns are Associated to nothing, or "none." Changing the association from "none" in these columns to a grouped column will most likely create a confusing result for a user.

Note

This works well only in the situation that was described in the last chapter when a column has a one-to-one relationship with a grouped column.

Other Ways of Adding Totals

Until this point in the chapter, point and click was the only way of adding summaries to a report. Now, you get to learn the other ways of adding summaries to a report.

Two other ways to add summaries are

- Using the Insert.Calculation.
- Using the QDB.

Create a Total Using Insert.Calculation

This technique is the same one used when you inserted a calculation in Chapter 7. The only difference here is that you know more about Impromptu, and you have experience in building totals. Knowing how to create a calculation and having some knowledge of totals, you can dive right into creating totals using Insert.Calculation.

Report Requirement

Boss: *The total Sale Amounts are nice, but can you add a total Qty just for each Product?*

Analysis

This request calls for a simple addition of a Summary, which can be translated into: *Total (Qty)* for each Product.

Steps to Use Insert.Calculation in a Summary

1. Select Insert. Calculation from the Menu bar. This allows you to place the calculation.

You can now place this calculation wherever you wish on the layout of the report. As you move your cursor around, you will notice either a dashed box or a vertical dashed line. The dashed box signifies that this is a grouped level, most likely a footer, but if you added a header to the report, the same rule applies. When the cursor is a dashed vertical line, Impromptu is letting you know that this will be interpreted as a column. Impromptu is waiting for you to find a place and click to let it know when you choose a spot.

2. For our example, place it in the Product footer.

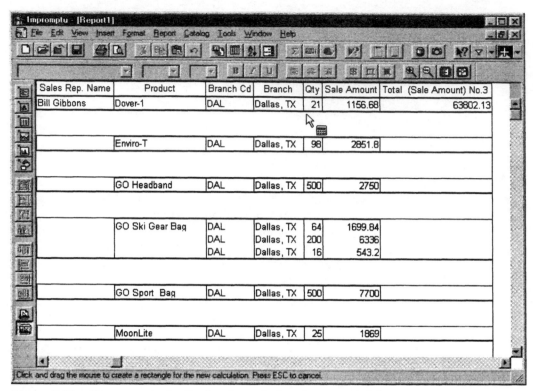

Figure 9.38   The cursor in the Product footer before the mouse click.

Immediately you will see the Calculation Definition box appear. This is where you will create the new total.

3. Name this Total Qty.
4. Expand the "Summaries" folder.
5. Double click on the Total summary (Figure 9.39).

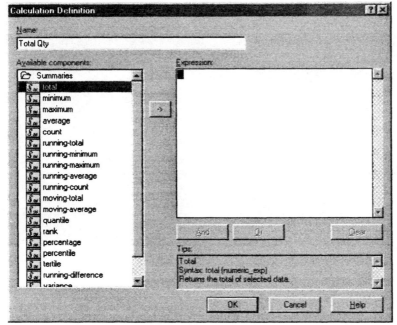

Figure 9.39
The summaries folder contains several summary calculations, which are discussed later in this chapter.

6. Expand the Report Folder.
7. Select the Qty column (Figure 9.40).
8. Click OK to run the report.

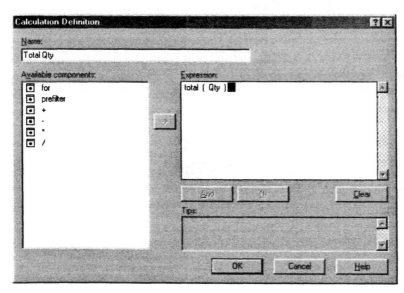

Figure 9.40
The finished calculated column.

And the Results Are...

	Sales Channel	Sales Rep. Name	Product	Branch Cd	Branch	Qty	Sale Amount	Total (Sale Am
	Direct Sales	Bill Gibbons	Dover-1	DAL	Dallas, TX	21	1156.68	
						21		
			Enviro-T	DAL	Dallas, TX	98	2851.8	
						98		
			GO Headband	DAL	Dallas, TX	500	2750	
						500		
			GO Ski Gear Bag	DAL	Dallas, TX	64	1699.84	
				DAL	Dallas, TX	200	6336	
				DAL	Dallas, TX	16	543.2	
						280		
			GO Sport Bag	DAL	Dallas, TX	500	7700	
						500		
			MoonLite	DAL	Dallas, TX	25	1869	
						25		

Figure 9.41   The report results with Total Qty calculated.

Once you press OK, Impromptu takes this new calculation, places it in the query, and sends a request off to the database. When the data comes back, Impromptu places the new value where you choose to put it. After this is done, you can format it and move it around to the exact position you desire.

Creating a Total Using the QDB

The final way to create a Total is by way of the QDB. This ability to create totals in the QDB is an extension of the ability to create calculations from the Data tab. Since summaries are an extension to a calculation, it makes sense to give a report developer the ability to do this from the QDB.

Report Requirement and Analysis

Instead of adding another report requirement, let's just add the Total Qty column again to the report. Remember, you can add as many columns as you like.

Steps to Create a Summary in the QDB

1. Open the QDB and select the Data tab if it is not already selected.
2. Expand the Orders folder.
3. Expand the Order Details folder.
4. Single Click on the Qty column in the Catalog.

> **Note**
>
> *Selecting a column from the Catalog enables the Summary button in the QDB.*

5. Click the Summary button.
6. Click the Total button in the "Summaries of…" window.

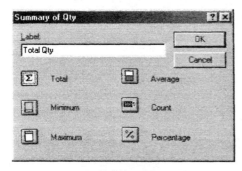

Figure 9.42
These are the Summary functions available directly from the QDB.

7. Rename the label "QDB Total Qty."
8. Click OK (Figure 9.43).
9. Click OK to run the report.

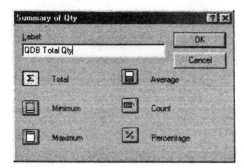

Figure 9.43
The completed "Summary of…" window.

And the Results Are…

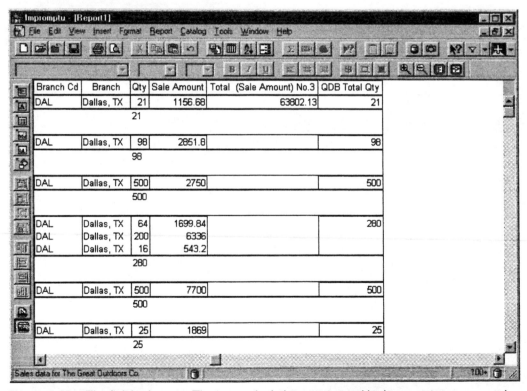

Branch Cd	Branch	Qty	Sale Amount	Total (Sale Amount) No.3	QDB Total Qty
DAL	Dallas, TX	21	1156.68	63802.13	21
		21			
DAL	Dallas, TX	98	2851.8		98
		98			
DAL	Dallas, TX	500	2750		500
		500			
DAL	Dallas, TX	64	1699.84		280
DAL	Dallas, TX	200	6336		
DAL	Dallas, TX	16	543.2		
		280			
DAL	Dallas, TX	500	7700		500
		500			
DAL	Dallas, TX	25	1869		25
		25			

Sales data for The Great Outdoors Co.

Figure 9.44   The finished report. The new calculation was treated by Impromptu as a normal column to be inserted to the report and a Smart Summary to the lowest grouped column.

Impromptu runs the report and places the calculation as if it were just another column to be displayed. From earlier in this chapter, you should be comfortable with moving the column around into a footer if you like.

Summaries: More Than Just Totals

Now that you are familiar with Totals, let's take a look at some other options available to use in the summaries folder. Not only can Impromptu add items up and put them in a calculated column, but it can also use totals in calculations, in functions, and in filters.

Different Summaries

Impromptu can do more than just create totals. Inside the Summaries folder, you can see that there are quite a few options, 20 to be exact.

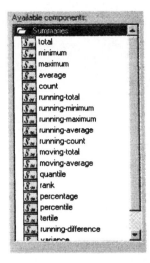

Figure 9.45
The expanded
Summaries section.

The first five summaries listed are basic summaries that Impromptu can pass on to the database, so it can do the calculating. The rest of the summaries listed are performed by a combination of Impromptu processing and database processing. These may take a little longer to process on some reports, but that is OK, considering what has to be done to perform some of these calculations. The extra time is well worth it.

Report Requirement

Boss: *I would like a count of the number of sales per Product.*

Analysis

This request calls on one of the new summary calculations: Count. Go ahead and create this new summary using the calculation button from the QDB.

Steps to Create "Different" Summaries

1. Open the QDB.
2. Select the Calculate button.
3. Name this column "Count Sales."
4. Expand the Summaries folder.
5. Select the Count summary function.
6. Expand the Report Columns folder.

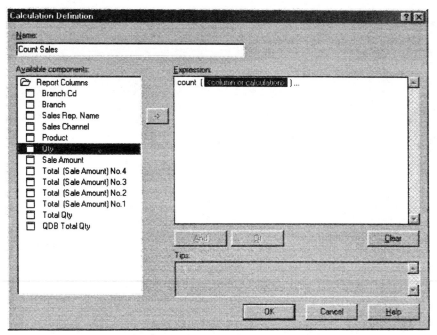

Figure 9.46   The list of columns from the query includes numeric, string columns, and even the totals.

Note

Notice how the selection list is not limited to numeric columns—that just means you can count either numeric items, like Sale Amounts, or text descriptions, like Branches.

7. Select Qty.

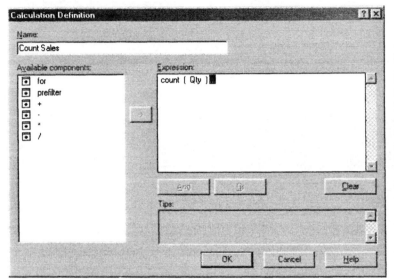

Figure 9.47
The completed Calcu-
lation Definition win-
dow. Notice how here,
you do not have the
option to select which
grouped item to asso-
ciate with; it is auto-
matically associated to
the lowest grouping:
the Product column. If
you want to control it,
you would have to
"Edit Definition" the
new column after it is
created to change it to
a desired association.

8. Click OK to complete the new calculation (Figure 9.48).
9. Click OK to run the report.

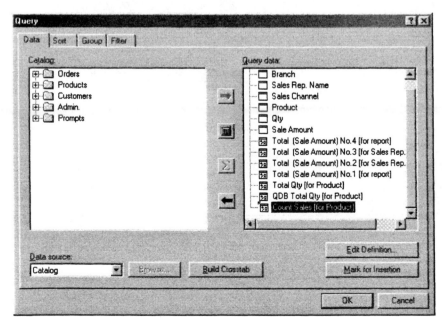

Figure 9.48
Since the
Product is the
lowest level of
grouping, this
Summary cal-
culation
defaults to it.

And the Results Are…

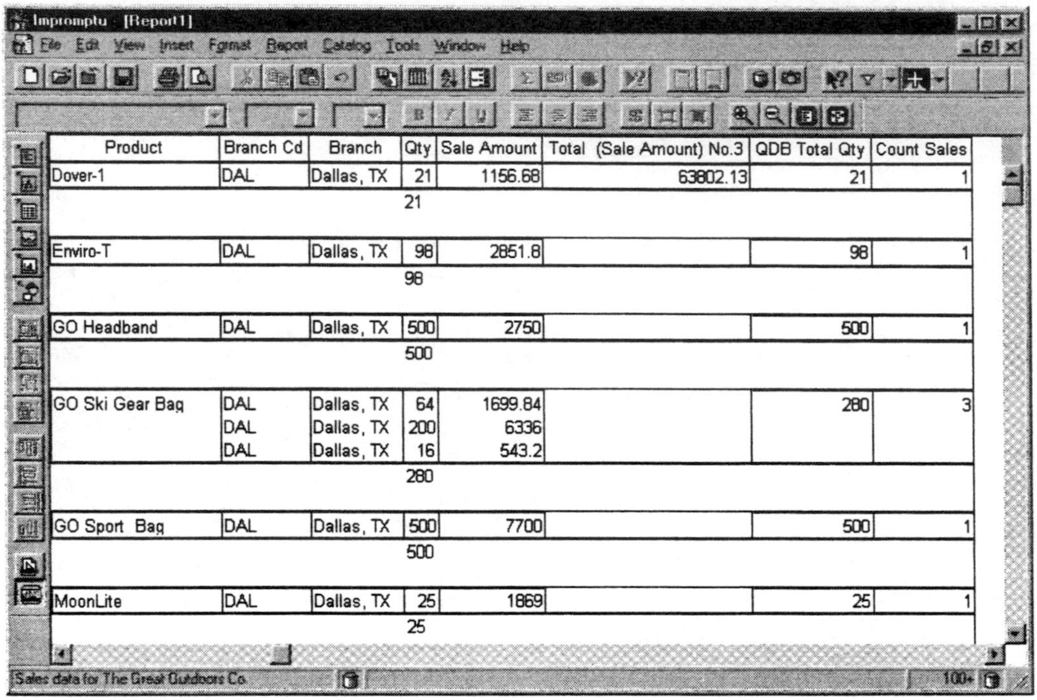

Product	Branch Cd	Branch	Qty	Sale Amount	Total (Sale Amount) No.3	QDB Total Qty	Count Sales
Dover-1	DAL	Dallas, TX	21	1156.68	63802.13	21	1
			21				
Enviro-T	DAL	Dallas, TX	98	2851.8		98	1
			98				
GO Headband	DAL	Dallas, TX	500	2750		500	1
			500				
GO Ski Gear Bag	DAL	Dallas, TX	64	1699.84		280	3
	DAL	Dallas, TX	200	6336			
	DAL	Dallas, TX	16	543.2			
			280				
GO Sport Bag	DAL	Dallas, TX	500	7700		500	1
			500				
MoonLite	DAL	Dallas, TX	25	1869		25	1
			25				

Figure 9.49 The report results.

Impromptu runs the report and inserts the new calculation as a column in the report. If you do not like this here, you can move it wherever you like. Remember, however, it was created as an Automatic association.

A Complete Totals Report from Scratch

You have learned how to create summaries many different ways in an existing report. Now, let's create a new report and build a summary calculation before we run the query even once.

What you will be building is a Summary Report. The easiest way to explain this type of report is to build it and explain it as we go along. Here's the requirement to complete the exercise.

Report Requirements

Boss: *Create a product total sales report by Sales Rep, Product Line, and Product.*

Analysis

In your analysis of this requirement, you can conclude that the hierarchy is Sales Rep, Product Line, and then Product. Also, it appears that the only number required is a total sale amount for the lowest level of grouping, Product. So, you're looking at three columns, all grouped, and then one total calculation, associated to the lowest level of grouping.

Steps to Build a new Summary Report

1. Click the New report button from the toolbar to create a new simple list report.

Populate the report with the first three columns, in the following order:

2. Expand the Orders folder.
3. Expand the Additional Info folder.
4. Select the Sales Rep. Name.
5. Expand the Order Details folder.
6. Select the Line No.
7. Select the Product.

Create the Summary:

8. In the Order Details folder, single click on the Sale Amount column in the Catalog.
9. Click the Summary button.

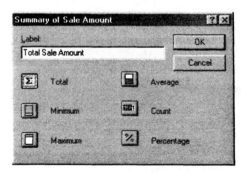

Figure 9.50
The "Summary of ..." window.

Summary Function	Description
Total	Creates a Total for the associated grouping.
Minimum & Maximum	Selects the minimum/maximum value from a grouping it is associated with.
Average	Calculates the average of the value based on the grouped column that this summary will be associated with.
Count	Counts the occurrences of the selected value for the grouped column that it is associated with.
Percentage	Same as the Average button; it takes the column and displays its percentage of the grouped column this Summary is associated with.

10. Click the Total button.

11. Click OK.

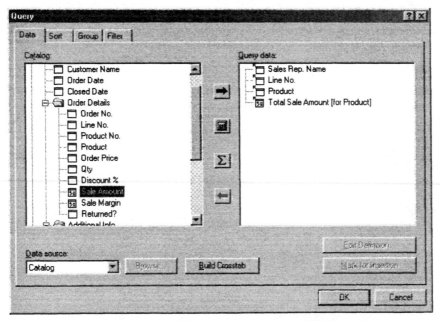

Figure 9.51   The completed QDB for the Summary report.

By default, this new summary calculation is turned into a Smart Summary.

Question	Answer
Hey, isn't a smart summary associated with a grouped column? We haven't grouped any columns yet, so how can it be associated to Product?	This is a part that needs a one-time explanation; after that, it is perfectly clear. So far, you have built a report by selecting several columns and grouping by one lone summary calculation. Since everything in your report is either being grouped on or is a summary calculation, you have a summary report. This is the definition of a summary report, and when Impromptu can identify this, it looks to do this whenever possible.

The key behind automatically grouping all columns is a check box in the Group tab.

12. Select the Group tab and look at the check box at the top.

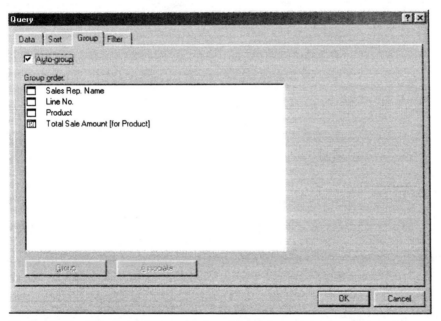

Figure 9.52   When the Auto-group is selected, Impromptu recognizes that you wish to turn this into a summary report anytime you create a summary calculation from the initial creation of a report.

You can turn this off anytime you wish. When this feature is turned off and you insert a summary calculation from the QDB's Data tab Summary button, the newly created Summary will *not* become a smart summary for the entire report, since there are no columns to be automatically grouped and associated.

13. Click OK to run the report.

And the Results Are...

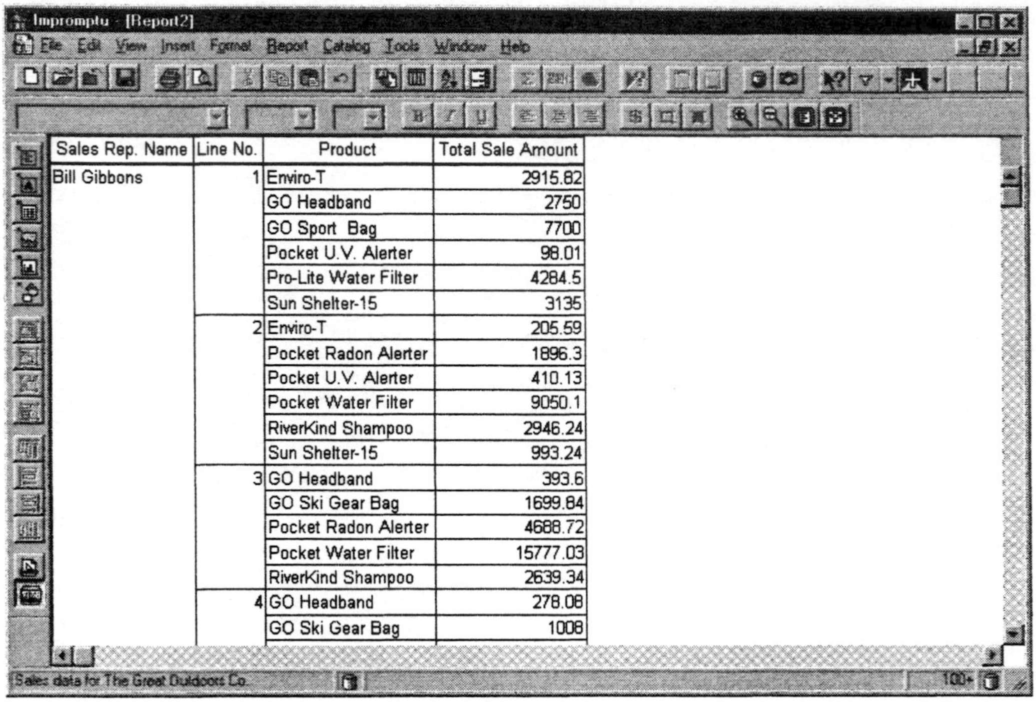

Sales Rep. Name	Line No.	Product	Total Sale Amount
Bill Gibbons	1	Enviro-T	2915.82
		GO Headband	2750
		GO Sport Bag	7700
		Pocket U.V. Alerter	98.01
		Pro-Lite Water Filter	4284.5
		Sun Shelter-15	3135
	2	Enviro-T	205.59
		Pocket Radon Alerter	1896.3
		Pocket U.V. Alerter	410.13
		Pocket Water Filter	9050.1
		RiverKind Shampoo	2946.24
		Sun Shelter-15	993.24
	3	GO Headband	393.6
		GO Ski Gear Bag	1699.84
		Pocket Radon Alerter	4688.72
		Pocket Water Filter	15777.03
		RiverKind Shampoo	2639.34
	4	GO Headband	278.08
		GO Ski Gear Bag	1008

Figure 9.53 The report results.

Congratulations, you have built your first summary report. Every calculation was executed before the first query was requested by Impromptu to the database. Once you become more comfortable with Impromptu, building reports, and most important, converting requirements into reports, you will build more and more of the report before you "run" the report for the first time.

Summary

The main points we learned from this chapter are:

1. How to create a summary.
2. What a smart summary is.
3. How to move summaries around in the layout of a report.

4. How associations are applied to other cases.

5. What other summary functions are available.

6. How to create a summary report.

Here you had to thoroughly know groupings and association as explained in a previous chapter before making sense of summaries. And even during the explanation of summaries, it took an entire chapter of building on information and knowledge acquired previously before you could arrive at a complete picture of Impromptu's full summary capabilities.

Advanced Impromptu Reporting

Stopping here and diving into building your reports is a fine decision. You have all of the tools to build 80% of all the reports you need. Put the book up on the shelf... for a while. This will give you the time you need to let everything sink in. There is so much to Impromptu; you should not expect to learn everything in a day either.

When you do come back, take a peek at these chapters. I have to warn you though, once you look at just one of the topics, you might find yourself covering the entire chapter. The next thing you know, you will be at the end of the book, and you will have a ton of new ideas for reports, and, unfortunately, more work.

Prompt Reporting

Impromptu provides you with an automated way to select the filter criteria for a report called a Prompt. Prompting allows you to write one report and have users see results based on the Prompt's filtering criteria selected. This is an extremely powerful and flexible feature. Impromptu provides the report developer with an easy-to-use dialog box to set up Prompts and create a Prompt without any programming. And, as you can guess, Impromptu is not shy about providing several different means to include Prompting in a report.

This chapter looks at the powerful features of Prompting, including the following:

- Examining an existing Prompt Report
- Building a Basic Prompt Report
- Multiple Prompts on one report
- Different types of Prompts
- Prompts in Catalogs
- Unique ways of using Prompts in filters

First, Let's See a Finished One

This chapter starts with opening an existing Prompt report. For Prompts, I like to walk through an example to explain what is happening before we create a new one. After viewing the existing report, we will build a basic report to be used throughout the chapter. In this basic report, we cover the steps and techniques of creating Prompts.

Impromptu comes with several examples of highly involved reports, and some have excellent examples of Prompting. You will see how a user interacts with a Prompt, learn how Prompts are used in the development of a report, and open up a Prompt. The report used is an example of an advanced Prompt report. It contains logic that is described at the end of the chapter. Let's open this Prompt report and step through it to see an end result.

Note

The report we will use is part of the samples loaded in a typical Impromptu installation. If you did not load them or deleted them from your disk drive, take a moment to retrieve them by going through a customized installation and selecting only the samples to install. Trust me; interacting with this report and those in the other chapters in Part 3 is well worth every second.

Opening Your First Prompt Report

1. Open Impromptu.
2. Select from the Menu option File.Open.
3. Select from the directory structure:

   ```
   <drive you installed Impromptu>:\Program Files\Cognos\cer1\Samples\
   Impromptu\Reports
   ```

4. Open report: Product Quantity Sales (Prompt) and log on to the Catalog if required. You are immediately greeted with your first Prompt:

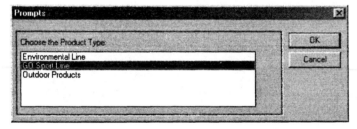

Figure 10.1
The first Prompt.

Each Prompt contains a message created by the report developer describing the particular Prompt request. This is the area where you, the report consumer, may choose the selection. Once the selection has been made, you may click OK.

Note

This Prompt allows you to choose more than one Product Type. This is done by holding down either the Ctrl or the Shift key. Remember, the Ctrl key allows for individual multiple selections, and the Shift key selects all of the columns between the current selected column and the next one you select.

5. Let's keep it simple the first time around, and just choose one: Select "GO Sport Line."

6. Click OK to continue running the report.

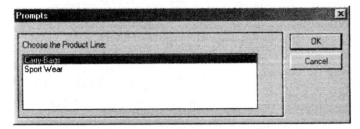

Figure 10.2
Again, we can select more than one option.

You are greeted with another Prompt. This time the report is asking you to choose a line from Products listed. You do not have to know this, but the product lines described here are only lines within the "GO Sport Line." The first Prompt told the second Prompt what to ask for.

7. Choose only the "Carry-Bag" from this filter.

8. Click OK to run the report.

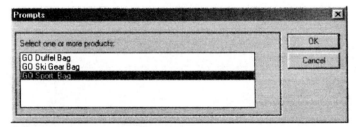

Figure 10.3
The third Prompt for just the products.

Another Prompt! OK, this is the last one. First we narrowed down our criteria from all Product Types to "GO Sport Line," then, we wanted to see only the "Carry-Bags"; now, we can choose which bag we wish to see for this report.

9. Select the "GO Sport Bag."

10. Click OK (Figure 10.4).

The report you are now looking at is an advanced Prompting report. It used such elements as multiple items selects and nested Prompts. The basic principle of Prompting, however, was displayed well.

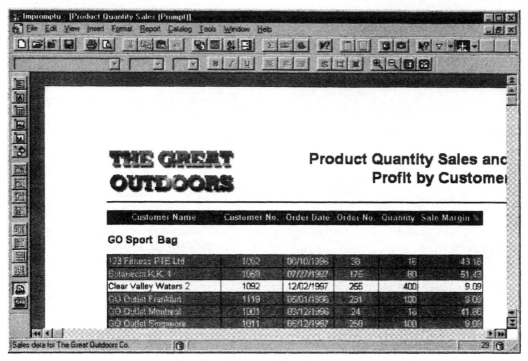

Figure 10.4   The report result. The Prompting trimmed down the report to the specific product.

Question	Answer
Why don't we just create one report for each Product? Then when you want a specific product, you just run that report.	There are two reasons why we used a Prompt report here: 1. There are 35 unique Products across the three Lines within this theoretical Great Outdoors Company. This Prompting saved us from having to build 34 additional, nearly identical reports that you would have to make changes to if something needed changing. Having one report cuts that task down to one report to maintain. 2. With the multiple selection, you can choose any combination of Products, and get the report results.

Under the Hood of the Prompt

Now, that the Prompt report is finished, take this opportunity to see where this Prompt thing is. Prompts are used to either filter in desired/wanted information or filter out unwanted information. This depends solely on how they are set up in the report. They key point here is that Prompts are used in the Filter tab of the QDB, which is where we will find our Prompts.

Try This:

1. Open the QDB.
2. Select the Filter tab.

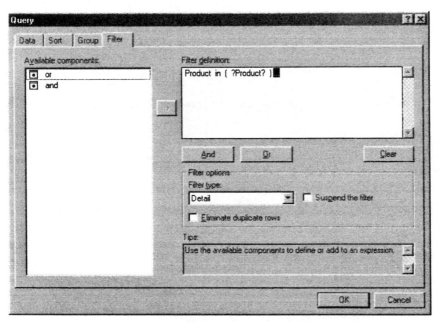

Figure 10.5   We can quickly identify that this is a Prompt Filter because the item in the parenthesis is not a column but has question marks before and after the word Product.

Even though there were three Prompts when you ran this last report, for the purpose of this chapter, we will look at just the last Prompt displayed in that series of Prompts. Because of the nature of Nested Prompts, there is only one Prompt in this report, the last Prompt for Product. This is explained completely further in this chapter.

One thing to keep in mind here is the use of the "in" operand in the filter comparison. The "in" operand allows for multiple items to be compared. This was what made it possible to select more than one product at a time.

Finally, let's see what the development screen looks like for a Prompt.

3. Double click on the Prompt '?Product?'.

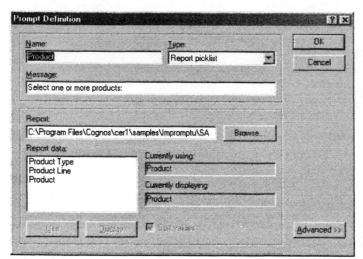

Figure 10.6
The Prompt Definition
window.

For now, we will only point out the more obvious part. Later, we will get under the hood to look at the details. The first part is the label of the Prompt as we saw it in the Filter Definition. You can change this label as often as you like and whenever you like. Any changes made to the name will be passed throughout the report, wherever the Prompt is used, automatically by Impromptu.

The second obvious part is the Prompt message. This is the message that instructs us on what to do with this Prompt. Like the Prompt name, this can be changed at any time.

To get out of the Prompt area of the report

1. Click Cancel.
2. Click Cancel to not run the report.

Question	Answer
I saw only one Prompt in the Filter Definition. When we opened the report we had to answer three different Prompts. Where are the other two?	The other two Prompts were part of an elaborate nesting of Prompts called cascading Prompts. The Prompts are real, they exist, but in a place outside the current Product Quantity Sales report. Without going into a detailed explanation, the ?Product? Prompt we looked at called up another report that had a Prompt in it as well.
	The same applies to that report; it had a Prompt in it asking for another report, which also had a Prompt in it, thus giving a total of three Prompts. When we run our report, each one of these Prompts must be satisfied in order for our filter to be populated.

Now that we are done looking at an elaborate Prompt report, leave it open because we will look at this report later in the chapter. Let's continue with the basics of building a Prompt report.

Building a Basic Prompt Report

To build a Prompt report, we need to identify when a report requires Prompts. In most real-life cases, users are not going to come right up to us and say "Hey, how about whipping together a Prompt report for me?" More often, we as report developers have to identify from a reporting requirement whether to use Prompts. This may mean following up with a user to make sure the report that you're developing will answer their needs.

Take a look at a report requirement and determine whether it needs a Prompt.

Report Requirement

Provide a report showing for each product, the Product Type, the Product, who sold it, who bought it, when it was ordered, the sale amount, and whether it was returned.

Analysis

This requirement has the potential for being a Prompt report; however, a savvy report developer will ask a follow-up question, such as:

> *Would you like to be able to choose a specific product one at a time or do you just want to see all of the products all of the time, but grouped together.*

This follow-up question provides some insight into how the report consumer plans on using the report. The answer to a question like: "*...choose a specific...one at a time or...all of the products...*" can determine if a filter is even needed. *One at a time* translates into using a filter and the "=" operand, while *all of the products* translates into no filter and grouping the products.

Based on the report user's answer, we may or may not have a Prompt report. For this example, let's assume that the user replied to the follow-up question with this response:

> *It would be nice to be able to go in and select just one or even a couple at a time. You know, I get this old report, and it just dumps out all of the products. I don't even know half of the stuff listed. Just look at the stack of paper in my recycling bin just from this morning.*

Well there you have it, a Prompt report waiting to happen. From the user's response, we are even able to discern what type of operand to use in the filter: "*in,*" because of the report consumer's phrase "*even a couple at a time.*"

Let's start by converting the initial requirement into a Report requirement; we can use

- Product Type (product type)
- Product (product)
- Sales Rep Name (who sold it)
- Customer (who bought it)
- Order Date (when it was ordered)
- Sale Amount
- Return? (when it was returned)

Since there was no mention of creating a total for Sale Amount, normally we would go back to the user and ask if he or she would like to see special groupings and any totals. Because we are focusing on Prompts, we will skip this follow-up question.

I break down building a Prompt report into two steps:

1. Building the basic report
2. Creating the Prompt

Step 1: Build the Report

Now, to build the report, create a Simple List report with the following columns:

1. Click the new report toolbar button.

   In the QDB:

2. Expand the Products folder.
3. Select the Product Type column.
4. Expand the Order folder, and then the Order Details folder.
5. Select the Product column.
6. Expand the Additional Info folder.
7. Select the Sales Rep Name.
8. Scroll back up to the main Orders folder.
9. Select Customer Name.
10. Select Order Date.
11. Scroll back down to the Order Details folder.
12. Select Sale Amount.
13. Select Returned? (Figure 10.7)

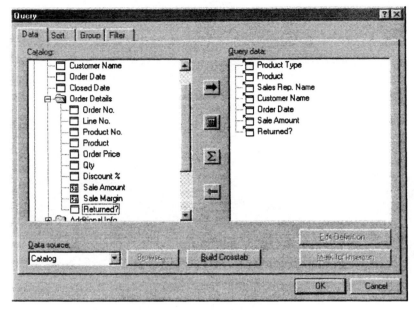

Figure 10.7
Data tab with all
of the columns
selected.

Going back to the requirements, we see that the report consumer wanted to be able to select one or more products. For this to work, we really should group on Product.

Go ahead and group the Product column:

14. Click on the Group tab.
15. Double click on Product.

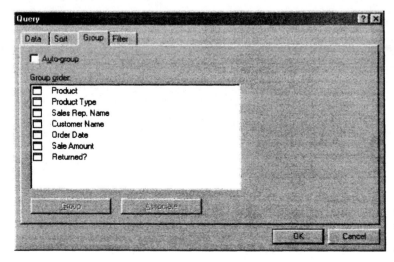

Figure 10.8
Group tab with
Product grouped.

Step 2: Create the Prompt

Before you click OK to run the report, first set up the Prompt Filter. To meet the report requirements, the Prompt Filter must be able to filter on one or more products. This is achieved by using the "in" operand. Writing out the filter beforehand gives us something like this:

> Product in (?Product Prompt?).

While still in the QDB,

16. Click on the Filter tab.
17. Open the Report Columns folder.
18. Select Product.
19. Go back into the recently changed Available Components Toolbox and select the "in" operand.
20. Select the open parenthesis "(".
21. Double click on the Prompt Manager.

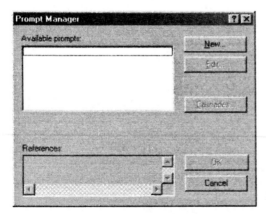

Figure 10.9
Prompt Manager—You may initially
see this window for only a second.

The Prompt Manager takes care of all of the Prompts for this report. There's a flicker of the screen, and then you see the Prompt Definition window. Initially, the Prompt Manager opens, recognizes that this report does not have any Prompts, and quickly displays a blank Prompt Definition window (Figure 10.10).

The Prompt Definition window is another interactive window. The contents of the window depend on the selection of the Type dropdown selection box. Initially, the box's default Type appears, a "type in" Prompt. There are four different types of Prompts used by Impromptu. Each one is available from this dropdown selection and is covered subsequently.

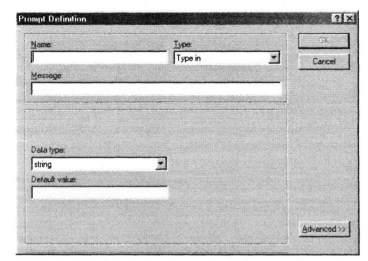

Figure 10.10
The Prompt Definition
window.

22. Give this Prompt a name: Product Prompt.
23. Change the type of Prompt from "Type In' to 'Catalog Picklist."

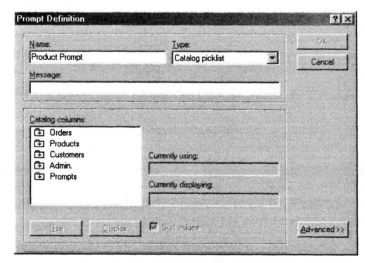

Figure 10.11
The Prompt Definition as it
changed to a Catalog Picklist
type.

Note

The Catalog Picklist allows the report developer to identify a column from the Catalog to be used to populate the Picklist. This populated list is displayed when the users view this Prompt. The Catalog points directly to the database, and therefore the Prompt is continuously populated by the most current Products list available. Getting the data to populate the Picklist does two things:

1. *It ensures that the Prompt displays the exact values from the database.*
2. *It ensures that the users of the report will choose the correct values, which in turn will provide an accurate filter.*

When the Catalog Picklist type is selected, the interactive window changes. The bottom half of the Prompt Definition window changes to allow a report developer to choose a column from the Catalog. The Catalog seen here is the same Catalog you have been working with in other areas of Impromptu. Nothing has changed, because we are now in the Prompt Definition window.

Next, select the proper column to use in the Prompt:

24. Expand the Order folder.
25. Expand the Order Details folder.
26. Since this Prompt shows the Products, click on Product once.

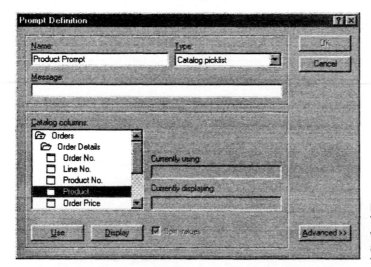

Figure 10.12
The Catalog Columns section with use and display buttons and side labels.

There are two buttons beneath the Catalog column selection box. They are Use and Display. The Use button relates to what Catalog column the Prompt will use back in the Filter Definition. The Display button controls what Catalog column is presented to the report consumer.

Question	Answer
Why have two different columns?	The separation of these two is important for the scenario in which user of the report understands only products, not the product numbers. In this case, the report filters on product numbers. Separating the two allows the user to understand the Prompt, using the Display column; and the filter to perform a comparison, using the Use column.

In this Prompt, we are concerned only with the Product:

27. Click the Use button.

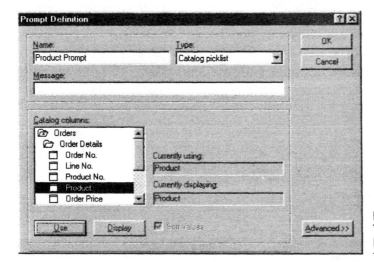

Figure 10.13
The bottom half of the Prompt Definition.

When you select the Use button, Impromptu defaults the column you have highlighted to both the Use and Display items, in this case as a Product.

Before we are finished, there is one more thing to do:

28. Type in a message for the users: Select one or more Products (Figure 10.14).

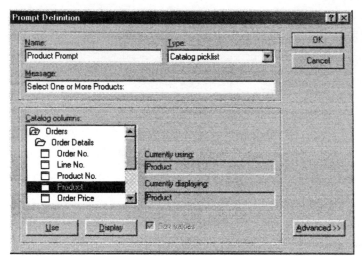

Figure 10.14
Congratulations! You have
developed your first Prompt.

29. Click OK to complete the Prompt Definition.

This takes you back to the Prompt Manager, and as you can see, there is now one Prompt for this report, called "Product Prompt."

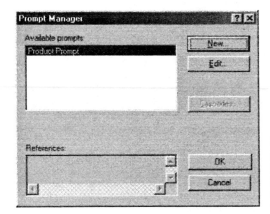

Figure 10.15
As you add more Prompts to this report,
they will appear in this list. Whether you
use them or not, they are in the report
until you delete them.

30. Since this is the Prompt we want, click OK.

31. From the toolbox, Double click the ")" close parenthesis.

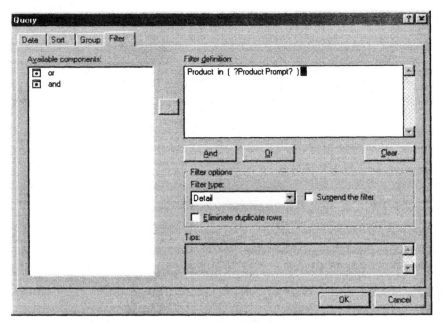

Figure 10.16   The completed Filter Definition.

32. Click OK to run the report.

Impromptu immediately goes out to the database, as the Prompt instructs because of the Catalog Picklist, and populates it with a list of unique products.

1. Select the Day Tripper and hold down the Ctrl key and select the Enviro-Kit.
2. Click OK to finish the Prompt, and run the report.

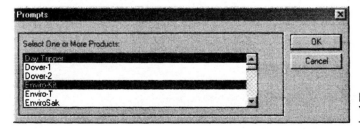

Figure 10.17
Your first Prompts window.

And the Results Are...

Product Type	Product	Sales Rep. Name	Customer Name	Order Date	Sale Amount	Returned?
Outdoor Products	Day Tripper	Bjorn Flertjan	GO Outlet Kista AB	08/11/1996	80.36	N
Outdoor Products		Thomas Brigade	Rock Steady 3	08/15/1996	340.2	N
Outdoor Products		Henri LeDuc	Clear Valley Waters 2	02/17/1996	10.64	N
Outdoor Products		Malcom Young	OutBack Pty 2	09/28/1996	81.34	N
Outdoor Products		Kaley Gregson	OutBack Pty 1	03/04/1996	179.2	N
Outdoor Products		Lyn Jacobs	GO Outlet London	05/02/1996	206.08	N
Outdoor Products		Thomas Brigade	GO Outlet London	04/03/1996	11.2	N
Outdoor Products		Henri LeDuc	Kay Mart 4	02/17/1996	45.36	N
Outdoor Products		Torey Wandiko	OutBack Pty 4	07/27/1996	130.2	N
Outdoor Products		Malcom Young	OutBack Pty 2	10/30/1997	142.8	N
Outdoor Products		Lisa Testorok	New Wave Wilderness 2	09/16/1997	32.76	N
Outdoor Products		Lisa Testorok	New Wave Wilderness 2	04/01/1997	103.32	N
Outdoor Products		Thomas Brigade	Trees to Seas Ltd	05/01/1997	76.44	N
Outdoor Products		Tony Armarillo	Pro Form Supplies 4	07/03/1997	48.16	N
Outdoor Products		Bill Smertal	Act'N'Up Fitness 3	02/18/1997	83.3	N
Outdoor Products		Dave Mustaine	Act'N'Up Fitness 1	02/17/1997	34.86	N
Outdoor Products		Malcom Young	OutBack Pty 2	12/20/1997	91.14	N
Outdoor Products		Inigo Montoya	Ultra Sports 1	02/13/1997	68.04	N
Outdoor Products		Kaley Gregson	OutBack Pty 3	08/17/1997	147.84	N
Outdoor Products		Gilles Turcotte	GO Outlet Paris	08/20/1997	114.8	N

Figure 10.18   The report results. It looks a little raw without a proper header, but we are concerned at this time only with what the details look like.

Congratulations, you have built and run your first Prompt report. Take a moment and review the tabs in the QDB. The report you just created is the most common Prompt report built in Impromptu.

Tip: Re-Query the Report

What if you wanted to see another product, or you inadvertently selected the wrong product and you wanted to rerun the Prompt.

It's quite easy. There are two ways for you to re-Prompt the report:

- From the toolbar, Press the Prompt button ![Prompt button], or
- From the Menu, select Report.Prompt.

And you will be re-Prompted; you can select an entirely new Product for this report. The Prompt values will be put into the filter, and the outgoing request to the database and the report results will be changed.

Prompt Manager

Now that we have gone the entire way through building a Prompt report, we can discuss maintaining the Prompt over time. This means that there may be changes to the Prompt, the report may require more Prompts to further satisfy the users, or the Prompt may not be needed anymore. All of these situations can be dealt with by using the Prompt Manager.

Let's go inside the Prompt Manager:

- From the Menu bar, select: Report.Prompt Manager...

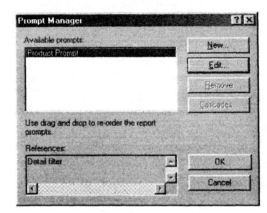

Figure 10.19
The Prompt Manager.

In the last exercise, you created a Product Prompt and used it in the report. The reference tells us where the Prompt is being used. Your first Prompt is the detail filter, which is where we have built all of our filters so far. At the bottom of the Prompt Manager, you can create a new Prompt, one that does not even have to be used immediately in the Filter Definition. The Edit button allows you to enter back into the Prompt Definition window to make any necessary changes.

Notice in the Prompt Manager how the Remove button is grayed out, or disabled. This is because this Prompt is actively being used in the logic of our report, so we cannot remove it. Notice also how the Cascades button is grayed out. This is because this report does not use cascading Prompts. Cascading Prompts are described later in this chapter.

When you have multiple Prompts in one report, the Prompt Manager gives you the ability to arrange how they appear when users see the Prompt window. This is performed the same way you arranged the order of columns in the Sort and Group tabs. This will become more evident in the next exercise.

Adding Another Prompt and Filter

Technically, it is not that difficult to add another Prompt to a report, which we will learn here. The real challenge is applying multiple Prompts to benefit the report consumer in answering a reporting need.

For our exercise, let's use the following business case:

Report Requirement

Report consumer: *The new Prompt report looks great, but I can never remember which product is in which Product Type. Would it be possible to also pick the Product Type like I can pick the products?*

Analysis

Looking at this request, you see that the report consumer just wants to be Prompted with a list of Product Types. Therefore, the report should filter both "Product" and "Product Type." Not a problem. Impromptu can handle multiple Prompts in one report.

The trickiest part of including this Prompt is understanding how it relates to the other filters. Going back to the analysis, you determined that the report is to be filtered by both Product and Product Type. For this, think back to Chapter 6 and Filters. Chapter 6 covered both the "and" and the "or" operands. Including both Prompts in the Filter Definition requires joining the two with an "and" operand.

Adding this Prompt involves two steps:

1. Adding the filter in the Filter Definition
2. Creating and adding the Prompt to the Filter Definition

Step 1: Adding the Filter

The first part is setting up the Filter Definition:

1. Open the QDB.
2. Select the Filter tab.
3. Click the "and" button.
4. Expand the Report Columns folder.
5. Select the Product Type column.
6. Select the "in" condition to allow the report consumers to select multiple Product Types.
7. Select the open parenthesis.
8. Double click the Prompt Manager.

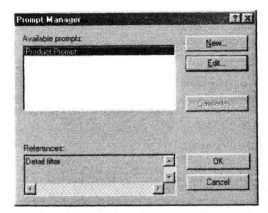

Figure 10.20
The Prompt Manager again.

Step 2: Creating and Adding the Prompt

Here, instead of a new Prompt Definition, just the Prompt Manager comes up. This appears because there are already Prompts for this report, and Impromptu cannot determine whether you should or will want to create a new Prompt. In this case, it displays the Prompt Manager to let the report developer make that choice. The report developer makes the decision whether to use an existing Prompt or to create a new one. For this report, you will create a new one.

9. Click the New... button.
10. Give the new Prompt the name Product Type.
11. Select Catalog Picklist from the Type dropdown. This Prompt Type creates a Prompt just like the Product Prompt.
12. Type in a message to assist report consumers: Select one or more Product Types.
13. Expand the Products folder from the Catalog Columns box.
14. Double click Product Type.

Note

The Sort Value checkbox is selected. This organizes the Prompt values to be displayed in alphabetical order in the value selection box.

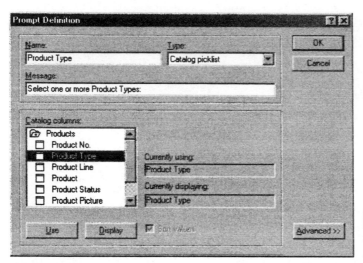

Figure 10.21
The finished Product
Type Prompt Definition.

Tip

At the bottom of every Prompt Definition is a button called Advanced. Advanced is used to iden-
tify a data type for a stored procedure parameter. Stored procedures are used to perform addi-
tional features in the database, as opposed to Impromptu. This feature should be used in
conjunction with experienced Impromptu and Database administrators only.

---

15. Click OK to close the Prompt Definition window.
16. Click OK to close the Prompt Manager.
17. Select the close parenthesis: ")" (Figure 10.22).
18. Click OK to run the report.

This procedure will run two separate queries against the database to fill the two
Prompts with values from Product and Product Type. The report consumer now has a choice
of any Product and any Product Type.

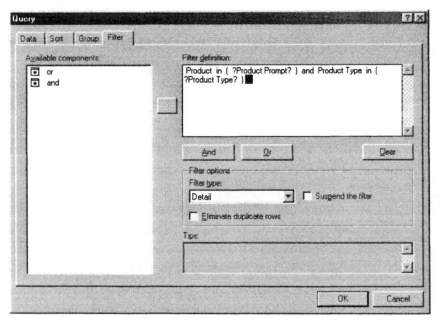

Figure 10.22   The completed Filter Definition.

19. Choose the original two Products: "Day Tripper" and "Enviro-Kit."
20. Choose all of the Product Types.

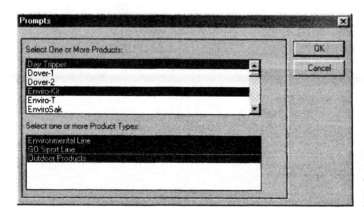

Figure 10.23
Show completed Prompt
window with selections
highlighted.

21. Click OK to run the report.

And the Results Are...

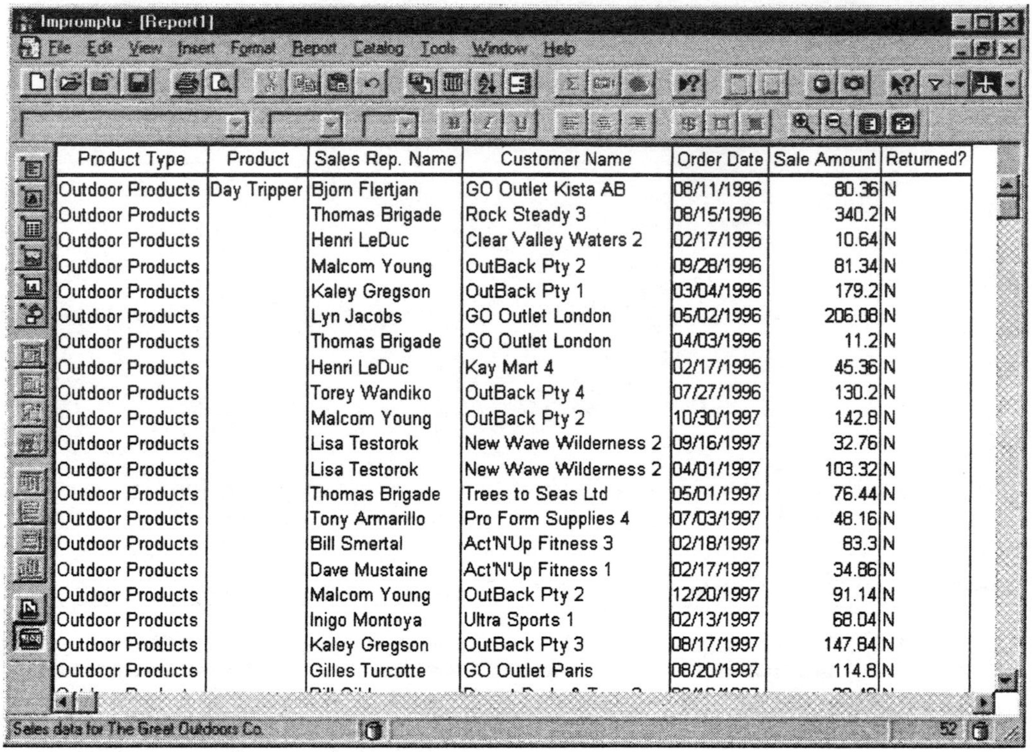

Figure 10.24 The report contains only the Products that matched the selected Prompted Products and only the Product Types that match the Prompt selection. Both had to be valid to be displayed on this report.

The results are the subset of products and product types that matched both the Prompt selections.

Debugging a Broken Prompt Report...

Take a moment to go forward in time with this report. Suppose that you cleaned up the report, added a fancy header, and the report results look good. The report consumer is happy. Then one day, the report consumer may leave you a voice mail message:

> *Hi, this is Jim. Remember that Product and Product Type Prompting report you built a while back? Well, it does not work. I tried bringing up the Dover series of products in the "GO Sports Line," and the report just dies. Fix this ASAP; I have a meeting in two hours, and I need this report.*

I'm not kidding. There will come a time when you, as a report developer, will get at least one of these messages in your life. Let's analyze Jim's problem. He tried running the report with the Dover Products: "Dover-1" and "Dover-2" and the product type: "GO Sports Line" and "*it dies.*"

In debugging problems like these, the best way to start is to try to do exactly what the report consumer did. This does two things:

1. It verifies that the report consumer followed the right steps.
2. You understand exactly what the report consumer is trying to do.

Steps to Debug a Prompt Report

So, since the report is still open, let's re-create this report by selecting the same Prompt values Jim did:

1. Re-Prompt the report by either:
   - Clicking on the Prompt button on the toolbar, or
   - From the Menu bar: Report.Prompt
2. Select both "Dover-1" and "Dover-2" from the Product Prompt box.
3. Select "GO Sport Line" from the Product Type Prompt box.

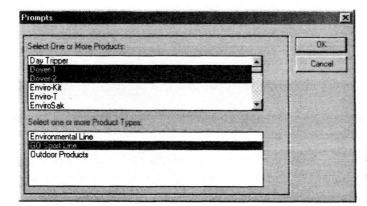

Figure 10.25
The completed Prompt box with selections before the report runs.

4. Click OK to run the report.

And the Results Are...

Notice Gil swimming in the Status bar. That lets you know the report is running, and Impromptu is waiting for results to be returned back from the report. When Gil stops and the Status bar shows the Report Data Source drum, Impromptu is done.

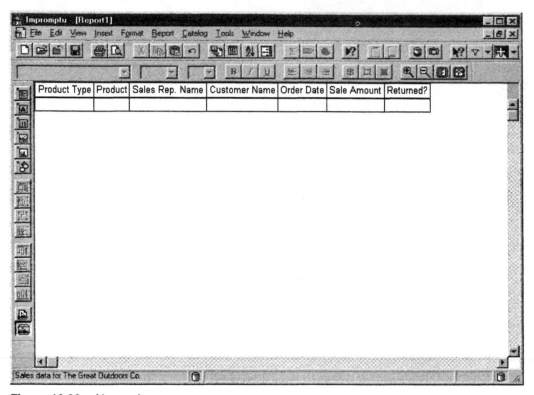

Figure 10.26   No results.

But wait! No results were returned? That is right, no results were returned from the database because there are no matches. The "GO Sport Line" product type does not contain any Dover products. Dover products fall under a different product type. So, when Jim and you selected the combination there were zero columns that matched both Prompt Filters. That's why the report "died"—the data selected was not accurate.

Now, that we figured out what the issue is, let's bring this to the attention of the report consumer, Jim. His reply: *Darn, I know that. I meant to hit Outdoor Products, but the phone rang, and it was Bill, and he invited me to the game. Then Fred called, and he was talking about the new Dover line of products. I wanted to select "Day Trippers." They are Outdoor Products. What was I thinking?"*

Error-Free Prompt Reports

What you just experienced was an example of a report consumer "breaking" a Prompt report. Jim found a way to request a report that did not make sense. He chose a Product Type and Product combination that did not have a result set to display on the report.

Analysis of Jim's Bug

To avoid this problem, you can develop something called a Cascading Prompt report. This is in the same vein as the advanced report that you ran at the beginning of the chapter. Here are the high-level steps involved:

1. Develop a two-column, single-Prompt report for the higher-level item (in this database, it is the Product Type). The columns are
   - Column 1: the column you will Prompt with
   - Column 2: the column that the next report will use to populate the Prompt list.
2. Develop a second report addressing the report needs, and have a Report Picklist type of Prompt Filter to further narrow down the list.

This report is pretty simple to build. You need to know what has to go into it. To map this out from the high-level steps presented above, you will need the two columns. But how do they map?

The first column is the column you Prompt, which is the Product Type:

- Column 1: Product Type
- Column 2: Product

After that is where Cascading Prompts get tricky. In Cascading Prompts, one report (the Prompt report we have used until now) uses the details value of another report (the one we are now building) to supply the Prompt value list. So, in our original Prompt report, we need a list of Products that exist as the result of the new Prompt report. That means the new report must contain Product Type and the list of Products.

To recap, the new Prompt Report requires

- Product Type (product type)
- Product (product)
- A Prompt selecting one or more Product Types

Step 1: Building an Additional Prompt Report

1. Create a new Simple List report.
2. Expand the Products folder.
3. Select Product Type.
4. Select Product.

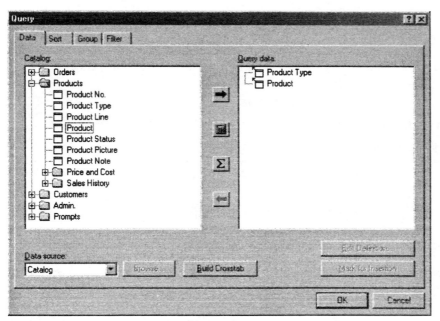

Figure 10.27   The finished Data tab.

The columns in the Simple List report should be grouped. This report needs to see only one occurrence of each column, and grouping provides this.

5. Select the Group tab.
6. Group first on Product Type and then by Product.

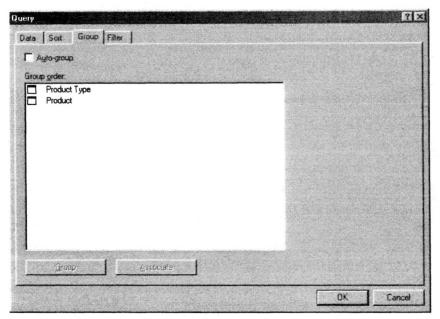

Figure 10.28   The finished Group tab.

Now, the Filter for this report needs to be built.

7. Select the Filter tab.
8. Expand the Report columns folder.
9. Select the Product Type column.
10. Select the "in" condition.
11. Select the "(" parenthesis.
12. Select the Prompt Manager.
13. Give the new Prompt the name Product Type.
14. Select the Type "Catalog Picklist."
15. Type in the following message: Select one or more Project Types:
16. Expand the Products folder from the Catalog Column box.
17. Double click on Product Type.

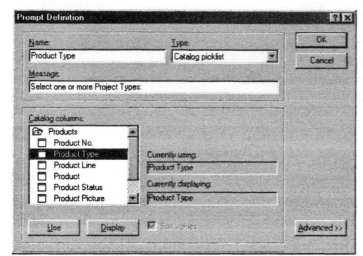

Figure 10.29
The finished
Prompt Definition.

18. Click OK.

19. While in the Prompt Manager, Click OK.

20. Select the ")" parenthesis.

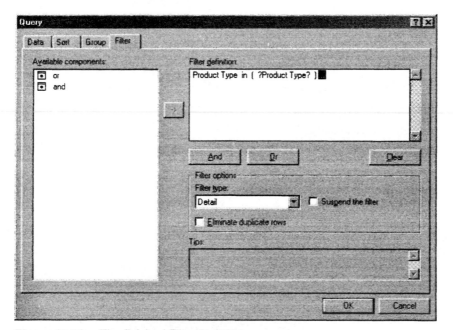

Figure 10.30   The finished Filter Definition.

21. Click OK to run the report.

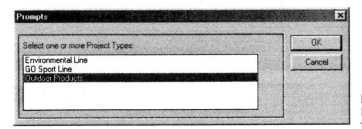

Figure 10.31
Prompt we just created.

Impromptu runs the report, and the Prompt appears asking the report consumer to select one or more Product Types.

22. Select the Outdoor Products.
23. Click OK.

And the Results of Step 1 Are...

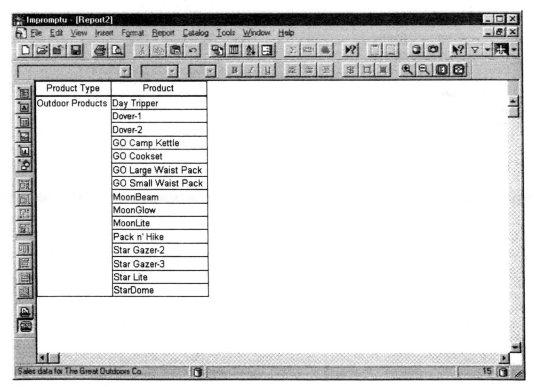

Figure 10.32   The report results.

Look at the results to determine whether this was what you were expecting. Yes, the report does supply a list of Products. This result will be used by the original report to populate its Prompt list. Next, save the report to be used in the next report.

24. Click File.Save As.
25. Use the default subdirectory, and name the Prompt report: Chapter 10 Prompt.

Now that you are done with building this report, you do not have to keep it open.

26. Click File.Close.

Note

Remember, this is only the first half of building a cascading Prompt. Our next step is to integrate this with our original report.

Step 2: Integrate the New Prompt

Next, we go back to our original report that Prompted on both Products and Product Types. This report now needs to integrate the newly created Product Type Prompt report into its Prompting strategy. Instead of having two Prompts here, only the Product will be necessary.

The adjustments to this report are not complex. The current Product Prompt now uses the report titled *Chapter 10 Prompt* to obtain the list of products for the user to select. The Product Type Prompt is no longer needed because the Product Type Prompt filtering is being handled by the new report.

Our first step is opening the QDB of the report you have been working on since the first exercise.

1. With the first Prompt report you built, open the QDB.
2. Select the Filter tab (Figure 10.33).

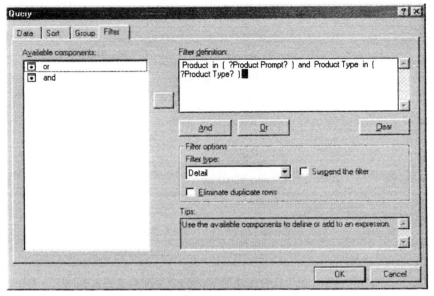

Figure 10.33   The Filter tab of the report first built.

3. Click on the "and" operand.

4. Press the Delete key until the entire second Prompt is gone, as shown in Figure 10.34.

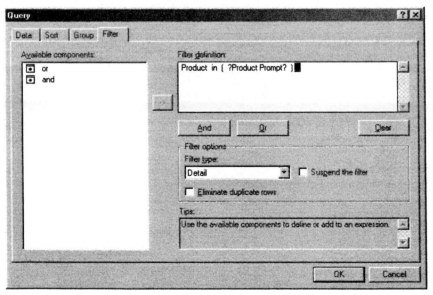

Figure 10.34   The Filter tab without the Product Type Prompt.

We are now ready to change our Product Prompt from a Catalog Picklist to a new Prompt type: a Report Picklist.

A Report Picklist works exactly the same way a Catalog Picklist works, but instead of retrieving data to populate into the Prompt value list, Impromptu opens a report and uses values from that report's result set to populate its Prompt value list.

To change the Product Prompt from a Catalog Picklist Prompt to a Report Picklist Prompt, follow these steps:

5. Double click on '?Product Prompt?'.

6. Change the Type to Report Picklist.

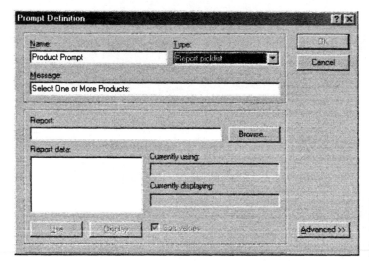

Figure 10.35
Notice how the Prompt Definition window has changed.

Since the Prompt Type has changed, the source of the Prompt value has to be established. This is where the Product Prompt identifies the values from the new Prompt report, *Chapter 10 Prompt*.

7. Click the browse button.

8. Find and select Chapter 10 Prompt.

Notice that instead of a Catalog column list, you are now looking at the query list of the Chapter 10 Prompt report. For this filter, you need the Product column.

9. Double click on the Product column (Figure 10.36).

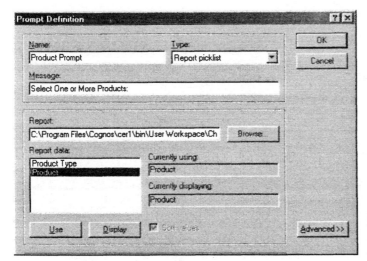

Figure 10.36
The finished and changed
Product Prompt Definition.

10. Click OK to complete the Prompt definition change.
11. Click OK to run the report.

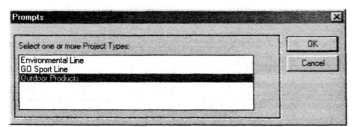

Figure 10.37
The Prompt from the new
Prompt report asking for a
Product Type.

12. Select "Outdoor Products," and click OK.

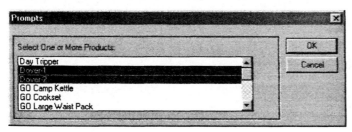

Figure 10.38
The Product Prompt is now
populated with Products
derived from the previous
Prompt.

This list of Products is a filtered list because the "Product Type Prompt" report filters the list of Products by the Product Types selected, which we just used.

13. Select the following Products: Dover-1 and Dover-2.

14. Click OK to run the report.

And, Finally, the Results Are...

Product Type	Product	Sales Rep. Name	Customer Name	Order Date	Sale Amount	Returned?
Outdoor Products	Dover-1	Kurt Gruber	Ultra Sports 3	12/16/1996	1201.2	N
Outdoor Products		Tony Armarillo	Pro Form Supplies 4	02/27/1996	967.2	N
Outdoor Products		Lyn Jacobs	GO Outlet London	05/02/1996	3796	N
Outdoor Products		Sally Strandherst	Wally Mart 2	03/02/1996	1560	N
Outdoor Products		Kaley Gregson	OutBack Pty 3	08/05/1996	2538.9	N
Outdoor Products		Bill Gibbons	GO Outlet Irving	08/26/1996	2293.2	N
Outdoor Products		Kurt Gruber	Supras Camping Supplies 8	02/24/1996	3264.3	N
Outdoor Products		Lee Chan	Kay Mart 5	12/08/1996	3075.8	N
Outdoor Products		Kurt Gruber	Sportwaren G.m.b.H. 1	12/10/1996	2020.2	N
Outdoor Products		Charles Loo Nam	123 Fitness PTE Ltd	07/31/1996	904.8	N
Outdoor Products		Conrad Bergsteige	Vacation Central 2	07/06/1996	1830.4	N
Outdoor Products		Bjorn Flertjan	GO Outlet Kista AB	04/10/1996	4080.7	N
Outdoor Products		Bjorn Flertjan	Tregoran AB 1	10/13/1996	2347.8	N
Outdoor Products		Lisa Testorok	Clear Valley Waters 3	07/28/1996	743.6	N
Outdoor Products		Ingrid Termede	Pro Form Supplies 3	07/19/1996	3732.3	N
Outdoor Products		Gus Grovlin	Florida Sun Sports 2	11/26/1997	1938	N
Outdoor Products		Conrad Bergsteige	Wilderness Wonderment Ltd	04/26/1997	1370.88	N
Outdoor Products		Torey Wandiko	OutBack Pty 1	03/26/1997	4743	N
Outdoor Products		Conrad Bergsteige	Rock Steady 4	07/08/1997	2264.4	N
Outdoor Products		Lisa Testorok	New Wave Wilderness 2	04/01/1997	461.72	N

Figure 10.39   The report results.

What you see here is a report that will not deliver to report consumers empty report results. If a report consumer selects a Product Type, the only choice available in the second Prompt is to select the Product(s) for that (those) Product Type(s).

Tip

The report is now a Cascading Report. In the Prompt Manager, you can see exactly which additional reports are used in the cascading hierarchy:

1. Select Report.Prompt Manager.

2. *Click on the Prompt that contains the Cascading Prompts. Notice how the Cascades...*
   button is now enabled.

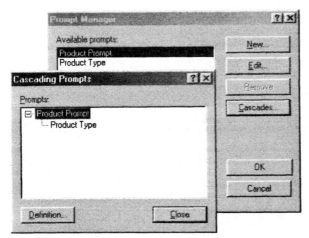

Figure 10.40
Cascading Prompt window.

3. *Click on Cascades...*
4. *Expand the Prompt to see the cascading effect, also shown in Figure 10.40.*

Here you can select a Prompt and look at its Prompt definition without having to open that report.

Different Types of Prompts

As we mentioned earlier in the chapter, there are four Prompt Types:

- Catalog Picklist
- Report Picklist
- Type In
- File Picklist

We covered, in great detail, the first two—Catalog and Report Prompts—in the exercise. Now you are familiar with how Prompting works for those. A discussion of the other two Prompt Types follows.

Type-In Prompts

The name alone for "Type-in" Prompts indicates clearly what this Prompt is all about. The Type-in Prompt, shown in Figure 10.41, allows report consumers to manually type in a value to be used in the generation of the Impromptu report. This is an extremely flexible Prompt. Here the report consumer controls exactly what is to be used in the Prompt filter.

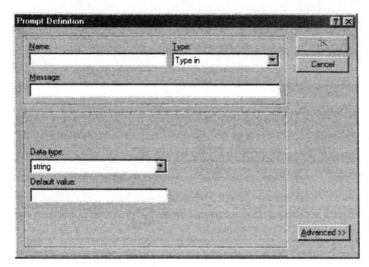

Figure 10.41
The basic Type-in
Prompt Definition.

The top section is the same as every other type of Prompt. Each Prompt needs a name and a message giving the report consumer instructions. In the bottom of the window, the dropdown selection allows the report developer to select the data type the Prompt will be. The default value allows the report developer to have a default value present when the Prompt initially appears. This is convenient because it can give a report consumer additional help in determining the format required by the Prompt.

The Prompt accommodates for any data type used in the Filter Definition. Additionally, you can apply a Type-in Prompt to either a detail filter or a summary filter. The Type-in Prompt is primarily used in singular conditions such as greater than, equal to, etc.

File Picklist Prompt

The File Picklist, shown in Figure 10.42, works just like the Report Picklist.

The top section is the same as every other Prompt. The Prompt needs a name and a message. The selection content is similar to the Report Picklist. Here the user has several file formats to choose from to obtain a list of values. Additionally, the File Picklist requires you to select the data type the report consumer will be selecting. This is determined by what data type the Prompt is being compared with in the Filter Definition.

This Prompt is useful when the Prompt needs to be a value coming from outside of the database, and you want to compare that data with data in the database through a Filter. The File Picklist Prompt can be used effectively by both singular conditions (e.g., greater than) as well as multiple comparison conditions (e.g., an "in" condition).

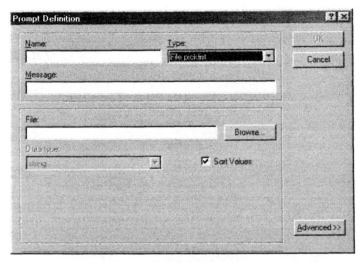

Figure 10.42
A File Picklist Prompt
definition.

Prompts in the Catalog

Impromptu provides an administrator the ability to store Prompts in the Catalog. Before Impromptu stored Prompts in the Catalog, there was no easy way to transfer a Prompt from one report to another except by keeping one report with the set of Prompts already stored in it.

As you can see from this chapter, Prompts are a really nice feature, and they are not that hard to construct from scratch. They do, however, take some time. As you start to incorporate Prompts into more and more reports, you will find yourself using a constant group of Prompts. Changing them on occasion can become a bit of a hassle. If you have a Prompt you plan on using over and over when creating reports, just have the Impromptu administrator store the Prompt in the Catalog, and you can use it anytime you like.

Prompts in Complex Reports

The following report is a complex report to say the least. Not only does it show you how Catalog Prompts look and work within a report, but it also is a crosstab report. Here, you get a sneak peek at how a crosstab displays results on a report. The details of how the crosstab report works are discussed in Chapter 13.

Steps to Open a Complex Report

1. Select File.Open.

   From the default subdirectory:

   ```
   <drive you installed Impromptu on>...\Cognos\cer1\samples\
   Impromptu\Samples\Reports
   ```

2. Select the report Sales Performance by Branch.

The report immediately requests data for the Prompt, and the report consumer is presented with a familiar Prompt, a Product Type Prompt.

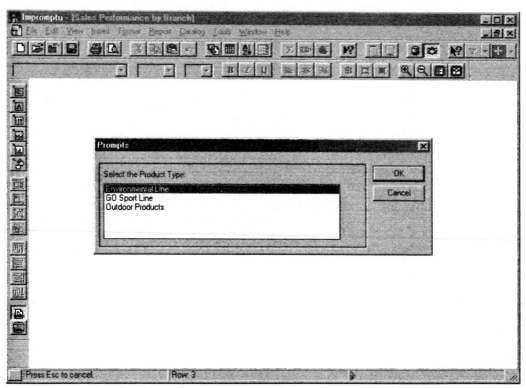

Figure 10.43   The Product Type Prompt.

3. Select just the "Environmental Line."
4. Click OK. The report runs and retrieves data from the database....

And the Results Are...

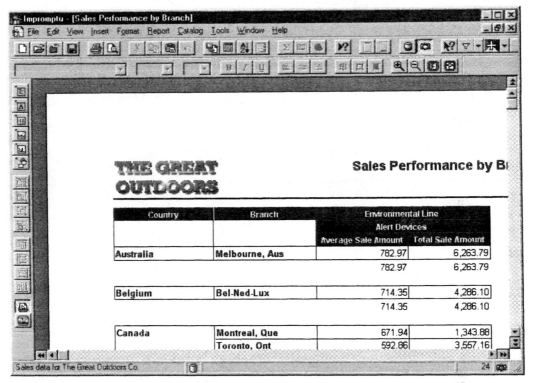

Figure 10.44 A Crosstab report.

This is a Crosstab report. But, staying away from the allure of the crosstab for a moment, focus on how this Catalog Prompt looks and works. See what the Prompt looks like in the Filter tab:

1. Open the QDB.
2. Select the Filter tab.

In Figure 10.45, the Prompt is highlighted. Here the Filter Definition uses the familiar "in" operand, which requires "("and")". Inside the parenthesis is our Prompt.

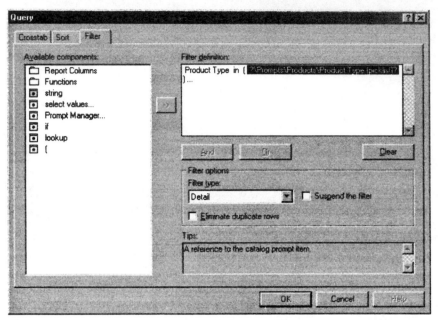

Figure 10.45   The Filter tab, with Prompt highlighted.

3. Single click on the Prompt to highlight it in its entirety.

Notice how the Prompt name has a directory path–like beginning "\Prompts\Products\...", and the name appears to be "Product Type (picklist)." The path–like beginning is the folder location of the Prompt in the Catalog (i.e., is where you can find it). The name is the actual name as it is stored in the Catalog.

Now, see what this Prompt looks like.

4. Double click on the Prompt, to see the Prompt Definition (Figure 10.46).

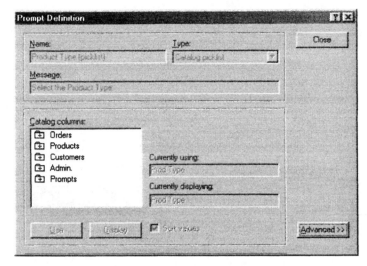

Figure 10.46
The Prompt Definition.

The Prompt we are looking at is a typical Catalog Picklist. The only thing different about this one is the way it got into our report. Here, the Prompt Definition window is locked. The report developer cannot change anything about this Prompt.

5. Click the Close button on the Prompt Definition window.

Another way to see how this Catalog Prompt is stored and viewed in the report is through the Prompt Manager.

1. Cancel the QDB.
2. Select Report.Prompt Manager.

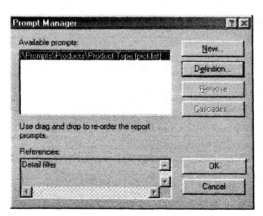

Figure 10.47
Notice instead of an edit button beneath the New button, this is now called Definition. This is because report developers cannot make a change to a Catalog Prompt; only the Impromptu administrator can.

This is the default way to go directly to the Prompt Manager. Even though you are outside the QDB, any changes here can cause Impromptu to either rerun the query or rerun the Prompts.

3. Click the Definition button.

The Prompt Definition window is exactly the same as it is when we looked at it through the QDB Filter tab—it is the same definition after all.

One More Prompt Tip...

The concept is called "Collar a Date." It comes from the real estate concept of collaring an interest rate. In reporting though, it allows a user to control a beginning and ending date. This is an extremely helpful tip to answer date-driven Prompt reporting.

Let's use a report request to describe how to collar a date.

Report Requirement

Boss: *Build a report such that a report consumer can select a range of order dates that will produce a sale amount total by product type, line, and product. For example, a report consumer wants an all-products sales summary for the first quarter of 1996. But the report consumer also wants the flexibility to enter a specific date range. For example, the company went through a promotional campaign during time period x; the report consumer would like to enter that date range to see what the sales figures are for that period.*

Analysis

First, determine what columns are needed for the report. After dissecting the request, you see that the report must display the following items:

- Product Type (product type)
- Product Line (line)
- Product (product)
- Total (Sale Amount) (sales summary)

Notice that the display list did not mention Order Date. The user did not mention in the request the need to display the order date range in the report. So, the display list does not include it.

The next step is to sketch out the filter and the Prompts. The user wants to compare the order date in the database with a beginning and ending date. So the report filter should look something like:

Order Date between *A Beginning Date Prompt* and *An Ending Date Prompt*

Step 1: Create the Report

Now that all of the requirements are mapped out, it's time to build the report:

1. Create a new Simple List report.
2. Expand the Products folder.
3. Select the Product Type column.
4. Select the Product Line column.
5. Select the Product column.
6. Expand the Orders folder.
7. Expand the Order Details folder.
8. Single click the Sale Amount.
9. Click the Summary button.
10. Click the Total button.

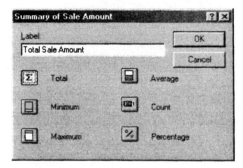

Figure 10.48
A completed Summary of... box.

11. Click OK (Figure 10.49).

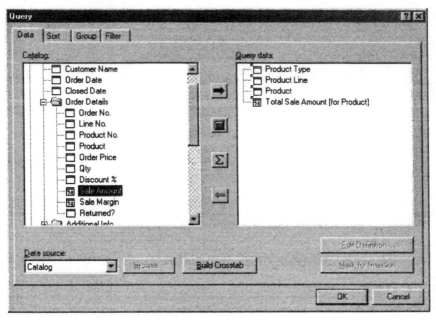

Figure 10.49   A finished QDB Query Data tab.

Step 2: Create the Filter and the First Prompt

Remember the Summary report from the previous chapter? You are applying the same principle here in this Date Collar report.

12. Select the Filter tab.
13. Expand the Catalog columns… folder.

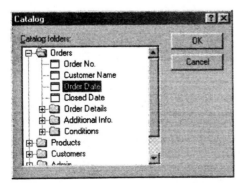

Figure 10.50
The Catalog Column window.

14. Expand the Orders folder.

15. Double click on the Order Date column.

16. Select "Between" from the Available Components Toolbox.

17. Select the Prompt Manager. This opens the Prompt Manager and goes directly to a new Prompt Definition.

18. Give our first new Prompt the name Beginning Date

19. Keep the Type as "Type In."

20. Create the message: Enter the Beginning date:

21. Check to make sure that the Data Type dropdown box is correct: "Date."

22. Change the default value to: "1996-01-01."

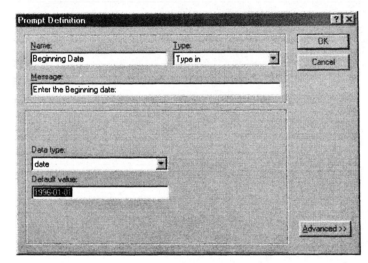

Figure 10.51
The finished first Prompt Definition window.

23. Click OK, to complete the Prompt Definition.

24. Click OK, to close the Prompt Manager.

To finish the "Between" component:

25. Select the "and" operand.

Step 3: Create the Second Prompt

Here you will create the second Prompt.

26. Select the Prompt Manager.
27. Click the New button.
28. Give the new Prompt the name Ending Date
29. Keep the Type as "Type In."
30. Create the message Enter the Ending date:
31. Check to make sure that the Data Type dropdown box is correct: "Date".
32. Don't change the default value. The Prompt will use it as the default.

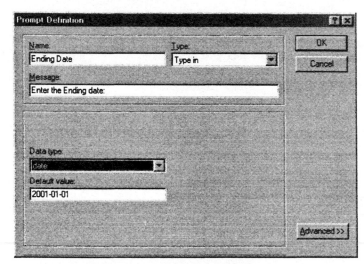

Figure 10.52
The finished second
Prompt Definition window.

33. Click OK to close the second Prompt Definition window.

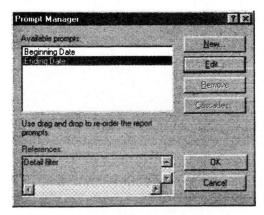

Figure 10.53
Prompt Manager with
both Prompts.

Make sure the new "Ending Date" Prompt is highlighted, because whatever is high-lighted will be used in the Filter Definition.

34. Click OK.

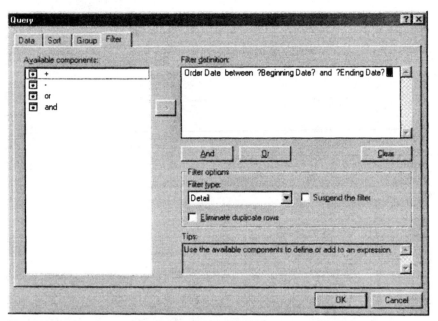

Figure 10.54   The finished Filter Definition box.

Now, that the report is built, let's run it.

35. Click OK.

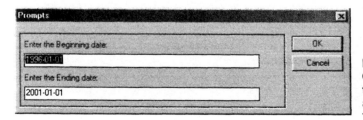

Figure 10.55
Our new Prompt con-taining both Beginning and Ending date.

To be quick, let's use the default dates and just click OK.

And the Results Are...

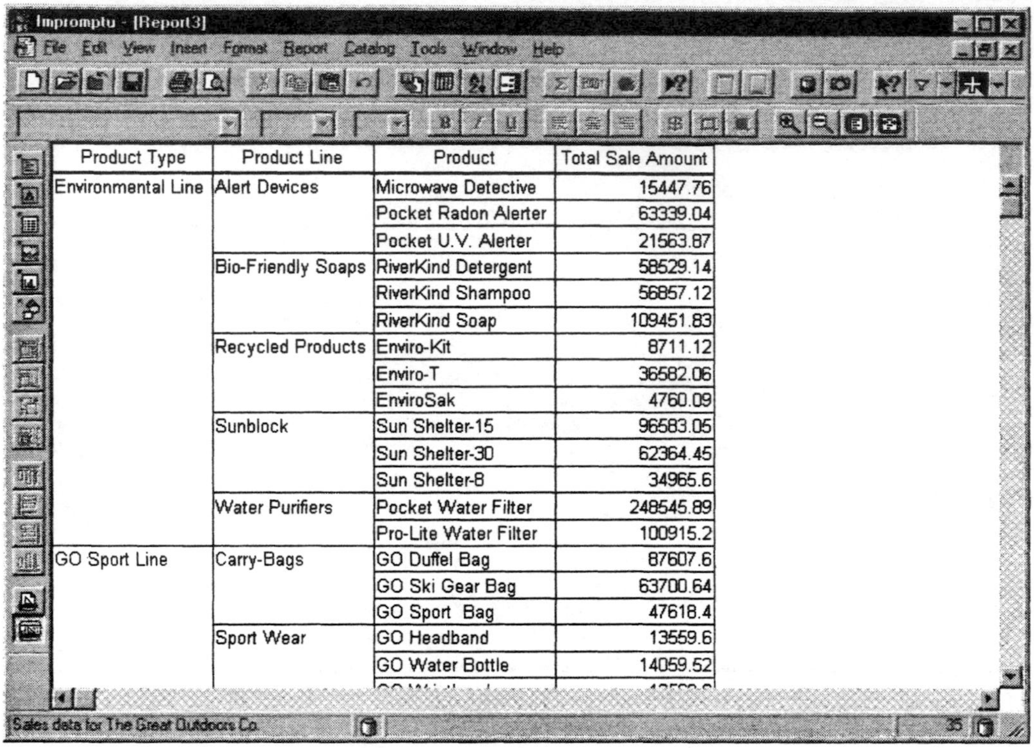

Product Type	Product Line	Product	Total Sale Amount
Environmental Line	Alert Devices	Microwave Detective	15447.76
		Pocket Radon Alerter	63339.04
		Pocket U.V. Alerter	21563.87
	Bio-Friendly Soaps	RiverKind Detergent	58529.14
		RiverKind Shampoo	56857.12
		RiverKind Soap	109451.83
	Recycled Products	Enviro-Kit	8711.12
		Enviro-T	36582.06
		EnviroSak	4760.09
	Sunblock	Sun Shelter-15	96583.05
		Sun Shelter-30	62364.45
		Sun Shelter-8	34965.6
	Water Purifiers	Pocket Water Filter	248545.89
		Pro-Lite Water Filter	100915.2
GO Sport Line	Carry-Bags	GO Duffel Bag	87607.6
		GO Ski Gear Bag	63700.64
		GO Sport Bag	47618.4
	Sport Wear	GO Headband	13559.6
		GO Water Bottle	14059.52

Figure 10.56 The report results.

Summary

Things to keep in mind:

- You can Prompt a report consumer to
    - Type in a value to filter on in the report.
    - Select from a list of values from a database, a report, or even a separate file.
- You can have a report consumer select multiple Prompts in one report.
- You can have standard Prompts stored in a Catalog to be used over and over.

The ability to build a report and choose what values populate the report can be a new concept. This is a very valuable concept and has many uses. Give it some time to sink in. Don't be afraid of even coming back and skimming through this chapter again. Features, like Cascading Prompts, don't just jump out at you in the business world right away.

Advanced Layouts
and Frames

$\mathbf{T}$his chapter describes the layout of Impromptu. Until now, you have worked within a simple premise of reporting. Just run list-oriented reports, aka Simple List reports. Although these reports serve a useful purpose, the Impromptu reporting environment extends to serve further needs.

This chapter will change your perception of what Impromptu is and what it can do. Specifically, it covers:

- What a frame-based report is
- The different frames on a simple list report
- The frames in an advanced report.
- Each type of frame available in Impromptu
- Report layout options

A General Description of Frames

Impromptu uses the term "frame" to describe the elements of a report. To give a better sense of how Impromptu uses frames, step away from Impromptu for a second and look at another application of frames.

A general definition of a frame is "a way of putting a boundary on something." A residential house serves as a basic example. A whole house is considered a framed structure. There are defined boundaries: outside and inside. Within the house, there are many different types of rooms. Each room has its own defined frame: what is inside a room and outside the room. The room contains a number of walls, usually four. A wall has a defined top, bottom, and sides. In construction, a wall is even commonly referred to as a frame.

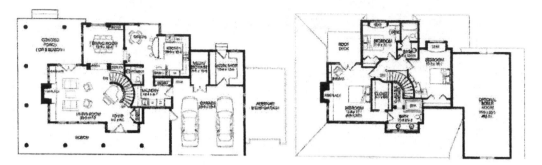

Figure 11.1   This entire structure is a frame that contains many different types of frames within it.

What is important about this example is the notion of a frame as an independent entity that can reside within another frame. Another way of describing this relationship is a parent-child relationship. Applying this terminology to our house example:

- A wall is a child to a room.
- A room is a parent to its walls, and at the same time, it is a child to the house it resides in.
- A house is a parent to all the rooms within it.

In Impromptu, a frame-based report is one in which the elements that make up and shape the report are described as frames. These elements can be as simple as a picture or as complex as an entire list of values. Also, some of these elements have the ability to be parents to other elements, as is shown in the next section.

Frames and Simple List Reports

Now, the layout starts to make more sense. All this time we were working in a frame-based environment without realizing it. Well you did, in a way. You knew that you were working with elements of a report and that everything you did, everything you added to the report, was part of the report body—its frame. To make this clear, open a sample report and take a look at the frames involved.

Open the first report you looked at in Chapter 2: the Product Type Sales report.

1. Select File.Open and choose the Product Type Sales (Figure 11.2).

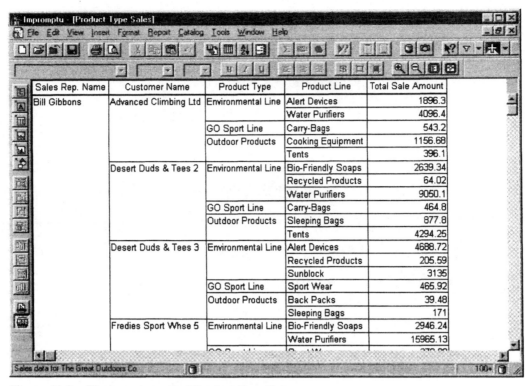

Figure 11.2 The report result of Product Type Sales.

Looking at the report, initially you do not see any frames. What you do see is a report with columns, Column headers, Page headers, and a lot of white space on the right-hand side.

For starters, select just one cell from this report:

2. Select the "Recycled Products" cell

You know that this is one cell for the Product column, and if you modify the format of this one cell, the entire column's layout changes. This cell relates to the column and the report in a frame perspective.

In the house example, a wall is a child of a room, and a room is a child of a house. Applying this concept to a report, what is this cell a child of? Or in other words, what is the parent of this cell?

The parent of a cell or a column is the List. The List in this report is also a frame of the report.

Note

The List frame gives the impression that it is the entire report; this is a little misleading. The size of this List frame fills the entire viewing area of the screen. This just happens to be the layout of this report. The List frame spans the height and width of the report. So, it gives the impression that nothing else exists. As you might guess, part of the List frame includes the scroll bar to the right, and the bottom. This is why they are included if the entire List is highlighted.

Selecting a Parent Frame

There are several ways to go about determining the Parent Frame:

3. Using the menu, select: Edit.Select Parent.
4. Using the Layout toolbar, select the Select Parent button.

Sales Rep. Name	Customer Name	Product Type	Product Line	Total Sale Amount
Bill Gibbons	Advanced Climbing Ltd	Environmental Line	Alert Devices	1896.3
			Water Purifiers	4096.4
		GO Sport Line	Carry-Bags	543.2
		Outdoor Products	Cooking Equipment	1156.68
			Tents	396.1
	Desert Duds & Tees 2	Environmental Line	Bio-Friendly Soaps	2639.34
			Recycled Products	64.02
			Water Purifiers	9050.1
		GO Sport Line	Carry-Bags	464.8
		Outdoor Products	Sleeping Bags	877.8
			Tents	4294.25
	Desert Duds & Tees 3	Environmental Line	Alert Devices	4688.72
			Recycled Products	205.59
			Sunblock	3135
		GO Sport Line	Sport Wear	465.92
		Outdoor Products	Back Packs	39.48
			Sleeping Bags	171
	Fredies Sport Whse 5	Environmental Line	Bio-Friendly Soaps	2946.24
			Water Purifiers	15965.13

Figure 11.3   The Select Parent button.

Try This:

5. Select a cell that contains "Recycled Products."
6. Select Edit.Select Parent.

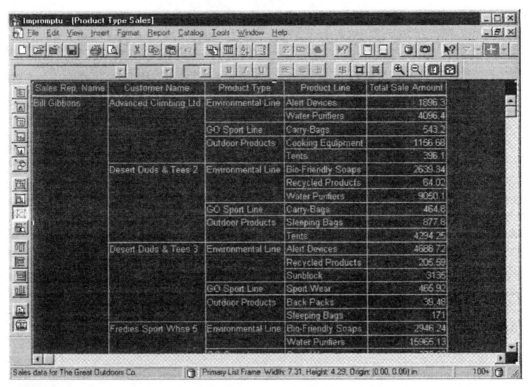

Figure 11.4   The report with the entire Primary List frame highlighted.

Note

Notice how the entire report is now selected. But, what exactly is selected? Looking at the Status bar, you see that the "Primary List frame" is selected, as shown in Figure 11.5. A Primary List frame is just that: the primary frame for this report. Each report must contain at least one primary frame, and for this report, it is a list frame. A primary frame is the default for the report and is the initial point for processing.

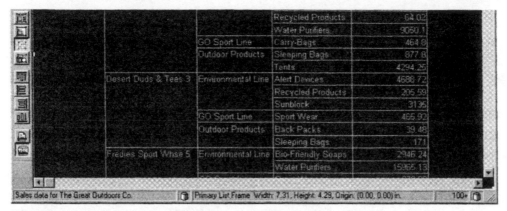

Figure 11.5 Remember, the Status bar provides identification of items selected.

Question	Answer
So, that's why when I try to uns-elect something on a report and I click on the white space the entire report gets highlighted?	Yes, by clicking on that white space, you are actually select-ing and highlighting the report's List frame, not "nothing."

The Report Body

Question	Answer
Does the list frame have a par-ent?	Yes, that is the Report Body itself. It is as high as you can go with parents; it is the equivalent to the house in the previous example. To see just what the Report Body is, select the par-ent again.

7. Edit.Select Parent (Figure 11.6).

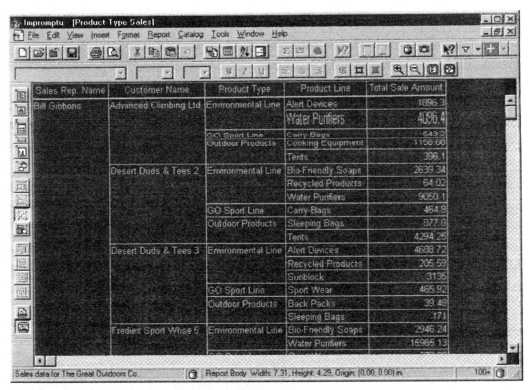

Figure 11.6 The report with the entire body present.

There is not that much difference between the way the List frame looked versus the Report Body. This is because the List frame consumes nearly all of the Report Body.

Select Another Detail Level Cell

To become a little more comfortable with this child and parent concept, try another route. Not only can cells/columns have parents, but everything else on the report also has a parent hierarchy that goes up to the top, the Report Body.

Steps to View the Parents of Another Cell

1. Click on the header: Customer Name (Figure 11.7).

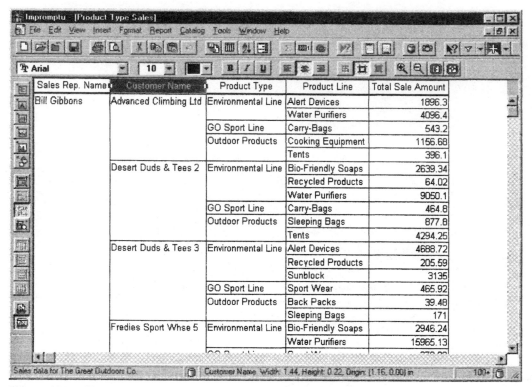

Figure 11.7   The report showing the Customer Name header highlighted.

Clicking on a detailed item in the report, even though it is not a cell or column but in a header, removes focus from what was selected previously. Now, let's see what the parent is:

2. Select Edit.Select Parent (Figure 11.8).

Now, the entire row of Column headers is selected. The one header is a child of the entire group of headers.

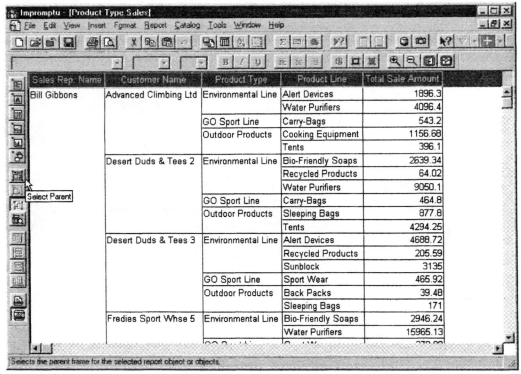

Figure 11.8   The highlighted Column header.

To see the group Column header's parent, select its parent:

3. Select Edit.Select Parent again (Figure 11.9).

The List frame is the parent of the Column headers. As you already know, the Report Body is the parent of the List frame. Now that you see the frame relationships of a simple list report, it is time to try a complex report example.

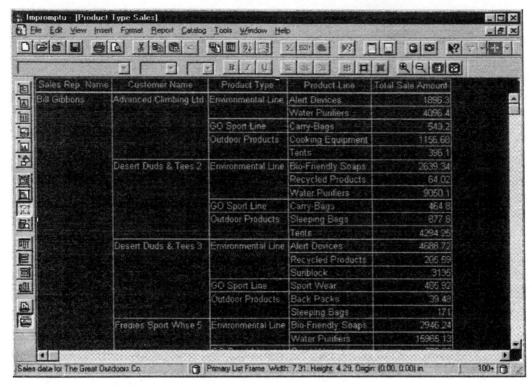

Figure 11.9   The highlighted List frame.

Open an Advanced Layout

This section introduces you to all the advanced layout features available in Impromptu. More than everything you have seen in the previous chapters, it is these layout features that lead many people to use Impromptu. As powerful a reporting tool as Impromptu is, its strength is not always in the way numbers are calculated, but how information is displayed. Because of the evolution of the graphical user interface environment, people are demanding to be impressed visually while being served a growing volume of information.

With that said, the advanced layout features described in this section will provide the foundation for you to build eye-catching, interactive reports.

Steps to Open the Advanced Layout Report

1. Select File.Open
2. Choose the same report: Annual Product Sales (Figure 11.10).

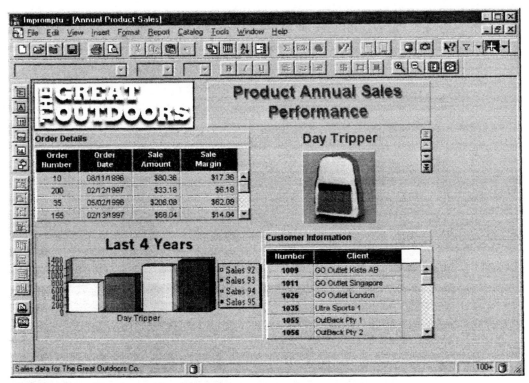

Figure 11.10 The Annual Product Sales report results.

Wow, this definitely is not a Simple List report. The following sections explain each of the frames you see here. Keep in mind a few simple things:

1. Even though the report looks different, Impromptu is still performing the essential task: retrieving data from the database and displaying it.
2. The Report Body contains everything—every cell, every frame, every picture.
3. The Status bar still works and is more useful than ever in this type of report.

At first glance, you will see that this report contains all the major elements of an Impromptu report:

- List frames
- Text frames
- Picture frames
- Chart frames

Additionally, this report combines formatting features discussed earlier as well as something new, called a Form frame, which is discussed later in this chapter.

Common Frame Properties and Formats

There are a couple of things common to all frames. Every frame, whether it is a Chart, a Picture, or a List frame, has both a Properties window and a Format window. And with every frame, the easiest way to go directly to these windows is by right clicking on the frame and selecting the window you want.

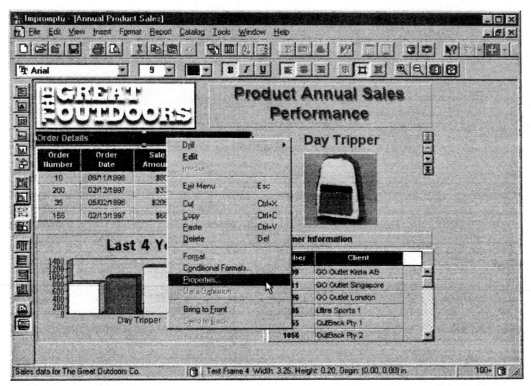

Figure 11.11   Right click on any frame and arrow point to both Properties and Format.

Frame Properties

The Properties window allows the report developer the ability to control the basic size and location of the frame. The Properties window contains four common tabs that are used by all frame objects. In addition to the basic tabs, Impromptu may add special tabs to display information specific to one particular frame or another. These specific instances are discussed in the detailed discussion of each frame. The four basic tabs are as follows.

Align Tab

The Align tab, shown in Figure 11.12, controls how a frame aligns itself with other frames within the report. The Align tab does not have other variations; either you can align the frame with frames or not. If you decide to align a frame, the options available are left, center, right, top, bottom, and middle of related frames and/or this frame's parent. This depends on what frame or combination of frames you have selected.

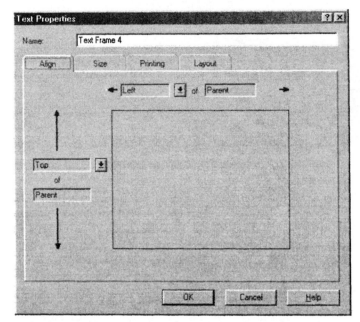

Figure 11.12
A typical Align tab.

Size Tab

The Size tab, shown in Figure 11.13, adjusts the size, both height and width, of a frame. This is the alternative way for the report developer to adjust these parameters. Traditionally, the report developer adjusts the frame's size in the report, by using on-screen mouse movements. Here, though, the report developer can choose to set a specific size, or have the size snap to the parent's size, either height or width.

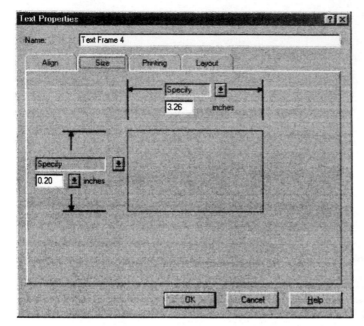

Figure 11.13
A typical Size tab.

Printing Tab

The Printing tab controls when this frame is printed. The Printing tab has two main layouts to control what exactly is to be printed. One layout is specific to a List frame, discussed in the List properties section, and the other is for the other frames, as shown in Figure 11.14. The left side of the typical Printing tab contains checkbox controls. These controls manage the printing direction: top-to-bottom or left-to-right. On the right is a preview of where the frame would print on a multiple-sheet printout. To interact with this window, a report developer would choose the print direction by selecting the checkboxes on the left and reviewing the results in the preview pane on the right.

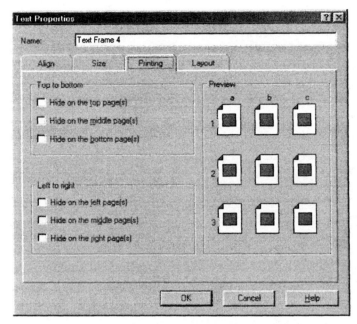

Figure 11.14
Picture of a Printing tab.

Layout Tab

The Layout tab, shown in Figure 11.15, is the least common of the four tabs. The example below is the Layout tab for a text frame. The Layout tab differs from frame to frame, based on the specific needs of that frame. The Layout tab is described specifically for each frame.

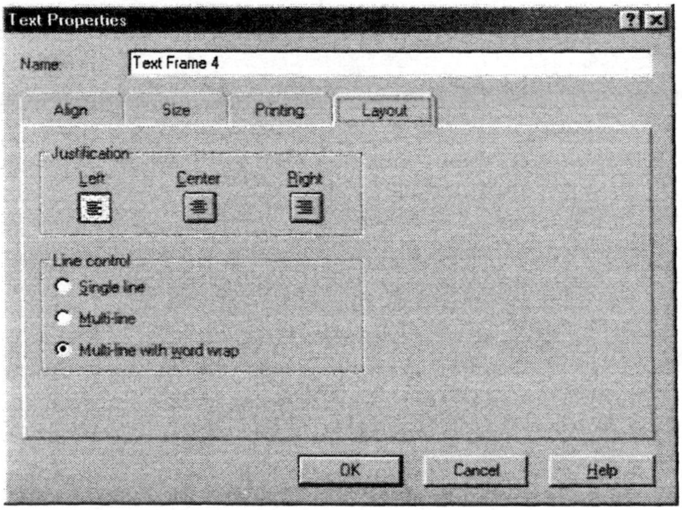

Figure 11.15
A Text frame Layout tab.

Frame Format

The Format window that you see when you select a frame and right click and choose Format, shown in Figure 11.16, is the same Format window described in Chapter 5. For the most part, the only thing new here is how these tabs are applied to different frames. There are a few exceptions, and we will discuss those in their respective frame areas.

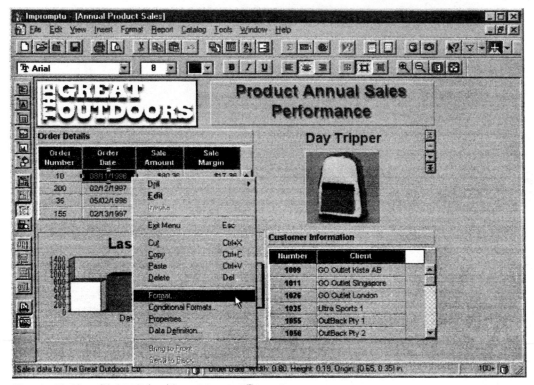

Figure 11.16   Right click with cursor over Format.

For a quick review, here are the Format window tabs.

Data Tab

The Data tab, shown in Figure 11.17, describes how data is displayed on the report. For example, a date column is stored in a database as 1999/12/02, but you want to display only the month/year. The Formats' Data tab provides you with the ability to do this formatting. Because not all frames have data to display (i.e. pictures), not all frames use the Data tab.

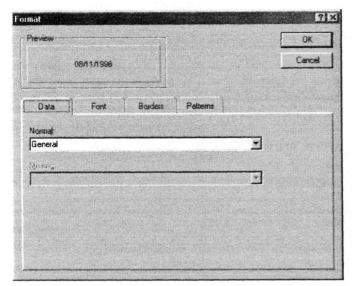

Figure 11.17
A Data tab.

Font Tab

Just as the Data tab describes how data elements are displayed, the Font tab, shown in Figure 11.18, formats how those data elements are viewed. The different characteristics of a frame, Font, Style, Size, and Color are all managed from this tab. Also, as with the Data tab, because not every frame contains data, the Font tab is not used with every frame.

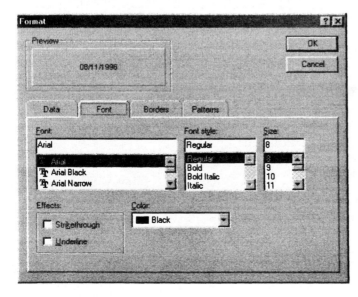

Figure 11.18
A typical Font tab.

Borders Tab

The Borders tab, shown in Figure 11.19, is available to every frame, because every frame has a border, regardless of what the frame has to display. The tab is arranged to give the report developer control over the style and color of each side of a border. Also available are two frequently used options: one to clear the border of all edges, and the other to place the selected style and color on all four sides of the frame.

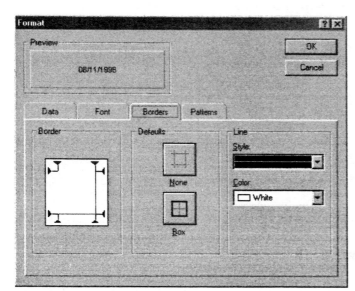

Figure 11.19
A typical Borders tab.

Patterns Tab

Used by most frames, the Patterns tab, shown in Figure 11.20, provides the report developer the ability to select a color background scheme for the given frame. For more information on this frame, refer back to Chapter 5.

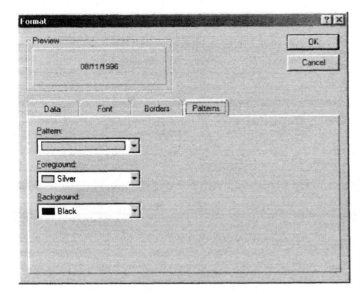

Figure 11.20
The Patterns tab.

Specific Frames

Each frame has a unique purpose in Impromptu. This requires each frame to have unique differences from one to another. These differences are spread throughout the Format and Properties windows. The following section identifies these differences, subtle or not, for each type of frame.

Text Frames

Text frames are the easiest to understand. They are simply line(s) of text that report developers enter to describe something, whether it is a Text frame describing a graph, a Text frame describing a page, or a Text frame displaying an informational message. Text frames have their own properties to manipulate everything from the font size to the background.

Adding a Text frame is easy to do, and it can be placed anywhere in a report, as shown in Figure 11.21. Text frames can be added as a column, in a grouped header or footer, or even anywhere on a different layout, as you have seen in the Annual Product Sales report.

Properties

First, look at the properties of the "Product Annual Sales Performance" text box:

1. Click the Cancel button or hit the Esc key to clear any window open.
2. Right click on the "Product Annual Sales Performance" text box.
3. Select Properties.
4. View the Align tab and then the Size tabs.

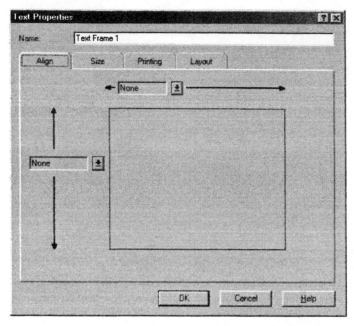

Figure 11.21
The Text frame uses a standard Align tab.

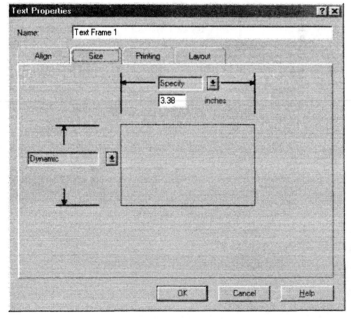

Figure 11.22
The Text frame also uses a standard Size tab.

5. View the Print tab and then the Layout tab.

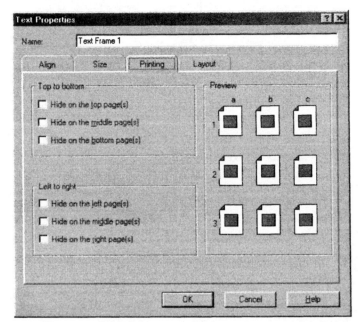

Figure 11.23
The typical view of a Print tab—gives the report developer the ability to manage where the Text frame prints.

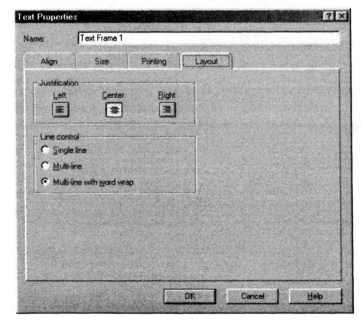

Figure 11.24
The Layout tab controls the text justification and the line control.

Note

One special note about the line control; the difference between multiline and multiline with word wrap is that the word wrap option automatically controls the wrapping of text entered, whereas the word wrap with the regular multiline option is manually controlled by the report developer.

Format

Look now at the Format window of the "Product Annual Sales Performance" text box.

1. Click the Cancel button or hit the Esc key to remove any opened windows.
2. Right click on the "Product Annual Sales Performance" text box.
3. Select Format.
4. View the Font tab and then the Borders tab.

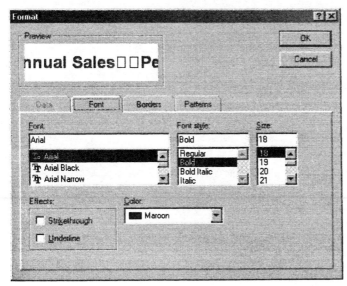

Figure 11.25
The Text frame does not use a Data tab, since there is no data in the text, but it still uses a standard Font tab.

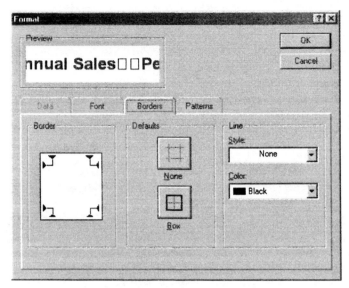

Figure 11.26
The Text frame also uses
a standard Borders tab.

5. View the Patterns tab.

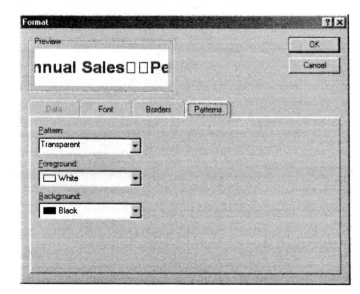

Figure 11.27
The typical view of a Patterns tab.

> **Note**
>
> *The two square boxes that are visible in the preview window represent a carriage return (enter) keystroke in the report. What is interesting about the carriage return with this Text frame is:*
>
> *• It is multiline word wrap, as we noticed from its Layout tab.*
>
> *But...*
>
> *• The report developer forces a second line with a carriage return between the words "Sales" and "Performance." This was done to force the layout you see here.*

Picture Frames

Picture frames are almost as easy as Text frames. There are two examples of this in the report. One Picture frame covers a static graphic being imported into the report, the logo of the company. The other Picture frame obtains a picture dynamically by using a column of data to determine which picture to display. The easiest way to explain this is to describe the static graphic and then discuss how the dynamic one works. They both use a new tab in the Properties window called "Source," which directs Impromptu where to find the picture, but the static and dynamic pictures use different features of this tab.

Properties

First, look at the properties of the corporate logo for Great Outdoors:

1. Click the Cancel button or hit the Esc key to remove any opened windows.
2. Right click on the company logo picture.
3. Select Properties.
4. View the Size tab.

The two options at the bottom of the Size tab control give the report developer the ability to let Impromptu keep the integrity of the picture, or not. When you initially create a Picture frame, you essentially draw a box of a certain size by clicking to anchor one corner, and dragging the cursor to create the desired size of the picture frame. This size, more than likely, will not be to the exact dimensions of the image you wish to use. Impromptu sizes the picture to exactly what you draw. It cannot assume the size of the picture you want to use. So the option to "Scale image to fit" makes sure the image you plan on using in this frame fits the initial frame size without distorting the integrity of the picture.

Once the "Scale image to fit" is selected, it gives the user the option to select the second option: "Maintain width/height ratio." This option forces Impromptu to keep the ratio of height and width. When a report developer resizes the picture, Impromptu is required to keep the height and width in the same proportion.

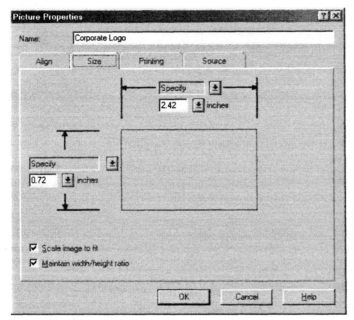

Figure 11.28
There is one difference with the Picture frame's Size tab. It includes in the bottom left corner two options. The Picture frame uses a standard Align tab, so it's not shown.

5. View the Source tab.

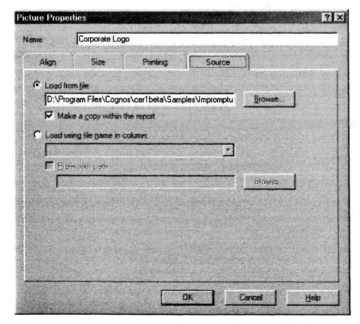

Figure 11.29
This is the Source tab. The two radio buttons control how the image is loaded into the Picture. This example uses the top radio button to directly load the image. The Printing tab (not shown) is typical.

How the Source Tab Works for the Company Logo

The static "Load from file" image uses a specific image from the subdirectory path and displays it on the page. That's it, nothing more, nothing less, just one picture for this picture frame. The checkbox beneath it tells Impromptu to save a copy of the image in the report. This allows the image to be viewed by a report consumer who may not have access to the subdirectory in which it is stored.

1. Click the Cancel button or hit the Esc key to clear any window open.
2. Right Click on the picture of the backpack.
3. Select Properties.
4. Click the Source tab.

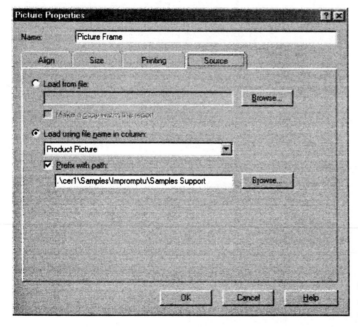

Figure 11.30
The same Source tab used for a dynamic picture display.

The Product Picture image has the same properties as the corporate logo Picture frame, with one small exception. The product picture uses a column from the database to determine the image name to be displayed.

Here's how it works in this example. The column in the dropdown "Product Picture" is a column in the database that contains only names of files. These file names are the names of pictures of the product that happen to be stored elsewhere. When a report developer selects this option, Impromptu takes this name, and follows the subdirectory path in the text box below to find where the image is stored. Then, each time a new Product Picture column is displayed in this report, there is a different picture. The key to the success of this report and displaying each one of the Product Pictures is how the report is set up with groupings and displays.

Note

The column may contain the subdirectory path or, as it is called here, the prefix. If this is the case, you just unselect the checkbox and the column from the report will tell Impromptu exactly where the image is: subdirectory and filename.

Format

Look at the Format window of the Company logo picture.

1. Click the Cancel button or hit the Esc key to remove any opened windows.
2. Right click on the company logo.
3. Select Format.
4. View the Border tab.

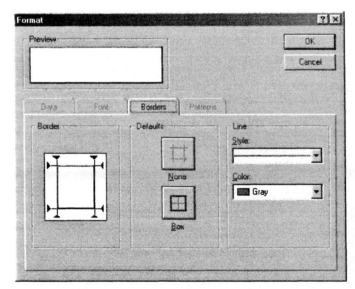

Figure 11.31
The typical view of a Border tab. The Border here, with different right and bottom edges, gives the Picture frame the beveled look.

Additionally, because in the Size tab the "Scale image to fit" was selected, you do not need to use the Pattern tab. Otherwise, you would have the ability to change the background pattern. This is available in the "Product Picture" Picture frame. The other two tabs, Data and Font, do not apply to pictures; accordingly, they are grayed out.

Chart Frames

Chart frames require even more intricate explanation because here Impromptu is displaying information in an entirely different format with this frame. In order to perform these tasks, the Properties window contains two new tabs. With these two new tabs, you will find that some pretty impressive charting can be performed by Impromptu.

Properties

The first three tabs, Align, Size, and Printing, are the same as you have seen and require no further explanation. The focus of the Properties windows is on the Data and Format tabs. Open the properties of the "Last Four Years " Chart frame:

1. Click the Cancel button or hit the Esc key to remove any opened windows.
2. Right click on the chart.
3. Select Properties.
4. View the Data tab.

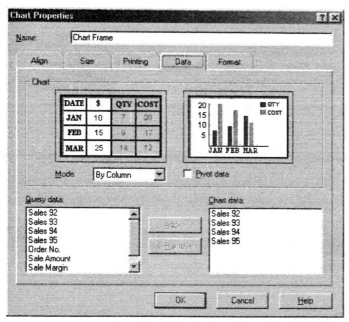

Figure 11.32
The Data tab manages what data goes into the chart and its mode or how the data is used in a graph vertically or horizontally.

Initially, the Data tab looks overwhelming. There are two graphs at the top and two text boxes at the bottom, but the goal is quite simple. The top half grouped by the chart helps a report developer see how the data is going to be viewed as population points in a graph. The "sample" list of data represents how we would see our data: a column of months, a column of $, a column of Qty, and a column of Cost. Notice how the two highlighted columns are measured items on the sample graph to the right. A couple of additional features are included:

1. The Mode dropdown box determines whether the chart will be graphing the data as a comparison of rows or displaying data one row at a time.
2. The checkbox below the sample graph gives the report developer the ability to Pivot or swap the columns being measured with the *x*-axis.

Still on the Data tab but below the chart group is the environment in which the report developer controls what columns from the report are to be used for the chart. Here you have the same environment as when you selected columns from the Catalog into the report. Now you are choosing which items to be used in the chart. Click and drag works between the two columns as well as selecting columns from one side and using the Add or the Remove buttons.

5. View the Format tab.

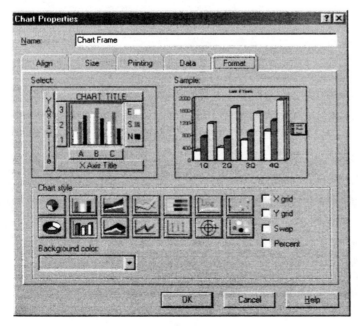

Figure 11.33
The Format tab controls which chart style to use and manages the labeling around the chart.

The Format tab is an interesting and interactive tab. The premise behind this tab is this: The report developer selects a "part" of the chart to modify in the area on the upper left side. Once selected, the bottom half of the tab displays the environment in which the report developer controls the components of that part.

For example, the tab opens by default, with the chart itself selected. At the bottom, the report developer can choose between several chart styles, from a pie chart to a logarithmic curve.

- Select a different section, the Chart Title.

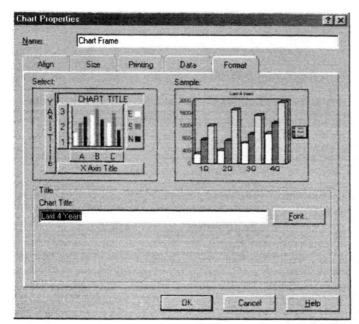

Figure 11.34
The Format tab has changed to allow the report developer to modify the elements of the Chart Title.

In the Chart Title variable, you have the ability to provide the specific title and control the font characteristics of that title, separate from the other aspects of the chart. For each button-like section of a chart, there is a separate area to control each aspect of a chart: from the legend to the x- and y-axes. Take a moment to interact with this tab and become acquainted with its features.

Format

In addition to specific format tab capabilities, there is a further use for the Format window. Here, since all of the specific formatting is done in the Chart Properties window, the only thing left for the Format window to manage is the Borders of the frame. Open the Format window of the chart.

1. Click the Cancel button or hit the Esc key to remove any opened windows.
2. Right click on the Chart.

3. Select Format.

4. View the Border tab.

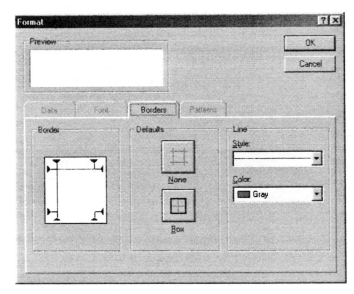

Figure 11.35
The only available option is
the Borders tab. This is shown
to give another example of
beveling a frame to enhance
the viewing appearance.

List Frames

List frames are what you have been working almost exclusively in the examples throughout
the book, so you should be fairly comfortable with what a List frame does. In the context of
properties and formats, Impromptu needs a few new tabs. One is a different view of a familiar tab in the Properties window, and the other is a new tab in the Format window.

Everything you are able to do at the cell/column level is available here from a formatting perspective. Additionally, you are able to manipulate the layout of the each element of
the frame from one tab.

Properties

First, the Properties of the "Order Details" List frame:

1. Click the Cancel button or hit the Esc key to remove any opened windows.
2. Select any cell in the List frame below the Text frame "Order Detail."
3. Select Edit.Select Parent.
4. Right click on the highlighted List frame.
5. Select Properties.

The Align and Size tabs are standard for their functionality. So, we will press on to the other two tabs.

6. View the Printing tab.

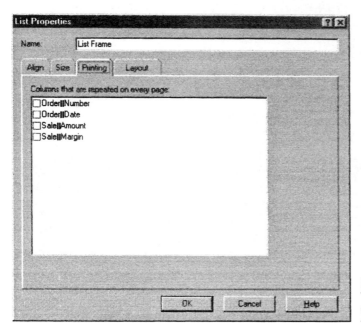

Figure 11.36
The Printing tab of the
Order Details List frame.

The Printing tab provides different functionality for printing than other tabs. The text box in this tab allows the report developer to choose which columns from the list will be repeated on every page. As you can see in this report, both List frames are scrolling frames, which means there are more records to be displayed than are allowed by the size. Checking the repeated checkbox tells Impromptu to keep printing the current page until the all of the rows from the List frames are printed.

Note

The double bar between each word represents a carriage return, as you can see by looking at the Column Headers of the list frame on the report.

7. View the Layout tab (Figure 11.37).

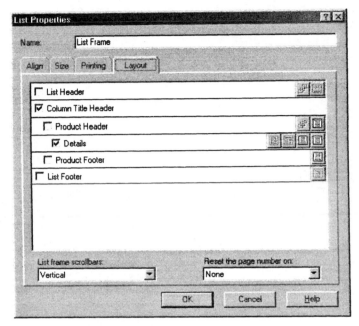

Figure 11.37
The Layout tab of the
Order Details List frame.

The Layout tab for the List frame is, to say the least, a breakthrough in innovation. The Layout tab is also one of the two most complex tabs in Impromptu. Prior to the current Layout tab design, performing these features took multiple tabs as well as some intricate and manual processes. Now, the Layout tab in the List Properties window handles this feature and a few more.

What you see on this tab is a bunch of rows representing items in the List frame: columns, grouped Column headers and footers, details of the report, and List headers and footers. These items are nested, staggered inward, to show a hierarchy. The most inner item will always be the details of the report. Directly to the left of each item is a checkbox indicating whether you see the item on the report. For example, if you were to uncheck the Details option, the List frame will not display the detail rows of the columns being displayed.

Remember from Chapter 8, that when you grouped on an item while in the report, the header appeared automatically. The Layout tab allows the report developer to manually control which grouped columns have their header or footer appear as well as Column headers and List headers and footers. In the report you have open now, there is only one grouped column: Product. So, you only have the ability in the Layout tab to select the Product header and footer. That is why we see two Product items in the Layout tab, one for the header and one for the footer.

Additionally, each of these items has one or more "buttons" to its right. These features are as follows:

- **Repeat Header on every page.** Selecting this button causes the header, whether it is the List header or a Column header, to appear on every page.
- **Pager Break After.** This forces a page break after the item that this button resides on changes.
- **Page Break Before.** This forces a page break before the item that this button resides on begins. You can use this option or the Page Break After option, or you can use both at the same time.
- **Keep Details and Headers Together.** This forces a page break after the item that this button resides on changes.
- **Keep Details and Footers Together.** This forces a page break before the beginning of a new set of grouped data. Either this option can be used or the Header option (above).

Also on this tab are two dropdown selectors. One dropdown controls the scrollbars on the List frame itself. This gives you the ability to control whether the report consumer is allowed to scroll up/down and left/right in the List frame. Careful consideration needs to be made when deciding to turn off this feature. For example, if you have a small List frame size like you have here, and the results of the List frame, the number of rows, exceeds the size the List frame allows, and you have "turned off" the list bars, the report consumer will not be able to view the rows not viewable through the List frame.

The other dropdown control gives the report developer the ability to reset the page count from the selections available. What goes into the dropdown is any grouped column that has a page-breaking button selected.

Format

To view the Format window of the List frame,

1. Click the Cancel button or hit the Esc key to remove any opened windows.
2. Select any cell in the "Order Detail" List frame.
3. Select Edit.Select Parent.
4. Right click on the highlighted List frame.
5. Select Format.

For the List frame, there are only three tabs available in the Format window. The first two, Border and Pattern, are exactly the same as you have seen in the past. The new one is the Grid tab.

6. View the Grid tab (Figure 11.38).

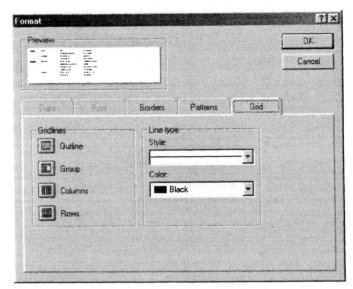

Figure 11.38
The List frame has a
new tab, the Grid tab.

The Grid tab allows you to select a line style using a dropdown selector, similar to the one used in the Border tab. The button group on the left allows you to determine where on the list's grid you want a line and what color of line. This can be any combination of the outline, the groupings, the columns, or the rows. The colors used in this report do not permit you to see the effect of selecting different combinations. When you get a chance, look at this feature and some of these combinations in a basic, simple list report.

Note

You know by now that the List frame is a parent of the column residing in it. You should also know that there is one tab unique to the List Column. It is the Column Title tab in the Properties window (Figure 11.39).

Here, you can type in a name to use for this column's header. Impromptu also provides a checkbox to override the value in the Column title text with the name of the query data item.

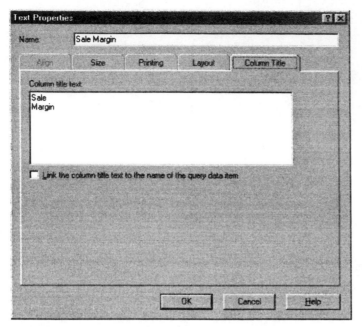

Figure 11.39   The Column Title tab is in the List Column's Properties window.

Form Frames

We now examines the last major frame: the Form frame. The objective of a Form frame is to control the layout of the entire report that you are seeing. The Form frame is a versatile object used in many situations to "form" a report to match the desired layout.

Also introduced with the Form frame is the notion of nesting entire frames within another frame. To see this in action,

1. Click the Cancel button or hit the Esc key to remove any opened windows.
2. Click on any area between the List frame on the left side of the report, the one you were just looking at, and to the right of the Picture frame, which showed a backpack when you first opened the report (Figure 11.40).

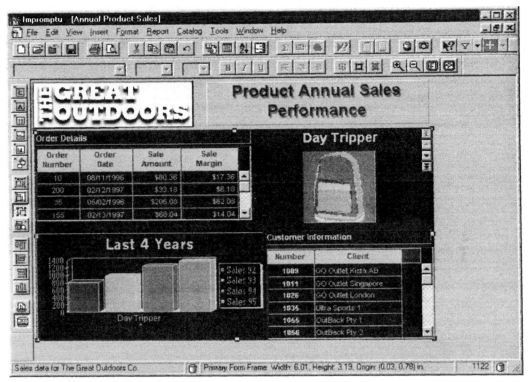

Figure 11.40   The entire Form frame.

What seems to be the entire report is now highlighted, and some of the frames you just examined reside inside the boundaries of the Form frame. These frames, now residing in the Form frame, are anchored in their location within the Form frame. If you move the Form frame around by clicking and dragging, the placement of the frames inside will remain. Figure 11.41 shows a Form frame moved from one side of the screen to the other. Note how the frames inside remain in the same position relative to the Form frame.

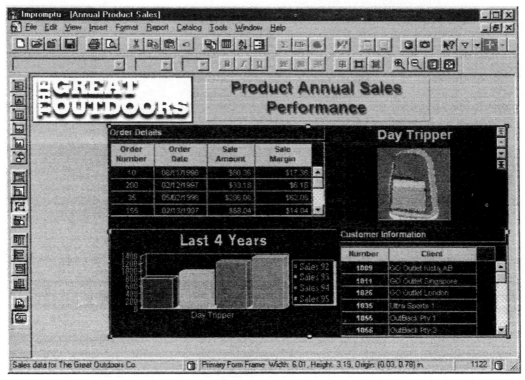

Figure 11.41   The entire frame contents or "children" included, moved.

Properties

To view the properties of the Form frame,

1. Click the Cancel button or hit the Esc key to remove any opened windows.
2. Right click on the Form frame.
3. Select Properties.

In the Properties window, three of the four tabs are available. The Align and Size tabs are identical to the ones seen before.

4. View the Layout tab (Figure 11.42).

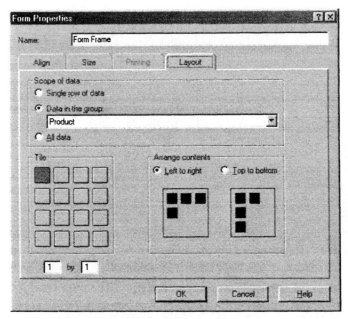

Figure 11.42 The Layout tab for a Form frame.

Again, the main goal of the Form frame is to control how a report displays information differently. What the Layout tab does is tell Impromptu what information to display within the frame. This is referred to as the *Scope of Data*. The Form frame controls the context of data being displayed at any given time in the frame. The three options to control the scope are Single Row of Data, Data in the Group, and All Data.

Single Row of Data.   This option tells Impromptu to display only one row of data inside the frame. This controls what data is displayed in other frames, such as the List frame. To see the impact of this,

1. Select the Single Row of Data option.
2. Click OK (Figure 11.43).

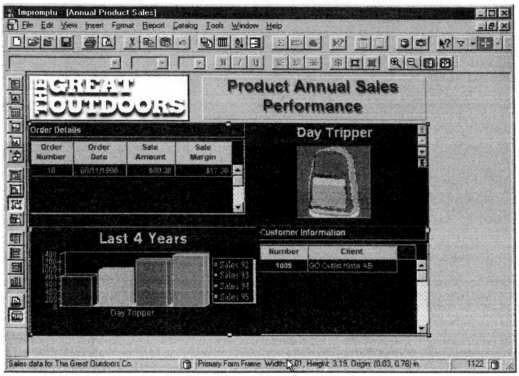

Figure 11.43 Notice how the two List frames show just one row of data each. This is because the Form frame allows only one row of data to be displayed.

Question	Answer
So, how can I see the other Products?	The dial buttons in the upper right corner of the Form frame control scrolling through the different values of the column selected in the Data in the Group (Figure 11.44).

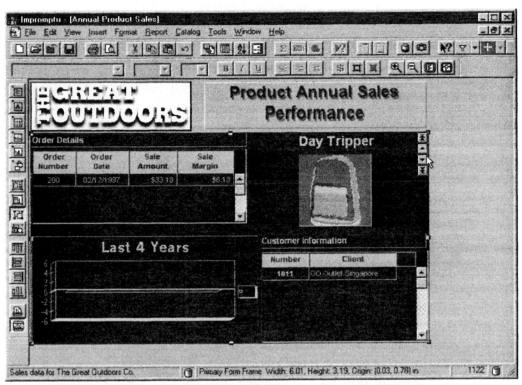

Figure 11.44   This gives the report consumer the ability to jump to the first row of data, next and previous, and to the last row.

By scrolling through the list of rows, you will be scrolling through each instance of a Product in the query. Since the Products are not grouped in this layout, you will see one occurrence of a product at a time.

Data in the Group.   The Data in the Group option allows the report developer to control how the data are displayed. The dropdown menu allows you to select a grouped column. Then the Form frame will show all the rows of the query results in the group. This is the option used in the Annual Product Sales report. This means that all the rows from the Order Detail List frame are orders based on the grouped column, which is the Product column. So, the list of Orders is specific to the product being viewed by the Form frame.

To see the impact of this,

1. Right click on the Form frame.
2. Select Properties.
3. Select the Layout Tab.

4. Select the Data in the Group option. This is the first column displayed in the grouped column Products.

5. Click OK.

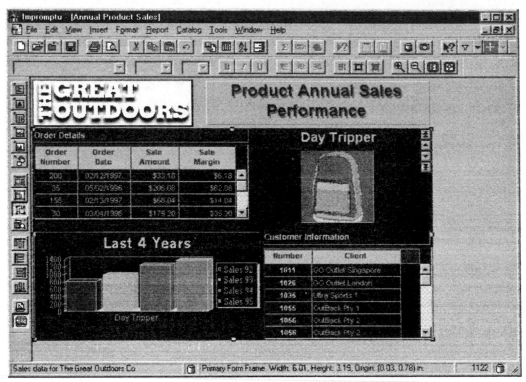

Figure 11.45   Notice how the two List frames now have multiple rows of data populating them.

Note

There is nothing prohibiting you from selecting a column that currently is not grouped. If you were to select a column from the dropdown that is not grouped, that column will become automatically grouped, and the layout and associated frames will display the query results accordingly. Since the report selected the Products column, the Products column is already grouped and sorted alphabetically. By scrolling from one to another, you are scrolling through the Products alphabetically.

All Data.   The final option in the Layout tab is the All Data option. This option "opens the floodgates" of data to the Form frame. This selection returns every row available to the layout of the report.

Try This:

1. Right click on the Form frame.
2. Select Properties.
3. Select the Layout tab.
4. Select the All Data option.
5. Click OK.

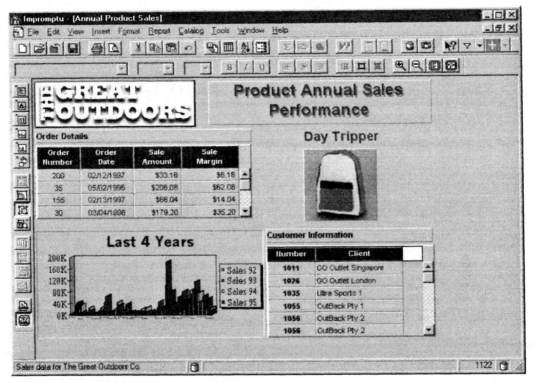

Figure 11.46 Impromptu displays all of the records.

The report layout doesn't change a whole lot, except for the difference in the Chart frame. Since Impromptu is sending all the rows to the layout, instead of comparing the Product sales from the past four years, the chart compares the past four years of all the products.

Note

The All Data option is the default Scope of Data for the Form frame. Initially, this is very similar to the Single Row of Data option. Don't be fooled!

Format

Only the Border and Pattern tabs are available for Form frames. These two tabs perform exactly as they do elsewhere in Impromptu frames, so refer back to the Format description in the Picture frame section.

More Objects

Since the discussion has revolved around identifying the frames and different objects in the Annual Product Sales report, let's take a minute to talk about what else can be added to reports. Impromptu has created an environment in which a report developer can access many other "objects" to add to a report. These objects range from standard and useful reporting components (e.g., page numbers) to more Impromptu-specific objects (e.g., Database Name and Catalog Name). The objects can be placed anywhere in the layout of the report.

There are more than 20 additional options Impromptu makes available to the report developer. These options are available by

- Selecting Insert.More Objects.

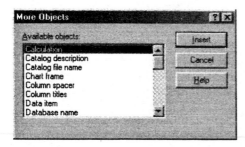

Figure 11.47   The More Objects... window provides the full list of objects available.

All the objects are available through the More Objects window. Once you select the object you want, you are required to place it on the report. This is just like the other frames you have worked with in this chapter, and just like the data columns and calculations you have used in previous chapters.

Here's a list of objects that will provide extra features to the format of a report. Each of these can be used anywhere in the report from the Report Body, like inside a Form frame, to a header or footer of a Simple List report.

System Objects	*Report-Specific Objects*
• System Date	• Detail Filter Text
• System Time	• Summary Filter Text
• Database Name	• Drill Through Filter Text
• Database User ID	• Prompt Variable
• User Class	• Report Description
• OLE Object	• Report File Name
	• Column Spacer
	• Row Number
Impromptu Objects	*Impromptu Format Objects*
• Catalog Description	• Rectangle
• Catalog File Name	• Page Number
	• Running Page Totals
	• Total Pages

Another Example: The Mailing List

Now that you have a good feel for all the reporting features, frames and objects, take a moment to look at another report, a Mailing List report. This report is a valuable example of the different types of "report" that can be developed within Impromptu. This uses another aspect of the Form frame's Layout tab.

Try This:

First, open the report.

1. Select File.Open: Customer Labels.
2. Click Open (Figure 11.48).

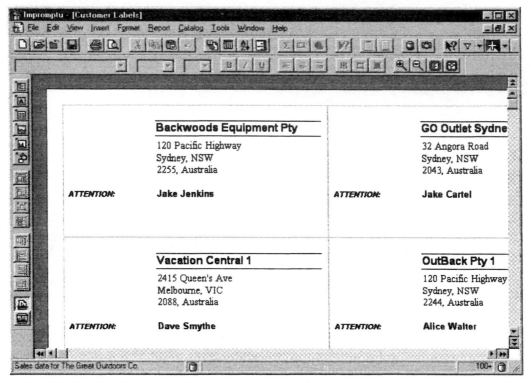

Figure 11.48   The Customer Label report.

This report shows six address labels on one page. Each label is part of one Form frame. To see this, go into the Form frame's Properties Layout tab.

3. Right click on any one of the frame's "labels."
4. Right click, Select Properties.
5. Select Layout tab.

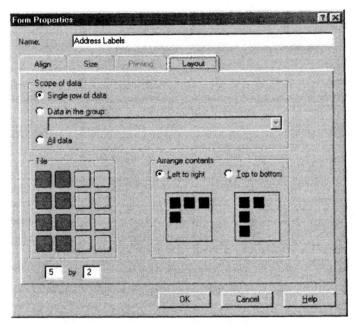

Figure 11.49
The Layout tab.

First look at the Scope of Data. This report uses the first option, single row of data. By using this, Impromptu places one row of data in one Form frame. Next, below the Scope of Data, is the Tile section. The tile feature determines how many frames to display on one page of a report. To control how many forms there are, you can either click on the button, which represents an instance of a tile, or enter in the text box below the exact number of rows and columns on the report. In this example, there are a total of 10 forms, 5 rows of 2 forms.

With the Single Row Scope of Data, one row of data is displayed per frame. When the report has multiple frames on one page, the report developer can control the directional flow of the data. To the right of the tile selection area, you can control the flow of data by selecting either left to right or top to bottom. In this example, there really isn't an advantage to having the order one way or another, so the default of left to right is used.

Summary

The main points learned in this chapter include

1. What a frame is
2. Formats and Properties that control a frame
3. The different frames that are available
4. How frames can enhance a report aesthetically and functionally

There you have it—advanced layouts and formatting at their best. In this chapter, you saw how all these advanced features such as Form frames, Chart frames, and Picture frames can be used to present information in an exciting and attractive way. There are additional examples in the sample reports to give you plenty of ideas to build your own unique reports.

Drill Through Reporting

$\mathbf{T}$his chapter covers the concept of drilling through from one report to another. This concept widens the scope of what can be accomplished with reporting. An entire reporting environment can be developed with the menu of that reporting environment being just one useful report itself.

The goal of this chapter is to introduce both the report developer and report consumer into the world of Drill Through reporting. Drill Through reporting is going from one report to another for more specific information about one topic or another; it is a way to accomplish what many people toil over in their daily activities.

For example, a production manager is looking at a weekly task report describing all the orders needing to be filled. The manager immediately needs to determine whether the raw materials are available to make a certain part. Instead of printing the report to get the part numbers, or writing down the part numbers for a separate report, the manager clicks on the part number, drills through, and launches an inventory report to determine the quantity on hand of the parts. A far-fetched notion? Not after this chapter.

Drill Through Evolution

The concept of drilling through from one report to another evolved from the analytical tool developed by Cognos called PowerPlay. In PowerPlay, one of the many features available is the ability for a report consumer to look at results on a screen and "drill down" from a high level of summarized information to a lower level of information. This concept caught on to the extent that this Drill Through functionality became required for the PowerPlay analysis tool to be able to use certain criteria and "drill down" to another tool, Impromptu. Analysts received their wish to be able to drill through from an analysis in PowerPlay to the detail-level reporting tool in Impromptu. PowerPlay was enhanced to send specific criteria to Impromptu. Impromptu would then use these criteria as a filter in a predefined report and run that report.

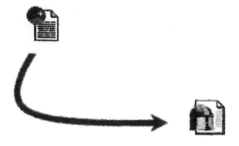

Figure 12.1
The PowerPlay to Impromptu Drill Through.

This was so popular that Impromptu report consumers wanted to have the ability to drill through from one Impromptu report to another. They wanted to look at one Impromptu report and point to a certain piece of data in that report and use that value to filter or drill through to another report. Thus, "drilling through to another report" was born.

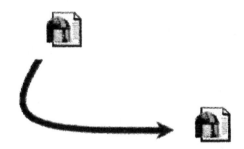

Figure 12.2
The Drill Through from Impromptu to Another.

How Drill Through Works

To show how this works, open a report and do a few Drill Throughs. Impromptu comes with a useful example to give you a solid background to execute your own Drill Through reports.

The initial report used is the Customer Orders Drill Through report.

With Impromptu open,

1. Select File.Open.
2. Open the report: Customer Orders Drill Through (Figure 12.3).

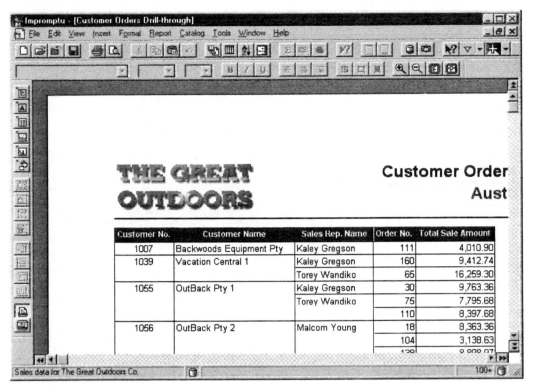

Figure 12.3   The Customer Orders Drill Through report.

The report appears fairly simple upon initial inspection. It looks just like any other Impromptu report you have opened in the past. It becomes interesting when you start drilling through to other reports. There are a lot of questions associated with this new topic, but first, let's walk through one Drill Through.

3. Select the first Order Number in the list: 111.

4. Click the Drill Through button (Figure 12.4).

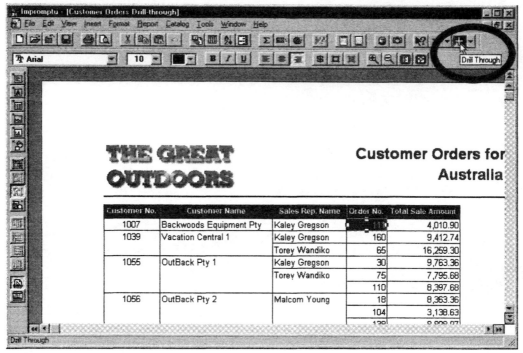

Figure 12.4   The Drill Through button.

The Drill Through button is a combination button; like the Filter button. It has the normal button function—press it, and it does its function. Then, there is the dropdown arrow to the right. It performs similarly to the Dropdown Filter: it provides extended features for Drill Through.

Impromptu opens the Customer Orders Drill Through 3 report and runs it with a filter: Order No. = 111 (Figure 12.5).

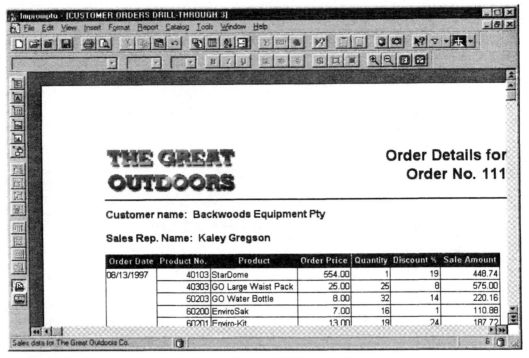

Figure 12.5 The new report: Customer Orders Drill Through 3.

Pretty neat. You just selected a cell from a column on one report, and it became the filter criterion on another. The new report ran, and it is displayed ready to be viewed. The original report, Customer Orders Drill Through, still exists because Impromptu can open multiple reports at once.

Note

One thing to keep in mind is that Impromptu does not label or put a special "tag" on this Drill Through report. There are no visual identifications to let the report consumer know that this report is a result of a Drill Through.

Note

In this chapter, instead of using the traditional Report Requirements and Analysis, the focus shifts to addressing business needs. Drill Through capabilities extend beyond the specific report requirements and address the larger issue of meeting business needs.

What Was My Drill Through Filter?

You ran the Customer Orders Drill Through report. You then performed a Drill Through to another report, Customer Orders Drill Through 3. Suddenly, you get a phone call or remember a meeting or are pulled away because of a crisis. The point is, you leave your desk and forget where you were. And when you get back to your desk....

"Where was I? Was this a Drill Through? What did I use when I drilled?"

Steps to See the Drill Through Filter

Impromptu stores the Drill Through filter in the new report as a filter separate from any others that may have been used for this report. Here's how to see it:

1. Select any cell in the Customer Orders Drill Through 3 report
2. Right click.
3. Choose the Drill option (Figure 12.6).

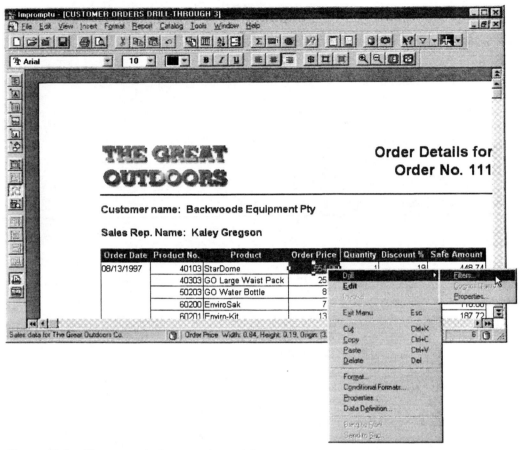

Figure 12.6   The expanded options for Drill Through.

4. Select "Filter...".

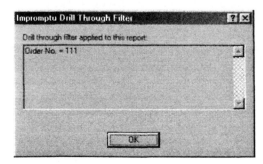

Figure 12.7
The Filters used in the Drill Through.

The result is that the report consumer sees the Drill Through filters being used in this report.

Tip:

Another way to see what Drill Through filters are being used is by selecting from the toolbar.

1. Choose the Drill dropdown option.

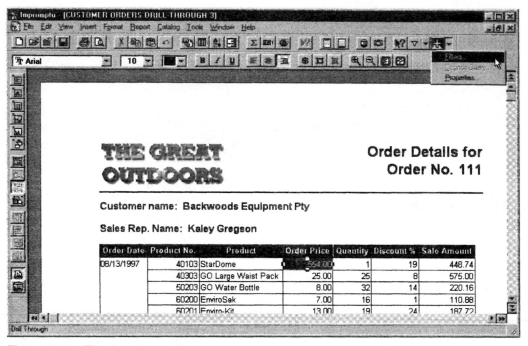

Figure 12.8 The dropdown options.

2. Select "Filter…".

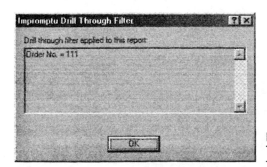

Figure 12.9
The filters used in the Drill Through.

Not Too Bad, Let's Do Another!

Yes, this is pretty cool stuff. The first Drill Through looked at the Order Number = 111. Now you want to do the same Drill Through for Order Number = 30.

Try This:

Start from the original report:

1. Select Windows. Customer Orders Drill Through report.

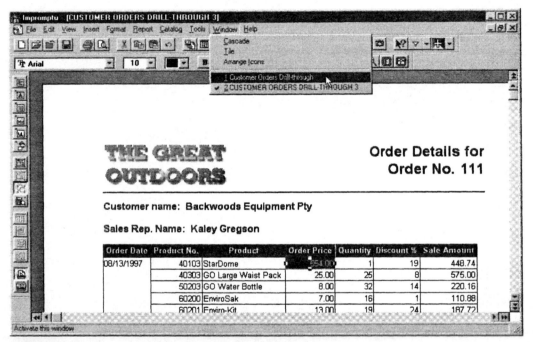

Figure 12.10   The Windows menu contains a list of all the reports open.

This takes you back to the original report opened at the beginning of the chapter. Nothing has changed with this report. It is left as it was before the Drill Through.

There is nothing special involved in drilling through to the same report using a different value. You can do this as often as you like. The following example uses another way to launch a Drill Through request.

Try This:

1. Right click on the cell that contains Order Number 30.
2. Select Drill from the pop-up menu.

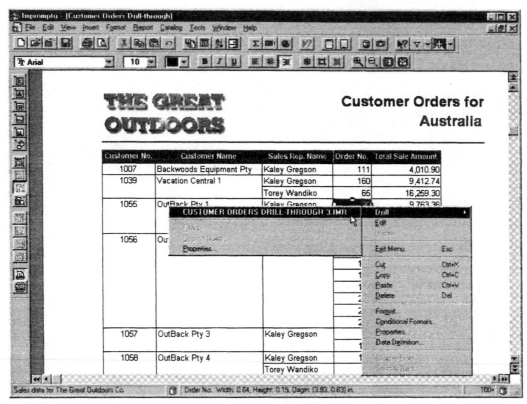

Figure 12.11   The pop-up menu gives you the ability to launch the Drill Through.

3. Choose Customer Orders Drill Through 3.imr (Figure 12.12).

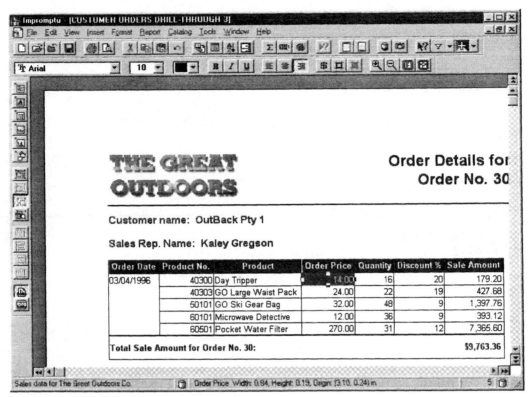

Figure 12.12 Drill Through report results.

The report runs again. Instead of using the previous filter criteria, Order Number = 111, Customer Orders Drill Through 3 replaces it with Order Number = 30.

Filter on a Different Column

The last Drill Through report works well for finding out the order details on a particular order. But say you wanted to look at the total sales for a particular salesperson instead. You would have to drill through to another report. Drill Through reports are not limited to only one Drill Through report per report column. In fact, you can drill through to multiple reports from just one column.

On the first page, Kaley Gregson has her name on a couple of sales orders. Use this Sales Rep Name to drill through to a different report that covers all her orders.

Steps to Drill Through to a Different Report

1. Select the Customer Orders Drill Through report.
2. Right click on a cell containing Kaley Gregson.
3. Select Drill.

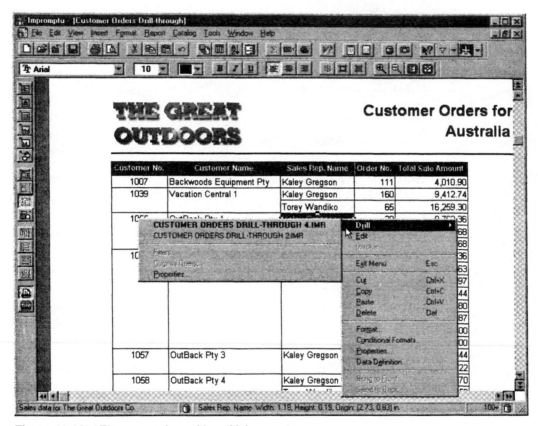

Figure 12.13   The pop-up box with multiple reports.

Here's a new twist: when setting up a column to have Drill Through capabilities, you can set up a column to have multiple report destinations.

4. Select the Customer Orders Drill Through 2 report (Figure 12.14).

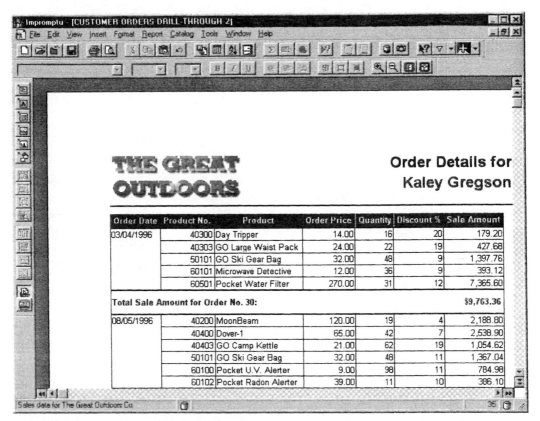

Figure 12.14   A different Drill Through report.

The new destination report displays all of the Order details for Kaley Gregson, grouped by Order. The other Drill Through report option you saw was the default Drill Through report. The default Drill Through is the first choice of Drill Through when a column has multiple Drill Through destinations.

Only One Column per Drill Through?

In the previous examples of Drill Through reporting, the action of drilling used one column name and value as the only parameters being passed from one report to another. Although this is the case 90% of the time, a Drill Through from one report to another can pass multiple columns from one to another.

A moment ago, you saw how one column drills through to multiple reports. But how can a Drill Through request send multiple columns to a destination report?

Before we go into the details of how to do this, take a look at an example of the end results for Kaley Gregson, the same salesperson used for the previous Drill Through.

On the initial report, Customer Orders Drill Through, there are a couple of occurrences of Kaley Gregson. What would be useful is to be able to Drill Through to some report using, for example, both the customer Backwoods Equipment and salesperson Kaley Gregson.

A Drill Through is a specific request. A report consumer cannot select multiple items from a column or columns and pass them on to another report; that is not the intent of Drill Through. The intent is to be able to select a specific item and use that as a filter for another report.

So, Impromptu does not allow the report consumer to pass multiple items from one report to another. It does allow the report developer to build this into the Drill Through filter definition of a Drill Through destination report. In this example, the destination report to answer the above question has been developed, even though the report consumer will use only one cell value to drill through.

Steps to Run a Multiple-Column Drill Through

1. Select the Customer Orders Drill Through report.
2. Right click on customer Backwoods Equipment.
3. Select Drill.
4. Choose the other report, Customer Orders Drill Through 4 (Figure 12.15).

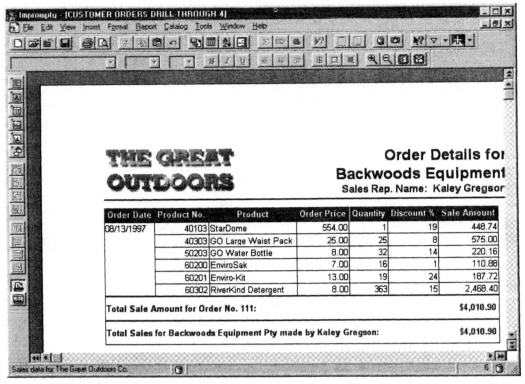

Figure 12.15   The Drill Through destination report.

A visual inspection of the results of this report show that the results are exactly what were asked. Both the Sales Rep Name column Kaley Gregson and the Customer Name column Backwoods Equipment are part of the filter.

To see the filter,

1. Right click on any column.
2. Select Drill.
3. Choose Filters... (Figure 12.16).

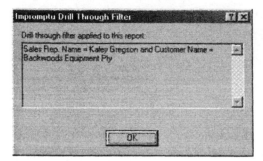

Figure 12.16
The Drill Through filter.

Question	Answer
Hey, the Drill Through filter has two filter criteria in it. But, the report consumer selected only one column. What is the deal, you said only one column can be passed to the destination report?	As a report consumer, you are only able to select one column and then pass it off the destination report as a Drill Through. Behind the scenes, the report developers set up the Drill Through of the Customer Name to send both the Customer Name and the Sales Rep Name. For a report developer, the next step is to learn how to set up what actually gets sent from the origination report to the destination report.

How it's Done

You all have been anxiously waiting to learn how to set up the Drill Through. It's quite simple. The interface is easy enough to use. You do not have to be a programmer to set up a Drill Through report. In fact, the interface used to develop the Drill Through is also what report consumers can use to determine which column on a report has Drill Through capabilities.

It all revolves around the Drill Through Properties of a report. In the Properties, you can link any column or combination of columns in the current report to any report that has been developed.

The three ways to get to the Drill Through Properties are as follows:

1. Right click
   • Right click on a cell.
   • Select Drill.
   • Choose Properties.
2. Toolbar
   • Click the Drill Through dropdown.
   • Choose Properties.

3. Report Column
- Double click on the cell you want to Drill Through.

Try This:

Go back to the original Customer Orders Drill Through report.

1. Select the Customer Order Drill Through report.
2. Hit the Esc key to ensure that nothing is highlighted.
3. Click the Drill Through button.

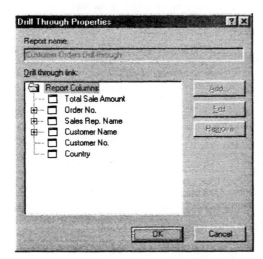

Figure 12.17
The Drill Through Properties window.

The Drill Through Properties window is the environment in which it all happens. In this window, you see:

- Each column of the report that you are currently in, regardless of whether it is a calculation, a total, or not shown
- Whether a column is grouped or associated
- Which columns have Drill Through links

This window allows report developers and report consumers both to see what is linked and to provide the environment to create and manage links. The set of buttons to the right of the list allows a Drill Through report to be added or a current one to be edited, and the bottom button allows you to remove an existing Drill Through report. Additionally, here you can add multiple Drill Through destination reports for each column.

The linked columns can be identified initially by the plus signs appearing next to them. Expanding the first one, Order No., you see that there is a report tie beneath it called Customer Orders Drill Through 3.imr, as shown in Figure 12.18. This is the Drill Through report you used when you selected the column in the first example.

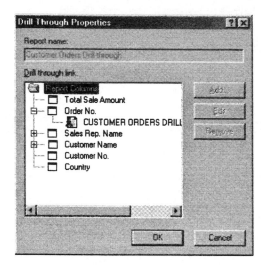

Figure 12.18
The expanded Order No. column.

View an Existing Drill Through

First, I recommend looking at an existing Drill Through. For this example, continue working with the Order No. Drill Through. With the Drill Through destination report selected, click the Edit button.

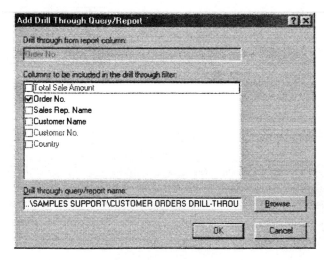

Figure 12.19
The selection criteria and report name for the Drill Through report.

In this window, several things can be identified. First, in the Columns to Be Included box, some columns are black and some are grayed out. The grayed-out columns are not available in the destination report, so it would be useless to select these columns. They are disabled. The black columns are columns in the Drill Through destination.

Next, you choose the Drill Through query here. This holds the complete path and file name for the query. There are two types of queries available for Drill Through. One is the IMR report you have been using throughout this book. The other is a report extension called IQD.

Create a Drill Through

To create a Drill Through is remarkably simple. While in the Drill Through Properties window, you can add a Drill Through to any report. The only requirement in creating a Drill Through is that the destination or target report must be already developed. The report must exist before you can select it as a Drill Through destination report.

Steps to Create a Drill Through

The following steps are all that is needed to create a Drill Through:

1. Click the Order No. column.
2. Click the Add...button.

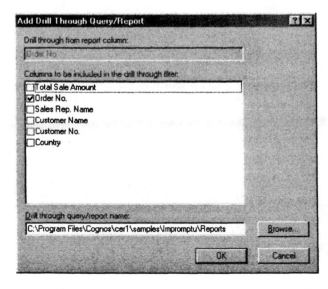

Figure 12.20
The Add Drill Through
Query/Report window.

The window used to add a Drill Through report is almost self-explanatory. In the main text box are all the columns used in this report, and the Order No. column is, by default, selected. Here is where you are able to select multiple columns from a report's row to be passed to a Drill Through report. Just select the checkbox next to the columns you wish to pass to the Drill Through report, and they will be passed along.

For this exercise:

3. In addition, choose Customer Name.

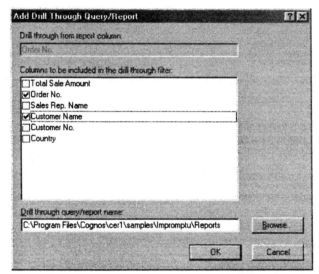

Figure 12.21
Customer Name is now also selected.

At the bottom of the window, there is a subdirectory path and a Browse button. This lets the report developer either type in the path and report name or select a report from anywhere in the network using an Open Dialog box, like the one used by many other Windows applications.

Note

Columns in a report can contain multiple Drill Through reports or destinations. They are listed in the Drill Through Properties window in the order in which they appear in the pop-up menu. Also, the first one in the order is the default Drill Through report. In the Drill Flyout menu, the destination report name is bold to indicate that it is the default.

The report developer may alter the order of the Drill Through reports in the same drag-and-drop manner used in other portions of Impromptu. The report name is selected and dragged to the place in the order the report developer prefers. Unfortunately, you are not allowed to move the report from one column to another.

4. Press the Browse button to find a destination report, as shown in Figure 12.22

When you select the Browse button, Impromptu opens the Open Dialog box and performs several passes of the files included in the directory. Impromptu is looking for IMR reports that contain both columns Order No. and Customer No. When finished, it will return all reports matching the criteria.

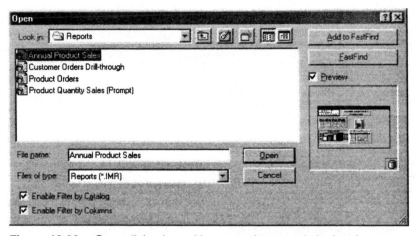

Figure 12.22   Open dialog box with reports that contain both columns.

5. Select Annual Product Sales.
6. Click OK to close the Add Drill Through window.
7. Click OK again to close the Drill Through Properties window and return to the report.

Note

Even though you have changed "the report," you did not change the specific query. Consequently, Impromptu does not have to re-query and rerun the report.

Test New Drill Through

Go ahead and test the newly created Drill Through:

1. Select the Order No. of 65.
2. Right click.
3. Select Drill.
4. Select Annual Product Sales.

And the Results Are...

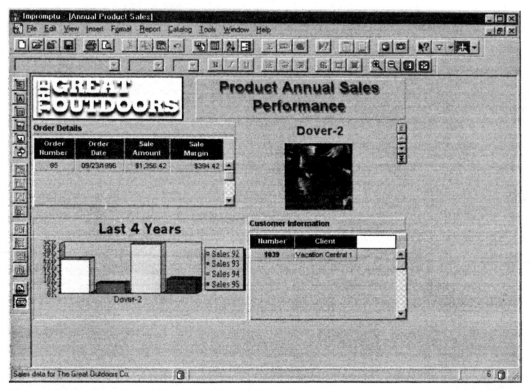

Figure 12.23   The Annual Product Sales report.

The report you are looking at is a specific Annual Product Sales report just for the one Order No. and Customer No. combination. As you can see, with Drill Through reporting your imagination is the only limit.

Summary

The main points covered in this chapter are

1. What Drill Through means
2. How Drill Through works
3. How to create a Drill Through

The concept of drilling through from one report to another and passing along values is, as you found in this chapter, a very simple yet powerful feature. Creating a reporting environment from inside reports is a refreshing concept, compared with the not-so-long-ago days of subdirectory nightmares.

The really exciting aspect of Drill Through reporting is the ease with which it can be implemented. There is no real "implementation process" to bog down an organization. No high tech consultants, no project plans, no meetings to discuss topics for planning meetings—just tie one report to another. Impromptu put a great deal of power in the hands of the right people with Drill Through: the people who need it!

Crosstab Reports

This chapter covers a very challenging topic: Crosstab reports. Crosstab reports are easy to construct from a functional aspect, but the concept, logic, and decisionmaking behind them is the real challenge. The display of a Crosstab report is always appealing to a report consumer. The challenge comes in developing a Crosstab report that both meets the users' needs and is an efficient query for the database. A poorly designed and developed Crosstab report is something to avoid.

There are three common ways a report developer interacts with Crosstab reports. Covering the following topics will prepare you for any report request that is thrown your way:

1. Opening up an example Crosstab report
2. Creating a Crosstab report from scratch
3. Converting a Simple List report to a Crosstab report

Crosstabs: The Basics

First, what is a Crosstab? A Crosstab report is a report that shows information summarized based on data organized in rows and columns. These rows, columns, and summarized values are all common values within a data column. The most common equivalent to a Crosstab report is a spreadsheet. A spreadsheet typically looks at information on an x- and y-axis. For example, a Crosstab report could be a report showing Sales Total with Products identifying the rows (x-axis) and by Sales Channels (y-axis).

Building Crosstab reports requires the same steps as building Simple List reports. Follow those steps just as if it were any other type of report.

1. Gather report requirements from users.
2. Ensure that the data are accessible (make sure that the columns are either in the Catalog or that they can be built using calculations).
3. Build the report for functionality (build just what the reporting requirements ask).
4. Validate the results:
   a. Run quick-and-dirty Test reports to verify results of sections of the main report.
   b. Verify the results with the user.
5. Clean up the report (apply formatting).

The approach taken in this chapter on Crosstabs is the same as in teaching past topics: Using an example from the sample reports provided by Impromptu, I describe the environment and the basics.

When to Use a Crosstab Report?

Properly identifying whether a report needs to be a Crosstab report or a Simple List report is essential. Here are a few simple guidelines for determining when to use a Crosstab report template:

- When a report is described with unique row and column identifiers
- When a user describes a report with terms such as Matrix, Grid, Intersecting totals, or even crisscross.
- Usually, when an existing report has months, years, or date groupings across the top.

Opening an Existing Crosstab

In the preceding chapters, an existing report showcasing the features of the upcoming chapter is discussed. This chapter follows a similar pattern by opening an existing Crosstab report. The twist here is that the report is not just a Crosstab report. It is a Crosstab report that incorporates a Prompt. This sample report provides a solid example, not only of an Impromptu Crosstab, but also of using different features in Impromptu to answer a reporting request.

Open the Report

The sample report used here is the Total Sales Over (Prompt). With Impromptu open, follow these steps to open a Crosstab Report:

1. Select File.Open.
2. Open the report Total Sales Over (Prompt).

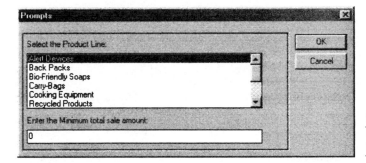

Figure 13.1
The Total Sales Over (Prompt)
report Prompt.

The report runs as it is supposed to and then asks you to fill the Impromptu Prompt.

3. Click on "Back Packs."

4. Hold down the Ctrl key and click on the "Carry-bags."

5. Let go of the Ctrl key.

6. Type in 14000 for the minimum Total Sale Amount.

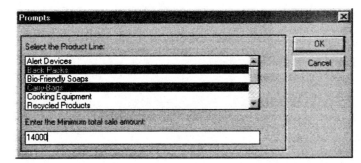

Figure 13.2
The finished Prompt box.

7. Click OK (Figure 13.3).

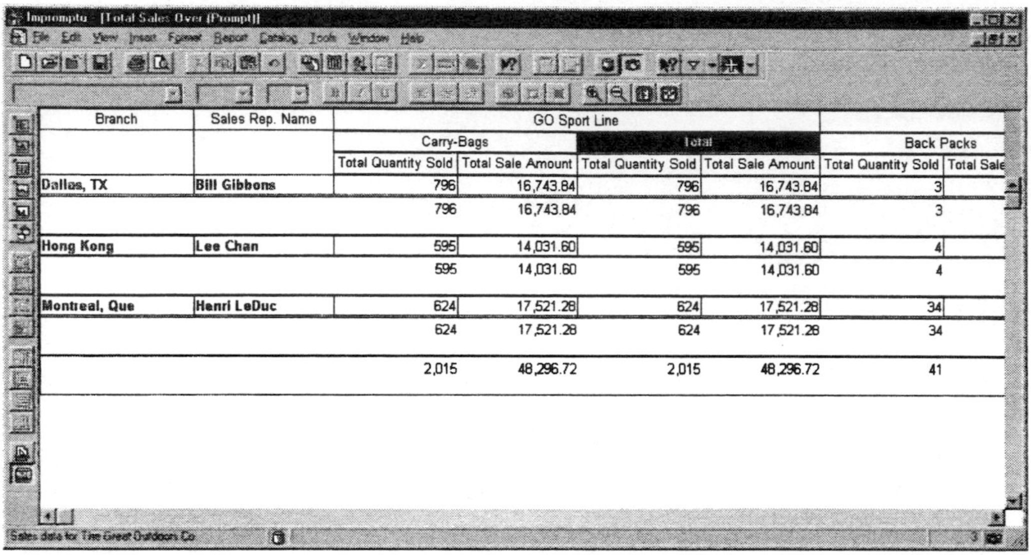

Branch	Sales Rep. Name	GO Sport Line					
		Carry-Bags		Total		Back Packs	
		Total Quantity Sold	Total Sale Amount	Total Quantity Sold	Total Sale Amount	Total Quantity Sold	Total Sale
Dallas, TX	Bill Gibbons	796	16,743.84	796	16,743.84	3	
		796	16,743.84	796	16,743.84	3	
Hong Kong	Lee Chan	595	14,031.60	595	14,031.60	4	
		595	14,031.60	595	14,031.60	4	
Montreal, Que	Henri LeDuc	624	17,521.28	624	17,521.28	34	
		624	17,521.28	624	17,521.28	34	
		2,015	48,296.72	2,015	48,296.72	41	

Figure 13.3   The report results in Screen layout. If you have a Page layout, you will see only part of the results.

Overview of Result Layout

Here you see the results of a Crosstab report. Notice that along the rows, you see the hierarchy of Branch then Sales Rep, and then on the top, you see the hierarchy of the products. These are natural groupings in the database that Impromptu is taking advantage of. Keep this tip in mind. When you build Impromptu reports, always try to utilize natural groupings and hierarchies,

Inside the QDB

Take a second to look into the QDB.

- Open the QDB, and look at the Data tab (Figure 13.4).

    The QDB has been modified to properly display a working environment in which the report developer has populated the proper columns, rows, and cells. Each of these elements of a Crosstab tab will be fully explained when a new report is developed. Only the Sort and Filter tabs are available. In a Crosstab report, there is no need for a Group tab, because the Crosstab groups the rows and columns.

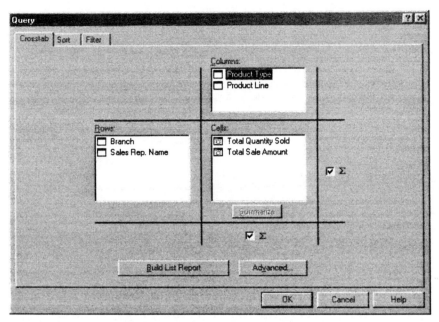

Figure 13.4   The QDB has changed. Instead of a Data tab, there is a Crosstab tab.

Creating a Crosstab

One of the critical elements to building a Crosstab report is developing a sound set of report requirements. To set up the first Crosstab report, use the following business request:

Report Requirement

Boss: *"I need a grid-like report that shows the Qty sold for sales reps and by Sales Channel."*

Analysis

Short and sweet; if only all the report users described their reports like this. In most cases, there is a lot more that comes with a report request. For the purposes of this exercise, however, I did not want to bore you by explaining why the boss needs this report. So, breaking down the report requirements, the needs are simple. The report consists of three columns:

- Sales Rep
- Sales Channel
- Qty

Question	Answer
Is this a List report or a Crosstab?	Since the topic of this Chapter is Crosstab reports, obviously this report is an example.
	But note that in the description, the report consumer did not even know to say Crosstab report. Instead, the consumer used a more descriptive term: "grid-like." This term is used frequently by report consumers, because initially they are unaware of the proper terms for different elements and features of Impromptu reports. As consummers evolve and become more knowledgeable about Impromptu, these odd descriptions will dissipate.

Steps to Create a Crosstab Report

With Impromptu open, use a Crosstab template to build this first Crosstab report:

1. Create a new report using File.New.
2. Choose the Crosstab template.

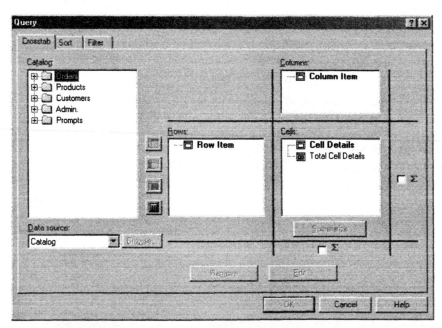

Figure 13.5   The initial QDB for Crosstab reports.

Hey, look; the QDB has changed. It had to. This isn't your standard list report anymore. A Crosstab report is a whole new breed of report. The most significant change with the QDB for a Crosstab report is the layout of the Data tab, which is now the Crosstab tab. This is the most important change. The layout of this screen serves two purposes. One, it provides an accurate place for the report developer to put rows versus columns. Two, it helps the report developer visualize the rows, columns, and cells, and how they will be displayed.

Crosstab reports display the intersection of a row and column as a cell. This is more than just a value of a column in a Simple List report. It is a numerical summary of an intersection of two columns of data, whether it is a numeric column or a count of some alphanumeric column's occurrences.

Cells? Yes, Crosstab reports not only display results in a different manner visually, but they must be thought of in different terms to build them. In the chapter on Summaries, groupings and totals were discussed, and the concept of a Summary report was introduced. Summary reports are reports that deliver results based solely on the groupings of the columns not being summarized. This holds true for Crosstab reports also—Crosstab reports are advanced Summary Reports.

There are two main ways to populate the elements of a Crosstab report:

- **Click and Drag.** This method requires the report developer to place the column from the Catalog directly on the Placeholder in the Crosstab report.
- **Buttons.** This option takes care of aligning the column in the proper location in the Crosstab report; the report developer just selects a column from the Catalog and clicks the desired area of the Crosstab.

Figure 13.6
Column button: Places a column from the Catalog into the Column box.

Figure 13.7
Row button: Places a column from the Catalog into the Row box.

Figure 13.8
Cell button: Places a column from the Catalog into the Cell box as a total or a count.

Figure 13.9
Calculator button: Takes the report developer to a Calculation Definition box, and then prompts you to place the calculation in the row, column, or cell.

Back to building your first Crosstab report.

3. Using any way you choose, move the following columns to the respective part of the Crosstab report, as shown by the examples in Figures 13.10 and 13.11.

- Sale Rep Name –> Row
- Sales Channel –> Column
- Qty –> Cells

When finished, the Crosstab QDB will look like Figure 13.12.

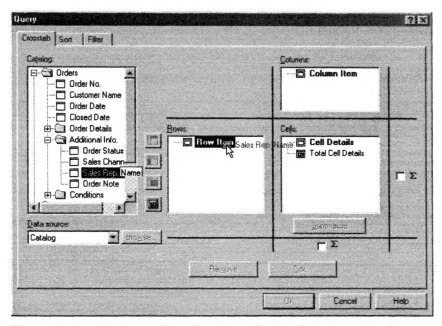

Figure 13.10   Moving the Sales Rep Name Catalog Column over the Row Placeholder.

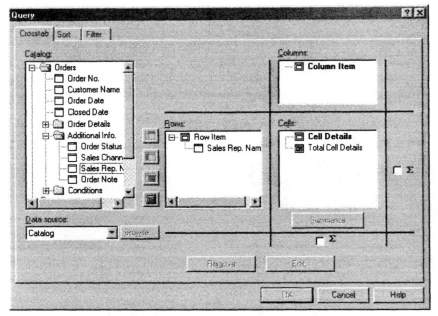

Figure 13.11 When the mouse is let go, the Sales Rep Name Column fits under the Row Placeholder.

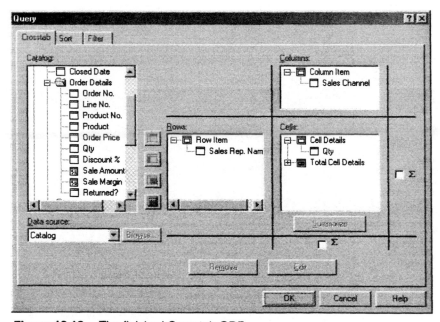

Figure 13.12 The finished Crosstab QDB.

Notice that when the Qty column was placed as a "cell" detail, Impromptu added a plus sign to the "Total Cell Details." The plus sign lets you know that you can expand this cell. This is a default setting establishing a total to be placed as an intersection for grouped rows and columns.

4. Click OK to run the report.

And the Results Are...

Sales Rep. Name	Direct Sales	Mail Sales	Telephone Sales
Bill Gibbons	1639	241	1310
Bill Smertal	1916		
Bjorn Flertjan	2094	1451	574
Carlos Rodriguez	2551		412
Charles Loo Nam	2449	513	517
Chris Cornel	705	515	448
Conrad Bergsteige	1113	509	1413
Dan Chancevente	797	738	798
Dave Mustaine	1580	592	1457
Francoise LeBlanc	328	1011	1394
Gilles Turcotte	1279	131	576
Greg Torson	401	563	348
Gus Grovlin	983	161	865
Hari Krain	1243		657
Henri LeDuc	1844	876	715
Henry Harvey	326	334	147
Ingrid Termede		291	1314
Inigo Montoya	112		123
Jane Litrand	753	387	982
Kaley Gregson	1388	589	433

Figure 13.13   The report results.

At first glance, it does not look all that exciting. But, upon closer observation, you see that the column headers, Direct Sales, Mail Sales, and Telephone Sales, all have values beneath them. In the database, those headers are all values within a specific column called Sales Channel. In the Crosstab report you are looking at, they appear as column headers for the values. Pretty neat, but pretty deceiving.

Enhance a Basic Crosstab

Go back to the QDB for the Crosstab report, as shown in Figure 13.14. Notice that the placeholders are now gone, no longer needed. Something is different; the single entity Qty is gone. Looking at the rows and columns, we see that something else is new also: these two columns have the bands across the top, and they are grouped!

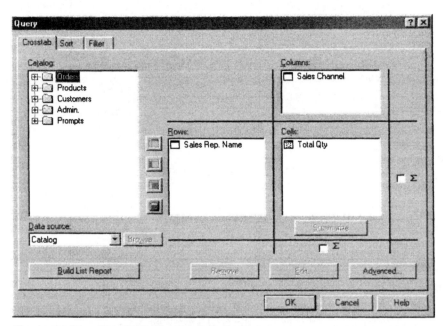

Figure 13.14 The QDB after the initial report was run.

Thinking it through, it makes sense. With both the rows and columns grouped, the only way to accurately display the cell value is by totaling it. This is the value that the Crosstab QDB provides: it offloads some of the thought from the report developer.

Now, let's enhance this Crosstab report and add a column to it.

Report Requirement

Boss: *"I like the Sales Rep Qty report by Sales Channel, but I'd like to see the Qty by Product Type for the Sales Rep as well."*

Analysis

From this statement, you gather that the Boss wants to see each sales rep's Qty broken out by Product Type. To solve this request, the report needs to display the Product Type as a nested grouping under the Sales Rep Name column. In other words, the Product Type column should be grouped beneath the Sales Rep Name column.

Steps to Enhance the Crosstab Report

With the QDB open:

1. Select the Crosstab tab.
2. Expand the Product folder in the Catalog.
3. Highlight the Product Type column.
4. Click the Row button.

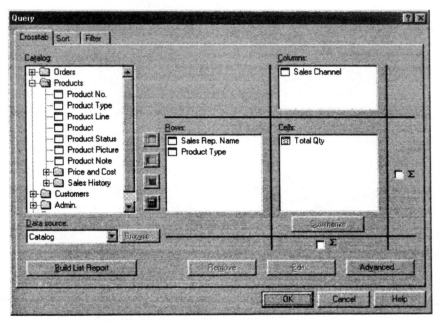

Figure 13.15   The new QDB with Product Type added.

Notice how the Product Type automatically slips beneath the Sales Rep Name and is grouped. This happens automatically, because the report is, in fact, a summary report. Every column in the report is either grouped or summarized.

5. Click OK.

And the Results Are...

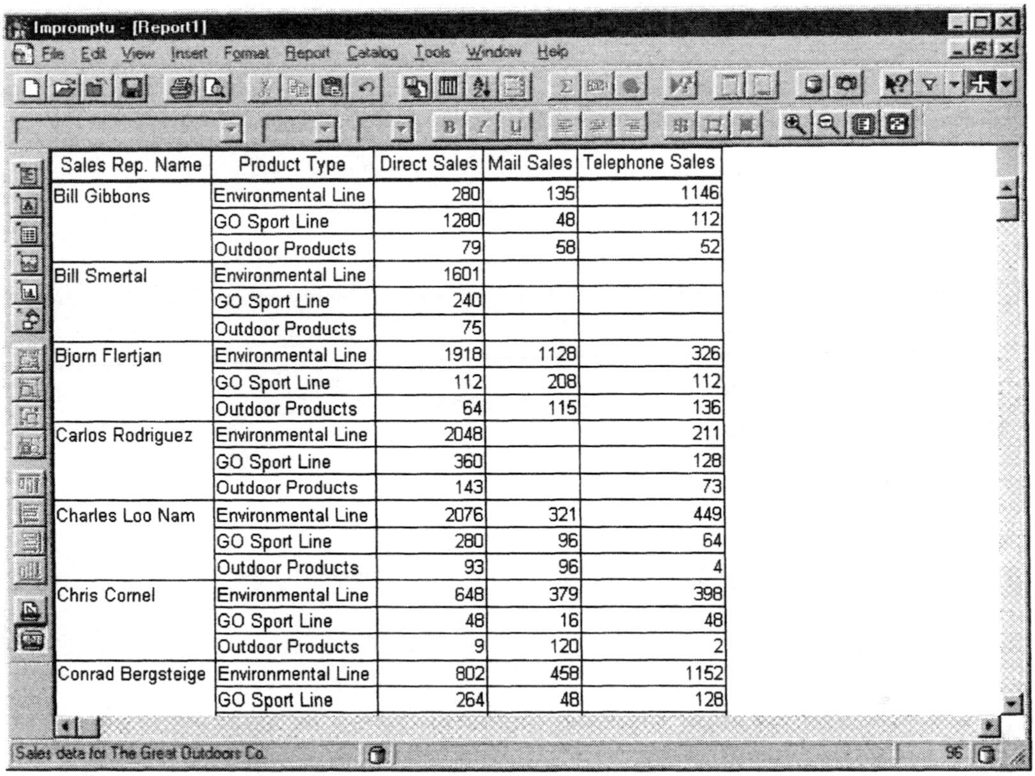

Sales Rep. Name	Product Type	Direct Sales	Mail Sales	Telephone Sales
Bill Gibbons	Environmental Line	280	135	1146
	GO Sport Line	1280	48	112
	Outdoor Products	79	58	52
Bill Smertal	Environmental Line	1601		
	GO Sport Line	240		
	Outdoor Products	75		
Bjorn Flertjan	Environmental Line	1918	1128	326
	GO Sport Line	112	208	112
	Outdoor Products	64	115	136
Carlos Rodriguez	Environmental Line	2048		211
	GO Sport Line	360		128
	Outdoor Products	143		73
Charles Loo Nam	Environmental Line	2076	321	449
	GO Sport Line	280	96	64
	Outdoor Products	93	96	4
Chris Cornel	Environmental Line	648	379	398
	GO Sport Line	48	16	48
	Outdoor Products	9	120	2
Conrad Bergsteige	Environmental Line	802	458	1152
	GO Sport Line	264	48	128

Figure 13.16 The report result broken out by Product Type.

The report delivers exactly what the boss requested. The Product Type falls beneath the Sales Rep Name. All the report developer had to do was bring the Product Type into the row area, and Impromptu did the rest.

Adding Cells

This section addresses adding additional cells to a report. Can a Crosstab report have more than one cell? Yes, it is possible to have an intersection of a row and column result in two distinctly different values. Here is how Impromptu manages this request.

Report Requirement

Boss: *"Qty is nice, but can I have Total Sale Amounts in the Crosstab, too?"*

Analysis

The report request is actually calling for two things:

1. The boss is asking for another measure: Total Sale Amounts.
2. This report request, as simple as it is, is letting you see how report consumers become more adaptive to an environment. They start to expand their vision of what they want and need. They start using Impromptu terms. By just adding the "Total" description, they are internalizing what they are seeing.

Steps to Add Cells to the Crosstab Report

1. Open the QDB.
2. Expand the Order folder in the Catalog.
3. Expand the Order Details folder.
4. Highlight the Sale Amount column.
5. Click the Cell button.

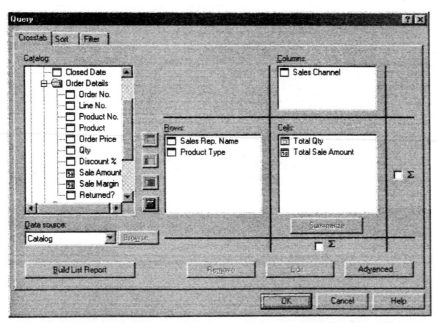

Figure 13.17   The finished QDB.

The Sale Amount blends into the bottom of the cells list. Visually, the calculate icon next to the name in the cell box is different. It is not an automatic Summary, nor is it associated with any row or column. Don't worry, this is applied by Impromptu upon running the report.

* Click OK.

And the Results Are...

Sales Rep. Name	Product Type	Direct Sales		Mail Sales		Telephone	
		Total Qty	Total Sale Amount	Total Qty	Total Sale Amount	Total Qty	Total
Bill Gibbons	Environmental Line	280	22174.13	135	1091.25	1146	
	GO Sport Line	1280	19029.04	48	393.6	112	
	Outdoor Products	79	22598.96	58	3265.68	52	
Bill Smertal	Environmental Line	1601	17278.22				
	GO Sport Line	240	1912.8				
	Outdoor Products	75	9516.29				
Bjorn Flertjan	Environmental Line	1918	22362.32	1128	9977.81	326	
	GO Sport Line	112	1630.24	208	4981.92	112	
	Outdoor Products	64	5315.1	115	19552.76	136	
Carlos Rodriguez	Environmental Line	2048	26773.58			211	
	GO Sport Line	360	7011.04			128	
	Outdoor Products	143	19078.68			73	
Charles Loo Nam	Environmental Line	2076	17482.49	321	7757.49	449	
	GO Sport Line	280	7953.12	96	732.16	64	
	Outdoor Products	93	11844.36	96	8821.47	4	
Chris Cornel	Environmental Line	648	4992.38	379	2019.81	398	
	GO Sport Line	48	790.88	16	134.4	48	
	Outdoor Products	9	2117.36	120	20242.06	2	
Conrad Bergsteige	Environmental Line	802	8562.99	458	8156.77	1152	

Sales data for The Great Outdoors Co   96

Figure 13.18   The report result with the new cell.

What is interesting about this report result is how Impromptu positioned the new total. The report display has been updated to categorically identify the different cells in the body of the Crosstab. Instead of assuming the cell is one value, Impromptu has to visually identify each cell. It does so by adding column headers to separate them for the report consumer. Don't let this fool you into thinking that the new cell was converted to a column; it wasn't. This is just how Impromptu distinguishes the different cells.

Summarizing the Crosstab Report

So far, this chapter has yet to cover summaries in the Crosstab reports in any degree of detail. Now is the perfect time. Summaries are a vital part in Crosstab reports. From the ccell, to row and column totals, this section discusses the role and functionality of summaries in Crosstab reports.

Basics of Summaries

The basic way of summarizing a Crosstab report is by using the checkboxes in the QDB. Using the checkboxes gives the report developer the ability to total at every grouping level in the Crosstab report. With the checkbox, either all totals are engaged, or none. This applies to both Row and Column Summarize checkboxes. Let's go ahead and do one.

Report Requirement

Boss: *"Report looks good. But, I was wondering if I could see the totals for each Sales Rep Name. That seemed to go away when you broke them out by Product Type."*

Analysis

Remember, reports are never really done. This is the one constant—change. Here, the Boss is asking for a total for Sales Rep Name. The requirement can be accomplished by using the Summarize checkbox in the QDB.

Steps to Summarize the Crosstab Report

Open the QDB for the Crosstab report:

- Click the Summarize button for rows (Figure 13.19).
- Click OK, to run the report.

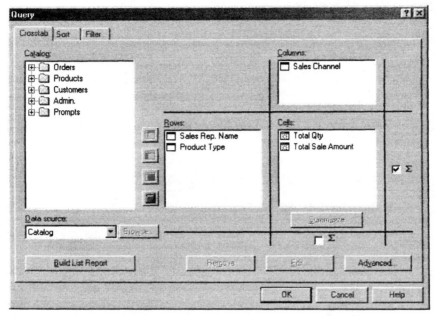

Figure 13.19   The QDB with the Summary checkboxes checked.

And the Results Are...

irect Sales		Mail Sales		Telephone Sales		Total	
Total Sale Amount	Total Qty	Total Sale Amount	Total Qty	Total Sale Amount	Total Qty	Total Sale Amount	
410.13	11	98.01	279	2946.24	339	3454.38	
1699.84	48	393.6	32	278.08	144	2371.52	
911.68	13	829.92	2	142.4	17	1884	
4279.08					422	4279.08	
419.04					48	419.04	
495					1	495	
1378.26	36	1053	201	916.56	484	3347.82	
102.4	48	2311.68	48	307.2	112	2721.28	
401.28	1	435.12	7	4261.95	12	5098.35	
1279.68			11	81.18	135	1360.86	
808.96			64	506.88	96	1315.84	
5553.9			1	521.7	35	6075.6	
1791.72	87	775.17	101	1194.83	566	3761.72	
394.24	64	486.4	64	556.16	144	1436.8	
5273.4	1	516.6	3	33.18	38	5823.18	

Sales data for The Great Outdoors Co.

Figure 13.20 The report result with summaries applied to both rows and columns.

The steps Impromptu took to derive this result are

1. Added a Sales Rep Name Footer
2. Created three summaries of each Sales Channel column for each Sales Rep Name
3. Added a List footer to the report
4. Created three summaries of each Sales Channel column for the entire report

Advanced Summarization

You might have noticed while looking at the QDB, that there is a Summarize button beneath the "Cells" list box. Its default position is unavailable; to enable it, a cell item must be highlighted. The Summarization window contains a feature to control how the summarization of the cells is applied to the Crosstab report.

In the Summarization window, the report developer controls two things:

1. What Summary Type is to be used
2. Where to apply the new summary to the report

What Summary Type to Use

There are five options, shown in Figure 13.21, available to the report developer in the Summarization window. These are the five basic summaries available throughout Impromptu. They correspond directly to common database summary functions.

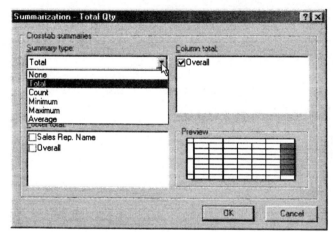

Figure 13.21
The Summarization window.

- **Total.** The Total Summary Type adds the existing cell creating a total at that location of the Crosstab report.
- **Count.** This feature counts the occurrences of the items for that location.
- **Minimum.** This takes the lowest value from the list and displays it.
- **Maximum.** The Maximum performs in the same manner as the Minimum option, but uses the highest value.
- **Average.** This calculates an average based on the values in its location on the report. In the example, Impromptu totals three Qty totals. Then it divides the result by 3.

Where to Apply Summary

The Summarization window gives the report developer the ability to control which row, column, or Overall to apply a summary. Just select a checkbox next to the column or footer to which you want a Summarization to be applied (Figure 13.22).

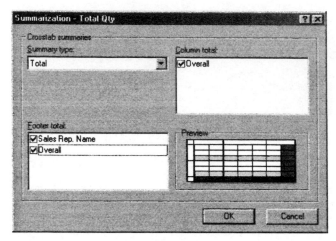

Figure 13.22
The Summary button with
every row and column checked.

A useful component of the Summarization window is the Preview panel. When a report developer selects to apply a summary for a column or footer, the Preview window highlights where the summary will be applied to the report, as shown in Figure 13.23. This gives the report developer the ability to get a sample understanding of where the summarizations will be placed.

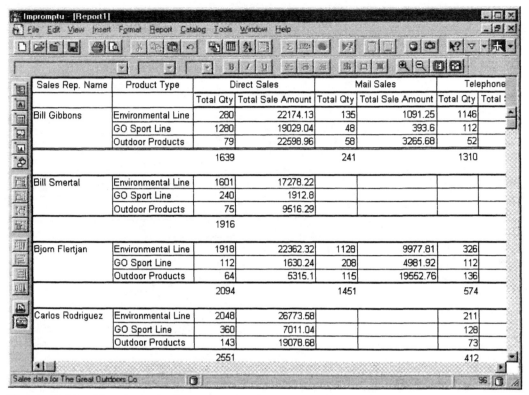

Figure 13.23   The result of selecting all the rows and columns in the Summarization button.

Moving Items Around in the Crosstab

The basic report you have been working on provides an excellent report to practice this topic with. Because Impromptu is a point-and-click-oriented tool, moving items from rows to columns is a fairly simple process. Also, as with many other features within Impromptu, there two ways to perform this task. This section describes specifically how to navigate rows and columns in a Crosstab report.

First Way: Layout Exchanging Rows and Columns

The first way to move rows and columns is by clicking and dragging. The easiest way to do this is by using the Screen layout of the report:

- Click and select any value of Product Type.
- Drag it to the top of the report, even above the Sales Channel header values.

Sales Rep. Name	Product Type	Direct Sales		Mail Sales		Telephone	
		Total Qty	Total Sale Amount	Total Qty	Total Sale Amount	Total Qty	Total
Bill Gibbons	Environmental Line	280	22174.13	135	1091.25	1146	
	GO Sport Line	1280	19029.04	48	393.6	112	
	Outdoor Products	79	22598.96	58	3265.68	52	
		1639		241		1310	
Bill Smertal	Environmental Line	1601	17278.22				
	GO Sport Line	240	1912.8				
	Outdoor Products	75	9516.29				
		1916					
Bjorn Flertjan	Environmental Line	1918	22362.32	1128	9977.81	326	
	GO Sport Line	112	1630.24	208	4981.92	112	
	Outdoor Products	64	5315.1	115	19552.76	136	
		2094		1451		574	
Carlos Rodriguez	Environmental Line	2048	26773.58			211	
	GO Sport Line	360	7011.04			128	
	Outdoor Products	143	19078.68			73	
		2551				412	

Figure 13.24 The changed cursor indicates that you are about to rotate a row to a column or vice versa.

Once the mouse button is released, Impromptu re-queries the database and recalculates the Crosstab report.

Note

There are two visual indicators that you are performing this correctly:

1. The Pivot cursor icon.

2. A wider dotted line than normal.

And the Results Are...

Sales Rep. Name	Environmental Line						
	Direct Sales		Mail Sales		Telephone Sales		
	Total Qty	Total Sale Amount	Total Qty	Total Sale Amount	Total Qty	Total Sale Amount	Total (
Bill Gibbons	280	22174.13	135	1091.25	1146	38694.14	1
Bill Smertal	1601	17278.22					1
Bjorn Flertjan	1918	22362.32	1128	9977.81	326	7270.2	3
Carlos Rodriguez	2048	26773.58			211	5392.02	2
Charles Loo Nam	2076	17482.49	321	7757.49	449	4678.31	2
Chris Cornel	648	4992.38	379	2019.81	398	3255.24	1
Conrad Bergsteige	802	8562.99	458	8156.77	1152	8574.98	2
Dan Chancevente	742	8074.8	655	8528.67	654	11138.03	2
Dave Mustaine	1197	21255.99	472	3850.46	1187	19173.16	2
Francoise LeBlanc	184	7802.1	942	6546.58	1003	13229.73	2
Gilles Turcotte	1048	13974.47	64	2338.52	363	6371.39	1
Greg Torson	295	9882.85	474	8831.68	266	3346.42	1
Gus Grovlin	727	10858.39	101	5911.84	744	8718.07	1
Hari Krain	754	14470.13			568	4896.39	1
Henri LeDuc	963	21578.86	753	8361.54	563	4067.73	2
Henry Harvey	302	9970.14	270	1683.04	50	7564.3	
Ingrid Termede			253	2524.64	1006	11076.57	1
Inigo Montoya	38	6643.8			31	4225.17	

Sales data for The Great Outdoors Co.

Figure 13.25 The report results with the Product Type in the new location.

Second Way: QDB Exchanging Rows and Columns

The second way of moving rows and columns around in the report is by using the QDB. To show this, move the Product Type from above Sales Channel to below the Sales Channel.

1. Open the QDB.

2. Click to select the Product Type column in the Columns box.

3. Drag it below the Sales Channel column.

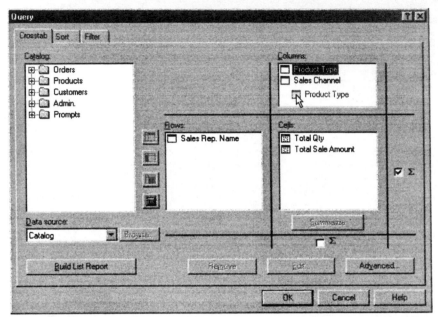

Figure 13.26   The Sales Channel is now above the Product Type in the column order.

Note

The cursor has to be completely below the Sales Channel for it to work properly.

4. Click OK, to run the report.

And the Results Are...

Sales Rep. Name	Direct Sales						
	Environmental Line		GO Sport Line		Outdoor Products		
	Total Qty	Total Sale Amount	Total Qty	Total Sale Amount	Total Qty	Total Sale Amount	Total (
Bill Gibbons	280	22174.13	1280	19029.04	79	22598.96	1
Bill Smertal	1601	17278.22	240	1912.8	75	9516.29	1
Bjorn Flertjan	1918	22362.32	112	1630.24	64	5315.1	2
Carlos Rodriguez	2048	26773.58	360	7011.04	143	19078.68	2
Charles Loo Nam	2076	17482.49	280	7953.12	93	11844.36	2
Chris Cornel	648	4992.38	48	790.88	9	2117.36	
Conrad Bergsteige	802	8562.99	264	5111.84	47	4859.3	1
Dan Chancevente	742	8074.8	32	227.84	23	2878.8	
Dave Mustaine	1197	21255.99	288	6648.64	95	22020.26	1
Francoise LeBlanc	184	7802.1	48	926.72	96	6466.75	
Gilles Turcotte	1048	13974.47	128	2358.4	103	22456.73	1
Greg Torson	295	9882.85	48	1458.24	58	1246.1	
Gus Grovlin	727	10858.39	144	2303.04	112	21177.02	
Hari Krain	754	14470.13	344	7712.32	145	25041.11	1
Henri LeDuc	963	21578.86	656	11968.96	225	21654	1
Henry Harvey	302	9970.14	16	133.76	8	491.4	
Ingrid Termede							
Inigo Montoya	38	6643.8	48	299.52	26	7657.47	

Figure 13.27   The new report with a different order in the column headers.

As before, Impromptu re-queries the database and recalculates the Crosstab report.

One thing to keep in mind when gathering reporting requirements: always try to be as specific as possible. Using our example from Moving Items Around, there were a couple of possibilities as to where the Product Type could have been placed, each giving a completely different answer in the result set.

Convert a List Report to a Crosstab

Looking back at the Crosstab report you just built, you may have noticed a button in the QDB Crosstab page beneath the Catalog box called "Build List Report." Impromptu gives the report developer the ability to convert the Crosstab report back to a List report at any time. Likewise in a Simple List report, there is a button letting you convert to a Crosstab report at any time. Converting from a Simple List report to a Crosstab report is a more challenging effort. So, in this section we will first build a Simple List report and then convert it to a Crosstab.

Building the List Report

You might have already had this happen to you, but the requirement I am going to use for this exercise starts out simple enough; then the request gets complicated.

Report Requirements

Boss: *"I need a report that shows the branch sales broken out by Product Type for 94 and 95."*

Analysis

I won't make a novel out of this, but assume you asked the Boss several follow-up questions about the requirements—for example, whether she would like to see the results in a *grid*-like format—and determined that she wanted only a Simple List of Sales 94 and 95, grouped first by Product Type and then by Branch.

Tip

This deserves mentioning again: the requirements gathered determined that there was no need for a Crosstab. If there is no need for one, why build a Crosstab report? A Crosstab report inherently requires more processing time and space from both the database and Impromptu. Always try to provide the simplest solution first.

Steps to Build the Initial Report

Now, build the report using the following columns:

1. With Impromptu Open, Click the New Report button on the toolbar.
2. Expand the Products folder.
3. Add Product Type to the report.
4. Expand the Customers folder.
5. Expand the Customer Site folder.
6. Add the Branch Column.
7. Go back to the Products folder.
8. Expand Sales History.
9. Add both Sales 94 and Sales 95 (Figure 13.28).
10. Click OK.

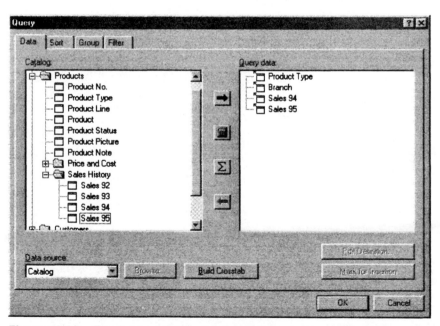

Figure 13.28   The finished QDB, showing all the columns in the query.

And the Results Are...

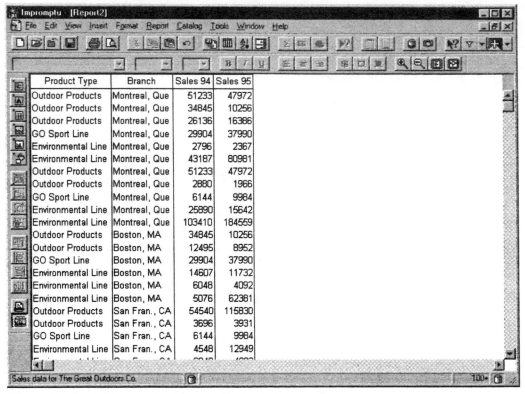

Figure 13.29   The report results—a plain simple list report.

Show the Report to the Boss

After showing it to the Boss, you find out that, even though it was firmly decided that the report was a Simple List, it now has to be a Crosstab report. The rows will be the Branches, and the columns will be Product Types. The cells of the new Crosstab report will be the two sales totals, Sales 94 and Sales 95.

Convert to a Crosstab Report

Converting this Simple List report into a Crosstab report is an easy process. Take a look and see how Impromptu interprets the conversion.

1. Open the QDB.
2. At the bottom, click the "Build Crosstab" button.

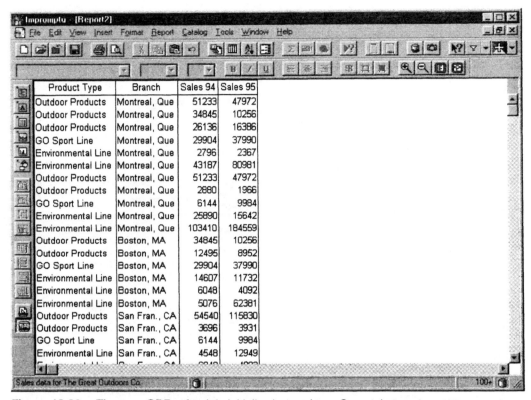

Figure 13.30   The new QDB, after it is initially changed to a Crosstab report.

Keep in mind that Impromptu takes a guess at what should be where. As we can see, it takes reports like these and assumes that the last column from a list report is the only "cell" value. This may look like a mess, but this is a wonderful time to put in place the skills you just learned about using the Crosstab tab.

There are a couple of things that need to be done to get the report in shape, but there are not that many steps. The steps required to clean up this report are:

1. Move Product Type to the Column box and the Branch to the Row box.
2. Double-check the numbers.
3. Fix any discrepancies.

Each step has only a couple of tasks involved, but the real focus here is taking a report that looks one way and converting it to a completely different format. This skill comes with time and experience, but a little practice never hurts.

Step 1: Putting Things in Place

The first task at hand is placing the Product Type in the Column box:

1. Click and drag the Product Type beneath the Branch column in the Column box.

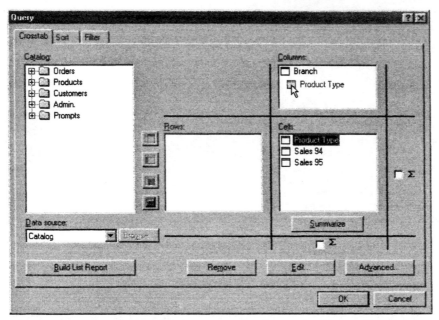

Figure 13.31   The Column box now contains the Product Type column.

The only thing left to do is to place the Branch column in the correct box.

2. Click and drag the Branch data column to the Row box (Figure 13.32).

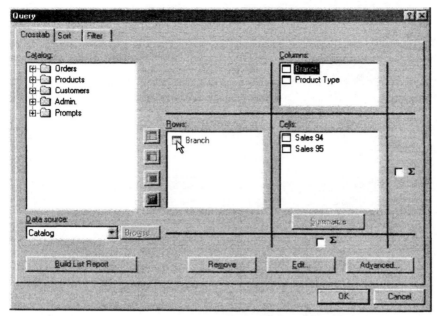

Figure 13.32 The Rows box now contains the Branch column.

Finally you can run the report.

3. Click OK, to run the report.

And the Results Are...

Branch	Environmental Line		GO Sport Line		Outdoor Products	
	Sales 94	Sales 95	Sales 94	Sales 95	Sales 94	Sales 95
Bel-Ned-Lux	2796	2367	6144	9984	2880	1966
Boston, MA	4548	12949	4864	9152	2880	1966
Chicago, IL	2796	2367	4864	9152	1242	1375
Dallas, TX	5076	62381	6144	9984	1242	1375
Denver, CO	2796	2367	6144	9984	3696	3931
Frankfurt, Ger	2796	2367	4864	9152	2880	1966
Hong Kong	6048	4092	6144	9984	2880	1966
London, U.K.	2796	2367	4864	9152	1242	1375
Los Angeles, CA	2796	2367	4864	9152	2880	1966
Madrid, Spain	2796	2367	4864	9152	1242	1375
Manchester U.K.	2796	2367	6144	9984	2880	1966
Melbourne, Aus	2796	2367	4864	9152	1242	1375
Mexico	4548	12949	6144	9984	2880	1966
Miami, FL	2796	2367	4864	9152	3696	3931
Montreal, Que	2796	2367	4864	9152	1242	1375
New York, NY	2796	2367	4864	9152	3696	3931
Paris, France	2796	2367	4864	9152	1242	1375
San Fran., CA	2796	2367	6144	9984	1242	1375
Seattle, WA	2796	2367	10280	7216	5109	8941

Figure 13.33 The correct Crosstab report result.

The report ran successfully—well almost. You are not expected to know this, but the numbers seem a little low for Total Sales, for a year, for a Branch, and for a Product Type. How can anyone be sure? To be sure, double-check with a small quick-and-dirty report to verify the numbers.

Step 2: Double-Check the Numbers

These are the steps to build a quick-and-dirty report to double-check the numbers in the new Crosstab report. This may seem a bit odd, to check numbers from a Crosstab report with numbers from a Simple List report, but you can do that. Here's how:

1. Create a Simple List report in the QDB.
2. Expand the Products folder.
3. Add Product Type to the report.

   4. Expand the Customers folder.

   5. Expand the Customer Site folder.

   6. Add the Branch Column.

   7. Go back to the Products folder.

   8. Expand Sales History.

   9. Click once on the Sales 94 column.

   10. Click the Summary button between the Catalog and the Query boxes.

   11. Click the Total

   12. Click OK to build the Total Sales 94 column.

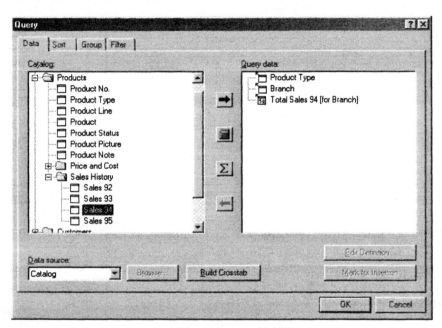

Figure 13.34   The finished QDB, just three columns.

   13. Click OK, to run the report.

And the Results Are...

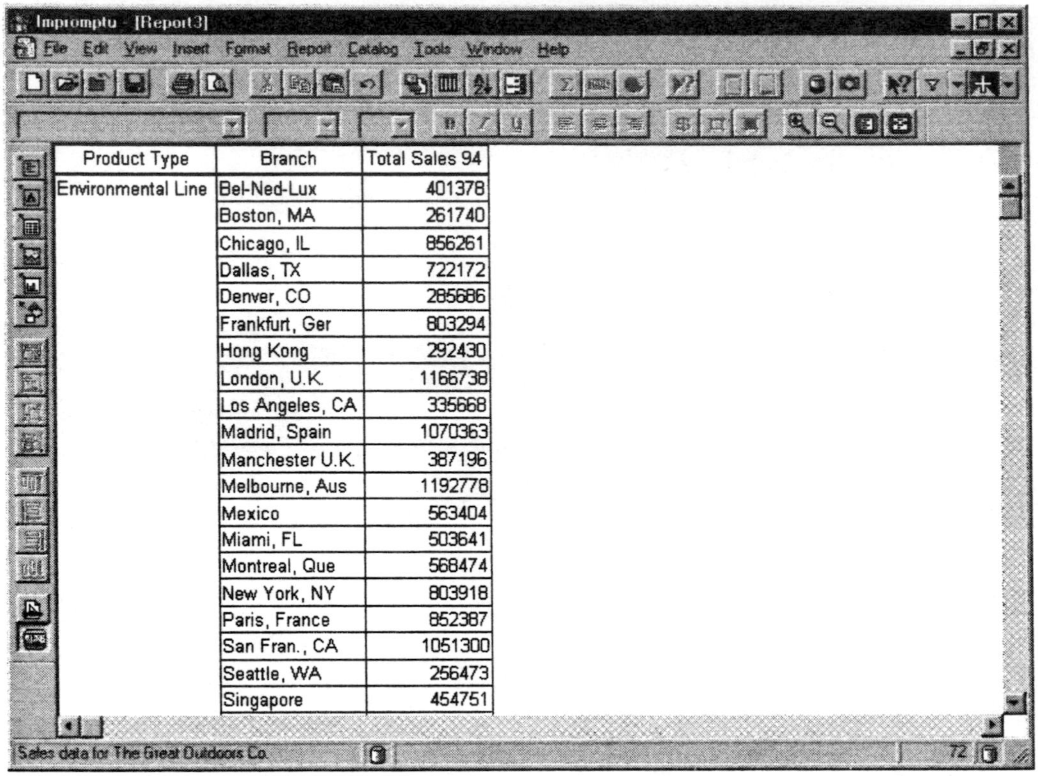

Product Type	Branch	Total Sales 94
Environmental Line	Bel-Ned-Lux	401378
	Boston, MA	261740
	Chicago, IL	856261
	Dallas, TX	722172
	Denver, CO	285686
	Frankfurt, Ger	803294
	Hong Kong	292430
	London, U.K.	1166738
	Los Angeles, CA	335668
	Madrid, Spain	1070363
	Manchester U.K.	387196
	Melbourne, Aus	1192778
	Mexico	563404
	Miami, FL	503641
	Montreal, Que	568474
	New York, NY	803918
	Paris, France	852387
	San Fran., CA	1051300
	Seattle, WA	256473
	Singapore	454751

Figure 13.35 The quick-and-dirty report results.

The report that was just created is a summary report, and every column is either grouped or a total. This gives us a picture of the total sales for a year, for a branch, and for a Product Type. As you look here and compare the results of both the Crosstab and the quick-and-dirty lists, there are noticeable differences. Take one example (Figure 13.36):

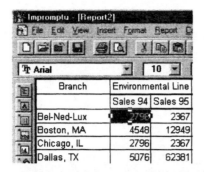

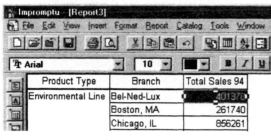

Figure 13.36
The Sales 94 total for Bel-Ned-Lux in the Crosstab report is 2796, while in the quick-and-dirty List that same value is 401378.

Step 3: Fix the Cells

From looking at the quick-and-dirty report, it seems that the Sales 94 cell values in the Crosstab were not made as summarized values when the report was converted to a Crosstab. Given that the Sales 95 numbers are similar to the Sales 94 numbers, it is a safe assumption that the Sales 95 numbers were not summarized as well. That is OK. All you have to do is make both Sales 94 and Sales 95 summaries.

Specifically, the definitions of the two cells need to be changed. The values need to be totals, so the Total Summary function must be added.

1. Open the QDB for the Crosstab Report.
2. Click on the Sales 94 cell column.
3. Click the Edit button to edit the definition of this column.

   In the Data Definition box:

4. Click on the Sales 94 column in the expression.
5. Expand the Summaries folder.
6. Select the Total Summary function (Figure 13.37).

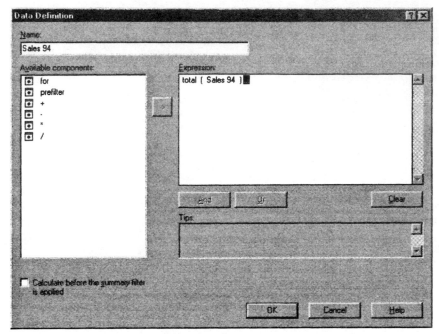

Figure 13.37   Data definition with new Summary function added to Sales 94.

7. Click OK, to finish edit on Sales 94.

8. Click on the Sales 95 cell column.

9. Click the Edit button, to edit the definition of this column.

    In the Data Definition box:

10. Click on the Sales 95 column in the expression.

11. Expand the Summaries folder.

12. Select the Total Summary function (Figure 13.38).

13. Click OK, to finish the edit on Sales 95.

14. Click OK, to run the report.

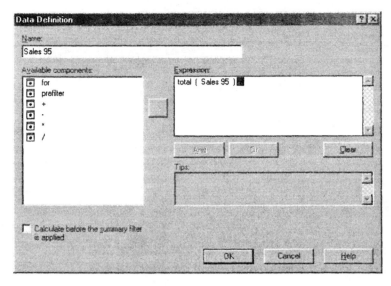

Figure 13.38
Data definition with new Summary function added to Sales 95.

And the Results Are...

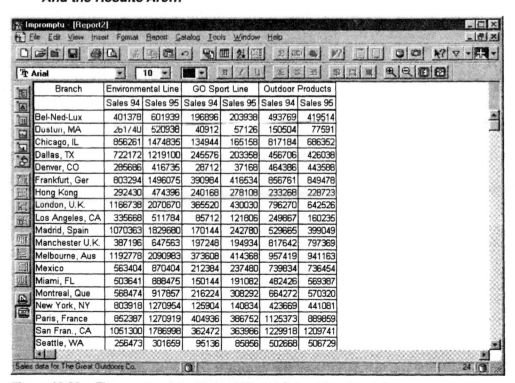

Branch	Environmental Line		GO Sport Line		Outdoor Products	
	Sales 94	Sales 95	Sales 94	Sales 95	Sales 94	Sales 95
Bel-Ned-Lux	401378	601939	196896	203938	493769	419514
Boston, MA	261740	520938	40912	57126	150504	77591
Chicago, IL	856261	1474835	134944	165158	817184	686352
Dallas, TX	722172	1219100	245576	203358	456706	426038
Denver, CO	285686	416735	28712	37168	464386	443588
Frankfurt, Ger	803294	1496075	390984	416534	856761	849478
Hong Kong	292430	474396	240168	278108	233268	228723
London, U.K.	1166738	2070670	365520	430030	796270	642526
Los Angeles, CA	335668	511784	85712	121806	249867	160235
Madrid, Spain	1070363	1829680	170144	242780	529665	399049
Manchester U.K.	387196	647563	197248	194934	817642	797369
Melbourne, Aus	1192778	2090983	373608	414368	957419	941163
Mexico	563404	870404	212384	237480	739834	736454
Miami, FL	503641	888475	150144	191082	482426	569387
Montreal, Que	568474	917857	216224	308292	664272	570320
New York, NY	803918	1270954	125904	140834	423669	441081
Paris, France	852387	1270919	404936	386752	1125373	889859
San Fran., CA	1051300	1786998	362472	363986	1229918	1209741
Seattle, WA	256473	301659	95136	85856	502668	506729

Figure 13.39   The report result with the adjusted Sales 94 and 95 columns.

The next step is to double-check again with the quick-and-dirty report. The numbers match, and all that is left is some formatting of the report. The most important part is done—the validation of the numbers.

Advanced Calculations

Now that you have a functional understanding of Impromptu's Crosstab reporting, it is time to cover the advanced calculating features within Crosstabs. As you have seen, there is a great deal involved in being able to create a Crosstab report. Additionally, the report developer needs an established foundation of Crosstab concepts to be able to effectively implement advanced calculation features.

There are two concepts involved in using calculations in Crosstabs. The first is, using the Calculate button on the QDB not only to create cell values, but to create rows and columns as well. The other is the ability to create calculations from rows, columns, and cells generated from the Crosstab report itself.

Calculate Button

The Calculate button is a very nice feature that, in the spirit of Impromptu, provides more than just traditional calculating features. The Calculate button allows report developers to perform the same features as they would in Simple List reports. What is different in Crosstab reports is determining where the newly created calculation goes—to the Rows, Columns, or Cells box?

Here is an additional report requirement to show how to use the Calculate button:

Report Requirement

Boss: *"In addition to the Sales 95 and Sales 94 columns, can you put a new column next to them showing the difference between the two?"*

Analysis

The boss is at it again. This time the request is asking for a calculated column to be placed in the Cells box.

Steps to Add the New Column

1. Open the QDB.
2. Click the Calculate button.
3. Give this new calculated column the name Yearly Change.
4. Expand the Report Columns folder.
5. Select the "Sales 95" column.

6. Select the minus sign from the Toolbox.

7. Expand the Report Columns folder.

8. Select the "Sales 94" column.

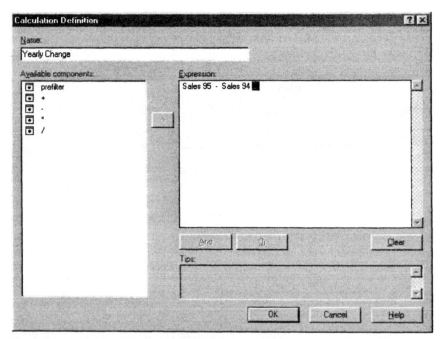

Figure 13.40   The finished new calculation to be used in the Crosstab report.

9. Click OK, to finish the Calculation box.

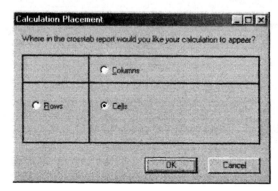

Figure 13.41
The Calculation Placement window gives the report developer a way to place the calculation.

The Calculation Placement box prompts the report developer to choose where to put the newly created calculation in the Crosstab report. This is important, because not all calculations go directly into the Cells box.

10. Click OK, to run the report.

And the Results Are...

| Branch | Environmental Line | | | GO Sport Line | | | Out |
	Sales 94	Sales 95	Total Yearly Change	Sales 94	Sales 95	Total Yearly Change	Sales 94	Sales
Bel-Ned-Lux	401378	601939	200561	196896	203938	7042	493769	419
Boston, MA	261740	520938	259198	40912	57126	16214	150504	77
Chicago, IL	856261	1474835	618574	134944	165158	30214	817184	686
Dallas, TX	722172	1219100	496928	245576	203358	-42218	456706	426
Denver, CO	285686	416735	131049	28712	37168	8456	464386	443
Frankfurt, Ger	803294	1496075	692781	390984	416534	25550	856761	849
Hong Kong	292430	474396	181966	240168	278108	37940	233268	228
London, U.K.	1166738	2070670	903932	365520	430030	64510	796270	642
Los Angeles, CA	335668	511784	176116	85712	121806	36094	249867	160
Madrid, Spain	1070363	1829680	759317	170144	242780	72636	529665	399
Manchester U.K.	387196	647563	260367	197248	194934	-2314	817642	797
Melbourne, Aus	1192778	2090983	898205	373608	414368	40760	957419	941
Mexico	563404	870404	307000	212384	237480	25096	739834	736
Miami, FL	503641	888475	384834	150144	191082	40938	482426	569
Montreal, Que	568474	917857	349383	216224	308292	92068	664272	570
New York, NY	803918	1270954	467036	125904	140834	14930	423669	441
Paris, France	852387	1270919	418532	404936	386752	-18184	1125373	889
San Fran., CA	1051300	1786998	735698	362472	363986	1514	1229918	1209
Seattle, WA	256473	301659	45186	95136	85856	-9280	502668	506

Sales data for The Great Outdoors Co.

Figure 13.42   The report with the new calculation.

Advanced Calculations

The Advanced Calculation option is an extremely powerful feature that can go completely unnoticed. The main purpose of this button is to allow the report developer to create calculations with the results of the Crosstab report. From this button, Impromptu treats the Crosstab result set as a Simple List report and provides each "column" in this version of Report Columns. The advantage of this feature is the ability for the report developer to create, in most cases, a summarized calculation of the entire report after everything else is done.

Report Requirement

Boss: *"Can I see an overall average of the Total Sales, (combine 94 and 95) for each Branch?"*

Analysis

Unfortunately, the Calculate button cannot perform this type of summary, which is a summary of the Total Sales 94 and Total Sales 95. Only the Advanced... button can do this calculation. Let's walk through the steps now.

Steps to Add an Advanced Calculation

1. Open the QDB.
2. Click the Advanced... button.
3. To get a sense of what is available at this level, click the checkbox at the bottom.

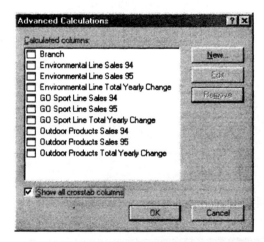

Figure 13.43
The Advanced Calculations window.

4. Click New...
5. Give this Advanced Calculation the name Grand Totals.
6. Expand Report Columns.
7. Select Environmental Line Total Sales 94.
8. Add the plus sign.
9. Select Environmental Line Total Sales 95.
10. Add the plus sign.
11. Select GO Sport Line Total Sales 94.
12. Add the plus sign.

13. Select GO Sport Line Total Sales 95.

14. Add the plus sign.

15. Select Outdoor Products Line Total Sales 94.

16. Add the plus sign.

17. Select Outdoor Products Line Total Sales 95.

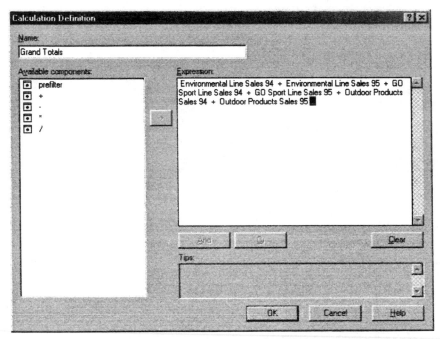

Figure 13.44   The completed Advanced column Calculation Definition.

18. Click OK.

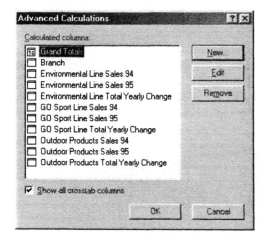

Figure 13.45
The Advanced Calculations window
with Grand Totals.

19. Click OK to return to the Crosstab QDB.

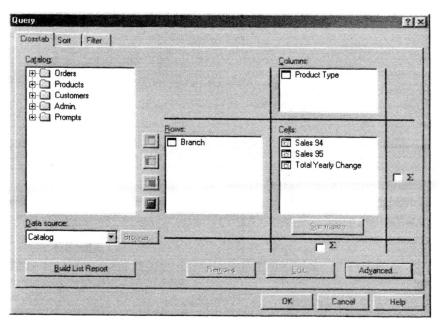

Figure 13.46   Notice the Crosstab QDB does not show the Advanced Calculations.

And the Results Are...

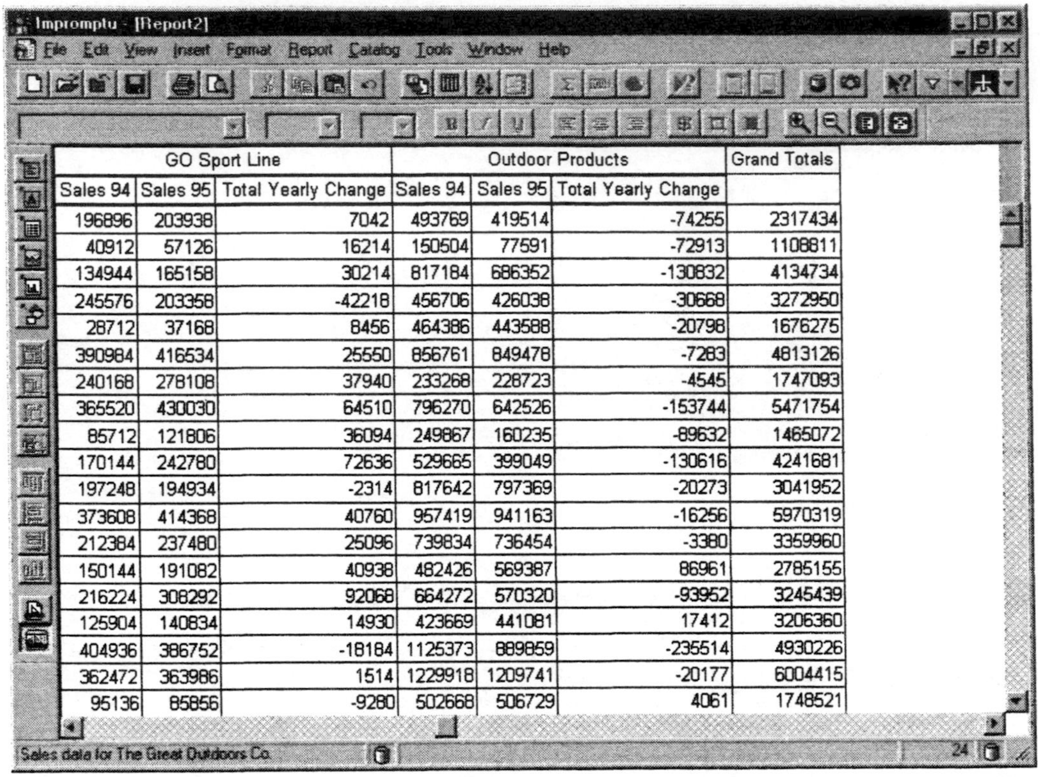

GO Sport Line			Outdoor Products			Grand Totals
Sales 94	Sales 95	Total Yearly Change	Sales 94	Sales 95	Total Yearly Change	
196896	203938	7042	493769	419514	-74255	2317434
40912	57126	16214	150504	77591	-72913	1108811
134944	165158	30214	817184	686352	-130832	4134734
245576	203358	-42218	456706	426038	-30668	3272950
28712	37168	8456	464386	443588	-20798	1676275
390984	416534	25550	856761	849478	-7283	4813126
240168	278108	37940	233268	228723	-4545	1747093
365520	430030	64510	796270	642526	-153744	5471754
85712	121806	36094	249867	160235	-89632	1465072
170144	242780	72636	529665	399049	-130616	4241681
197248	194934	-2314	817642	797369	-20273	3041952
373608	414368	40760	957419	941163	-16256	5970319
212384	237480	25096	739834	736454	-3380	3359960
150144	191082	40938	482426	569387	86961	2785155
216224	308292	92068	664272	570320	-93952	3245439
125904	140834	14930	423669	441081	17412	3206360
404936	386752	-18184	1125373	889859	-235514	4930226
362472	363986	1514	1229918	1209741	-20177	6004415
95136	85856	-9280	502668	506729	4061	1748521

Figure 13.47 The report result.

The report results show an additional column added at the end of the list of columns. This is the Advanced calculation you just added. The options available with the Advanced button are endless because of the incorporation of the Calculation Definition box and the Available Components Toolbox.

Summary

This chapter covered

1. What a Crosstab report is in Impromptu
2. How to create a Crosstab report
3. How to modify a Crosstab report

4. Converting Simple List reports to Crosstabs

5. Adding Advanced calculations to a Crosstab report

That is a lot of content for one type of report. Crosstab reports are a very compelling report to deliver to a report consumer. Developing these reports requires careful consideration of the placement of report requirements and the elements available in the database. By the time you are building a Crosstab report, you should have a clear understanding of the database you are working with and a good feel for the abilities of Impromptu. Have fun!

Sub Reports

I considered not having this chapter in the book. It covers an extremely advanced topic. You have learned so much and come so far since the first chapter. Would this be too much? When is it enough? I can add chapter after chapter, going deeper and deeper into Impromptu and uncovering all the little nuggets of gold, but when does the value diminish?

I spoke with a few colleagues about this concern. Their consensus was, "You have to have a Sub Reports chapter: when people see what they can do with them, their eyes light up." And they are right. I have not seen a report developer to whom I showed Sub Reports who didn't literally jump to the edge of his or her chair with eyes wide open. Now, I cannot guarantee you'll be dancing in your office after reading this chapter, but if you have read thus far, you will definitely appreciate the value that Sub Reports provide to reporting solutions.

The topics covered in this chapter are

- What a Sub Report is and when to use it
- Opening an existing Sub Report
- Creating a Sub Report
- Two types of Sub Report

A Sub Report Is...

What exactly is a Sub Report? There is no template, there is no special QDB as with a Crosstab report. It is very fitting that this is the last chapter, because a Sub Report calls for you to use all the skills you have learned thus far. To effectively build a Sub Report, you need to use several topics covered in this book (e.g., Filters, Frames, and the QDB). To understand the application of Sub Reports, you must have an understanding of these concepts.

Specifically, a Sub Report contains at least two separate queries displayed in one IMR report, where the values of one query are filtered by the values of another query.

This is not a new concept for providing information in the business world. The common term used by most people for this type of report is a Master/Detail report or a Master/Detail screen for information, not printed but viewed within a traditional computer application. The Master/Detail concept is actually quite simple: for every Master record (result set of one query) there is a group of one or more detail records (results from another query). There is a one-to-many relationship between these two queries. Remember that each query, even if there are four or five separate queries, resides within one Impromptu report. That is correct—more than one query in the same report. Impromptu handles the multiple queries, as you would expect. It assigns every new query to a report its very own QDB.

Note

Here, Impromptu relies on your working knowledge of a QDB and a query.

The link between each query is established through a filter. In every Impromptu report, there is a Main query and then one or more sub-queries. The Main query is the first query developed in the building of an Impromptu Sub Report. These sub-queries are linked to the Main query by filtering on like columns or else the sub-query is an independent query returning to the report results independent of anything else.

Note

To link queries together, Impromptu relies on your working knowledge of filtering.

In addition to holding the queries in multiple QDBs, there is the matter of displaying multiple queries on one report. You worked with a Multiple Frame report in Chapter 11. The preferred method of building an Impromptu Sub Report is having different frames display data from different queries.

Note

This requires you to understand the frame-based nature of Impromptu and how to apply multiple frames to a report.

When to Use a Sub Report?

Just as in Crosstab reporting where you had to determine whether a report is a Crosstab or not, properly identifying whether a report needs to be one query or multiple queries is essential. Here are a few simple situations that call for using a Crosstab report template:

- A report needs to total two similar values using separate grouping orders.
- A report needs to show one set of information, while at the same time displaying another set completely separately.
- A report has one master row of information to display in one location and a filtered list of detail rows to display separately.

There are many more situations than just mentioned, but use these as a starting point for evaluating whether your next reporting requirement is asking for a Sub Report or a Crosstab, or even just a plain old Simple List Report.

Opening an Existing Sub Report

As in the rest of the chapters, we will open an existing report to see how it was built. The value in opening up an existing report shows what it looks like on the outside (layout) and on the inside (QDB). A Sub Report looks just like any other report. The only major difference is in the way the information is gathered.

The report used here is a very interesting one. It is another combination report, showing a Crosstab and a Summary. The Sub Report includes a query for the Summary Report and a query for the Crosstab. In this example, both queries, although they represent similar features, are separate queries that do not require the results from one another to process information.

With Impromptu open, follow these steps to open the Sub Report:

1. Select File.Open.
2. Open the report Crosstab Sub Report (simple) (Figure 14.1).

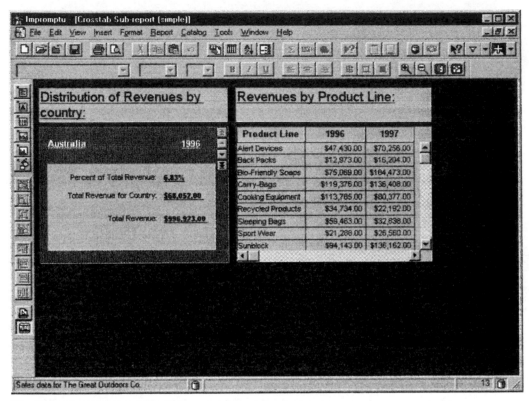

Figure 14.1   The Crosstab Sub-report (simple) report.

Even though it is a Sub Report, it runs just like any other Impromptu report. The results you are looking at are the result of a combination of two frames displaying two separate queries. The frame on the left displays a Form frame, and the frame on the right is a List frame displaying a Crosstab.

Impromptu allows the report developer to choose the specific query a couple of ways. They are the same ways you are accustomed to. But because there are multiple queries, there are some added rules.

- **Toolbar selection of a query.** This is allowed, but Impromptu is sensitive to what is selected on the layout of the report. If you have a column or a cell or an object related to one particular query, then when you click on the toolbar QDB button, you will see the QDB for that query. If you do not have an item selected that is related to one query or another, then the Main query is displayed.
- **The Menu selection.** The Menu gives you direct access to the specific query you want. When you select "Menu. Report," you now have a Flyout menu for the option

of picking one query or the other, as shown in Figure 14.2. In this Flyout, you can also choose to bring up a list box showing all of the queries. This can aid in selecting a specific query when the list becomes lengthy.

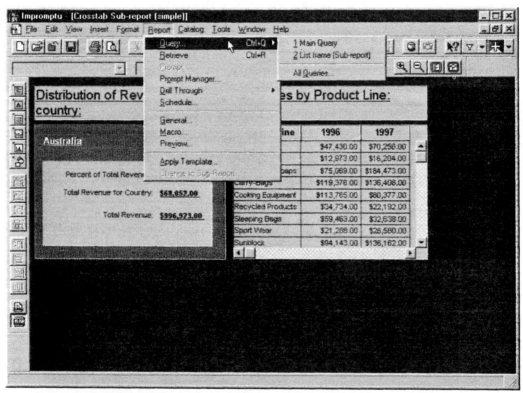

Figure 14.2   The Flyout option shows the options to selecting a specific query.

Building a Sub Report

Now, that you have seen an existing Sub Report, it is time to build one. When building a Sub Report, the main issue is where to start. This is important, because the first query you develop is the Main query. Then every query afterward will be a sub-query. So, choose the Main query first, then build the sub-queries.

Getting Started: The Requirements

Let's not beat around the bush, especially in the final chapter. For the first Sub Report, here is the business's reporting request:

Report Requirement

Boss: *"I want to be able on one page to see an order and all of the line items associated with it in a list format. Just like in that one software package we bought not too long ago."*

Analysis

What you see here is a user, wanting to see a report similar to a screen that can be found in most computer systems or software packages used by the general business community. This is a common report request. What the report consumer is describing is a typical Master/Detail Sub Report. The Boss left a lot of room for creativity in the report, so instead of spending time creating the requirements for this report, the columns will be identified when the report is created. This is done here to get directly to the focus of the chapter—building Sub Reports.

To build a Sub Report, several incremental steps must be performed. Unfortunately, you cannot just click a button and create a whole slew of QDBs, tie them together, and click one OK button to run everything. In building a Sub Report, the following steps will be followed:

1. Create the Main query.
2. Develop the layout for that query on the report.
3. Create a sub-query.
4. Relate the sub-query to the Main query. (Optional)

> **Note**
>
> Steps 3 and 4 are performed as many times as there are additional sub-queries to add to the Impromptu Report.

Step 1: Create the Main Report

With Impromptu open and the "Sales Data for the Great Outdoors Co." Catalog open,

1. Create a new report using File.New.
2. Choose the Blank Report template.
3. Click OK.
4. Expand the Orders folder.
5. Select the four columns there:
   - Order No.
   - Customer Name
   - Order Date
   - Closed Date

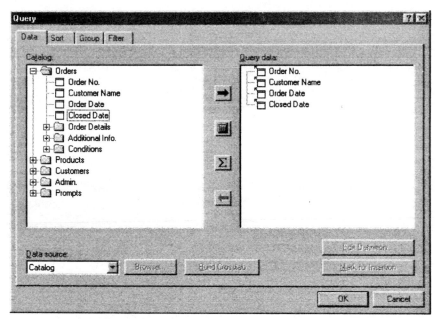

Figure 14.3   The QDB of the Main query.

6. Click OK to run the report.

And the Results Are...

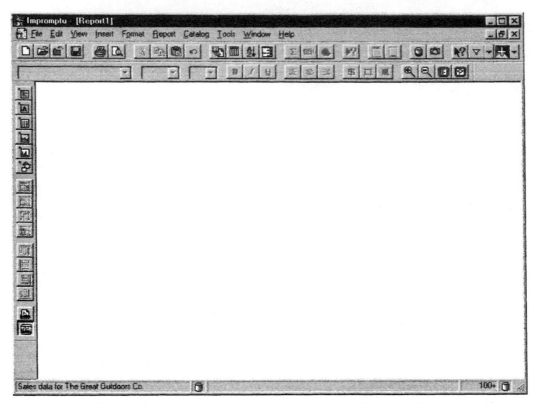

Figure 14.4   The report results—a blank report does not have a frame to show report values.

The report is empty. That is because the report type selected is a blank report. You see nothing, even though the columns you selected were "Marked for Insertion." A Blank report template does not have any frames initially to place columns from a report. The Blank report contains just the Report Body.

The next step is to add a Form frame to the Report Body and columns from the Main Query to that frame.

Note

Make sure the report is in Screen layout for this entire chapter.

Step 2: Create the Layout of the Main Query

1. Select from the menu Insert.Form Frame.
2. Move the mouse down to the Screen layout. Starting in the upper left corner, click and drag to the bottom right corner of the layout.

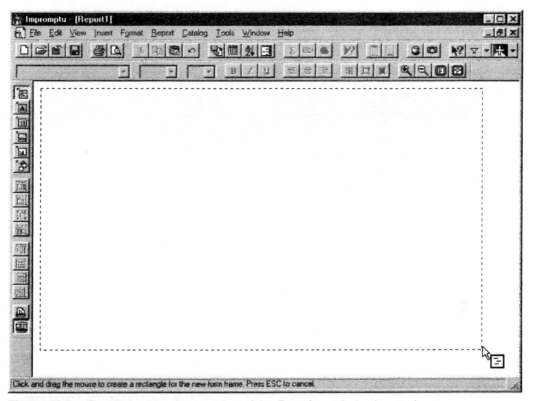

Figure 14.5 The dashed line is an outline of the Form frame being inserted.

3. Click anywhere in the space occupied by the newly created Form frame; this selects the Frame form.
4. Select Insert.Data.
5. Move the mouse to an area in the upper portion of the form frame and click to place the data columns (Figure 14.6).

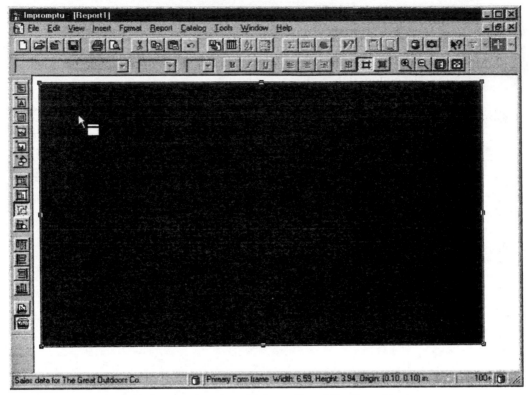

Figure 14.6   The data column being placed in a section of the Form frame.

6. With the QDB reopened, "Mark for Insertion" each Query Data column by either double clicking on each column or selecting each one of them and pressing the Marked for Insertion button.

7. Click OK.

And the Results Are...

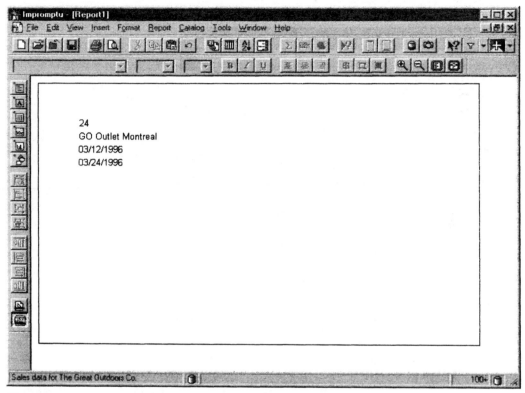

Figure 14.7 The report results showing just one row of data.

What you see here is one row of data being displayed on the Form frame. Unfortunately, that is all that the Form frame knows what to do with the data coming back from the database. Remember from Chapter 11 that the default layout for a Form frame is All Data where only a single row of data is displayed. Currently, this is the single row, the only row a report consumer can see. The next step is modifying the Form frame layout so that all report consumers can view any row of data.

This step shapes the layout of the Form frame. The data need to be grouped and displayed by the Order No. The following steps will achieve this:

1. Right click anywhere in the Form frame.
2. Select the Properties.
3. Select the Layout tab.

4. In the Scope of Data, choose the Data in the Group radio button.

5. In the Dropdown box, choose Order No.

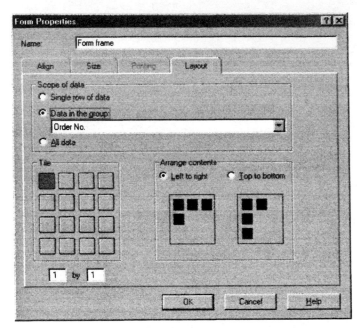

Figure 14.8
The completed Form
Properties box.

6. Click OK (Figure 14.9).

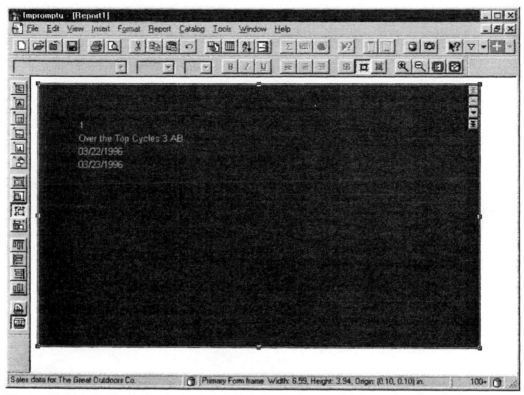

Figure 14.9 The Form frame now has the controls to toggle through the rows of data.

Step 3: Create the Sub Report

Now that the Main query has been built and the layout set, it is time to add a sub-query to the Impromptu report. Adding a sub-query is essentially adding additional data to the overall Impromptu report that does not otherwise fit into the scheme of the Main query. The new sub-query may be grouped differently. It may need a different summary value or use different parts of the database. There are many reasons to create a sub-query, and as a report developer, you just have to take each case as it comes and evaluate it.

In this part, you will create and populate a List frame with a sub-query of Order Detail data.

1. Select Insert.Sub Report.List Frame.
2. Move the mouse down and draw the boundaries of the new List frame (Figure 14.10).

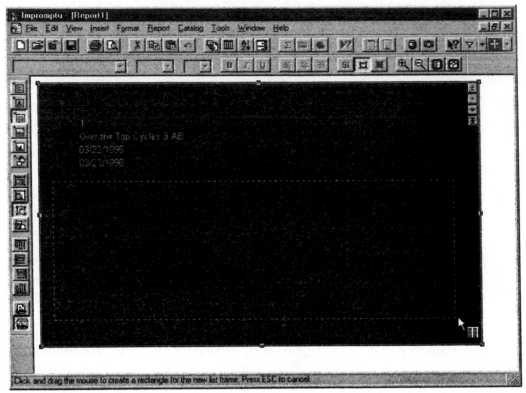

Figure 14.10   Like the dashed line of the Form frame, the dashed line here indicates the size of the List frame.

Note

The List frame does not have to be in the boundaries of the Form frame. I just like to do this to keep a sense of order within a frame and its borders.

3. With a New QDB open, expand the Order folder.

4. Expand the Order Details folder.

5. Select the following columns for this query:

   - Order No.
   - Line No.
   - Product.
   - Order Price.
   - Sale Amount.

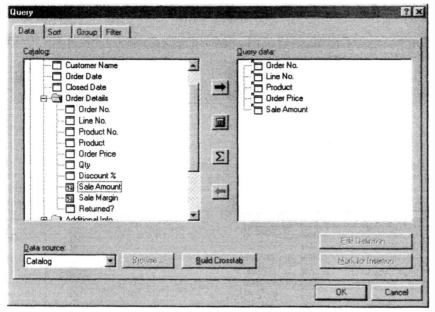

Figure 14.11 The finished QDB of the sub-query.

6. Click OK, to run the sub-query.

And the Results Are...

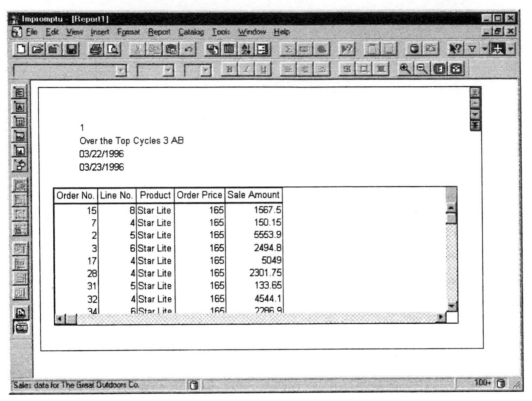

Figure 14.12   The sub-query results displayed in the List frame.

Considered from a user's perspective, the report makes no logical sense. The List frame has many Order Nos. displayed, while the Form frame just has one, Order No. 1. The reason for this is simple: the sub-query added is not linked to the Main query. There is nothing that ties the two together.

Step 4: Tie the Two Queries Together

To tie the sub-query to the Main query, the only thing needed is to make a filter in the sub-query. The sub-query has one column in common with the Main query, Order No. It is just a matter of joining the Order Nos. of the two queries together.

Follow these steps to join the two queries together:

1. Select Report.Query.2 List frame (Figure 14.13).

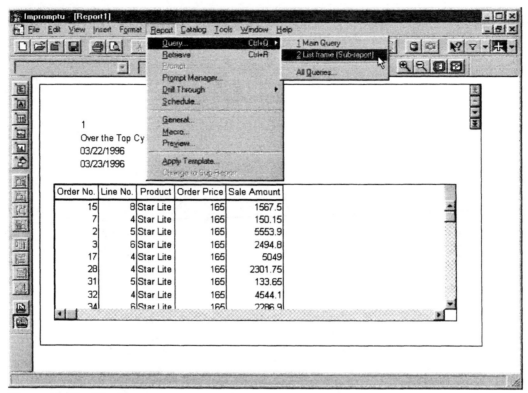

Figure 14.13 The Flyout menu to select the sub-query.

The joining of a sub-query to the Main query takes place in the Filter tab of the sub-queries QDB.

Tip

If a cell or column is highlighted, and Ctrl+Q or the Query button is selected, Impromptu displays the QDB related to the item selected.

Tip

If nothing is selected, and Ctrl+Q or the Query button is selected, Impromptu displays, by default, the Main QDB. The Main QDB is the first Query developed for this report.

Impromptu gives report developers access to the columns in the Main query to use in the Filter tab of the sub-query.

2. Select the Filter tab.

3. Expand the Report Columns folder.

4. Select Order No.

5. Select =.

6. Expand the Report Columns again.

7. Expand the Main Query.

8. Select Order No.

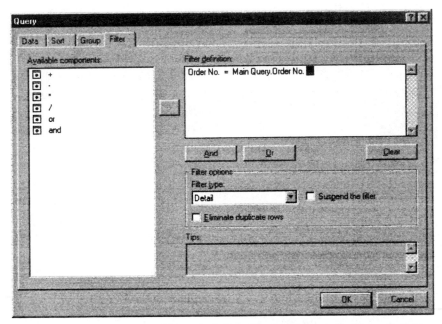

Figure 14.14   The finished Filter Definition filtering the value of the sub-query with a value from the Main query.

- Click OK, to run the report.

And, Finally, the Results Are...

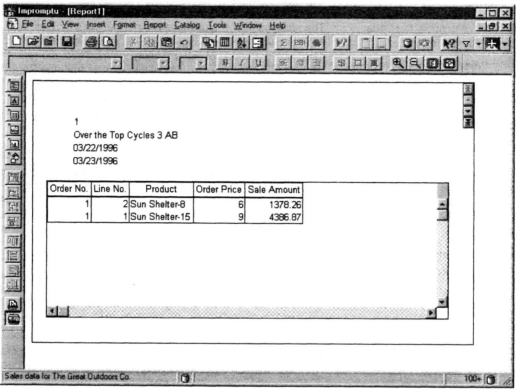

Figure 14.15   The report results now show the List frame showing only the rows for Order No. 1.

Now, the Form frame's Order No. filters the List frame. The report consumer is now able to see the specific Order Detail for the Order displayed in the Form frame. The report consumer can scroll through the values of the Form frame; each time the Form frame displays another Order No., Impromptu runs the sub-query again and displays new sub-query data. This sub-query is run every time a new Order No. is selected in the Form frame because the filter criteria in the sub-query has changed. Each new row in the Form frame changes the Main Query.Order No. value, from one Order No. to another, thus changing the filter criteria of the sub-query.

Did You Really Need...

Now that you have created a complete Sub Report on your own, take a look at one aspect of it: the filter in the second report. This filter uses a column from its own query and compares it with a column from the Main query. In both cases it is the same column: Order No.

But, here are a few questions to ask yourself when you build your own Sub Reports.

Question	Answer
Do I have to show the Order No. in the list report? Do I really need to have Order No. in the list report at all?	The answers to both questions are no. Here is why. Remember when you were working with filters, and inside the toolbox, there was the option of either getting columns from the report "Report Columns" or getting a column straight from the Catalog: "Catalog Columns?" You did not have to use a column being retrieved for the report to use in the Filter Definition.

The same holds true for Sub Reports. Even in the Filter tab of the sub-query, you can take a column directly from the Catalog and use it in the filter. To see that this indeed can be done, let's remove the Order No. from the sub-query.

Try This:

1. Open the QDB for the sub-query: From the Menu bar: Report.Query.1 List frame (Sub Report).
2. Select the Order No. column from the Query Data box.
3. Delete it.
4. Click OK (Figure 14.16).

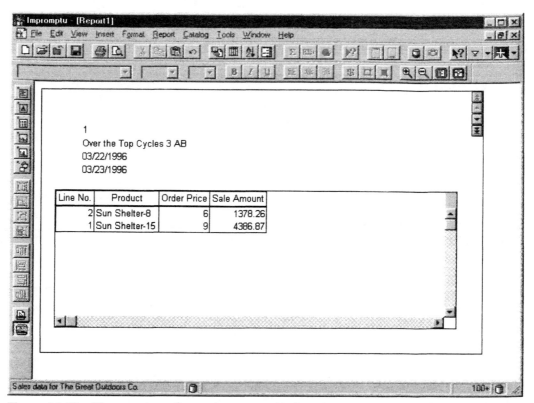

Figure 14.16   The report results are the same, with the minor exception of the List frame.

The report ran successfully. The List frame did not include the Order No. The Order No. is not needed as a column in the sub-query to be used in the Filter Definition.

Question	Answer
But, we used that Order No. from the second query in the filter to link it up with the Main query? Why did it work?	It worked because of the Catalog Column principle. In the root running of this query, Impromptu has to know where the column came from. In this instance, it comes from the same place (database and table) as it did when it was a column in the report. That did not change. The only thing that changed in the query is that Impromptu is not asking for this column back in the query data. It just uses that column in the filter part of the query.

Not Just Linked Together

Sub Reports can also be independent running reports, without a link to one another. Think back to the example from the beginning of this chapter. That report has two independent queries running. They are related in concept, but they have no interdependence in displaying information. Again think back to the preceding exercise, where you created the sub-query as an independent query. Initially, you did not filter the sub-query based on any column from the Main query. It returned exactly what it was asked for—everything.

Summary

This chapter covered

1. What a Sub Report is in Impromptu
2. How to create a Sub Report

There are many things you can do with Sub Reports, from Master/Detail reports, to Detail/Summary reports, to just different totals of the same information side by side, Impromptu provides Sub Reports to the report developer to enrich the report viewing experience.

As this chapter and book conclude, obviously not everything has been covered. To include every example and explanation of every subtle nuance in Impromptu would be overwhelming to the report consumer and the report developer. That would defeat the intent of this book: to teach you the mechanics and then let you go off and apply those to your environment. Good luck, and have success in your reporting environment.